New Constitutionalism an

This path-breaking collection analyzes the dialectic between the development of world order and neo-liberal legal, regulatory and constitutional innovations at local, regional and global scales. Such innovations are intended to shape the global political economy and limit policy options according to the intensifying demands of corporations and market forces in global market civilization. Contributors also consider whether the ongoing crises and contradictions of capitalism and geopolitics offer states and societies opportunities to regain policy autonomy and for the potential for challenges and alternative frameworks of constitutionalism to materialize. Integrating approaches from leading and emerging scholars, this is an innovative, indispensable source for policy-makers, civil society organizations, professionals and students in law, politics, economics, sociology, philosophy and international relations.

STEPHEN GILL is Distinguished Research Professor in the Department of Political Science at York University, Toronto.

A. CLAIRE CUTLER is Professor of International Law and International Relations in the Department of Political Science at the University of Victoria.

New Constitutionalism and World Order

Edited by
Stephen Gill and A. Claire Cutler

CAMBRIDGE
UNIVERSITY PRESS

University Printing House, Cambridge CB2 8BS, United Kingdom

Cambridge University Press is part of the University of Cambridge.

It furthers the University's mission by disseminating knowledge in the pursuit of education, learning and research at the highest international levels of excellence.

www.cambridge.org
Information on this title: www.cambridge.org/9781107633032

© Cambridge University Press 2014

This publication is in copyright. Subject to statutory exception and to the provisions of relevant collective licensing agreements, no reproduction of any part may take place without the written permission of Cambridge University Press.

First published 2014
First paperback edition 2015

A catalogue record for this publication is available from the British Library

Library of Congress Cataloguing in Publication data
New constitutionalism and world order / edited by Stephen Gill and A. Claire Cutler.
  pages cm
Includes bibliographical references and index.
ISBN 978-1-107-05369-4 (hardback)
1. Neoliberalism. 2. International organization. 3. Globalization – Economic aspects. 4. Globalization – Political aspects. 5. International relations. 6. World politics – 21st century. I. Gill, Stephen. II. Cutler, A. Claire.
JZ1318.N483 2014
342'.001–dc23
2013032796

ISBN 978-1-107-05369-4 Hardback
ISBN 978-1-107-63303-2 Paperback

Cambridge University Press has no responsibility for the persistence or accuracy of URLs for external or third-party internet websites referred to in this publication, and does not guarantee that any content on such websites is, or will remain, accurate or appropriate.

Contents

List of figures	page x
List of contributors	xi
Acknowledgements	xiii
List of acronyms	xvi

1 New constitutionalism and world order:
  general introduction   1
  STEPHEN GILL AND A. CLAIRE CUTLER
  Aims and considerations   1
  The historical context for new constitutionalism   5
  Criticisms of the new constitutional concept   8
  What is 'new' about the new constitutionalism?   11
  Themes, hypotheses and questions: overview of the contributions 14
  Hegemony, supremacy and the power of capital   14
  Law, legitimacy and legitimation   16
  Agency and contestation   17
  A note on the organization of this book   19

  Part I Concepts   23

2 Market civilization, new constitutionalism and
  world order   29
  STEPHEN GILL
  The constitution of market civilization: the old and the new   29
  New constitutionalism and the rule of law   34
  Three dimensions of new constitutionalism   37
  Measures to reconfigure state apparatuses   38
  Measures to construct and extend capitalist markets   39
  Measures for dealing with dislocations and contradictions   40
  Conclusion: from transformative resistance to the
    post-modern Prince   42

Contents

3	New constitutionalism and the commodity form of global capitalism	45
	A. CLAIRE CUTLER	
	Introduction	45
	Commodity fetishism and the commodity form of law	47
	The commodification of nature	50
	Contesting new constitutionalism	57
4	The rule of law as the *Grundnorm* of the new constitutionalism	63
	CHRISTOPHER MAY	
	The *Grundnorm*: from legal to political analysis	65
	New constitutionalism, market civilization and disciplinary neo-liberalism	67
	(Re-)producing the norm: maintaining the rule of law	70
	Professionalization	70
	Technical assistance	72
	New constitutionalism and the rule of law	74

Part II Genealogy, origins and world order   77

5	Toward a genealogy of the new constitutionalism: the empire of liberty and domination	81
	TIM DI MUZIO	
	The new constitutionalism	83
	Colonial elites and the American Revolutionary War	85
	The constitution of liberty and domination	90
	Conclusion	93
6	The origins of the new constitutionalism: lessons from the 'old' constitutionalism	95
	RAN HIRSCHL	
	The insurance logic of constitutionalization and judicial empowerment	97
	Back to the new constitutionalism	104

Part III Multilevel governance and neo-liberalization   109

7	When the global inhabits the national: fuzzy interactions	115
	SASKIA SASSEN	
	The global capital market: power and norm-making	117
	The partial disembedding of specialized state operations and non-state actors	118
	The state: one site for non-state actors	120
	Conclusion	123

Contents

8	**New constitutionalism and variegated neo-liberalization**	126
	NEIL BRENNER, JAMIE PECK AND NIK THEODORE	
	The global and the national in the new constitutionalism	127
	Geographies of neo-liberalization	129
	Modalities of neo-liberalization	130
	Pathways of neo-liberalization	131
	Toward a moving map of neo-liberalization	133
	Regulatory experiments	133
	Systems of inter-jurisdictional policy transfer	133
	Transnational rule-regimes	134
	Restless landscapes of neo-liberalization	134
	Scenarios of counter-neo-liberalization: toward a progressive new constitutionalism?	138
	Conclusions	142
9	**New constitutionalism and multilevel governance**	143
	ADAM HARMES	
	Introduction	143
	New constitutionalism and the neo-liberal separation of the economic and the political	144
	Neo-liberalism and 'market-preserving federalism'	147
	Market-preserving regionalism and globalism	152
	Social forces and multilevel governance	154
	Conclusion: prospects for progressive multilevel governance	156

Part IV Trade, investment and taxation   159

10	**How to govern differently: neo-liberalism, new constitutionalism and international investment law**	165
	DAVID SCHNEIDERMAN	
	Neo-liberalism under construction	167
	International investment law under construction	171
	Rolling back the new constitutionalism	175
11	**Trade agreements, the new constitutionalism and public services**	179
	SCOTT SINCLAIR	
	The GATS and the NAFTA	180
	Impacts on public services	182
	Confining public services within existing boundaries	183
	Increasing the bargaining power of global corporations	184
	Applying pro-competitive regulation to previously socialized services	186
	Locking in future privatization	188
	Shifting the balance against public services	189
	Dynamism of the agreements	190
	Trade negotiations between the EU and Canada	192
	Conclusion	195

Contents

12	New constitutionalism, international taxation and crisis DRIES LESAGE, MATTIAS VERMEIREN AND SACHA DIERCKX	197
	Introduction: new constitutionalism and taxation	197
	The political economy of global taxation after the crisis	199
	The crisis in/of neo-liberalism and taxation	199
	Taxing the financial sector	202
	Taxing the capital of wealthy citizens	205
	Corporate taxation	208
	Conclusion	210

Part V Social reproduction, welfare and ecology — 211

13	Social reproduction, fiscal space and remaking the real constitution ISABELLA BAKKER	219
	Introduction	219
	New constitutionalism, social reproduction and fiscal squeeze	222
	Expropriating the commons and extended commodification	225
	Enlarging spaces of resistance	228
	Creating fiscal space	228
	Remaking the real constitution	231
14	New constitutionalism, disciplinary neo-liberalism and the locking in of indebtedness in America ADRIENNE ROBERTS	233
	Introduction	233
	Debt and the reprivatization of social reproduction	235
	The new constitutionalism and bankruptcy protection	240
	The state, the law and the coercive relations of debt	242
	Conclusion	245
15	New constitutionalism, neo-liberalism and social policy JANINE BRODIE	247
	Introduction	247
	Globalization and social policy	249
	Predictions	249
	Outcomes	252
	An unsettled policy field	253
	New 'constitutions' of the social	254
	Epilogue: social policy and the Great Recession	258
16	New constitutionalism and the environment: a quest for global law HILAL ELVER	261
	Introduction	261
	Evolution of environmental law and constitutionalism	262
	Globalization, environment and inequality	263

	Environmentalism versus corporate governance?	266
	Voluntary codes of conduct	266
	Market-based regulations	267
	Public–private partnerships	268
	A new global challenge: climate change	269
	Responses to the environmental challenge	273

Part VI Globalization from below and prospects for a just new constitutionalism   277

17 Constitutionalism as critical project: the epistemological challenge to politics   281
GAVIN W. ANDERSON

Introduction	281
Political economy and constitutionalism	282
How *new* is new constitutionalism?	285
Struggles over hegemony: imagining post-imperial new constitutional forms	289
Conclusion	293

18 New constitutionalism and geopolitics: notes on legality and legitimacy and prospects for a just new constitutionalism   295
RICHARD FALK

Points of departure	296
Distinguishing legality and legitimacy	297
International law and the 'old' constitutionalism	299
Managing nuclear weaponry and new constitutionalism	303
International criminal accountability	305
The post-9/11 counterterrorist challenge	306
Imperial new constitutionalism	308
Neo-liberal globalization and the new constitutionalism	309
A concluding comment	312

Glossary	313
Appendix	326
Key questions and issues	326
Present and future prospects	327
Bibliography	328
Index	363

Figures

8.1	Historical geographies of modern constitutionalism	*page* 128
8.2	From disarticulated to deep(ening) neo-liberalization: a stylized outline	135
8.3	Counter-neo-liberalization: future pathways and scenarios	139
14.1	Uses of home equity extraction 2001–8	237
14.2	Average net worth of US households by race, 2005 and 2009	239

Contributors

GAVIN W. ANDERSON, Senior Lecturer, School of Law, University of Glasgow, Scotland.

ISABELLA BAKKER, Professor of Political Science and Trudeau Fellow, York University, Toronto, Canada.

NEIL BRENNER, Professor of Urban Theory, Graduate School of Design, Harvard University, Boston, USA.

JANINE BRODIE, Distinguished University Professor in Political Economy and Social Governance; Trudeau Fellow, University of Alberta, Edmonton, Canada.

A. CLAIRE CUTLER, Professor of International Law and International Relations, Political Science Department, University of Victoria, Canada.

TIM DI MUZIO, Assistant Professor in International Relations, University of Wollongong, Australia.

SACHA DIERCKX, Doctoral Researcher, Ghent Institute for International Studies, Ghent University, Belgium.

HILAL ELVER, Research Professor, Global and International Studies, University of California, Santa Barbara, USA.

RICHARD FALK, Albert G. Milbank Professor Emeritus of International Law and Politics, Princeton University; Visiting Distinguished Professor in Global and International Studies at the University of California, Santa Barbara, USA.

STEPHEN GILL, Distinguished Research Professor of Political Science, Communication and Culture, York University, Toronto, Canada.

ADAM HARMES, Associate Professor in Political Science, University of Western Ontario, Canada.

RAN HIRSCHL, Canada Research Chair Professor of Political Science and Law, University of Toronto, Canada.

DRIES LESAGE, Professor of Globalization and Global Governance, Institute for International Studies, Ghent University, Belgium.

CHRISTOPHER MAY, Professor of Political Economy, Lancaster University, UK.

JAMIE PECK, Research Professor in Urban and Regional Political Economy, Department of Geography, University of British Columbia, Vancouver, Canada.

ADRIENNE ROBERTS, Assistant Professor in International Studies, University of Manchester, UK.

SASKIA SASSEN, Robert S. Lynd Professor of Sociology and Co-Chair Committee on Global Thought, Columbia University, New York, USA.

DAVID SCHNEIDERMAN, Professor of Law and Political Science, Faculty of Law, University of Toronto, Canada.

SCOTT SINCLAIR, Senior Research Fellow, Canadian Centre for Policy Alternatives, Ottawa, Canada.

NIK THEODORE, Associate Professor of Urban Policy and Planning, University of Illinois at Chicago, USA.

MATTIAS VERMEIREN, Postdoctoral Researcher, Ghent Institute for International Studies, Ghent University, Belgium.

Acknowledgements

The critical project for this work was long in its gestation and will continue to develop well beyond the publication of this volume! That project is connected to theoretical and practical goals broadly shared by the editors and contributors:

1. To provide a means for facilitating new, critical theoretical syntheses to think through the interface between law, constitutionalism and patterns of political economy.
2. To chart historically and empirically the principal relationships involving new constitutionalism – i.e. the key changes in law, constitutions and regulation relative to the extension of the world market and the dominant patterns of geopolitics in the early twenty-first century.
3. To offer alternative constitutional frameworks to better promote democracy, social justice and sustainability.

Our method to address these objectives is therefore collaborative and combines thinkers from ethics, political economy, geopolitics, international and constitutional law, geography and sociology.

This volume was initiated as a result of Stephen Gill's successful application for a Social Science and Humanities Research Council of Canada Workshop Grant, number 646–2010–0033, an application that was developed and planned from its conception along with A. Claire Cutler. Subsequently the concepts and framework for the book were further defined over three days of intensive debates in the May 2011 Workshop, based on first drafts. Contributors then provided second drafts in 2012 and 2013, and with new editorial materials added, the work was reviewed and a contract offered by publishers.

Many people were involved in the project to develop this volume, and they include the following institutions and individuals.

First of all, the editors wish to acknowledge the financial support of the Social Science and Humanities Research Council of Canada, and especially to all the participants at that Workshop for their constructive engagement and hard work in writing and redrafting their contributions for this project. It was also made possible by the generous financial and in-kind support that came from many quarters of York University for this venture. In particular we are grateful to: the Office of the President, Office of the Vice President and Provost, Office of Vice President Research and Innovation, Office of the Dean of Graduate Studies, Office of the Dean of the Faculty of Liberal Arts and Professional Studies (and particularly the very helpful support of Associate Dean Barbara Crow), the Department of Political Science, the Office of the Dean, Osgoode Law School (and particularly Associate Dean of Law, Lisa Phillips) and finally, the Jack and Mae Nathanson Centre on Transnational Human Rights, Crime and Security, also at Osgoode.

Second, we also particularly thank the kind financial and intellectual support of Trudeau Foundation Fellows Professors Janine Brodie (University of Alberta) and Isabella Bakker (York University). Isabella Bakker also provided additional funds to help support the volume following the Workshop and provided editorial advice and inputs that have been invaluable throughout the entire development of this book.

Third, we also acknowledge the hard work and exceptional professionalism of the members of the Organizing Team for the SSHRC Workshop held during 26–28 May 2011 at York University in Toronto (for details see New Constitutionalism and World Order, http://pi.library.yorku.ca/ocs/index.php/ncwo/ncwo). That team included the following: the editors of this volume; and (from York University) Professor Bakker; Dr Paul Foley and Karl Dahlquist who both worked long hours to make the events a success (Paul and Karl were at the time of the Workshop both Doctoral Candidates in Political Science; Paul is now Assistant Professor at Memorial University, Newfoundland); Andrea Kosavic (Digital Initiatives Librarian) who developed superb website materials for outreach; Nadja Martin (Research Officer, Faculty of Liberal Arts and Professional Studies) who worked painstakingly on the SSHRC application; and Phyllis Lepore Babcock and Lia Novario (both Office of the VPRI) who were excellent in helping to administer the funds and organize the events. Other members of the organizing team who made valuable contributions were Dr Adrienne Roberts (Manchester University) and Janine Brodie.

The Workshop was preceded by a related one-day public event that involved several of the contributors to this volume, and it drew a very large audience. The event, *The Future of Global Governance?*, was held on 25 May 2011 at the McEwan Auditorium, Schulich School of Business, York University. For edited videos of the event, edited by Stephen Gill and Grant W. McNair of York University, as well as programme details see: http://www.yorku.ca/lefutur/. Karl Dahlquist painted and designed the excellent poster that advertised both the Workshop and public event and that is featured on the website. The event was graciously opened by Mamdouh Shoukri, President and Vice Chancellor of York, and closed by Patrick J. Monahan, York's Vice President Academic and Provost.

Fourth, at the SSHRC Workshop and afterwards we also benefited from the valuable assistance of Dr. Dan Bousfield (University of Western Ontario) and Dr Adrienne Roberts, and, as the manuscript developed, from the careful and constructive editorial inputs of Dr Hironori Onuki (Lecturer in International Relations, University of Wollongong, Australia). A. Claire Cutler also wishes to acknowledge the research assistantship of the following at the University of Victoria: Ingrid Philion, Michael Smith, Paul Donaldson and James Roy. In particular, Michael and Ingrid worked with A. Claire Cutler on early material for the SSHRC Workshop application. Dr Tim Di Muzio (University of Wollongong), one of the contributors, also performed the substantial and vital task of compiling the index.

We also wish to express our gratitude to John Haslam and his editorial, production and marketing colleagues at Cambridge University Press, in particular to Carrie Parkinson and Karen Oakes. We would also like to thank Jenny Slater and Gail Welsh for their work during the production stage. Finally, we are very grateful to four anonymous reviewers for their exceptionally useful advice, commentary and feedback on this book since its inception. The editors remain responsible for the work as a whole.

Acronyms

ABS	asset-backed securities
AEI	American Enterprise Institute
AKP	Justice and Development Party (Turkey)
ALBA	Bolivarian Alliance for the Americas
APEC	Asia-Pacific Economic Cooperation
ASEAN	Association of Southeast Asian Nations
BAPCPA	Bankruptcy Abuse Prevention and Consumer Protection Act
BIT	Bilateral Investment Treaty
CCCTB	Common Consolidated Corporate Tax Base
CDM	Clean Development Mechanism
CDSR	Cabinet Directive on Streamlining Regulation
CEO	Chief Executive Officer
CETA	Comprehensive Economic and Trade Agreement (Canada–EU)
CFC	chlorofluorocarbons
CMARPRP	Community-Managed Agrarian Reform and Poverty Reduction Programme
EC	European Commission
ECB	European Central Bank
ECJ	European Court of Justice
ETS	European Trading Scheme
EU	European Union
EUSTD	European Union Savings Tax Directive
FAO	Food and Agricultural Organization
FATCA	Foreign Account Tax Compliance Act
FTA	Free Trade Agreement
FTT	financial transaction tax
G20	Group of 20 (finance ministers and central bankers)
GATS	General Agreement on Trade in Services
GATT	General Agreement on Tariffs and Trade

List of acronyms

GDP	gross domestic product
GHG	greenhouse gases
GRAIN	Genetic Resources Action International
ICESCR	International Covenant on Economic, Social and Cultural Rights
ICJ	International Court of Justice
ICSID	International Centre for the Settlement of Investment Disputes (World Bank)
IFAD	International Fund for Agricultural Development
IFI	International Financial Institutions
ILO	International Labour Organization
IMF	International Monetary Fund
IR	international relations
JI	Joint Implementation
KMT	Kuomintang of China (Taiwan)
LDC	least-developed countries
MBS	mortgage-backed securities
MERCOSUR	Common Market of the South
MMT	methylcyclopentadienyl manganese tricarbonyl
NAFTA	North American Free Trade Agreement
NATO	North Atlantic Treaty Organization
NPT	Non-Proliferation Treaty
OECD	Organisation for Economic Co-operation and Development
OTC	over-the-counter
PCB	polychlorinated biphenyls
PPP	Pakistan People's Party
PRA	Portfolio Recovery Associates
PRI	Institutional Revolutionary Party (Mexico)
RAFI	Rural Advancement Foundation International
RAI Principles	Principles for Responsible Agricultural Investment
R2P	Responsibility to Protect
TINA	there is no alternative
TISA	Trade in Services Agreement
TRIPS	Trade-Related Aspects of Intellectual Property Rights
UDHR	Universal Declaration of Human Rights
UN	United Nations
UNASUR	Union of South American Nations
UNCTAD	United Nations Conference on Trade and Development

UNECE	United Nations Economic Commission for Europe
UNEP	United Nations Environment Programme
UNESCO	United Nations Educational, Scientific and Cultural Organization
UNFCCC	United Nations Framework Convention on Climate Change
UN-WIDER	United Nations University World Institute of Development Economics Research
USO	universal service obligation
VAT	value added tax
WB	World Bank
WEO	World Environmental Organization
WTO	World Trade Organization

1 New constitutionalism and world order: general introduction

Stephen Gill and A. Claire Cutler

This introduction sketches some of the book's central considerations and relates them to the immediate historical backdrop of this study. It highlights transformations that constitute the *new constitutionalism* of *disciplinary neo-liberalism*. We also respond to key criticisms of the concept of new constitutionalism and address whether its theory and practices are under challenge in crisis conditions. We then provide an outline of the principal themes and questions that the volume addresses, including: hegemonic and supremacist projects of rule; the power of capital; law, legitimacy and legitimation; contradictions, political agency and contestation. A detailed overview of each chapter is subsequently provided in separate mini-introductions to each of the six parts of this book.[1]

Aims and considerations

A central contention of this volume is that the new constitutionalism of disciplinary neo-liberalism can be conceptualized as a set of dominant political practices that, despite growing contradictions, are reconstituting political and civil society as well as the relations between humanity and the environment in fundamental ways. We believe that these developments mandate new forms of theoretical integration, for example between law and political economy, to better explain key aspects of the twenty-first-century world and some of its potentials for transformation. In that context our principal aim is to map out and explore a new terrain of enquiry in a synthesis of diverse forms of knowledge (law, politics, political economy, sociology and ecology) to seek to explain the reconstitution of power and governance in the emerging world order – one that is characterized by increasing crises, dislocations and political

---

[1] The editors are indebted to the anonymous reviewers, to participants at the York Workshop in May 2011, and especially to Isabella Bakker and Hironori Onuki for their painstaking and constructive comments on drafts of this introduction.

contestation in ways that are reframing the very meaning of traditional constitutionalism.

The term 'new constitutionalism' is used in a variety of related but different ways in the disciplines of political science and law (see Fitzpatrick 2006). For some, new constitutional forms are emerging from the expansion of constitution-making throughout the world, the increasing juridification of international trade and investment laws, the articulation of an autonomous *lex mercatoria* and the emergence of global administrative laws that are knitting the world together under the promise of the global rule of law (Kingsbury *et al.* 2005; Stone Sweet 2006).[2] Others emphasize the growing power of judiciaries, administrators and the 'new federalism' developing through the reorganization of power and authority within states (Hirschl 2004b). Yet others identify new constitutionalism with the pragmatic search for effective, efficient and 'good governance' (Elkin and Soltan 1993). These views are informed by various theoretical traditions that emphasize the global proliferation of democratic models of governance, evolutionary and functional theories that posit constitutional devolution as a matter of system differentiation, or models that regard constitutional evolution as driven by the search for economic efficiency (Hirschl 2004a).

This volume adopts a rather different approach. While we recognize that there is scepticism about the devolution of political powers to judges and administrators (see Hilbink 2008), this volume is inspired by a rather different and more critical tradition. This tradition is connected to the view that theories are not neutral but serve particular purposes or projects. This perspective was reflected in the well-known distinction made by Robert Cox (1996 [1981]) between two broad sets of theories, respectively: 'problem-solving' theory and 'critical' theory. The former 'takes the world as finds it, with the prevailing social and power relationships and the institutions ... as the given framework for action ... the general aim ... is to make [them] work smoothly by dealing effectively with particular sources of trouble' (*ibid.*: 88). In contrast, 'critical' theory 'stands apart from the prevailing order of the world and asks how that order came about ... [it] does not take institutions and social power relations for granted but calls them into question' with a view to revealing the conditions for their radical transformation (*ibid.*). This volume therefore contends that a critical perspective is crucial to the analysis of the constitution and relations of power in the emerging world order of the early twenty-first century.

---

[2] Terms such as rule of law and *lex mercatoria* are discussed in the Glossary.

The contributors to this volume differ in disciplinary origins and in the emphases and meanings they attach to constitutionalism. However, what unites them is an appreciation of the two types of theory noted above. Indeed, each reviews and critiques the problem-solving emphasis of those perspectives associated with extending or reinforcing new constitutionalism as a 'project' of governance of the global political economy (Schneiderman 2010). They develop their critiques to not only interrogate the structural changes in political economy, society and ecology that inform the new constitutionalism, but also to contribute to the transformation of those structures and practices. They seek to deconstruct how the project of new constitutionalism justifies the improvement of the currently dominant set of neo-liberal institutions and practices of global governance: in ways consistent with what the World Bank and the IMF refer to in more normative terms as 'good governance' (Esty 2006).

Thus a critical perspective, associated with the various arguments and approaches that unify this volume, brings ethics, power and political economy to the centre of its analysis. It seeks to reveal and question the purposes and interests served by new constitutionalism as a political and social project. It therefore asks: new constitutionalism of what and for whose benefit? It poses questions concerning law, legitimacy, human rights, political economy and world order. For example: how far and in what ways does the recent spread of rights discourse link to and help to extend the extension and deepening of capitalism by means of laws and regulations designed to remove barriers to the power and mobility of capital? Who benefits from such liberalization of trade and investment or more broadly from corporate expansion? A critical perspective not only seeks to identify the origins, lineages and form of the present world order and thus what is unique about the current period (what is 'new' about the new constitutionalism) but also its potentials for transformation and for alternative forms of constitutionalism to emerge. Constitutionalism as a 'project' more broadly has roots in earlier approaches to international law and organization that reflect the liberal belief in the perfectibility of the world through the development of international laws, institutions and regimes that are said to mute the effects of international anarchy (the absence of a world state or some overarching governing force in world order). In this context, several strands of legal theory are recording the global expansion of law. Domestic constitutional lawyers note the increasing number of states that are adopting domestic constitutional political orders, while domestic administrative lawyers and judges observe the global expansion of their fields (Kingsbury and Casini 2009). For some, this is a welcome movement toward a world governed by law and not by politics, while others applaud the functional efficiencies generated by disaggregated sovereignty, as experts and specialists become the centre of law-creation and enforcement (Slaughter 2004). Public international lawyers also record the global move to law, although some are sceptical of the resulting displacement of politics by managerial technocrats (Koskenniemi 2009). These various strains share faith in the law as the vehicle for the stabilization and legitimization of the existing order and the entrenchment of global 'best practices' in governance (Kennedy 2009). They stress the progressive values of legal process and procedures, many of which, however, are inspired by private, corporate actors and institutions (Dibadj 2008). Indeed, private transnational lawyers believe that their field has come into its own as a central pillar of the global legal architecture (Cutler 2003). The concepts of limited government as well as self-regulating business and finance are promoted as core principles in pro-market reforms and legal structures.

An initial task of a critical perspective is to highlight how new constitutionalism is not simply a set of neutral laws and mechanisms of regulation and governance associated with contemporary capitalism but also reflects a specific complex of dominant forms of political agency, as well as a set of actors, practices and forces in political and civil society – particularly large corporations. These practices have as a goal, at least in the terminology used by the World Bank (1997), the 'locking in' of neo-liberal frameworks of accumulation, with American geopolitical power as its ultimate guarantor.

A second task is to specify how such forms of political agency and the constitutional frameworks may constitute the juridical and political conditions for contestation over present and future development of alternatives, at least in the jurisdictions that have fully embraced market-enhancing, neo-liberal reforms. If so, what are the potentials for this situation to change? In responding to such questions this volume seeks to go well beyond those analyses of 'new constitutionalism' that have so far tended to focus on its *synchronic* dimensions – how it has become structurally entrenched in the global political economy – by systematically foregrounding its *diachronic* aspects, or their potentials for transformation (on this distinction see Braudel 1980 and Glossary). Therefore a key aim of this volume is to identify how the contradictions and contestations within the new constitutionalism of disciplinary neo-liberalism are calling forth new patterns of resistance and forms of insurgent power.

With such issues in mind, to give focus to this volume, we have developed three sets of related hypotheses for contributors to address.

1. We are living in an era in which there is a neo-liberal redefinition of the political on a world scale, linked to the emergence of a de facto neo-liberal new constitutional structure that is serving to define present and future, local and global, policies.
2. Some of the principal mechanisms for this redefinition are both public and private, and are drawn from constitutional, administrative, international and transnational laws. These operate within and across jurisdictions, thus mandating detailed research on such multilevel and multifaceted domains.
3. Contradictions, dislocations and inequalities associated with the new constitutionalism of disciplinary neo-liberalism and global crises are producing contestations linked to new patterns of resistance and insurgent power.

The historical context for new constitutionalism

It is widely acknowledged that a central characteristic in the world order today is how it has been shaped by a 'worldwide market revolution' associated with globalization and neo-liberalism. This characteristic refers to processes of economic integration beyond state borders culminating in a global marketplace of commodities, ideas and identities. The increasing prominence of transnational corporations and the mobility of capital through foreign investment facilitate this integration, as do the networks of trade in goods and services that span the globe (Cutler 2009a, 2009b; Kobrin 2004).

The historical context for much of this transformation was the end of the Cold War, and the ideological triumphalism of the West associated with Francis Fukuyama's eschatological claim that by the early 1990s we had arrived at the end of history, with liberalism as the only viable political alternative that would govern the future. This ideological moment was reflected in the famous dictum of Prime Minister Margaret Thatcher, vowing to destroy socialism in Britain, that henceforth 'There is no alternative' to conservatism and neo-liberalism. Thus the new constitutionalism can be traced back to not only the development of the world market and the particular responses of many ruling forces in the capitalist world to the crisis of profitability for capital in the 1970s and 1980s, but also to the geopolitical reconfiguration during that period. Then, the challenges of the Soviet bloc and the Third World to the dominance of the United States and its allies were firmly repelled; an era of neo-liberal supremacy, or what Stephen Gill (1995a) calls disciplinary neo-liberalism, began to emerge.

However, even today, there is far less recognition that this market revolution – and indeed the emergence of a wider 'market civilization' has been accompanied by the 'new constitutionalism', i.e. the legal and political frameworks that are equally significant in facilitating neo-liberal forms of global economic integration and the extension of the world market.

In this context we should underline that new constitutionalism (as a concept as well as a mode of law and legal regulation) is analytically separable from disciplinary neo-liberalism (understood as a concept of political economy as well as a set of social practices). However, the two concepts reflect different faces of a single neo-liberal political project – intended to extend and deepen the power of capital and to extend capitalist market civilization (Gill 1995a). New constitutionalism forms the political-judicial counterpart to disciplinary neo-liberalism, where the latter refers primarily to the processes of intensifying and deepening the scope of market disciplines associated with the increasing power of capital in organizing social and world orders, and in so doing shaping the limits of the possible in people's everyday lives.

In that context, we view new constitutionalism as involving many political-legal elements and regulatory mechanisms, encompassing hard and soft law that have developed unevenly across space and time (see particularly Chapter 3 by A. Claire Cutler). New constitutionalist pressures and constraints are not a uniform force field, nor a fully formed set of historical structures: they 'vary according to the size, economic strength, form of state and civil society, prevailing national and regional institutional capabilities, and the degree of integration into global capital and money markets' (Gill 2008: 142). This also means that constitutional forms are contingent: they vary to the degree to which they incorporate neo-liberal elements.[3] Nevertheless, one could argue that the emergence of new constitutionalism is part of a more general, albeit uneven, shift or transformation in forms of state, toward the neo-liberal form away from state capitalism and 'actually existing' communism, in a world where the commodity form has been extended into new avenues of accumulation and geographical spaces.

---

[3] Few countries in Latin America have gone as far as Mexico, which made 30 amendments to the nationalist revolutionary Mexican Constitution of 1917 – so that by 1994 it would be fully compatible with NAFTA's requirements concerning free movement of goods and services, extended protections for private property and privatization of common lands. Another extreme example was in 2003, when, following the Iraq War, the US Occupation Authority imposed new constitutional measures that replaced the previous Iraqi statutes, including new protections for private property rights and free movement of capital and goods.

Our definition of the new constitutionalism thus refers to a combination of various sets of processes:

1. The uneven emergence of a de facto constitutional governance structure for the world market (intended to operate regionally, nationally and globally) involving the interaction of public and private power, incorporating international organizations.
2. The neo-liberal reshaping of political subjects and restructuring of particular state forms, partly through constitutional and legal means, extending the orbit and interpellation of the commodity form and its legal codification, in order to extend capitalist markets and the sway of market forces in social and political life.
3. The specific locking-in mechanisms (laws, rules, regulations, procedures and institutions, such as independent central banks) associated with neo-liberal patterns of accumulation.
4. The 'new informality' involving proliferation of soft, self-regulatory and 'flexible' or 'double' legal standards.

In this volume, some of the contributors focus on the third and fourth of these processes in order to specify the operation of new constitutionalism in particular domains and activities. Others, such as Ran Hirschl, are concerned with the second set of these processes (relating to the constitutions of particular nations). Hirschl notes in Chapter 6 that over the last 30 years there has been a large-scale convergence toward constitutional supremacy worldwide, 'accompanied by the rise of what may be termed "generic" constitutional law – a supposedly universal, Esperanto-like discourse of constitutional adjudication and reasoning'; as of 2010, there were approximately 160 countries that subscribed to one form or another of the US model of constitutional supremacy. Moreover, despite numerous variations, judicial review – one of the key neo-liberal locking-in mechanisms identified by the World Bank – has become a fundamental force in determining global and domestic affairs.

Not only has there been a shift toward constitutional supremacy, but also, as Chapter 7 by Saskia Sassen notes, there has also been a general increase in executive, administrative and judicial power relative to that of legislatures. This can be seen as relating to the process that Robert Cox (1987) referred to as the 'internationalization of the state', whereby key agencies of government associated with the executive branch gain in power and increasingly seek to regulate their domestic political economies with reference to the exigencies of the world market (see also Brand *et al.* 2008; Demirović 2011). They do so partly by subordinating those elements of the state formation concerned with domestic welfare and production to ministries of finance and central banks. This pattern is clear if we analyze governmental responses to the recent global financial meltdown in the dominant capitalist powers and the consequent increase in power accruing to heads of state and specialized administrative bodies (Gill 2012).

Therefore if we look at these issues from the perspective of power, production and social reproduction as opposed to the traditional vantage point of constitutional law, we would observe that a large majority of those 160 states have not only moved toward US-style constitutional supremacy, but also reforms within the political economy have been largely consistent with creating the key domestic policy underpinnings of disciplinary neo-liberalism on a world scale. To go one step further, a condition of existence of the legal and political economy system we are describing is the willingness of states to defend it, and in particular the most powerful state in the world, the United States, which has probably greater military supremacy relative to other states than any other state in history, with the possible exception of ancient Rome at the zenith of its power. Moreover the US executive branch and administrative agencies are intertwined with and at the heart of the governance of the principal institutions of the global political economy.

Criticisms of the new constitutional concept

In addressing such issues, some contributions stress the uneven depth and complexity of neo-liberal transformations – what Neil Brenner, Jamie Peck and Nik Theodore refer to in Chapter 8 as the variegated spread of neo-liberal forms of state and regulation across different scales and transformations of society. This conception seeks to expand upon Gill's earlier work. Brenner *et al.* illustrate how new constitutionalism takes on different shapes and results in a variety of neo-liberal state forms. Indeed, in new ways, the contributors explore both horizontal and vertical aspects of new constitutionalism. These involve not only its global, regional, national and local elements but also its political economy elements that are considered alongside the more deeply sociological aspects of new constitutionalism.

Together with Neil Brenner *et al.*, some of the other contributors to this volume, such as Saskia Sassen, Adam Harmes and David Schneiderman, all critically reflect upon the adequacy of earlier formulations of the concept, seeking to extend and develop it in innovative ways.

By contrast other critics have been more dismissive of the new constitutionalist concept. For example, some have argued that the concept is too *structuralist*, pessimistic and deterministic – thus understating the transformative potential of law (Parker 2008; Strange 2002, 2006, 2011).

Others have argued almost the opposite – that it involves a reading of law that is too *instrumentalist* (Hartmann 2011). Other critics see the concept as ignoring soft-law and non-legal neo-liberal practices in ways that neglect opportunities for contesting and resisting neo-liberalism. We think such criticisms are somewhat misplaced and address them later in this section.

A second set of criticisms are more indirect and imply that the new constitutional concept may have been useful but it is likely to be of little relevance in analyzing current and future global transformations. Neo-liberalism (and with it implicitly new constitutionalism) is said to be under pressure as the ongoing financial crisis causes elites and ruling classes to reevaluate their policies. Indeed, some suggest the global financial and economic crises mark the 'end' of neo-liberalism (e.g. Krugman 2009; Nesvetailova and Palan 2010; Stiglitz 2010; Wallerstein 2008; Žižek 2009, 2010). We believe, however, that these economic crises form one part of a wider organic crisis; moreover we also think that like the announcement of Mark Twain's death, these conclusions may be premature. They also beg the following key questions: exactly what is neo-liberalism, how do we define it and how do we know when it has come to an end? Many economists treat neo-liberalism as simply a set of economic doctrines and policy formulas (also Žižek treats it as a form of ideology), whereas we see neo-liberalism as a conscious political project that is connected to an identifiable set of social forces and practices. Put differently, disciplinary neo-liberalism fosters and consolidates a possessively individualist, marketized 'common sense' that militates against solidarity and social justice; however, it also is a normative project, one that is contested yet still dominant and supremacist (rather than hegemonic) or widely viewed as legitimate (Gill 2012).

Indeed, neo-liberalism as a form of social and economic development is full of contradictions, crises and contingent practices, not least of which is the way in which it has gone with immense increases in inequality and social dislocation, while at the same time wealth and power is being concentrated in the hands of a global plutocracy. And in the most recent wave of capitalist crises, while the risks of large investors and firms have been socialized, the costs have been transferred to the public in the form of fiscal and sovereign debt crises, with widespread austerity measures imposed to finance government activities in the global economic emergency. Indeed it is doubtful that new constitutionalism as a strategy can either institutionalize or stabilize the crisis of social reproduction within neo-liberalism – let alone the global crisis of accumulation (Gill 2002: 63–4, 2008: 176, 2012). This is despite the fact that as Chapter 2 by Gill illustrates, new constitutionalism involves crisis management mechanisms and practices to try to contain dislocations and co-opt political opposition to prevent a backlash against neo-liberalism. Gill also underlines how new constitutionalism has a contingent, pragmatic and contested character.

However, this does not mean that disciplinary neo-liberalism has ended, although it may be in crisis; and indeed there is much to play for. We therefore see the present situation as still in flux but pregnant with new political possibilities. For example, in 2012 the European Union made efforts to further extend new constitutionalist frameworks via various measures including the new Fiscal Compact as well as the policies of the so-called 'troika' (IMF, ECB and European Commission) applied in Greece, Portugal and potentially in Spain (the Compact requires balanced budget amendments to national constitutions and greater control over national fiscal policies to the unelected European Commission). These new measures have emerged in the context of financial, banking, fiscal and sovereign debt crises. However, the austerity that has been imposed is deeply controversial and may be provoking a general crisis of legitimacy for the European integration project. It is an open question as to whether the European Union will be forced to abandon some of these new constitutional measures or face disintegration as a result of these struggles.

Other more global elements of new constitutionalism, e.g. bilateral trade and investment treaties, are proliferating but are also subject to some modification because of the contradictions associated with the multiple economic crises (see Chapters 3, 10 and 11 by Cutler, Schneiderman and Sinclair). Key elements of new constitutionalism associated with international taxation and the question of capital mobility have continued to be extended, despite some acknowledgement of the need for capital controls to deal with problems generated by capital flows under crisis conditions (see Chapter 12 by Lesage *et al.*). While there has been some (temporary) resistance from countries in the global South to a key aspect of new constitutionalism, that is the free movement of capital, 'it seems that all emerging markets still seem to agree on the final goal of full international capital mobility and of gradually liberalizing capital accounts' (Dierckx 2013: 13). The form and purpose of resistance is also important and involves 'those ... who reject US dominance, without necessarily envisaging more democratic control of capital, neither in the authoritarian Chinese regime, nor in Brazilian or Indian liberal democracy' (*ibid.*).

Because of such evidence, we suggest that it is no longer possible to think of constitutional transformations simply from within the confines of a nation state – that is from the vantage point of what might be called methodological nationalism. Indeed many international agreements and treaties have domestic constitutional status, and act as part of a transnational force field of laws, as well as patterns of incentives and constraints that serve to constitute global power relations and some of the governing institutions and structures of the global political economy. This of course does not mean that all constitutional forms are subordinated to neo-liberal ends, nor does it mean that there is no constitutional space, even in neo-liberal constitutional orders, for contestation, innovation and transformation.

Indeed, even those contributions that debate traditional dimensions of constitutionalism and the rule of law (May, Chapter 4), the relationship between legality and legitimacy (Falk, Chapter 18), judicialization (Hirschl, Chapter 6), and between property rights, security and the constitution of liberty (Di Muzio, Chapter 5) reveal how problematic traditional constitutional conceptions have become under the logic of new constitutionalism. They underscore the need for critical and innovative re-conceptualizations of the question of law and constitutionalism in order to capture contemporary transformations in political practices, state forms and not least how the law interpellates political and social subjects, and instantiates the commodity form across wider areas of social life and the environment (see Chapters 2 and 3 by Gill and Cutler).

What is 'new' about the new constitutionalism?

All this still begs the question what is *new* about the new constitutionalism? Perhaps the answer is *not everything is new*: the new constitutionalism combines both the old and new in a radically changed contemporary context whereby the forces of commodification are reaching ever deeper into new domains that have previously not been subordinated to capitalist market forces or encoded in contractual relations (not only life forms but even the weather are now subject to commodification via futures and derivatives sold on commodities exchanges; see in particular Chapter 3 by Cutler and Chapter 13 by Isabella Bakker). The chapters by Bakker, Adrienne Roberts, Janine Brodie and Hilal Elver in Part V all show, in different ways and at different rates of change, how commodification processes, locked in by new constitutional mechanisms, serve increasingly to reconstitute the nature of social reproduction, welfare and society, and the governance of the environment. Such contributions also reflect the fact that new constitutionalism involves dominant forms of agency: conscious projects to insulate the economy and private power from any potential for democratization of control and, if necessary, to do so with punitive disciplinary measures, such as those associated with the criminalization of poverty (see Chapter 14 by Roberts).

Other contributors address the 'new', highlighting how old political structures may adapt and maintain their resilience in the face of new political practices under the multilateral governance of neo-liberalism. For example, in Chapter 8, Brenner *et al.* illustrate the uneven, variegated and contested nature of new constitutionalism, a process that also challenges traditional conceptions of the state as an integral and sovereign political form.

Another difference, which combines the old and the new, is also highlighted in Chapter 3 by Cutler, and concerns the degree to which transnational forms of law and quasi-constitutional structures are coming, for many nations, to supervene over domestic constitutionalism, but not necessarily in ways similar to previous forms of imperialism or colonization: something new appears to be at work. Indeed, there is a discernible pattern in terms of a rules-based constitutionalism, which is reflected not only in the domestic adoption of charters and bills of rights, and mechanisms for judicial review, but also as addressed by Chapters 10 and 11 by David Schneiderman and Scott Sinclair: the proliferation of neo-liberal trade and investment frameworks, such as the North American Free Trade Agreement (NAFTA), the World Trade Organization (WTO), over 3,000 recently struck Bilateral Investment Treaties (BITs) and the Trade-Related Intellectual Property Rights (TRIPS) Agreement in the WTO.

Privatization trends and changes in public service provision are also indirectly related to other new constitutional developments – including trade- and investment-related aspects of education, healthcare and other public service sectors – despite variations across different scales of governance and jurisdiction (see Chapters 10, 11 and 13–15 by Schneiderman, Sinclair, Bakker, Roberts and Brodie). Such new forms of neo-liberal regulation as the General Agreement on Trade in Services (GATS) are intended to serve as neo-liberal 'pre-commitment mechanisms' with quasi-constitutional effects. Other examples include the legally binding trade 'disciplines' of NAFTA and the WTO, which build upon traditional liberal trade principles of non-discrimination (national treatment and most-favoured-nation) embodied in previous regimes, and that are now greatly strengthened with new forms of commitment and more powerful dispute settlement mechanisms. In this context, WTO signatories are formally committed to 'the progressive liberalization' of key areas of economic activity and social life that have been previously insulated from the full play of capitalist market forces.

What are much less frequently noted even in the political economy literature are the constitutional, legal and institutional changes in macroeconomic policy (and more generally concerning the commanding heights of economic policy), exemplified by the proliferation of politically independent central banks, currency boards and the widespread introduction of fiscal restraint and balanced-budget laws (Gill 1992a, 1998a). Of interest here are responses to the global financial meltdown of 2008, when central banks throughout the world, which had previously preached the disciplinary and market-enhancing virtues of sound money and anti-inflationary policy, reacted pragmatically and used their 'independence' on behalf of financial capital as they pumped huge bailout funds into their financial systems in order to avoid a great depression in the early twenty-first century. Indeed, the bailout measures just noted were extended not simply to financial capital but also, particularly in North America, to US automobile producers, in ways that were *not* extended to all foreign corporations operating within the United States and Canada – a prima facie abandonment of the key principles of non-discrimination in the trade and investment regime, signalling that *key aspects of new constitutionalism are either temporarily suspended or simply not sustainable in the context of deep financial crises.* Such examples show the *pragmatic* nature of systems of rule in actually existing capitalism – particularly when the system as a whole seems to be threatened. What needs to be emphasized here is how capitalist regulation and its institutional structure do not operate neutrally, as many liberal legal scholars seem to imply, but rather they operate systematically on behalf of particular interests, in this case large banks and other powerful corporations that benefit from enormous subsidies and bailouts.

Even mechanisms of judicial review highlighted by the World Bank (1997) as crucial for the credibility of new constitutionalism and governance, should be viewed in an equally pragmatic way. A study by Michael Mandel (1998) notes that the use of judicial review by what he calls the capitalist oligarchy depends entirely upon whether it is perceived as being useful for fending off democracy, and in particular for controlling representative organs. This position is also taken up and developed further in Chapter 6 by Ran Hirschl.

Finally, in the context of the debates concerning 'hard' and 'soft' law as aspects of the governance of the global political economy, it seems that it is no accident that new constitutional agreements tend to provide *hard* or *binding* rights for corporations and investors but only require *soft* or *voluntary* responsibilities of them. Why, for example, should environmental norms be soft, with international agreements concerning the stewardship of the environment based upon voluntary self-regulation by firms or nations? This question is taken up in Chapter 16 by Hilal Elver.

In sum, we suggest that the new constitutionalism appears to be emerging as a de facto governance structure for the global political economy, one that is premised upon *both* domestic constitutional transformation as well as 'progressive liberalization' of the global political economy. Here therefore, we are not simply interested in *de jure* constitutional change as normally addressed by constitutional lawyers, but also in de facto changes of governance that may serve to reconstitute political power on a world scale. Put differently, in the terminology of the neo-liberal theorists, does new constitutionalism create conditioning frameworks or binding constraints so that political contestation is isolated within the realms of 'ordinary politics' (Buchanan 1991) in ways that protect or cannot threaten private property rights and individual freedoms? And while Hirschl notes that new constitutionalism lacks many of the attributes associated with 'classical constitutionalism' and entrenched rules that shape what is politically possible, including: 'separation of powers; a hierarchy of institutions; an amending formula; or an aspirational preamble ("we the people ...") that defines and constitutes the polity' (Hirschl in Chapter 6 of this volume), we note that new constitutionalism does feature several key elements of traditional or classical constitutionalism, ranging from forms of judicial review to other quasi-constitutional structures that supervene over 'domestic' or traditional constitutionalism. The WTO, which was approved in 1994 as a Single Undertaking, has constitutional status for its signatories; and as we have noted above, it also has an overarching aspirational commitment to the 'progressive liberalization' of the global political economy.

Themes, hypotheses and questions: overview of the contributions

This section highlights other key themes that are shared across various contributions: hegemony, supremacy and the power of capital; the relationship between law, legitimacy and legitimation; and, questions of political agency and contestation.

Hegemony, supremacy and the power of capital

We suggest that new constitutionalism can be considered to be part of a broader supremacist (not hegemonic) project of rule, associated with extending the power of capital and the geopolitical reach of the United States, and not least with creating a global plutocracy, in the post-Cold War world order (Gill 1995b, 2004).

Bourgeois *hegemony* implies the rule and forward-looking leadership of a bloc of social forces drawn from political and civil society, which sustains the existing order by incorporating and gaining the consent of subordinate social classes, presenting its leadership as legitimate and operating as if it is in a general or universal interest. At the global level, hegemony is rarely if ever achieved, since it necessarily involves inequalities of inter-state and social power that are experienced by subordinated nations and peoples as forms of imperialism. Nevertheless efforts to institutionalize the rule of law and to contain the use of organized violence, such as the creation of the United Nations, can be conceived of as attempts at creating a more legitimate or hegemonic global order. *Supremacy*, by contrast, involves rule by a bloc of forces that clearly serves partial or particular interests, and that is experienced by subordinates as involving coercive, corrupt forms of rule that lack legitimate appeal and credibility. Supremacy can continue to exercise dominance over politically fragmented or atomized populations until a coherent form of opposition emerges that might provoke a crisis of authority and a challenge to supremacist leadership. Such a challenge might, therefore, reverse growing inequalities of power and the deterioration in the conditions of existence of a majority of people (Gill 2008, 2012).

The new constitutionalism as a governance and geopolitical project therefore represents a major component of the 'really existing' response to the problem, on a world scale, of securing the conditions for extended capital accumulation in the contemporary period – however, one that lacks a hegemonic quality. As Neil Brenner noted, 'It is ... not the only response, but because of its "parameterizing" properties and tendencies, it is a response that has massive implications for other responses to this dilemma, as well as to any counter- or anti-capitalist projects to challenge the structural power of capital at any spatial scale.'[4]

Indeed, any research programme on this question would need to note nevertheless that it is very difficult to contest the structural power of capital. In turn, the idea of capital mobility itself ultimately rests upon the direct power of capital, in the form of the national and international legal frameworks and forms of state action that inform, codify and protect private property rights: without such private property rights in place, capital mobility does not exist; investors seek legal guarantees when they make decisions on whether to move capital into and out of jurisdictions. Indeed, the structural power of capital is also vividly illustrated in Chapter 12 by Dries Lesage, Mattias Vermeiren and Sacha Dierckx on new constitutionalism and the global tax regime. Thus research must take account of the structural dimensional of the power of capital and how this is precisely locked in, consolidated and ultimately normalized so that it becomes 'constituted power'.

---

[4] Correspondence from Neil Brenner to the editors, 28 May 2011.

As Adam Harmes notes in Chapter 9, neo-liberal intellectuals have linked these developments to the promotion of a particular kind of market-extending federalism that incorporates inter-jurisdictional competition to discipline governments so they compete to attract mobile capital and investment, while providing holders of capital with the exit option of moving from one jurisdiction to the next if the business climate in that location deteriorates. In this sense the direct power of capital, which is manifested in the creation of institutions and laws, including property rights (private property rights are a necessary legal counterpart to international capital mobility), is umbilically linked in neo-liberal theorizations to extending the structural power of capital. The latter partly depends upon the inter-jurisdictional mobility of capital, which acts to discipline governments and workers. Chapter 10 by David Schneiderman, on the global investment regime, directly addresses the linkage between the neo-liberal forms of state and the power of investment capital.

Law, legitimacy and legitimation

Critical political economy starts from the premise of the historicity of capitalism: the power of capital does not spring spontaneously as if from the virgin soil, but has historical as opposed to natural roots. Moreover capitalism as a system does not automatically reproduce itself but requires the ongoing application of political power to make private accumulation possible. Therefore it involves both political and material structures of production/reproduction and mechanisms for the legitimization of private accumulation (see Cutler in Chapter 3).

As several of the contributions to this book seek to show, in effect what is being analyzed and described here consists of elements of a *de jure* but ultimately a de facto constitutional structure that is emerging for global capital accumulation in our present historical moment. New constitutional principles and institutions serve not only conservatively to lock in existing entitlements to private property, but also innovatively to create new forms of private property in ways that allow capital to overcome limitations and barriers to accumulation.

Yet at the same time questions about contradictions and inconsistencies in the law arise: the *hard* legal disciplines locking in neo-liberalism exist dialectically with *soft* laws – for example, the laws governing corporate social responsibilities for the environment, human rights and labour are soft and non-binding. Indeed laws may either have non-existent or very weak binding mechanisms, and where they are soft they assume voluntary compliance by corporations. As soft laws they also function flexibly, as safety valves for capitalism, 'allowing the law to be breached' when required (Cutler 2005: 539, quoting Poulantzas).

Thus we recognize the tendency to selective use of soft legal disciplines as a counterpart to the advent of flexible accumulation and strategies to further subordinate labour to capital (Harvey 1989; Scheuerman 1999). A dialectic between hard and soft law also works a legitimizing role by facilitating the enforcement of hard corporate rights (the right to property and to hire and fire workers) in the face of the soft corporate social responsibilities noted above.

Nevertheless, legitimization of new constitutionalism may also be achieved through the use of law to limit democratic challenges to protected private property rights (Di Muzio in Chapter 5; Hirschl in Chapter 6) and through the maintenance of federal-provincial arrangements that insulate economic relations from political accountability and controls (Harmes in Chapter 9). Christopher May (Chapter 4) also explores the social processes associated with professionalization and technical expertise, involved in advancing and legitimizing new constitutionalism as a global rule of law – a form of agency that is intended to transform the legal orders of the global South to make them more consistent with the new constitutionalism, perhaps serving to widen its legitimacy. Such mechanisms have frequently gone, however, with very detailed and coercive conditionality imposed on recipients of loans by the international financial institutions, particularly the World Bank (on this question see Ruckert 2009).

Indeed, as Chapter 18 by Richard Falk illustrates, the new constitutionalism is underpinned not only by US primacy and related geopolitical structures but also by double standards involving the selective application of law. This generates troublesome distinctions, ambiguities and relations between legality and legitimacy.

Agency and contestation

The current deep crisis in neo-liberal capitalism has placed new constitutionalist projects under scrutiny, and in important respects under challenge. As we have noted a critical perspective challenges liberal legalism's assumptions that new public or private modes of law-creation and adjudication are neutral or legitimate. A critical perspective, as discussed in Chapter 4 by May, raises the question of agency and asks who constructs and legitimates the rule of law as an integral dimension of new constitutionalism, and indeed who challenges the self-evidence and justice of its precepts (see also Cutler in Chapter 3). Indeed a critical perspective explores lineages and potentials for structures and relations of power, from the origins of modern capitalism (e.g. the genealogy of American constitutionalism in Chapter 5 by Di Muzio) to future prospects and potentials for transformation.

From our critical perspective we are thus interested in the dialectic between constituted and insurgent power, and how far and in what ways this dialectic may be intensified in an era of capitalist crises in ways that might give rise to transformation in the political 'limits of the possible'. The book is therefore concerned to both imagine and consider a series of alternative constitutional forms – including forms that may be more consistent with the democratic self-actualization of local and global communities and sustainable relations between human beings and nature (Sassen 2008).

The contributors note the existence of a variety of legal structures and institutions that facilitate capitalist accumulation through the constitution of new and expanding legal forms for appropriating property and by legitimizing this expansion as part of the 'common sense' of global capitalism. At the same time, the world is experiencing a wrenching set of economic crises that form part of a much more extensive 'organic' crisis (Chapter 13 by Bakker). This conjuncture raises important issues concerning whether new constitutionalism is in advance or decline and the prospects for transforming global leadership through challenges to neo-liberal discipline (Gill 2012).

With such issues in mind, some of the contributions of this book, such as Chapter 9 by Harmes and Chapter 12 by Lesage *et al.*, directly explore questions of agency, and how and with what consequences the new constitutionalism, multilevel governance and neo-liberal federalism projects may be connected to both the direct and structural forms of the power of capital and specifically to international capital mobility (see also Dierckx 2013).

In this conjuncture what is deemed to be politically possible is framed by what Fernand Braudel called the *longue durée*, or the historically constituted structures of world order and capitalism that have emerged over a considerable time span (Braudel 1980). These structures have been subsequently modified with the *conjoncture* associated with the emergence of disciplinary neo-liberalism over the past 30 years, e.g. via accelerations in time-space compression and mechanisms of dispossession, and by capitalist crises, as dominant elements seek to transform their preferred frameworks of rule into synchronic mechanisms of constituted power that serve to protect them from the contestation of emergent forces that experience subordination. Under certain conditions, however, diachronic elements or emergent forces produce contestations, such as those that may crystallize as insurgent power with new projects of governance.

Therefore contributors to this book seek to highlight alternative possibilities and those forms of insurgent power that are, or may be, emergent in the context of the global organic crisis. In that sense we are interested in change and transformation that goes beyond what Richard Falk has called the 'horizons of feasibility', that is the limits of what can be implemented politically given the constraints imposed by special interests and constituted powers that seek to stabilize the existing order. Indeed, a key political aspect of the global organic crisis is that it reflects an impasse, or what Falk calls the 'horizons of necessity': a moment when what must be done for the sake of sustainability and survival exceeds what is possible politically: constituted powers are trapped within horizons of feasibility. This volume therefore seeks to explore and imagine some of the means to go beyond this impasse and it invokes what Falk refers to as new 'horizons of desire'.[5] These new political intimations and forces are associated for example with what Negri (1999) has called the insurgent power of the subaltern, e.g. related to the quest for a 'just new constitutionalism' (Falk, Chapter 18) or as part of an 'insurgent alternative' associated with 'globalization from below' (Anderson, Chapter 17). Can these new horizons be linked to a wider democratization of global politics and society and the creation of more just constitutional forms? Might they involve a new 'environmental constitutionalism' as suggested by Elver (Chapter 16)? Sassen (Chapter 7) emphasizes the role that national actors play in driving forward new constitutionalism, while others emphasize that local- and national-level practices are unpredictable and varied (Brenner *et al.*, Chapter 8). How far and in what ways does the new constitutionalism of disciplinary neo-liberalism limit and contain demands for change, and channel and serve to co-opt them into the systemically supportive political forces? This is only one of a series of questions raised by this collection.

A note on the organization of this book

This book therefore addresses one part of the *problématique* of the neo-liberal governance of global capitalism. The emergence of the new constitutionalism has coincided largely with the global expansion of the

---

[5] Richard Falk, 'Horizons of Global Governance'. Lecture delivered at the conference 'The Future of Global Governance?', York University, Toronto, 25 May 2011. Available online at: http://stephengill.com/news/2011/07/re-imagining-the-future-videos-of-yorks-the-future-of-global-governance.html (accessed 13 July 2011).

power of capital, in general, and of large corporations in particular. It has involved the extension of private property rights and investor freedoms, locked in by hard, binding forms of law as well as by other rules and regulations. The growing power of transnational corporations in turn raises questions of legitimacy and agency in global capitalism.

We suggest that the developments discussed above may constitute a *global redefinition of politics and governance*, involving significant geopolitical changes with associated processes of privatized and multilevel governance. We also think that many of the changes in the nature and form of constitutionalism suggest *ontological* and *epistemological shifts* in world order that are highly differentiated, and certainly not monolithic. They involve multiple contradictions and contestations, many of which arise directly from neo-liberal capitalism across different scales and regulatory domains such as trade, investment, taxation, welfare, education and health, as well as security. Some of these contestations stem from the effects of the progressive commodification of production and social reproduction in a process that involves the contradictory restructuring of societies that have been heretofore organized on a variety of different social principles. Nevertheless, such de facto neo-liberal constitutionalism and its counterparts in the emerging forms of privatized economic governance have been palpable in shaping global public policy in ways intended – through the variety of lock-in mechanisms noted above – to have long-term effects. Whether this can remain the case in light of the deepest global economic meltdown since the 1930s is a moot point.

From a theoretical viewpoint, therefore, we believe this mandates a critical reconsideration of the ontological and epistemological bases of comparative and international constitutionalism, and of political economy, as well as reflection on the significance of such legal and institutional changes in governance for what feminists call the institutions of social reproduction – that is those associated with public services, care, education, and common goods and resources (Bakker and Gill 2003).

We are in a period in which the political economy, legal frameworks and regulatory institutions of capitalism – and the frameworks of new constitutionalism – may be up for revision. The deep and wrenching crisis of global capitalism has, in effect, created a conjecture that offers us a unique opportunity to interrogate the nature and sustainability of new constitutionalism, and also initiate groundbreaking contributions to the reconsideration of key mechanisms governing our political economies and societies.

This volume is structured as follows: Part I: Concepts; Part II: Genealogy, origins, and world order; Part III: Multilevel governance and neo-liberalization; Part IV: Trade, investment and taxation; Part V:

Social reproduction, welfare and ecology; and Part VI: Globalization from below and prospects for a just new constitutionalism. Each part has a short mini-introduction that briefly summarizes each chapter and helps guide the reader through this volume. The mini-introductions were written by Hironori Onuki under the guidance of the editors. Each highlights the main arguments and themes addressed in the various chapters. Finally, we have included a Glossary of technical and conceptual terms used throughout and a short Appendix listing key questions and themes addressed by the authors in preparing their contributions for this work.

This volume, we think, has allowed for imaginative and innovative contributions that seek to interrelate and integrate knowledge drawn from ethics, law, political economy, society, welfare and ecology, in a forward-looking way. As noted, many of the chapters (not simply those in Part I) introduce conceptualizations: they often cut across themes and issues. As critical thinkers, the contributors have sought not only to identify the potentials for transformation of neo-liberal new constitutionalism but also to outline and develop new intimations for alternative ethical and political forms that can contribute to a more just and sustainable world order.

Part I

Concepts

The aim of Part I is twofold. First, it seeks to outline some of the issues surrounding the collective critical effort of this volume to interrogate and underline the importance of law and constitutionalism for the study of global political economy. Second and more specifically, it seeks to outline how new constitutionalism operates within the dynamics of emergent global market civilization as the 'common sense' for ordering the neo-liberal restructuring of local and global political economies and societies. There are four main themes to Part 1:

1. Conceptualization of the law as an active governing technique that is productive of political authority;
2. Expansion of the commodity form of law and new constitutionalism in the social reproduction of capitalist market civilization;
3. Globalization of the neo-liberal rule of law as a project to strengthen and legitimate the power of capital and to secure the absolute sovereignty of private property rights; and
4. Possibilities for the development of alternative or insurgent forms of constitutionalism to advance a more just, democratic and progressive world order.

Stephen Gill in Chapter 2 seeks to go beyond dominant understandings of law as either a 'superstructure' or as an external mechanism of authority and regulation that operates in a neutral manner within a relatively self-regulating capitalist economy. Legal relations, as he stresses, are 'central to the constitution of the power of capital as well as neo-liberal forms of state, or political and civil society, in the emerging world order'. From this perspective, he highlights the emergence of new constitutionalism as a de facto political-juridical structure that intensifies and 'locks in' powers and disciplines of capital in social relations – what he calls 'disciplinary neo-liberalism'. New constitutionalism and disciplinary neo-liberalism form part of a wider market civilization that has emerged during the long history or *longue durée* of modern capitalism. Gill shows how the emergence of market civilization forms part of the constitution of capitalist social and power relations in an historical process that involves ongoing processes of dispossession and proletarianization. He argues that the global extension and social reproduction of the capitalist market civilization are also intimately tied to geopolitical changes in both the global North and global South since the 1970s, particularly since the end of the Cold War, as well as to transformations in the political economy characterized by shifts toward flexible accumulation and the development of neo-liberal forms of state. To bring important historical changes into relief, he outlines the principal ideal-typical features of neo-liberal state forms and the rule of law. The neo-liberal rule of law or 'new' constitutionalism formally defines and limits the scope and purpose of state action in the form of limited government, and in so doing promotes the autonomy of private corporations through the separation of public and private, or state and civil society. In the neo-liberal rule of law, mechanisms such as judicial review are designed to limit executive and legislative power and to preserve the separation of the 'economic' as a 'private sphere' outside of the 'political'. Put alternatively, neo-liberal forms of state facilitate the decentralization of power, affirming the rights of private enterprise to create 'private laws' to govern the organization of firms and production, as well as consolidating other private property rights.

Gill further elaborates that to guarantee extended protection for private property rights and investor freedoms across national borders now and in future, new constitutionalism involves three interrelated sets of measures, or what he calls 'productive constraints' that shape neo-liberal governance of the global political economy and strengthen the power of capital:

1. Measures to reorganize state apparatuses through not only the liberalization of trade and investment but also the privatization of public resources and services, in a process that is underpinned by various legal mechanisms including judicial review as well as multilateral, regional and bilateral agreements.
2. Measures to create and expand capitalist markets by rewriting laws and statutes to extend the scope and scale of accumulation and to intensify the prerogatives of the holders of private property rights over labour, environmental and other human rights.
3. Measures to maintain depoliticization of the 'economy', especially within the management of the current crisis of accumulation, through legitimating the removal of strategic economic policy from political contestation while attenuating and co-opting popular democratic forces and potential opposition.

In this light, Gill addresses the possibilities for transformative resistance to the power of capital under the conditions of an emerging global organic crisis. Drawing on his notion of a 'post-modern Prince' that refers to the potentials for a set of left forces to organize an emerging and variegated form of progressive global leadership, he emphasizes the need to not only critically explore the contradictions in global market civilization but also for progressive and left forces to coalesce into a new radical democratic organization as a means to creating more just, sustainable and human forms of constitutionalism.

Further noting the limitations of conceptualizations of legal relations as simply a 'superstructure' of capitalism, in Chapter 3, A. Claire Cutler highlights how new constitutionalism is a juridical foundation for the global expansion of capitalism and market civilization. She argues that the globalization of the commodity form of law has not only served as a necessary precondition for the emergence of transnational market civilization that is unifying diverse peoples and places through the logic of commodification, but also that it has established new privatized modes of appropriation and legitimation. As Cutler elaborates, these systems of private transnational governance privilege the rights and interests of transnational over national capital. Providing evidence from a range of locations in the global South, Cutler outlines the relationships between patterns of primitive accumulation and dispossession, and their links to World Bank structural adjustment policies, which have sought to reconfigure local legal frameworks governing property rights. Such measures and forms of legal reconstruction subordinate local economies and societies to delocalized and denationalized laws, and legitimize and enforce knowledge and power structures that enclose common property into private property regimes.

Cutler then shows how this process is extending to encompass ever-expanding dimensions of nature that are transformed into tradable commodities. In so doing, Cutler addresses the question of what is 'new' about the new constitutionalism. While the enclosure of nature as private property through the commodity form of law is not a historical novelty, her discussion of the commodification of land, the atmosphere and water precisely shows how the new constitutionalism combines the 'old' or traditional technique of enclosure, by which capitalism transcends and disassembles limits to private appropriation, with the 'new' form of neo-liberal enclosure. Neo-liberal enclosures push back the frontiers of commodification into new spheres of nature and society in a process that is 'predicated on Lockean understandings of property that assess value in pure economic terms of improvement, displacing non-economic measures of value and utility'. This process has therefore rapidly deepened the penetration of neo-liberal market disciplines into new areas of resource extraction and into social activities that have hitherto not been subordinated to capitalist market forces or encoded in contractual relations.

For example, Cutler describes the ways in which the adoption of the Kyoto Protocol in 1997 has been linked to the commodification of the atmosphere, resulting in the creation of a 'new carbon economy' in which actors can buy and sell carbon credit or carbon offset credits in capitalist markets. The commodification of CO_2 emissions can be regarded as a highly privatized mode of governance that decentralizes significant authority over the atmosphere to markets and to supranational and non-state actors. As Cutler notes, it also forces communities in the global South to receive 'unequal benefits from offsets and emission trading' under the neo-colonial systems of property rights.

The transformation of the natural environment and resources from public to private goods through the commodity form of law has not gone unchallenged. Drawing on E. P. Thompson's understanding of the double face of the law that instantiates class power but also creates legal forms that restrict that power, Cutler suggests that 'resistance that redefines the meaning of law' is possibly one of the most powerful means to contest further enclosures of common property and expansion of the commodity form of law. This form of resistance, as she underlines, requires the reconstitution of legal relations by 'recasting private property rights to nature as shared collective property rights of use, conservation and preservation', in ways that fundamentally challenge the principles of the new constitutionalism of disciplinary neo-liberalism.

Chapter 4, by Christopher May, builds upon Gill's earlier discussion of the neo-liberal rule of law and explores the ways in which the rule of law has been conditioned by the prevailing logic of the new constitutionalism. More specifically, May directs attention to the issues of legitimation and political agency by addressing the question: how and who constructs and legitimates the rule of law in capitalist market civilization? May reminds us that the justification or legitimation of any specific legal system as a technology of governance cannot be achieved simply through coercion exercised by the governing class but must receive the consent of the governed. Therefore, what initially needs to be recognized is that the establishment and reproduction of a particular form of the rule of law that serves as the *Grundnorm* of the new constitutionalism is driven by a specific political project. This project serves the particular interests of dominant capital and its operating agents. It seeks to sustain itself as a form of 'common sense', namely an understanding of the rule of law largely accepted by those it governs as uncontroversial and non-problematic: a self-evident foundation for the organization and understanding of their everyday lives and more broadly for global politics. The central purpose of this project, as May notes, is, however, not to promote an active citizenry but to depoliticize its particular form of the rule of law as central to its systems of governance. In this way 'the *pre-commitment* to the rule of law' limits and shapes the political limits of the possible, constraining potential transformations of current and future social and world orders.

For May, along with Gill, the spread of the rule of law as an increasingly legitimated norm and as a form of rhetoric can be also attributed to the rise of supremacist American power and the diffusion of liberal forms of identity in the twentieth century. Particularly since the post-Cold War geopolitical shift to a more neo-liberal world order, there has been a transformation in questions of democracy and governance. May is concerned with a combination of two complementary practices that reinforce this neo-liberal shift: professionalization and technical assistance to former communist and to Third World countries. Both play a key role in the neo-liberal reconstitution of the rule of law as the current 'overarching norm of global politics'. One of the consequences of this shift is that social problems are increasingly not addressed through democratic deliberation or treated as politically contentious issues. Rather they are conceived as involving narrow technical choices between rules and jurisdictions, in a process managed by lawyers who are often part of a professionalized transnational legal-commercial community. Indeed this community engages in extensive programmes of technical assistance – many of them sponsored by international organizations such as the World Bank – which seek to inculcate and (re-)establish the rule of law in communities that have historically developed different legal norms. These programmes are based on the claim that 'the rule of law represents a global consensus concerning the technical problems of governance and not the imposition of a particular political system'. May concludes, nevertheless, by suggesting that the process of maintaining the new constitutionalism is incomplete and still lacks legitimacy. It therefore allows spaces for alternative projects of law and society to emerge, precisely because its *Grundnorm*, the rule of law, is highly contested.[1]

---

[1] Editors' note: the World Bank has sought to maintain depoliticization of economic policy, partly by means of its conditionality agreements that are counterparts to the 'technical assistance' programmes noted by Christopher May. Incorporation of social policies and poverty reduction strategies by the World Bank into its efforts to restructure state forms involves attempts to 'deepen the hegemony of neoliberal policies in developing countries, by selectively combining coercive (increased conditionality and monitoring) with consensual (better inclusion) political strategies'. Put differently, 'macro-structural elements of disciplinary neoliberalism are … increasingly complemented by various micro-political policing tools for regulating and monitoring the behaviour of the poor' (Ruckert 2009: 56). See also Chapter 14 by Adrienne Roberts on strategies to incorporate and discipline the poor in the United States.

2 Market civilization, new constitutionalism and world order

Stephen Gill

This chapter advances several hypotheses concerning market civilization and then identifies key ideal-typical features of neo-liberal forms of state, and three principal elements of new constitutionalism[1]. The latter furnishes central juridical and institutional mechanisms that underpin the power and discipline of capital in social relations (what I call disciplinary neo-liberalism). In my argument the law is not simply understood as 'superstructure' or indeed as a set of constraints on the exercise of authority of government; rather, law is seen as an active governing technique that is productive of political authority: it is seen as central to the constitution of the power of capital as well as neo-liberal forms of state, or political and civil society, in the emerging world order.

In that context, the principal hypothesis that guides this chapter is that we are living in an era in which there is an uneven, multi-scalar, crisis-driven and contradictory neo-liberal redefinition of the political on a world scale, consistent with the spread of an emergent global market civilization. With this in mind, and particularly in the conclusion, I address some of these contradictions and the potential for contestation and transformative resistance to disciplinary neo-liberalism, associated with the intimations of a post-modern Prince as a means to creating alternative forms of civilization and world order.

The constitution of market civilization: the old and the new

Fernand Braudel once noted 'it would be pleasant to be able to define the word "civilization" simply and precisely, as one defines a straight line, a triangle or a chemical element' (Braudel 1994: 3). While civilizations

---

[1] This chapter draws partly on sections from Gill 2002 and 2004. My sincere thanks go to the participants at the May 2011 SSHRC Workshop, and especially to Isabella Bakker, A. Claire Cutler, Ran Hirschl and Saskia Sassen, for their insightful comments – only a few of which I was able to address in this version.

exist in space and time, in specific although sometimes overlapping geographical areas, Braudel notes that the vocabulary of the social sciences scarcely permits a 'decisive definition': civilizations are complex and contested entities. To explain them involves all of the social sciences: history, geography, sociology, political economy and 'collective psychology'. The latter refers to how people internalize certain perspectives on the world and society and its institutions forming 'collective mentalities' that from time to time 'dominate the whole mass of society' (*ibid.*). This is what Gramsci called the 'common sense of an epoch', something he contrasted with 'good sense' (the latter corresponds more to the conventional English usage of the term) (Gramsci 1971: 323–43).

This provides us with some of the clues that we need to decipher some aspects of the constitution of subjects, political identities and specifically the 'common sense' associated with key notions such as state, civil society, the rule of law and rational action in neo-liberal market civilization. I suggest such neo-liberal common sense has multiple, ongoing, sources of constitution. For example, it is associated with:

1. the validation of possessively individualist, materialistic and ecologically myopic modes of thought and action;
2. the idea of 'limited' government, that is one subordinated to civil society and to patterns of economic growth that rely on the capital accumulation driven by market forces and corporate power;
3. a monoculture dominated by capital and consumerism linked to specific patterns of production and distribution intended to increase the turnover time of capital (e.g. in agribusiness, energy, military-industrial development, fashion, computing, pharmaceuticals, retailing more generally);
4. predominance of the commodity form of law, embodied in contracts and private property rights, which supervenes over other forms of law (see Chapter 3 by A. Claire Cutler);
5. the institutionalization of a hierarchical, disciplinary and materially unequal world order increasingly dominated by capital, reified as the 'international community' in the dominant discourses of global politics.

In sum, the 'common sense' of market civilization involves a geopolitical structure, a political economy structure, a structure of laws and a cultural structure premised upon the ethical and moral rectitude and rationality of the capitalist world market as its primary governing force.

As Polanyi pointed out, this type of civilization is historically unique. Indeed, it was the late eighteenth and nineteenth centuries that first saw the emergence of a civilization in which social practices and political institutions came to be subordinated to capitalist market forces (Polanyi 1944/1957). Furthermore, as Di Muzio (2011) has underlined, market civilization is a 'petro-market civilization' with significant ecological consequences since it entails unsustainable (and expanding) consumption of fossil fuels. Particularly over the past 30 years, this market civilization has come to globalize and thus mediate the everyday lives and life chances of a growing proportion of the world's population.

In what follows I briefly underline some features of the historical constitution of market civilization. We first note its roots in a triple dispossession: of the Catholic monasteries; the producers on the land; and finally the Crown itself. In Tudor England, Henry VIII's dispossession of the monasteries transferred monastic wealth to not only the Crown but also to the Whig dynasties that came to use that wealth to dominate nascent British capitalism. They accelerated the enclosure (expropriation) of the common land, dispossessing the peasantry. In the century prior to the Glorious Revolution of 1688, in the context of civil war, the bourgeoisie finally expropriated power from the Crown: parliament subordinated the prerogatives of the Crown and created a new sphere of freedom for the propertied to flourish, a sphere called 'civil society'. The bourgeoisie were thus protected from not only the whims of kingly sovereignty, but also from threats to their power and property stemming from democratic or popular forces such as the Diggers or Levellers, a point I develop below (Gill 2008: 47–51).

Thus market civilization forms part of the *longue durée* of modern capitalism, which itself is the product of a variety of long-standing political struggles over the nature of property, forms of livelihood and political representation, over the nature of rights, freedoms and responsibilities.

In this context, the modern form of what Marx called original or primitive accumulation was built on the enclosure movement and extended through colonization and imperialism. In this process, local producers and aboriginal peoples were expropriated – partly through the use of law in a process that was violent – from their direct and customary access to the means of livelihood and subsistence (including access to water), a process that continues in a variety of new ways (Prudham 2007; Swyngedouw 2005; White *et al.* 2012).[2] This ongoing process of

---

[2] Bourgeois colonization not only brought the imposition of racist ideologies but also the imperialism of new liberal epistemologies, and with them alien concepts of private property, the commodity form and contract law: these then supervened over the customary laws, rights and duties of the indigenous peoples. Such forms of epistemological enclosure went with the more directly coercive and violent mechanisms of conquest, occupation, displacement and elimination. On these questions see, in this collection, Chapter 5 by Tim Di Muzio and, on the epistemological impacts that subsequently shaped many

dispossession and proletarianization forces producers to become 'free' wage labour in order to survive – an element of the reproduction of capitalist social relations that has been associated historically with the contestations over dispossession that have configured a long, complex and conflict-ridden set of historical processes (De Angelis 2004; Federici 2004; Harvey 2003, 2004). Today, it is reflected in diverse and ongoing social struggles over the conditions of livelihood, e.g. recently involving the Chinese peasantry moving into the cities to look for work in the factories as their previously socialized mechanisms of reproduction have been replaced by private market forces, a process prompting innumerable localized protests and resistance concerning exploitation, living conditions and corruption.[3]

Primitive accumulation points to contradictory developments: on the one hand toward greater possibilities for the organization of workers (for example in China, where worker militancy is growing), on the other social dislocation, atomization and anomie, e.g. in the huge shantytowns that encircle many of the megacities of the Third World, which are now flooded with new dispossessed migrants from the countryside looking for work.

It is important to remember, then, that at its core the social reproduction of a market civilization involves the process through which people are dispossessed of their means of livelihood, generating the compulsion to depend on the market for subsistence and survival.

Today, much of the material and political base for the reproduction of global market civilization rests on the power of giant oligopolistic firms, e.g. those that sub-contract Chinese firms and workers to produce the goods that flood affluent supermarkets worldwide. These firms have powerful links to and influence within state apparatuses and international organizations. The social nucleus of market civilization is the relatively small percentage of affluent people who are the primary beneficiaries of neo-liberal political economy. It includes not only privileged workers and owners of giant corporations but also sub-contractors, stockbrokers, accountants, consultancies, lobbyists, educational entrepreneurs, architects, designers and stars of celebrity culture.

---

of the post-colonial constitutional forms after the Second World War, see Chapter 17 by Gavin Anderson.

[3] Illustrating the crisis of social reproduction in China, the government estimates that 58 million 'left-behind children' (almost 20 per cent of all children and half of the children in the countryside) now live with grandparents or in foster centres because their parents have left to earn income in the factories and cities. What Mao failed to achieve – the destruction of the family structure via forced collectivization – is now being accomplished by primitive accumulation (Hille 2011).

In this context, many of the political precepts of market civilization link the effective rights of representation to ownership of private property and, as such, hark back to the pre-democratic age. This is why, with the emergence of modern forms of state and political struggle, neo-liberal constitutionalism has to acknowledge that democracy continues to involve universal normative aspirations that need to be incorporated or attenuated in new political forms and laws (Gill 1995a, 1998b).

Further, it is worth noting that the neologism 'market democracy' (some might call it an oxymoron) was coined by US leaders to denote the strategic objective of the restructuring of the former Soviet Union, and the new Russia, following the *coup d'état* in 1993 led by Yeltsin when he turned the cannons on the parliament, with the support of the West. Yeltsin then promulgated a liberal-authoritarian constitution modelled on that of Pinochet's Chile, which was designed by Chicago School neo-liberals (Mandel 1998). The new Russian Constitution enshrined contract laws, safeguards for private property, privatization of state property, and measures to allow for the extended commodification of labour, social institutions and the environment. Thus President Clinton's former Treasury Secretary, Robert Rubin, on joining the board of the world's biggest financial conglomerate, Citicorp in 1999, spelled out the geopolitics of this project (Citicorp was subsequently quasi-nationalized following the 2008 financial collapse). Rubin explained that the strategic goal of US policy toward the former East bloc was not to create liberal democracy as such but 'market democracy'. He then outlined how new constitutionalist strategy would be applied in post-communist Russia:

Contract law and property rights would have to be created from scratch. Institutions to develop and enforce market regulations would have to be established. Judges to interpret the laws and regulations would have to be trained ... The rule of law is not established overnight. Nor is a market democracy. These are long-term objectives. (Rubin 1999)

Such developments indicate a geopolitical effort to attenuate and commodify democracy. To grasp the scale of what is involved, we might remember that the universal ambit of liberal capitalist market forces was fundamentally constrained after the First World War by the creation of the Soviet Union and the rise of fascism, the abandonment of the gold standard and the institutions of liberal capitalism in the Great Depression of the 1930s; and after the Second World War various forms of state placed significant constraints on liberal frameworks of accumulation. However, since the 1970s, there has been acceleration in the development of neo-liberal forms of state, and a shift toward flexible accumulation and extended commodification of political and civil society. In this sense neo-liberal market civilization is the cultural and social counterpart to a geopolitical shift that has transformed world order and the global political economy.

However, political alternatives to market civilization not only exist, but also new ones are being forged. Disciplinary neo-liberalism is under challenge in a number of parts of the world, such as Latin America, largely because intersecting global crises (of livelihood, political representation, leadership, of social reproduction and ecological sustainability) that go well beyond the global crisis of accumulation have emerged since 2008 – comprising what I have called an emerging global organic crisis (Gill 2012).

Indeed, because of the dislocations and social inequalities these processes engender, neo-liberal market civilization is heavily contested. In some parts of the world, for example in Latin America, many of the principles of neo-liberalism are now openly repudiated, and innovative, progressive constitutional and political forms are being created, premised upon what has been called twenty-first-century socialism, involving new regional organizations and new principles of military security to deter imperial intervention – e.g. the Bolivarian Alliance for the Americas.

New constitutionalism and the rule of law

Today formal democracy has extended with relatively universal suffrage – citizenship rights are not formally premised on private property. Thus new constitutionalism now involves the need to attenuate, incorporate, co-opt or depoliticize democratic forces and potential opposition. As Mandel (1998) has argued, what is partly involved is a transformation in the relationship between the courts and representative institutions via constitutional limitations such as bills of rights or charters, often enforced by tribunals. Mechanisms such as judicial review are precisely constructed as antidotes to democracy to preserve the oligarchy of private property by declaring the economic as a 'private sphere' outside of politics, and as a realm of 'freedom'.

How in practice is this achieved? To make this as clear as possible, and not to deny considerable variation in state forms, I sketch an ideal-typical liberal form of state and, within it, the role of the rule of law.

Neo-liberal state forms, at least theoretically, involve limited government: a government ultimately subordinated to the private sphere, and as such, having limited legal competence to intervene in civil society and

Market civilization 35

the market. Such a state form can be vast and powerful (e.g. the United States), so 'limited' does not mean weak or small. It is 'limited' because the constitutional framework of a neo-liberal state is pluralist, with formal decentralization of power: the state is ultimately subordinated to civil society. This framework of power is the corollary of the sovereignty of private property rights and freedom of contract that are written into, and protected by, liberal and neo-liberal constitutional forms. Thus *freedom of enterprise appears as a constitutive element of the liberal rule of law*. In turn, the neo-liberal rule of law, and in particular the new constitutionalism, formally defines the actions of the state in terms of a separation of state and civil society, of public and private, and of statute and contract, with mechanisms of judicial review designed to maintain that separation. This formal analysis needs of course to be related to actually existing capitalism where there are large concentrations of private power with vast corporations. Nonetheless, the neo-liberal state cannot monopolize power and authority, which is in principle decentralized: concentrations of privately controlled capital largely define the distribution of power.

Within this context, the subject of the law is understood as a possessive individual who has full ownership of him/her self, and has formal equality before the law. He/she is assumed to have free will and thus the freedom to enter into contracts (as a citizen, or indeed as a corporation). This of course allows for the labour contract – as well as other contractual relations – to take place *as if* they involved free exchange between individuals exercising their will. At the same time contracts are the legal form that underpins the commodification of labour and of things, or more precisely the power to control the disposition of people relative to things (Edelman 1979). Military and police power protect this constitutional framework in an ongoing way both locally and, in the case of the United States, globally in the era of disciplinary neo-liberalism.

What this might ultimately mean in the context of a market civilization was imagined in Shakespeare's *The Merchant of Venice* (c. 1596), a work that interrogated the potential legal basis of an order based on the principle of the absolute sovereignty of property rights. A contract was signed that allowed Shylock the right to extract a pound of flesh from any part of Antonio's body if the latter were to default on payment of his debts. When faced with Antonio's plea of mercy Shylock argues that contract right is supreme and that the property holder holds this right as a 'sovereign' power. In this reading, private property rights assume the right to control the life of another person provided that such control was subject to a legal contract. At issue was how far private property rights included the right to treat people as disposable commodities. Resistance to absolute property rights was embodied in Portia, in the guise of Justice, who proposes constraints on, and if necessary confiscation of, such private property rights.

Thus much of the modern political struggle has involved the effort to extend and lock in rights and powers of capital (in so far as these tend toward sovereign rights of property) on the one hand, and those that seek to democratize, socialize and politically control capital on the other (the socialist project) (Gill 1998b). This is of course why the law usually has placed limits on the scope of contractual relations, for example forbidding an individual from selling parts of his/her body or genetic code, although today these limits are increasingly transgressed in market civilization.

Moreover I would add that the law *actively constitutes* the very subjects to which it refers, such as corporations and the parties to contracts, including labour contracts. In Althusserian terms the law *interpellates* individuals as subjects with certain attributes, powers and freedoms within the practice of law. Thus law is not merely an external mechanism of regulation but a constituent way in which social relations are lived and experienced. In this way, the form of the subject constitutes a basic grounding for the rights of property (and of political representation) in global capitalism (Hunt 1993).

This is also why Marx contrasted the formal freedoms of the law with the substantive inequality generated in the processes of production and exploitation, in which labour and capital are both legal categories involving bundles of rights that include employers' rights to control, exploit, and hire and fire labour, where the latter is understood as a commodity. The most important relations within capitalist society are moulded into the form of contractual relations; they rest ultimately upon the separation of public and private, or state and civil society in the constitutional and political structures of the state.

As Jean-Philippe Robé argues, full acknowledgement of private property rights means, therefore, that the owner (e.g. a corporation) is sovereign in his specific field of action – whatever the limited, constitutionally valid application of the state's legislative and regulatory powers may entail. This allows individuals to enjoy their property however they choose unless expressly prohibited. Indeed not everything can be prohibited. Thus power is decentralized in a liberal society principally through property, and this explains the high degree of autonomy of the corporation (and large property owners) relative to the state and the rest of civil society, that is the citizens. The rule of law allows the corporation the autonomy to make decisions concerning the disposition of its private property rights. As noted, the enterprise also commands the individuals under its jurisdiction as a consequence of the labour contracts they have signed, thus giving the employer authority and power over employees. The law assumes that employees have freely entered into the employment contract, thereby authorizing the command of the employer over the employee since the employer controls the property rights of the enterprise. 'Thus the existence and power of the enterprise derives from fundamental legal principles that guarantee private property rights as a part of liberal constitutions. The power of the enterprise is therefore built upon positive constitutional foundations by which the [neo-]*liberal* State *must* abide' (Robé 1996: 60, his emphasis).

In this way the neo-liberal state allows employers to create 'private' laws, the existence of which is accepted by the state since they derive from overriding legal principles that guarantee private property rights. Such private rights thus may tend to erode social or collective property rights, e.g. if democracy is redefined as 'market democracy'. Thus *the enterprise forms part of the constitutional structure of the exercise of power*, ultimately sanctioned by neo-liberal constitutions; therein firms are a form of private government since some of the legal rules they create are final and may not be reviewed by any public body.

We should also note that property is not so much a right 'over the thing itself as much as a right over the behaviour of others (including the state's agents and judges) in connection with the thing' (*ibid.*) and it encompasses a set of legal *relations* that involves a range of rights and freedoms, as well as certain limitations therein (Oakes 1981). Legal relations associated with property are connected to the behaviour of people relative to things, in the present and in the future, as well as to control over flows of income deriving from control over a commodity (an asset or investment).

In this context, a central geopolitical goal of new constitutionalism – associated with US and G7 strategic objectives since the 1970s – is to secure uncontested and extended protection for private property rights and investor freedoms on a world scale, locked in by basic laws, constitutions and treaties such that these rights are likely to stretch well into the future. Of course the precise form that such initiatives will produce varies in and across different political and civil societies, and as such there are often very important differences between jurisdictions, despite considerable evidence of convergence in practices (Schneiderman 2008; Chapter 6, this volume).

Three dimensions of new constitutionalism

So what precisely is new constitutionalism intended to do? From the viewpoint of the owners of capital, it helps to constitute and enlarge the world market and within it their freedom to acquire, exchange or move property. These freedoms also involve constitutional guarantees against expropriation of their assets or property. New constitutionalism also imposes what are theoretically *binding constraints* on states' macroeconomic, trade, investment and industrial policies. For example, devaluation or inflation may affect the capital value of an asset or investment; state industrial strategies may imply that domestic capital gains preferential treatment over foreign capital; national laws may have the same effect.

This is why neo-liberals such as Hayek and Buchanan have called for fiscal and monetary constitutions to remove important aspects of macro- and microeconomic policy from democratic scrutiny and contestation, while providing guarantees to private property holders that they are free to move their property across borders, with the state being constrained from nationalizing or expropriating their investments or engaging in policies inimical to capital accumulation. Meaningful rights for labour are not included in the neo-liberal agenda of constitutional reform.

In this light, new constitutionalism can be said to involve three interrelated sets of 'productive constraints' to shape neo-liberal governance of the political economy and underpin the power of capital.

Measures to reconfigure state apparatuses

These measures are intended to maintain the formal separation of the 'economic' and of the 'political', and of state and civil society under limited government to subordinate the state to dominant elements of civil society. This can mean a wide menu of mechanisms such as judicial review, federalism and multilevel governance (Harmes 2006, 2007, 2012; Chapter 9, this volume). It also involves the right of the state to take extraordinary (extra-constitutional) measures to protect capital in situations of emergency.

In addition, neo-liberal constitutionalism has sought to compel states to operate under greater market discipline. One method is to institutionalize or lock in free entry and exit options for mobile capital through investment agreements and other legal devices. Associated with this type of initiative is promotion of an ideology of 'best practice' or 'good governance' promulgated by the international financial institutions, which involves application of new systems of incentives and surveillance (panopticism) by private bond-rating agencies and decision-making by private neo-liberal epistemic communities (Gill 1995b). In addition to privatization, state agencies are made to compete with the private sector in, for example, service provision, and behave, at least in theory, as if they were marketplace actors.

These reforms are justified in the name of the three Cs of capital: creating investor *confidence*, which in turn rests partly on the *credibility* that governments will *consistently* assure political conditions to guarantee full security to the rights of property (Gill 1998b; World Bank 1997). However, what neither the World Bank nor the IMF emphasize is how these measures involve limiting mass popular-democratic or parliamentary influence over central aspects of economic policy, suggesting that what is being promoted by the IFIs are variants of 'market democracy'.

Measures to construct and extend capitalist markets

New constitutionalism serves to institutionalize liberalization and extension of markets for capital, goods and labour to permit extended capital accumulation. This includes rewriting laws and statutes to facilitate primitive accumulation, e.g. laws enabling privatization of state assets or alienation or dispossession of common lands, of public services and resources such as water, or publicly owned natural resources. Some of these practices have been likened to a new enclosure movement and to new forms of colonialism provoking armed resistance (for example in the Amazon and Chiapas).

An example of how new constitutional trade agreements can supervene over domestic law and act as mechanisms of dispossession is the Abitibi Bowater (AB) versus Government of Canada case. When the firm closed its operations in Newfoundland and Labrador in 2008, the provincial government expropriated some of its assets, offering compensation for some assets (the firm's land, buildings, equipment, etc.) but not the firm's water and timber rights, since they are not usually considered compensable rights in Canadian law. The firm then used the arbitration mechanism in Chapter 11 of NAFTA and won $130 million in compensation for expropriation from the federal government, despite the fact that its closure left severe environmental damage and significant costs to the province for severance and pensions of workers who lost their jobs. This example also reflects the fact that there is now a global web of new constitutional trade agreements, principally in the form of over 3,000 Bilateral Investment Treaties (BITs) (efforts to create multilateral agreement on investment have so far failed because of significant political resistance across the OECD).

More generally in international law, private property rights generally supervene over labour, environmental and other human rights.[4] Such

---

[4] See 'Public Statement on the International Investment Regime' 2008. Available online at: www.osgoode.yorku.ca/public_statement.

rights now include not only trademarks and packaging (e.g. for cigarettes) but also patents over seeds, genetic structures and drugs, which are usually owned by large firms. While such rights are institutionalized via BITs and in TRIPS (Trade-Related Intellectual Property Rights in the WTO) they have consistently been challenged by Third World governments for monopolizing cultural and technological knowledge and transforming it into a commodity (e.g. disputes over AIDS drugs between developing countries and the giant pharmaceutical firms). Here we might note that private medical research is skewed away from diseases that principally afflict the poor by the pharmaceutical industry. The result is a global medical research agenda in which only 18 of 1,556 approved drug patents issued in 1975–2004 were for use against tropical diseases and three against tuberculosis (Benatar *et al.* 2009).

Many of the arrangements just mentioned have facilitated small numbers of agribusiness corporations to obtain control of the world market in food, and thus to shape nutritional patterns (and concepts of food security) in a world where 25 per cent of the population is obese and 25 per cent starving, a situation with immense implications for global health. Again, this has prompted worldwide resistance from farmers and workers, e.g. from Via Campesina and many Third World governments (Albritton 2009). Concentration of control in agriculture is also related to destruction of biodiversity and growing use of monocultures in seeds and crops. There is also evidence of ever-reducing gene pools for the animals used by agri-corporations, e.g. in North American agribusiness, cattle are artificially inseminated by a few 'super bulls' with ominous genetic implications.[5] The conditions for such trends rest on control of various contracts and property rights over life forms. These are owned by giant life sciences and agro-corporations that are protected by the US and EU governments.

Such developments may be fundamentally at odds with global health, social justice, biodiversity and ecological sustainability, and have prompted growing global resistance from producers and environmentalists, and the development of agro-ecological alternatives worldwide.

Measures for dealing with dislocations and contradictions

Since contemporary capitalist development is punctuated by crises of accumulation, in order for those crises to be managed by neo-liberal

---

[5] The greatest genetic dangers probably lie in the breeding of pigs and poultry, since they offer the fastest turnover time of capital (Richardson 1996).

leaders requires that depoliticization of the 'economy' be maintained. This involves at least three aspects.

A primary element is to make legitimate the removal of democracy from key aspects of economic policy by means of participation in safely channelled areas, away from the 'commanding heights' of macroeconomic (fiscal and monetary) policy – an element of 'market democracy' (see also World Bank 1997). This effectively removes strategic economic policy and crisis management from almost any political contestation by popular democratic forces.

Second is a process that Gramsci called *trasformismo*, or incorporation of political tendencies that might generate a broad-based political backlash against liberal governance, such as occurred from left and right in the 1930s (Gramsci 1971). Indeed, the various crises and dislocations associated with the uneven and contradictory development of global capitalism over the past three decades have also gone with the incorporation of most stripes of social democracy into disciplinary neo-liberalism; this is reflected in political responses to the deep crisis of accumulation since 2008. What has emerged is a consensus on the part of conservative, liberal and social democratic parties on the need for deeper neo-liberal reforms to flexibilize and further weaken organized labour and socialist forces, and thereby to deepen disciplinary neo-liberalism by means of policies of austerity stretching well into the future to pay for the gigantic bailouts of capital.[6]

Third, and related to the above, is a process whereby economic questions are made to appear as technical questions beyond political contestability. A profoundly political process – e.g. massive socialization of the losses of giant corporations following the 2008 financial meltdown – is represented as a purely technical exercise conducted during an economic emergency by private, non-partisan experts or 'epistemic communities'. While central banks are independent of governments (and insulated from the influence of broader political forces) their governors are largely drawn from private financial interests – not from trade unions or the multitudes of very able progressive political economists. Meanwhile, risks for the majority are increasingly privatized, in the so-called 'self-help society' promoted by neo-liberal disciples of Hayek and Friedman from Margaret Thatcher onwards.

---

[6] See also on this question Chapter 8 by Neil Brenner *et al.* on how neo-liberalization has tended to deepen in and through economic crises; see also Chapter 15 by Janine Brodie on the G20 adoption of the so-called doctrine of 'expansionary austerity', an oxymoron also known as 'expansionary fiscal contraction'.

Thus in 2010 many G20 governments announced an era of fiscal austerity to pay for the massive bailouts of 2008–9, partly to satisfy the bond markets that governments would not default on debts or debt servicing, a policy that has continued in many G20 members, particularly in the European Union. Unprotected workers and poorly represented working people were, by contrast, badly hurt through cuts in public sector wages and jobs, in social and pension benefits, and health expenditures and because of further privatization of public services, assets and lands: an example of dispossession on a massive scale. The resemblance to typical forms of surplus extraction via prioritization of debt servicing that has characterized Third World public finances for much of the past three decades is, therefore, no coincidence.

Not surprisingly, there were demonstrations and strikes opposing neo-liberal policies and the new austerity strategies in many nations, including across Europe, for example in Greece, Spain and the UK, where after the financial meltdown a Conservative–Liberal coalition government came into power in 2010 and quickly announced that 500,000 public service jobs would be cut (350,000 held by women) in measures that would reduce public services for the needy as well as for policing. None of this had ever been mentioned during the election. Also, extensive organized resistance from workers preceded the mass demonstrations in Egypt in 2011, although much of what seems to have motivated the so-called Arab Spring were some of the values of the French Revolution, particularly the desire for political recognition and redistribution, reflected in the demand for post-authoritarian and post-neo-liberal constitutional forms and real democracy for citizens.

Conclusion: from transformative resistance to the post-modern Prince

This chapter has hypothesized a shift toward a more neo-liberal world order as, in part, a significant reflection of the massive geopolitical changes that have followed the collapse of many communist states and the end of the Cold War as well as the defeat of more progressive and militant Third World projects for a different kind of global order, e.g. efforts to create a New International Economic Order in the 1970s and early 1980s. Geopolitical change is also bound up with a general intensification in the exploitation of workers and of the ecological resources of the planet, allied to a worldwide process of dispossession of livelihoods in a new phase of primitive accumulation on a world scale.

In this context, market civilization has come to condition many of the alternatives – often as matters of life and death – that humanity faces as we look forward into the twenty-first century. A longer study could have outlined specific ways this has been occurring: e.g. over-consumption and irrational use of resources and the global food regime; hyper-exploitation of labour; the commoditization of the body (sex trafficking, pornography as well as commercial surrogacy and sale of body parts); the lionization of celebrity culture; and not least healthcare primarily geared toward caring for the minority affluent strata of the world's population, with public health systems defunded and privatized.

This is why our current predicament involves not only recurring crises of accumulation, but also deep structural crises that are simultaneously ecological, social, material and political: an emerging global organic crisis. Part of this involves the expropriation or forcible removal of human beings from their livelihoods and use of the commons, a process that generates intense social conflict and resistance.

This pattern seems, on the one hand, to be intensifying through a kind of path dependency, in which new constitutionalism locks in the neo-liberal pattern of global development (and the power and prerogatives of capital) making it more difficult for alternative solutions to common global problems to emerge. On the other hand, this pattern provokes 'transformative resistance' (Gill 2008). Here Brazil is an interesting case: the conditions of life have improved not just because of Lula's social redistribution policies (left-wing social democracy allied to neo-liberal principles of public finance) but also because of millions of landless peasants who formed political organizations linked with urban workers. They took advantage of a remaining clause from the Brazilian Constitution allowing for unproductive lands to be occupied and used by workers; that is the population of Brazil had a collective right to such land. This is an example of how a constitutionalism that is socially inclusive can mediate the pure right to private property. It also illustrates how the modern social struggle is connected to dispossession and proletarianization, a process in which the antagonist of capital is created as a result of (primitive) accumulation. The Landless Workers' Movement is part of the small farmer's global organization, Via Campesina, whose political slogan is 'small farmers can feed the world and cool the planet'; in this sense, in a situation of organic crisis, resistance is and must be organic or relatively permanent and broad based.

Thus, in today's world, we can identify multiple sources of resistance to the power of capital at all levels: by indigenous peoples; the intelligentsia; workers across a range of sectors and professions; and by new forms of state associated with socially and ecologically sustainable principles (e.g. Bolivia). They are already providing progressive forces with powerful new concepts to grasp the profound attack on the conditions of existence of a majority of the world's population associated with market civilization. They look beyond the present crisis of accumulation, crucial though it is, to address the reckless despoliation of the biosphere, intensified exploitation of human beings, and the spread of primitive accumulation in North and South. In this way, the lefts (in the plural) are actually promoting a new 'common sense' and forms of knowledge to challenge the hegemonic capitalist concepts – e.g. that the *credible* governments seek to generate the *confidence* of capital and ensure a favourable investment climate for the 'markets'. New forms of thinking suggest that credibility and confidence in government should be prudent, sustainable, equitable and just, delivering policies to address social needs, not the needs of capital, with the commanding heights of the economy brought under democratic control – not ceded to capital in 'market democracy'.

I have elsewhere identified the potentials of such a set of left forces as an emerging and variegated form of progressive global leadership, a leadership that is both collective and plural. I call it the post-modern Prince. A key question for the making of world order thus concerns how far transformative resistance and the political embryos of the post-modern Prince further develop and coalesce into more effective political organizations under conditions of organic crisis – otherwise neo-liberal crisis management will further compound the fundamental crises of livelihood and social reproduction that afflict a majority of the world's population. In this context, a central task for the lefts is not only to develop a critique of market civilization but also to foster a new and more radical common sense, to combine progressive forces in a new form of democracy based on principles of solidarity, justice and progressive constitutionalism (e.g. what Richard Falk, in Chapter 18, calls a 'just new constitutionalism'), thus to govern well and to generate new forms of society and civilization.

3 New constitutionalism and the commodity form of global capitalism

A. Claire Cutler

This chapter analyzes new constitutionalism as the juridical foundation for the global expansion of capitalism. It illustrates what is 'new' about new constitutionalism in terms of the constitution of new forms of private property rights that contribute to the expansion of capitalism. This is achieved through the progressive enclosure of public into private property and through the legitimation of private appropriation over previously non-commodified activities, processes and resources. More specifically, this analysis posits the globalization of the commodity form of international law as a necessary dimension of a transnational market civilization that is unifying diverse peoples and places through the logic of commodification. This logic is bringing hitherto untapped activities and resources into the ambit of capitalist production and reproduction and is affecting profound alterations in state–society relations throughout the world. New privatized modes of appropriation and legitimation are emerging as the commodity form of law achieves transnational scope and significance. Privatized systems reformulate public modes of governance and are naturalized and legitimized as public and 'constitutional' duties to enforce the rule of law. In doing so, they privilege neo-liberal market fundamentalism and the public protection of private interests as the common sense of market civilization. The chapter therefore explores how the 'new' of new constitutionalism combines with old legal forms to constitute novel forms of private property that are advancing the commodification of nature. The chapter also raises the possibilities for resistance to further expansion of the commodity form of law through the recognition of rights that challenge neo-liberal discipline and the disembedding of human relations from social control.

Introduction

Value ... does not have its description branded on its forehead; it rather transforms every product of labour into a social hieroglyphic. Later on, men try to

decipher the hieroglyphic, to get behind the secret of their own social products.
(Marx 1976 [1867]: 167)

Commodities, like persons, have social lives. (Appadurai 1986: 3)

This chapter argues that new constitutionalism 'constitutionalizes' the commodity form of capitalism as a necessary precondition for the emergence and expansion of a transnational market civilization that operates according to private, delocalized and denationalized systems of governance. These systems privilege the rights and interests of transnational over national capital, subordinating local economies and societies to denationalized and delocalized laws. It argues that the commodity form of law is the juridical equivalent of and homologous with the commodity form of capitalism. The commodity form of international law both mirrors and instantiates the commodity form of capitalism, the latter constituting 'the very *cell* of a capitalist society' (Balbus 1977: 573, original emphasis). The chapter suggests that while diverse activities and resources in many different locales throughout the globe are submitting to new constitutionalism and neo-liberal market discipline, there is a singular logic to the commodity form that is flattening out differences and reformulating state–society relations in a uniform way. New privatized modes of appropriation and legitimation are emerging as the commodity form of international law achieves transnational scope and significance.[1] These private systems rearticulate and often displace public modes of governance and acquire their authority through knowledge and power structures that enclose common property into private property regimes and then legitimate and enforce them as natural incidents of the public and now 'constitutional' duty to secure the rule of law. In doing so, they privilege neo-liberal market fundamentalism and the public protection of private interests as the 'common sense' of market civilization.

With such issues in mind, this chapter proceeds as follows. First, my discussion examines the nature of the commodification process and the relationship between the commodity form of capitalism and the commodity form of international law. Second, I focus on the commodification of nature: the growing dimensions of nature submitting to enclosure. Third, I explore possibilities for resistance to further enclosure and expansion of the commodity form of law.

---

[1] Space limitations preclude a review here of the burgeoning literature on the emergence and expansion of regimes of private transnational governance, but see Cutler (2012).

Commodity fetishism and the commodity form of law

In possibly one of the most insightful examinations of commodification, Karl Marx identified two sets of interrelated processes at work in the creation of production based upon commodity exchange. One set concerned the transformation in the social relations constituting the object of commodification, while the other set concerned the necessary recognition and legitimation of the agent of commodification, the juridical subject. Each will be addressed in turn.

Marx (1976 [1867]: 163–4) recognized the social character of commodities, which he defined as goods produced under the alienating conditions of capitalist production and labour. Marx (1976[1867]: 138) posited that commodities have a dual nature as 'objects of utility and bearers of value'. The 'use value' of a commodity embodies the human labour that went into its creation and reveals the social embeddedness of production, as well as the qualitative differences amongst things created through human production. In contrast, the 'exchange value' emerges upon the entry of the thing into the market and its transformation into a commodity that is objectified through its equalization with other commodities through the assignment of monetary value in the exchange relationship. Marx argued that this process of commodification alienates workers from the product of their labour and imparts to the commodity the appearance of being independent of the producer, with a life of its own. The process masks the exploitative social relations underlying production and the inequality between the producer of the commodity and the owner of the means of production, who reaped the surplus value of the commodity in the market. Marx (*ibid.*: 163–4) identified the appearance of independence as the fetishism of commodities, which he believed explained the 'enigmatic character', 'metaphysical subtleties' and 'mystery' of the commodity form under capitalism.

A necessary precondition for commodification is the recognition of a subject that can legitimately lay claim to the value produced through commodity exchange. Marx observed that this required the recognition of the 'juridical subject' or an individual vested with the legal right to claim the surplus value generated in the process of exchange. But the recognition of the juridical subject, in turn, assumed or required the existence of legal categories creating rights to private property and enforcing contractual arrangements and claims. However, Marx did not address the creation of the juridical subject in any great detail. Nor did he develop his analysis of the role of law in capitalism. These points have been subsequently taken up by others when analyzing the role of law in capitalist political economy.

Theorizing that capitalism does not simply emerge naturally, of its own accord, theorists identify material, institutional and ideological structures that enable the enforcement and legitimation of capital accumulation. Drawing upon the insights offered in a fragmentary way by Marx, Antonio Gramsci (1971) and Louis Althusser (1971), theorists in the 1970s and 1980s such as Isaac Balbus (1977), Duncan Kennedy (1985: 976–7) argued that the commodity system 'presupposes laws of contract and property that legitimate and enforce private ownership of the means of production and exchange. These laws neutralize the commodity system by presenting the communal protection of private property rights and entitlements as natural incidents of the rationalized commodity form.' Indeed, these theorists posited law to take on a specific form under capitalism, which they called the commodity form of law. Balbus (1977: 573) also identified an identity or homology between the commodity form of capitalism and the commodity form of law. Just as the commodity form of capitalism produces fetishized commodities, he reasoned that the commodity form of law produced equivalent fetishized legal categories that conceal both the exploitative social relations forming commodity exchange and the role that the rule of law plays in de-politicizing and neutralizing these relations. Many drew upon the work of Evgeny Pashukanis (1978), the Soviet legal theorist who argued that the agency of the juridical subject and the imputation of equality amongst legal subjects were preconditions for capitalist relations. Althusser (1971) possibly went the greatest distance in analyzing the process by which an *individual* is interpellated under capitalism as a *legal subject*.[2] Such theorists thus regard the legal structure, the legal subject and the rule of law as preconditions for the enforcement and legitimation of capitalist production.

Others have deepened this analysis by exploring how the legal structure and juridical subjects provide more than just the means for the enforcement and legitimation of private property rights.[3] The legal structure is seen as creating the very conditions of possibility for the emergence and continuing expansion of capitalism through the recognition of an ever-expanding scope of juridical subjects, property rights, and activities and

---

[2] See Cutler (2009b) for an Althusserian reading of the interpellation of the transnational corporation as the neo-liberal corporate subject.

[3] There has been a notable ambivalence amongst Marxists concerning the historical and material significance of law due to the influence of distinctions between the base and superstructure of capitalism and the tendency to conceptualize legal relations as superstructural and as analogous to ideology in terms of performing legitimating functions. This ambivalence has frustrated the development of an adequate understanding of the historical and material effectivity of law (see Cutler 2003, 2005).

The commodity form of global capitalism 49

resources that may be subject to private appropriation.[4] Law is conceptualized as significant in every step of commodification, which is regarded as a complex process imbricated in networks of social relations. The analytical challenge, as Marx put it in the opening quotation to this chapter, is to 'get behind' this social process.

We might begin to 'get behind' this social process by identifying its constituent elements and, rather, analyzing commodification as set of interrelated processes. These processes involve the continuous transformation of public or common property into private property that is recognized, legitimated and enforced by the state. Each process will be addressed in turn.

The continuous nature of commodification relates to the inherent tendency for capitalism to expand, extensively and intensively. David Harvey (2003, 2005) provides an insightful analysis of the inherent tendency for capitalism to expand, extensively, in the drive for new geographic spaces for capital investment and, intensively, in terms of the creation and legitimation of new methods of private appropriation. The geographic expansion of capitalism and its penetration into new modes of human activity are thus integral dimensions of commodification as a continuous process. But equally important is the continuity of the process of transforming or enclosing common or public property into private property. Massimo De Angelis (2004: 60–1) notes that 'enclosures are a continuous characteristic of "capital logic"' and he underlines 'the continuing relevance of "enclosures"' as a 'constituent element of capitalist relations and accumulation'.[5] Observing that this enclosure involves the continuous separation of the producer from the means of production, he quotes Marx from the *Grundrisse*: 'Once this separation is given, the production process can only produce it anew, reproduce it, and reproduce it on an expanded scale' (De Angelis 2004: 64 quoting Marx 1974 [1858]: 462). The process of separation is derived from the word 'to cern' or to encircle or enclose, and addresses the method by which something

---

[4] Pashukanis probably provided the first deep analysis of international law as a constitutive, historical force and sought to isolate the commodity form of law as homologous with the commodity form of capitalism. Like Marx, Pashukanis recognized the ontological priority of the juridical subject who could legitimately claim the right to private appropriation, secured through laws. China Miéville (2005, 2008) draws heavily upon Pashukanis and, indeed, defines international law in terms of the commodity form of law. This chapter seeks to develop the work they began and to suggest the possibility of resistance to the commodity form of law through rights that contest private property rights as the common sense of the time.
[5] De Angelis is here disputing the tendency to limit the significance of enclosures to primitive accumulation and making the case for the continuing relevance of the enclosures of common property to contemporary capitalism.

that has hitherto not been subject to private ownership is individuated, abstracted, privately appropriated and transformed into a commodity (Castree 1995: 27). This involves, inter alia, the systematic displacement of production for use by production for exchange, the mediation of value by money, and the recognition of new classes of goods and services as commodities (Prudham 2008). But the process also requires as a precondition the recognition of a juridical subject vested with the legitimate entitlement to claim the value generated by these commodities.

However, while the commodity form of law plays a central role in these processes, this is under-theorized and little understood. It is the legal form that in the first instance abstracts, individuates, encircles and displaces. The legal form articulates new forms of property through the expropriation of ever-new activities and resources from the common property of the public sphere. It is also the legal form that legitimates and in the last instance enforces commodified social relations at the behest of the state. The commodity form of law assists in the normalization of fetishized legal subjects through the normalization of enclosures, separations and displacements. It assists in providing a 'mantle of rationality' and projecting 'a vision of the future that *makes sense* to a multiplicity of concrete subjects' and serves to 'integrate the social body' and constitute 'social subjects who are normalized to the commodity-form, that is to stratified enclosures' (De Angelis 2004: 82, original emphasis). The discussion will turn to illustrate these processes at work in the commodification of nature.

The commodification of nature

Scholarship on the global political economy has developed considerable understanding of privatizing processes that are commodifying a number of human activities, including international trade (General Agreement on Trade in Services (GATS)) and the commodification of health, education and other services (Pollock and Price 2000; Scherrer 2005); Trade-Related Aspects of Intellectual Property Rights (TRIPS) Agreement and the commodification of new forms of intellectual property (Dickenson 2004; Strauss 2009); international investment (Bilateral Investment Treaties (BITs)) and the commodification of various natural resources (Leubuscher 2004; Razzaque 2004); international finance and the commodification of risk and debt (Cutler 2012); the commodification of international security (Cutler 2010; Krahmann 2008); and the commodification of food (Hauter 2007). In a number of cases, commodification is accompanied by the privatization of dispute settlement in investor-state regimes where arbitration tribunals operate outside the public rule of law in delocalized and denationalized institutions according to private procedures and standards (see also Chapters 10 and 11, this volume).

While many of these activities and resources intersect with nature, few studies seek to isolate the specificity of the legal forms at work and the ways in which the natural environment and resources are being enclosed as private property through law and transformed into tradable commodities. The commodification of nature is creating possibly the most pressing crisis facing human existence today. The transformation of parts of nature into tradable commodities pits the North against the South, elites against peasants, and transnational corporations against people. In some of these domains, the process is one of constitutionalizing corporate rights to exclusive access to things that had previously been held in common – a wave of new enclosures. In others, it is an issue of opening the market to domains that had previously been wholly under the control of the state. The commodification of land, the atmosphere and water provide vivid examples of the commodity form of law at work over nature.

The commodification of land through international law is taking place as states agree to adopt neo-liberal, market-oriented land reforms, either by selling state-owned land or by marketizing peasant land holdings, and allowing the land to be bought and sold on the free market. A famous example of this sort of process is the end of the *ejido* programme in Mexico. Recently, the process can be observed in India, Brazil, the Philippines and many other parts of the global South (Wolford 2007). Land reform in the global South is being advanced by the World Bank, through its policies of 'market-led agrarian reform'. Market-led agrarian reform has involved the removal of traditional or non-market systems of land tenure, basically as a new round of enclosures. The World Bank is facilitating a 'land grab' in the global South where agrarian reform is advanced through market-friendly policies that encourage foreign investment by transnational agro-food corporations to increase the efficiency of food production 'through a land-as-commodity framework' that requires formalization of land rights (Narula 2012: 19). Many of the agrarian communities that employ communal conceptions of ownership, which stress conservation and stewardship, are being deprived of their lands due to insecure claims – as defined by conventional Western property rights (*ibid.*). Such countries are encouraged to create investor-friendly legal regimes in the form of bilateral investment agreements that limit governments' abilities to regulate land use and that provide for binding dispute resolution in privatized arbitration settings that severely limit citizen participation (*ibid.*: 10).

The impact of these policies on the societies and political economies of developing countries has been profound in terms of creating a 'bifurcated' agrarian structure. Export-oriented capitalist farming undertaken by transnational agro-food corporations 'sits side-by-side with a "classic" peasant subsistence-oriented agricultural sub-sector that is not as strictly governed by the market' (Akram-Lodhi 2007: 1437).

For example, World Bank efforts at mandating market-based land reform in the Philippines were originally avoided by the government and social movement groups. But in 1999, lacking public funds, the government was forced to accept a proposal from the World Bank. However, this new Community-Managed Agrarian Reform and Poverty Reduction Programme (CMARPRP) project has tended to benefit elites, further hurting the poor. While the former policy had reflected a compromise between peasants and landowners, in 2005, the government announced plans to convert 2.4 million hectares of upland, affecting a million peasant households, into agribusiness plantations tied to multinational companies (Borras *et al.* 2007: 1560):

[t]he lands sold were public lands for which there were no titles, but where competing claimants already existed, including peasants claiming rightful ownership on the basis that they were the actual tillers ... [However] the CMARPRP process settled the matter in favour of elite sellers. Local government officials, not particularly interested in land reform, but instead in the possible inflow of funded projects ... tended to compel [by threats of eviction] peasant land claimants to drop legitimate claims in lands they have been tilling, and instead to recognise the dubious, untitled claims of elite actors and then [the tillers have] to agree to buy 'their own land' from the elite sellers at commercial rates. (Borras *et al.* 2007: 1570)

Similar criticism has been made of World Bank-sponsored reform in Brazil. It is said to have effected no redistributive reform at all, but simply involved 'the sale and purchase of land between private parties, with the addition of various subsidies for social and productive investments' (Sauer 2009: 138).

The financial and food crises of 2008 generated an escalation in large land transfers, prompted by perceptions of food scarcity and financial opportunities. The World Bank estimates that between 2008 and 2009 nearly 10 per cent of worldwide non-cultivated arable land was acquired by foreign investors, mostly in Sub-Saharan Africa (Narula 2012: 5).

What is important to note is that the enclosure of land through law is about more than the privatization of assets: 'the emergence of capital through processes of enclosure reflects deeper processes than simply the transfer of the private ownership of material assets at a given point in history' (Akram-Lodhi 2007: 1443). Enclosure of land, as with other resources and activities, is about the transformation and restructuring of social relations to nature (McCarthy and Prudham 2004: 277). Enclosure is the technique used when limits to the expansion of capitalism present themselves. Enclosure through law is the means by which capitalism overcomes and dismantles barriers to private appropriation (De Angelis 2004). Moreover, neo-liberal enclosure is predicated on Lockean understandings of property that assess value in pure economic terms of improvement, displacing non-economic measures of value and utility, such as stewardship and conservation, and privileging a commodified understanding of land (Wolford 2007). The implications for the transformation of peasant and collectivist agrarian societies are profound in terms of the rearticulation of state–society relations and the redefinition of the relationship amongst and between peoples and their natural environment. In an analysis of neo-liberal, market-based agrarian reform in Brazil, Wolford (2007) reveals the tensions created by ambiguous property rights, competing claims to land and the resulting climate of surveillance generated as the rural populations sought to secure rights to land in competition with the claims of others.

Contestation over the growing commodification of nature extends as well to the fruits of lands that are also being enclosed through private property laws. The genetic patenting of plant life, which is recognized and protected under the WTO's TRIPS Agreement, expands the 'scale and scope of commodity production and circulation' and has been criticized as a neo-liberal process that is 're-structuring social relations to biophysical nature' (Prudham 2007: 413). As one commentator notes, 'not many years ago, the world's major crops were considered the common property of humankind, along with water and air. Patenting them was out of the question' (Powledge 2001: 273). However, with perceptions of declining biodiversity and new developments in biotechnology, 'plant germ plasm – and water and clean air – stopped being thought of as common goods and became valuable assets' (*ibid.*: 274). Now, developing countries are contesting the operations of corporations that are harvesting their crops and are asserting sovereignty over their biodiversity and the indigenous knowledge to which it gives rise, generating a 'classic North–South fight over resources' (*ibid.*; and see Oguamanam 2006).

Commodification of the atmosphere involves the commodification of the physical space occupied in the atmosphere, as in the recognition of 'air rights' over it (e.g. over fly zones), the commodification of information about the atmosphere (e.g. weather reports, or information that can be used to alter market prices or property values) and the commodification of the actual gases in the atmosphere (and sequestering them for commercial purposes). The commodification of information about the atmosphere has become a major growth industry with the development of the global weather insurance market and the emergence of weather derivatives in 1997 in the US energy sector. Weather derivatives are used by companies to manage the financial risks posed by the changes in the weather. Energy, utility and insurance companies use a variety of derivative contracts to smooth out their earnings by transferring the risks associated with variable weather conditions to the market. Weather derivatives evidence a significant deepening of commodification and of capitalist social relations, as atmospheric conditions and resources are recast as financial instruments. This transformation is working a whole new wave of enclosures and creating new property rights that are capable of generating considerable profits through the commodification of weather risks.[6] Emissions trading and carbon sequestration schemes also commodify the atmosphere and have proliferated since the adoption of the Kyoto Protocol by the UN Framework Convention on Climate Change in 1997. In addition, emissions trading markets have been created in Canada, New Zealand, Australia and some American states, and there are voluntary carbon markets, such as the Chicago Climate Exchange and over-the-counter (OTC) markets (Corbera and Brown 2010: 1739). OTC markets are formed by networks of dealers who arrange the purchase and sale of securities through telephone, fax or electronic networks, rather than through a stock exchange.

These efforts record 'a sea change in environmental law and policy, marked by a growing interest in market-based instruments of environmental protection … approaches that explicitly commodify environmental impact by creating markets for their sale are on the rise' and have great impact on air pollution, natural resource extraction and the development of habitat (Salzman and Ruhl 2000: 609). For example, wetlands mitigation trading schemes permit developers to compensate for wetlands they destroy by paying for wetland restoration elsewhere. However, these schemes do not address the full environmental or social welfare impact of the arrangements, as not all wetlands are of similar nature or social welfare value (*ibid.*). Similarly, treating endangered species' habitats and fish stocks as tradable commodities flattens out important differences that are simply not addressed by market-based regulations that treat all commodities as fungible in nature (*ibid.*).

---

[6] Weather derivatives are listed on the Chicago Mercantile Exchange and allow hedging against the effects of the weather on the demand for a product or service. In 2005–6 US$45 billion worth of weather derivatives were traded, and multilateral organizations and global financial services are competing to broker these new opportunities for profit (Thornes and Randalls 2007: 275). See Cutler (2012) for further discussion of the nature and operation of derivatives.

Carbon commodification is giving rise to a 'new carbon economy' that is based on an exchange of carbon emissions through cap and trade and projects-based markets. Carbon markets exist where states and private actors are allowed to buy and sell carbon credits or carbon offset credits on a market. CO_2 emissions are made into a tradable commodity, which acts as a 'currency' for CO_2 emission allowances. Thus actors can buy CO_2 credits, allowing them to emit more. Actors can also accumulate CO_2 offset credits by making investments in projects that reduce a certain measurable amount of CO_2 in the atmosphere, which then can be sold on the market, or used as an allowance for further CO_2 emissions.[7]

Carbon commodification may 'be situated within a larger market environmentalism doctrine, current trends in marketized environmental governance, and the construction of a "neoliberal nature"' (Corbera and Brown 2010: 1742). Drawing on Harvey's analysis of accumulation through dispossession, carbon commodification has been referred to as 'accumulation by decarbonization' and as a new form of governance that devolves significant authority over the atmosphere to markets and to supranational and non-states actors (Bumpus and Liverman 2008: 127). Such analyses underline the dual nature of climate change as a threat to the accumulation of capital and as a potentially lucrative opportunity for profit. The processes involved in these schemes also illustrate the creation of legal rights in the ownership of carbon reductions and their individuation and abstraction from physical locations (*ibid.*: 136). Accumulation by decarbonization is big business, with the World Bank estimating the 2006 value of carbon trading at US $30 billion (*ibid.*: 136). In asking 'who benefits' by accumulation by decarbonization and carbon offsets, Bumpus and Liverman (*ibid.*: 142) argue that a redistribution of wealth is resulting between the North and South because carbon credits are worth more in developed markets. They identify communities in the South as receiving unequal benefits from offsets and emission trading and neocolonial systems of property rights.

Water privatization has been a global trend for the past decade or more and is enthusiastically advocated by the World Bank, the International Monetary Fund (IMF), the Organisation for Economic Co-operation and Development (OECD), and other global institutions. Transnational water corporations have actively advanced the agenda of privatizing water and have entered into partnerships with international financial institutions, including the Global Water Partnership and the World

---

[7] While there are several carbon trading schemes, domestically and internationally, the three most significant ones are the Joint Implementation (JI), the Clean Development Mechanism (CDM) and the European Trading Scheme (ETS). The first two are part of the Kyoto Protocol and the last one has been legislated by the European Community.

Water Council. These partnerships promote the neo-liberal agenda of water privatization and commodification in the broader context of marketized environmentalism and poverty reduction. The marriage of the market and development is heralded as the way forward to sustainable development in the South, but obscures the expansion and deepening of the commodity form. Critics caution that this marriage generates a 'market-oriented structure of ownership that disregards the social relations through which ownership patterns and processes of dispossession are legitimized' (Higgott and Weber 2005: 448). Indeed, the commodification of water is described as the new strategy for accumulation by dispossession and 'a process through which nature's goods become integrated into the global circuits of capital ... A local/global choreography is forged that is premised upon mobilizing local H_2O, turning it into money, and inserting this within transnational flows of circulating capital. Consequently, local resource systems become part of the strategic checkerboard of global companies' (Swyngedouw 2005: 87).

However, the commodification of water has not gone unchallenged. There is great concern that the General Agreement on Trade in Services (GATS), negotiated as part of the Uruguay Round of multilateral trade negotiations, will require states to liberalize and privatize their water sectors and that recasting water resources as 'services' subject to trade discipline is transforming elements of nature into tradable commodities (Lang 2005). Resistance to the commodification of water resources is evident in the 'water wars' in South America, Africa, and municipalities in Europe and North America (Holland 2005). Many states have learned that foreign investments in the water sector are big business; moreover, claims for compensation proliferate under bilateral investment treaties as states respond to failed water privatization initiatives or take measures to mitigate the effects of global financial crises. For example, there was a series of high-profile cases arising out of the Argentinian financial crisis of 2001–2. A number of foreign investors claimed that emergency measures adopted by the government to address the worsening economic situation in Argentina impaired their investments. These measures included the cancelling of water concessions granted to foreign investors that had resulted in hugely inflated and unaffordable water rates and generated profound civil discontent. The foreign investing companies initiated claims that Argentina breached obligations under the BITs governing their investment relations.

Throughout South America resistance to World Bank-inspired water privatization initiatives occurred. Similar legal actions have been launched elsewhere, and Bolivia, Ecuador and Venezuela eventually withdrew from the investor-state regime (Nolan 2012). Other communities are contesting neo-liberal discipline through the discourse of human rights: water privatization is being contested by claims of an international human right to clean water. These measures suggest that there are fractures in neo-liberal discipline and new constitutionalism.

Contesting new constitutionalism

The transformation of nature from public to private goods through the commodity form of law is not a new phenomenon. Indeed, in a seminal analysis of the emergence of market civilization in the nineteenth century, Karl Polanyi (1944/1957) went to great lengths to illustrate that each step in the creation of free markets for land and labour was mediated by extensive legislation. For example, the creation of free markets for land and labour, which Polanyi (*ibid.*) regarded as 'fictitious commodities', was predicated on extensive legislative reforms removing feudal entailments that restricted the transmissibility of real property.[8] Polanyi (1944/1957: 180) cites Jeremy Bentham's association of individual liberty and prosperity with the removal of 'entails', 'unalienable endowments', 'common lands', and 'rights of redemption' as the ideology informing legislation such as the Prescriptions Acts, the Inheritance Act, the Fines and Recoveries Act, the Real Property Act, the Enclosure Act and the Copyhold Acts of 1801, which were passed to remove feudal restrictions on the disposition of land. The scope of legislative interventions to create free markets in land and labour was so extensive in reach and intensive in penetrating into the fabric of society that Polanyi (*ibid.*) identified the great 'paradox' that '*laissez-faire* was planned'. It was 'the product of deliberate state action'. Polanyi (*ibid.*) emphasized that the 'road to the free market was opened and kept open by an enormous increase in continuous, centrally organized and controlled interventionism'. He attributed the continuous nature of this liberal project to the tendency of each legislative intervention to produce a countermove and resistance to the social dislocation resulting from the enclosure of common land and the creation of a wage-labour market. The moves to market civilization were thus met by countermoves seeking to mitigate the harsh effects of market discipline. However, the continuous nature of this project may also be attributed to the inherent tendency

---

[8] While Polanyi distances his analysis of the fiction of treating land, labour and money as commodities from Marx's analysis of commodity fetishism, it is difficult to interpret his criticism of subordinating the social relations constituting the 'human activity' associated with labour and the social context of human relations with land (which he defines as 'nature') to the market in any other way.

of capitalism, discussed earlier, to expand, seeking out new avenues of private appropriation and value – new enclosures of common property.

To what extent are we able to identify a countermovement to the contemporary operation of the commodity form of law? Has the ongoing global financial crisis opened up the possibility for re-examining the corporate practices that are contributing to the degradation of nature?

There is much pessimism about the possibility of major social revolution today in the face of the global expansion of capitalism and the entrenchment of powerful agents and institutions of private power and authority, such as transnational corporations. The barriers to developing counter-hegemonic international law are powerfully articulated by Bhupinder Chimni (2003) and Third World legal scholars. Calls for the establishment of 'new commons' are suggested by some as a 'counter-hegemonic project' to neo-liberalism and new constitutionalism, but many of these claims continue to reflect the fetishism of neo-liberalism in their fear and suspicion of the state and faith in some amorphous power of the commons (McCarthy 2005).

However, the 'collapse of more revolutionary images of social justice in favor of capitalism, democracy, human rights, and the rule of law' have directed attention to more 'bottom-up, small-scale changes' (Merry 1995: 15). Conceptions of 'international law from below' are contrasted with 'international law from above', while 'counter-hegemonic law' is contrasted with 'hegemonic law' (Rajagopal 2003; Santos and Rodríguez-Garavito 2005). These contrasts illustrate that law can work both oppressive and emancipatory ends; it can be used as a sword or as a shield. This was noted some time ago when E.P. Thompson (1975) raised the issue of resistance through law in his analysis of the Black Act that created draconian penalties for what was previously legal and allowed as a means of access to the commons, e.g. appearing in a park or warren or hunting (particularly if with a blackened face or in disguise). While Thompson acknowledged that the rule of law does instantiate class power, he believed that it also creates legal forms that pose restrictions on that power, such as trial by a jury of commoners. To be legitimate law must also be seen to be just.

That international law cannot rule legitimately through coercion alone but also must receive the consent of the governed reflects the double face of law, noted most acutely by Gramscian understandings of international law as a form of *praxis* that unites popular movements with emancipatory practices. In this vein we might distinguish resistance against law, resistance by means of law, and resistance which redefines the meaning of law (Merry 1995). Resistance against the law directly challenges the legitimacy of the law and is evident in Bolivia in the protests over the privatization of water services and in India in the protests against the Naramada Dam project (Rajagopal 2005: 372). Resistance by means of law is evident in the use of law to challenge exercises of power, which failed in the case of the Naramada Dam. Rajagopal (*ibid.*) notes that the project was associated with progress, development and nation-building, purposes that were just too hegemonic to allow for meaningful political resistance. Possibly most powerful in addressing the commodity form of law is resistance that redefines the meaning of law, for this directly engages the reconstitution of legal form itself. An illustration of this form of resistance is the successful challenge by Sandra Lovelace of Canadian legislation, the Indian Act, that denied her status as an 'Indian' for marrying a non-status man. She claimed that this was discrimination, for the same loss of status did not apply to First Nations' men who marry non-status women, and she took her case to the United Nations Human Rights Committee. She invoked the Covenant on Civil and Political Rights and the Committee agreed that Canada had breached significant rights provided for in the Covenant. The legislation was subsequently amended providing for equal treatment of First Nations' men and women.

Such resistance suggests that the process of 'commodification is an inherently unfinished tendency' (Prudham 2007: 413) that requires continuous reproduction. Like the rule of law and neo-liberal common sense more generally, the constitution of capitalist legality must be continuously legitimated and reinforced (Cutler 2012). The process of commodification requires ongoing abstraction, individuation and alienation (Prudham 2007: 414), all of which may be challenged by shifting commonsense understandings of the nature of the legal form from one of rights to private property to one of rights to common property.

The ability to challenge dominant power structures through appeals to rights is contested by some. China Miéville (2005) thinks it idealistic to believe that rights can speak to power and recalls Marx's caution in *Capital* (1976: 344) that 'between equal rights force prevails'. However, as Susan Marks (2007) notes, the emancipatory potential of international human rights law is not fixed, but is very much context-dependent. The ability of rights to speak to power turns on the complex of social forces that organize and mobilize across the body politic. The success of rights challenges to the Indian Act relied upon a broad mobilization of First Nations' peoples in a number of different national and global arenas and was supported by a growing transnational indigenous movement that is creating different conceptions of common sense that emphasize common property, conservation and stewardship as the dominant norms governing ownership.

For example, claims that access to water is a human right shift the terrain by revealing cracks in commonsense understandings about the privatization of water services by international institutions and powerful transnational corporations (Razzaque 2004). One of the goals in articulating the human right to water is to create mechanisms of accountability by establishing a duty of public authorities to protect and enforce access to clean water against corporate and international institutional encroachments on the right. The United Nations General Assembly adopted a resolution (UN Res. 64 2010) recognizing the right to safe and clean drinking water and sanitation as an essential human right and calling upon states and international organizations to assist in establishing the means for providing clean water to all countries. The United Nations Human Rights Council subsequently adopted a resolution that explicitly derives the human right to safe drinking water and sanitation from the existing human right to an adequate standard of living and the right to life and human dignity. This embeds the right to clean water in the fabric of international human rights law and assists in universalizing and communalizing conceptions about access to water.

Efforts to challenge claims to the legitimacy of private appropriation and the purchase and sale of land as a commodity are also being articulated in assertions of the 'right to food'. While the right to land is not codified under international law, land security is regarded as necessary for the attainment of other human rights, such as the right to water and the right to food. The right to food is recognized in the United Nations International Covenant on Economic, Social and Cultural Rights (ICESCR) (Article 11) and in the Universal Declaration of Human Rights (Article 25). However, sets of principles advanced by the United Nations (Eleven Principles), the World Bank Group, the United Nations Food and Agricultural Organization (FAO), the International Fund for Agricultural Development (IFAD), and the United Nations Conference on Trade and Development Principles for Responsible Agricultural Investment (RAI) do not articulate the right to food as an unequivocal right, but rather attempt to balance land-use interests with market considerations. In addition, the successful challenge of land reform policies through the investor-state regime under Bilateral Investment Treaties does not portend well for the right to food trumping the right to private property any time soon (Schneiderman 2008).

Similar efforts to re-conceptualize germ plasm as collective property that requires conservation and protection are taking place in the Andean Community, comprising Bolivia, Colombia, Ecuador, Peru and Venezuela (Powledge 2006). Farmers' movements in India, South America, Asia and the Pacific, and non-governmental organizations, such as the Rural Advancement Foundation International (RAFI), Genetic Resources Action International (GRAIN) and the Third World Network, are working with farmers and indigenous groups and have initiated legal challenges to existing patents for pesticide extracted from the neem tree, various varieties of the chamomile plant, and genetically engineered herbicide-resistant plants, which were historically regarded as common property. Mexican bean growers who make their livings selling yellow beans are now subject to legal challenges from an American farmer who patented beans he brought from Mexico and named after his wife 'Enola'. RAFI argues that the yellow beans are legally for the 'free use of mankind' because they are entered in a germ plasm bank as 'in-trust germ plasm' (*ibid.*: 274). Andean farmers are also battling patents on Quinoa, a traditional source of protein and considered sacred by the Inca. While the United Nations Convention on Biological Diversity negotiated as part of the 1992 Earth Summit recognizes the sovereign rights of states over their natural resources and their authority to regulate genetic resources, these rights are being indirectly or directly challenged by the 1994 TRIPS Agreement, which expands private appropriation of biodiversity through patents. At issue here is the balance to be struck between the private and public spheres.

Further attempts to redefine international law are being generated by the Bolivarian Revolution, which is articulating principles of solidarity that rival dominant international legal principles and the practices of hegemonic international institutions. The Bolivarian Alliance for the Americas (ALBA) is encouraging popular participation in international lawmaking and advancing a new 'paradigm of co-operation, justice and equity' as the foundation for a 'neo-humanism through law' (al Attar and Miller 2010: 361). The emphasis in ALBA is upon the destiny of a shared humanity, a notion that is at odds with new constitutionalism. This is because new constitutionalism sees no future, because it disciplines the collectivity by freezing and locking in protections for the private appropriation of nature and labour by a very select few. New constitutional discipline removes the private appropriation of land, air and water from social control. The challenge to new constitutional discipline involves recasting private property rights to nature as shared collective property rights of use, conservation and preservation. This is a daunting task. The first step in contesting new constitutionalism is to recognize the effects of the commodity form of law and the agency of those empowered to appropriate privately (such as transnational food, water and land corporations, international organizations and global financial institutions) on the rearticulation of social relations through the enclosure and privatization of ever-more dimensions of human activity. This is particularly urgent in the context of the commodification of nature, for it involves the future of the fundamental conditions of human existence. Surely, it is here, the rights to and, indeed, the very future of life forms, where the lines must be redrawn between private and communal rights in favour of the latter.

4 The rule of law as the *Grundnorm* of the new constitutionalism

Christopher May

In contemporary global politics there can be few more popular normative appeals than to the rule of law. Norms such as democracy and human rights are frequently expressed by global leaders and political activists, and alongside them, the rule of law has become almost universal in its invocation, despite much less agreement about its effective implementation. If the 'new constitutionalism' represents one part of the neo-liberalization of the global political economy, then this is founded on the establishment of the rule of law as (potentially) universal common sense. In his recent meta-history of Western civilization, for example, Niall Ferguson made the rule of law (linked with property rights) one of the six 'killer apps' of Western domination of the global system (2011: Chapter 3). Indeed, it is easy to find appeals to the value and necessity of the rule of law by a range of commentators, politicians and national or global technocrats in any given week.

Conversely, for a minority of critics, the rule of law is far from benign: Ugo Mattei and Laura Nader (2008) argue that the (pretended) universality of the rule of law, by excluding much that is local/regional and that which has been established under different legal norms, is undermined by the *actual* imposition of a Westernized rule of law that seeks to structure societies to enhance and facilitate plunder of the local resources. This imposition undermines the 'real' (localized and organic) rule enjoyed by various communities: the rule of law, although itself contaminated by imperialism at the global level, still has value for local societies, in the guise of the 'people's rule of law' (*ibid.*: 202–11). As this implies, on both the right and the left, the rule of law has become an important touchstone for contemporary global politics.

In the general introduction the editors argue that neo-liberalization has yet to establish a hegemonic global order; its political supremacy relies on (implied) force, to serve the particular interests of the dominant social class. Any attempt to establish hegemony requires the justification and legitimation of rule alongside the consent of those governed, which at the global level has not been fully achieved. Thus, despite a long history of jurisprudential debate about the meaning of the rule of law, the term itself has increasingly been deployed in global politics to define what is legitimate and what is illegitimate, in an attempt to replace political supremacy with legitimated hegemony.

This move shifts the mode by which law is constituted; if national laws have often reflected a Hobbesian need to maintain order, by force if necessary, some elements of the international realm have become less dependent on state authority of this sort. Certainly parts of the international order remain dependent on the recognition of state consent (and therefore on force, in the last analysis), but there is much of the international rule of law that is grounded in a claimed collective good; the ability to constitute an effective global system of governance (Orford 2012). The support for capitalist economic development has increasingly been seen by the United Nations and other global non-state actors as a key end for this global system of governance.

That the development and expansion of capitalism is linked with specific 'rational' forms of legality is hardly a novel insight; it is a central element to Max Weber's account of capitalism in *Economy and Society* (Trubek 1972). Indeed it is now a commonplace to claim that the rule of law plays a key structural role in the governance of capitalism: from property rights to contract law, from legal personality of corporations to the alienation of labour's outputs, law underpins and facilitates the operation of capitalist markets. On the one hand critics such as Michael Tigar (2000) have sought to unpick the normalization of a particular form of legality that supports capitalism and privileges certain (class) interests, while organizations such as the World Bank have sought to promote these forms of law as a depoliticized technology of economic growth (Shihata 1991).[1]

Indeed, the very fact that the structural power of capital requires specific legal mechanisms to be in place before any state can compete to secure the resources that capital can deploy has further prompted a convergence in legal forms. However, the legitimation of the (rule of) law as an acceptable technology of governance has not, and cannot, be achieved by force alone; law, by working through consent and acceptance of its demands on political behaviour, must always be hegemonic (in the editors' sense) not only supreme. Therefore my question is: in the neoliberalization of the global political economy and through the moves to

---

[1] Ibrahim Shihata was general counsel at the World Bank during the key period in which the Bank expanded its remit into the legal arena, partly based on Shihata's presentation of the rule of law as a technique of economic organization and not a political issue. A similar treatment of the need for the rule of law can be found in Chapter 5 of *From Plan to Market: World Development Report 1996* (World Bank 1996).

expand the realm of the 'new constitutionalism', what political processes have established the normativity of law as a legitimate and authoritative institution of (global) politics?

To explore this position, I start with Hans Kelsen's idea of the basic norm (or *Grundnorm*) in law, and suggest that the idea of the rule of law qua *Grundnorm* can help us understand the global politics of the project to establish a 'new constitutionalism'.[2] Then I ask how this *Grundnorm* has been (re-)produced; this is unlikely to have been a casual, organic or accidental process but rather a political project supported by a recognizable group of actors. Thus any structural account of the new constitutionalism needs to be leavened with an account of agency, and specifically the project of establishing the rule of law as a non-problematic foundation for the organization of contemporary (global) politics.

The *Grundnorm*: from legal to political analysis

In the debates about the character and justification of legal systems, Hans Kelsen argued that the system of law was based on a prior basic norm (or *Grundnorm*). This basic norm is:

> The highest rule of law creation, establishing the unity of the entire system, [and] is indeed on hand for the issuance of other legal norms, but it must itself be assumed to be *presupposed* as a legal norm and not *issued* in accordance with other legal norms. Its creation must therefore be seen as a material fact outside the legal system. (Kelsen 1923 [1998]: 13)

Elsewhere, Kelsen suggested that this basic norm be regarded as the original constitution, the establishment of a particular social order by force, or political revolution before which time political justification relied on different norms (1945 [1999]: 115–17); the *Grundnorm* is the manifestation of a political break point. Tony Honoré has likened this to the 'big bang'; it is postulated by physicists to understand subsequent developments, but its own causes are not amenable to explanation based on current forms of analysis (1998: 101–3). When we seek to justify the notion of legality, the 'rule of law' is a norm that is not produced as part of the establishment and reproduction of any specific legal system but rather predates it: *the initial social desire for the rule of law must precede its origin.*

---

[2] Here I do not set out the debates about the substantive content of the norm of the rule of law, but see May (2011) for a discussion based on Lord Bingham's formulation. Here I am concerned with the appeal to the rule of law as political totem rather than its contestable character, although any appeal to the norm also includes an implied characterization and often a more explicit set of assumed (and prioritized) elements.

In Kelsen's view, there can be no legal system without a prior assumption that a system of laws (the rule of law) will provide direction for how those governed ought to behave (1982: 69). This transcendental notion of the foundation of law suggests a depoliticization of law as a system of governance: the content of the law comes after the acceptance of the process of following the law itself. A basic norm/*Grundnorm* that presents the rule of law as a legitimate and effective practice prior to its actualization is essentially an act of faith, not politics (in his later work Kelsen began to refer to the *Grundnorm* as a necessary fiction). This principle is not subject to political argument or amendment, it predates debate about the content and particulars of any specific legality; it is apolitical, and is intended to be so in Kelsen's analysis. The belief in the value of compliance with the law is the basis on which any system of rules *must* rest for otherwise it could not be regarded as a system of regulation. This is the crucial a priori step for governance.

Kelsen's position solidified around the argument that positive law could only be so by including its establishing norm for which no legitimate authority could be claimed, as logically it preceded the ability to be so justified (a claim only available after the basic norm is/was in place) (Bindreiter 2001: 149–52). As Jacques Derrida puts it in his consideration of law (which parallels Kelsen's on this point): 'How are we to distinguish between the force of law of a legitimate power and the supposedly original violence that must have established this authority and that itself could not have been authorized by any anterior legitimacy?' (1992: 6). Here, the rule of law, and thus its role as *Grundnorm*, is always the contemporary manifestation of some initial (original) moment of force, or assertion of legitimate authority. Leaving aside the continuing debates about Kelsen's analysis of the *Grundnorm*,[3] this idea has something to offer the discussion of the 'new constitutionalism' in contemporary global political economy. The prior political move that precedes the neo-liberalization represented by 'new constitutionalism' can be understood as the establishment and (in the face of resistance) reproduction of the rule of law qua *Grundnorm*.

Once a constitution is regarded as problematic, justificatory arguments track back through the hierarchy of norms, leading to debate and contestation about the presumption that the basic norm is valid. However, as the basic norm cannot be justified within the (legal) system that it precedes, this shifts the question of its validity (back) into the realm of politics. Thus, if the *Grundnorm* remains uncontested it is able to depoliticize

---

[3] See, for instance, the essays in Paulson and Paulson (1998) or the discussion in Bindreiter (2001).

subsequent debates about law, but when questions arise about the validity of any constitutional settlement, a political defence of its basic norm must be articulated. The move from acceptance to contestability of the *Grundnorm* can illuminate the political activity that underpins the 'new constitutionalism'. However, it may be preferable for constituted power to meet criticism of capitalist development on the ground of the rule of law than elsewhere; law's plausible (if not consensual) presentation as a technique of just governance rather than as a political instrument can (partly) dissolve criticisms based on partiality or inequity, or challenges premised on insurgent reason.

New constitutionalism, market civilization and disciplinary neo-liberalism

In Stephen Gill's analysis of the 'new constitutionalism', globalization has involved the establishment of a globalized 'market civilization'; the latest phase of an expanding capitalist system rooted in the nascent liberal state that emerged in Britain in the seventeenth century and the subsequent internationalization of liberalism in the nineteenth century (1998b: 27–9, 2003: 118; see also his Chapter 2 in this volume). Drawing on Foucault, Gill sees the increasing marketization of social relations as driven by a set of 'disciplinary practices' (2003: 130) centred on the use of legal institutions to structure and shape political forms of regulation and governance. This leads Gill to define 'new constitutionalism' as:

A macro-political dimension of the process whereby the nature and purpose of the public sphere in the OECD has been redefined in a more globalized and abstract frame of reference ... [It is] the political project of attempting to make transnational liberalism, and if possible liberal democracy, the sole model for future development. (2003: 131–2)

It mandates a particular set of state policies geared to maintaining business confidence through the delivery of a consistent and credible climate for investment and thus for the accumulation of capital ... It stresses the rule of law ... [and expands] state activity to provide greater legal and other protections for business. (1998b: 38)

[It] involves *pre-commitment mechanisms* to lock in not only present governments and citizens into the reforms, but more fundamentally to prevent *future* governments from undoing the reforms. In this way its central purpose is to reconstruct the political and legal terms through which governance and accountability operate not only in the near term, but also in the longer run. (Bakker and Gill 2003: 30, emphasis in original)

Emphasizing 'market efficiency; discipline and confidence; economic policy credibility and consistency; and limitation[s] on democratic decision-making processes' this new discipline establishes 'binding constraints' on fiscal, monetary and wider economic policy (Gill 2003: 132). Crucially, this 'new constitutionalism' seeks to confer privileged rights of citizenship on global corporate capital, and establish mechanisms by which the commitment to these values is embedded in current and future political practice.

As Gill notes, 'traditional notions of constitutionalism are associated with political rights, obligations and freedoms, and procedures that give an institutional form to the state' (2003: 132). Although this 'new constitutionalism' proceeds at the global level, rather than focusing on the rights and obligations of the global citizenry relating to a globalized governing body (or bodies), it is concerned with a much smaller group: global capital and its operating agents, corporations (both national and multinational). It holds separate the political and economic to ensure that the economic remains uncontaminated by the political, and the rule of law stands between them: markets are facilitated by the legal structures of property, contract and other laws. Politics can add to these laws but their basic components represent the rule of law not of politics; the latter of which is limited to dealing with the effects of these rules (e.g. problems of market failure). In this sense, the *pre-commitment* to the rule of law limits and shapes any subsequent reformist dynamic.

The national governance practices that are promoted as 'benchmarks' or 'best practices' by the World Bank support this constitutional settlement in favour of private property rights, contract law and other constitutional elements by constraining political impulses to undermine the efficacy of a particular capitalist form of the rule of law (Gill 1998b: 32ff.). Thus, as noted in the editors' introduction, judicial review has become increasingly used to remove issues from the political realm. Here the rule of law through the independent judiciary's power to review policy is mobilized to ensure policy remains consistent with constitutional requirements to reinforce the commitments to further neo-liberalization. In effect this is an antidote to democracy (Mandel 1998), given that the rule of law indicates both that all must be subject to the law (including states' governments) and that the judiciary must be independent; provided the constitution is directed towards neo-liberalization (as it will be under the 'new constitutionalism'), judicial review will constrain democratic political resistance based on the need to uphold the constitution's *non-political* strictures.

The World Bank also identifies a key *external* 'mechanism of restraint'. As Gill notes, it suggests that international agreements help states 'strengthen commitments' by raising the (international) political costs of policy reversal. Through the 'new constitutionalism', specific forms of capitalist social relations are normalized by multilateral agreements on the rights of property owners and investors, and the domestic legislation implementing these agreements. Although requiring the recognition and protection of non-national property, mandating unrestricted access to national markets, and establishing compensation ('damages') for state actions that impede these rights, such benefits are all set out in supposedly neutral and technical, trading and investment agreements. They are local manifestations of the norm of the rule of law: these rights have been established via a legitimate constitutional/legislative process, and as such are tied up with a commitment to the rule of law, and are mostly abstracted out of the political realm. From this particular neo-liberal perspective, then, governance is based on the 'rule of law'. Thus the expropriation of private property is viewed as not only unjust but also as theft; that opening markets allows competition to bring efficiency, which, by definition, is socially valuable; further, some neo-liberals argue that the right to trade is a putative human right (Petersman 2002). Who could object to this conception of the rule of law?

However, for Gill, these legal mechanisms are intended to shield global capital from local democracy (threats from below) and to insulate property rights from nationally based interference (1998b: 25, 30). What is hidden by the appeal and commitment to rule of law is the manner in which powerful (class) interests shape the forms of political economic relations that *can* be established. A general legal context underpins political/economic power: disputes and conflicts play out within the limited field the legal system maps out through the rule of law and its constitutional articulation. Conversely, as debates about soft law (Shelton 2009) have demonstrated, the legal method can also be utilized beyond the confines of the formalized 'hard' law of legislated governance, suggesting that the rule of law has imbued legal process with a wider legitimacy in global politics than merely its utilization within formalized legal practice. Soft law encompasses legal practices but (when favourable to corporate interests) dispenses with legal obligation, and suggests that the rule of law is far from fixed or immutable. Nevertheless, if hegemony is about the construction of a common sense as uncontroversial (while serving and privileging the interests of a specific class or interest), then the 'new constitutionalism' by establishing a *pre-commitment* to the rule of law (in its Western particularity) as the *sine qua non* of development at the global level (and even a key element of 'civilization' in Ferguson's account) achieves the normalization of a skewed and exploitative global system.

The 'new constitutionalism' not only shapes and develops political structures to advantage certain groups/interests, it also limits the modes of political engagement to the *constitutional*. Criticism and resistance are channelled into the forms of amendment and accountability that are established within the constitution(s). Forms of political engagement that fall outside are rendered illegal, illegitimate or nonsensical, while those that conform to the rule of law's strictures about process and legality may be constrained in the range of alternatives that can be offered. If the rule of law is the *Grundnorm* on which the new constitutionalism finally depends, then given Kelsen's analysis of the origins of the *grundnorm*, we need to ask how the rule of law is inculcated in societies and cultures that hitherto had different normative commitments.

(Re-)producing the norm: maintaining the rule of law

Why is the rule of law an increasingly legitimated norm in global politics? If, as Paul Kahn contends, in general terms, American political identity is 'peculiarly dependent on the idea of law' (1999: 9), then the rise of American global power in the twentieth century might also be expected to have shaped how (global) politics was perceived and characterized. Certainly, Pierre Bourdieu agrees that the social and political role of law (and in his terms, the juridical field) is notably stronger in the United States than elsewhere, and hence the weight accorded the rule of law is that much greater (1987: 823). The rise of the rule of law as norm and rhetoric then simply could be attributed to the post-1989 establishment of a dominant (US-inspired) depiction of the (global) good society focusing on democratization and liberal market economy (Carothers 2006: 6–7); a form of functional explanation where 'at least some positive link [between law and development] appears plausible and is enough to animate many aid practitioners' (Carothers 2009: 50). In other words, the triumph of an American process of neo-liberalization of economic organization, and the concomitant defeat of communism, shifted the focus of developmental political economy, establishing a clear role for the rule of law, almost by definition. However, in this section I am going to suggest, albeit briefly, that the rise of the rule of law as an authoritative norm is likely a combination of two further factors: professionalization and technical assistance. The issue of hegemonic, American political identity is part of another (albeit parallel) discussion about US political economic hegemony, which has already received considerable attention, and thus here I shall focus on two practices of normative (re-)production that support this development.

Professionalization

Harold Perkin suggests that the professionalization of society includes a move from a focus on capital either as investment or activity based, to a focus on property (which is to say scarcity) in the delivery of services

(1990: 377–80, *passim*). The shift that Perkin charts for the UK can also be discerned more widely; a move in global politics from discussions of power based on territory and/or resources, to discussion of power based on knowledge and expertise, the very attributes claimed by the professional classes. Central to any 'professional project' is the promotion of a higher status for the profession in the socio-political order through the control exercised over the (re-)definition of the field in which they seek to operate (Macdonald 1995: Chapter 7). This control is then extended through a process of abstraction and reduction: particular problems are reconceived in abstract terms and then reduced to problems that fall within the jurisdiction of the profession (Abbott 1988: 98). The legal profession is one of the key professions that seeks to establish and maintain the scarcity (and thus value) of its expertise (Bourdieu 1987): social problems are re-conceptualized as issues of regulation, and then reduced to questions of the development, application and interpretation of law, where lawyers can claim expertise.

However, as Gerard Hanlon has argued, the contemporary form of professionalization in legal services is different from previous waves, which focused on lawyers' gentlemanly practice, and then on social value. In this new wave, neo-liberalization has fostered 'commercialized professionalism' favouring large corporate law firms and centred on commerciality of the practice/firm, and lawyers' own entrepreneurship (1999). Thus, one side of legal professionalization has been the careful fostering of a closed group (lawyers) alongside the promotion of their tool (law) as a solution to problems of order. The other has been the normalization of commercial practices and foci, at the expense of a concern for social benefit; lawyers are now often more focused on the commercial success of their practice, and are not only looking to corporations as clients, but are themselves often part of a transnational legal-commercial community of practice functioning in an international market.

In contemporary global politics, issues are increasingly rendered as questions about the choice of jurisdiction where international adjudication should be sought and the linked choice of which set of rules and/or organization can decide (Koskenniemi 2007). Lawyers are asked to pronounce on political issues, deploying a perspective that 'rescues' issues from politics by appealing to (nascent) cosmopolitan values and norms; what Koskenniemi has referred to as the 'politics of redefinition' (2011: 67–8). This has led to an interest in constitutionalism, seen either critically, as a move to establish the rule of capitalism across the global system (as in this volume), or as a response to the fragmentation of governance and the shift from states' sovereignty to a range of issue-based international organizations. As Jan Klabbers puts it: 'constitutionalism carries the promise that there is some system in all the madness, some way in which the whole system hangs together and is not merely the aggregate of isolated and often contradictory movements' (2004: 49). The pre-commitment to the rule of law, represented by the notion of an emergent global constitution, allows the continual competition for authority over contentious issues to be presented not as political contest, but rather as a legitimate choice between rules and jurisdictions, overseen by lawyers and technocrats, not politicians with sectional interests.

This is reinforced by the more general professionalization of global society (not least amongst civil society groups) that has led to a move to regard the legal terrain as increasingly important in political mobilization.[4] Transnational advocacy networks now expend significant energy on helping to draft new legal rules, before then (empowered by these very same rules) seeking to publicize where national and international practices fall short (Sikkink 2002). By normalizing the utilization of legal mechanisms to address political issues, these networks have prompted a further consolidation of the normativity of the rule of law. This is exemplified by the professionalization of French non-government organizations: Gordon Cumming (2008) suggests that this is leading to a development 'mono-culture', which has been supported (or even promoted) by states' governments (in this case France) seeking to distinguish those groups worthy of funds and those not. Responding to the fragmentation and diversification of advocacy and civil society groups alongside increasingly scarce resources to support this segment of the international policy community, the sector has been (re-)organized into a neo-liberalized mode of competition, emphasizing value for money and efficiency.

Thus, one element for understanding the rise of the rule of law norm is the professionalization of the global polity, which has moved legal forms of organization to the forefront, and firmly placed lawyers at the centre of the practices of the global political economy. The political self-maintenance of the legal profession and the (commercialized) professionalization of global civil society have reinforced each other to prompt the increasing *pre-commitment* to the rule of law.

Technical assistance

If professionalization has played a key role in the establishment of the rule of law as an overarching norm of global politics, this didn't happen

---

[4] The role of lawyers in developmental politics is explored across a range of case studies in Dezalay and Garth (2011).

spontaneously across the world. Rather, there have been, and continue to be, extensive programmes that seek to (re-)establish the rule of law in developing countries, in post-conflict societies and elsewhere.[5] Only in the post-colonial period did legal re-engineering move from imposed legal structures to a more negotiated mode of co-development of local legal regimes, although some might still regard this as a form of imperialism (see Mattei and Nader 2008). In the 1960s the 'law and development' movement drew on liberal views about the social value of law with a focus on the state as the agent of development (Trubeck 2006: 75). These efforts often reflected the wider global political (and geopolitical) aims of the donor countries; for instance, during the 1960s and 1970s the United States expended significant public and private resources to support the development of the rule of law in Latin America (Domingo and Sieder 2001) as part of a wider regional political strategy. However, given its relatively well-publicized failings in Latin America (Gardner 1980), it is perhaps little surprise that when legal assistance returned to the international political agenda, legal-technical assistance was relocated to a range of international organizations (from UN Transitional Administrations to the World Trade Organization) and non-government organizations (the American Bar Association, for instance). It also became a major (mostly, but not exclusively) regional activity of the European Union.

The political landscape of these technical assistance programmes is very different from what it was in the 1960s and 1970s; there is a more complex appreciation of the sequence of developments required to instigate a specific form of the rule of law within a particular state.[6] For instance, the EU's programmes recognize three key overlapping stages of development: rule adoption; rule implementation; and rule internalization. While forms of conditionality (tied to EU membership) have been important, a recent survey of these programmes concludes that for 'rule adoption' it is the willingness or otherwise of local elites to work toward these ends that is crucial (Magen and Morlino 2009: Chapter 8). The rule of law's technical elements (procedures) are dependent on a normative acceptance of the wisdom of adopting this mode of ordering in the first place: a *pre-commitment* to the rule of law.

International organizations are most likely to be able to substantiate a claim that the rule of law represents a global consensus concerning the technical problems of governance and not the imposition of a particular

---

[5] For a selection of surveys of this activity, see Bull (2008); Jensen and Heller (2003); Magen and Morlino (2009); Sriram *et al.* (2011).
[6] However, the debate about sequencing is far from settled; see Carothers (2009: 55–8).

political system. However, this has sometimes led to what Amichai Magen and Leonardo Morlino, in their study of EU legal programmes, have referred to as 'subversive compliance': the form of laws are adopted but politically emptied of content, specifically when the (new) outcomes do not accord with already established local political mores or political priorities (Magen and Morlino 2009: 243). Here the laws and forms of legality the EU requires are established, but without the social (or more accurately, elite) internalization of any substantive normative content; this would seem to suggest that the introduction of the 'new constitutionalism', while needing the rule of law as its *Grundnorm*, also requires further political work to consolidate its systemic impact: some form of inculcation. Likewise, in the development of the rule of law across Asian countries, conflicts remain between what some programmes seek to deliver and what recipients are willing to accept and adopt.[7]

Developing the political culture that supports and facilitates the rule of law as a central element of any constitutional settlement (national or regional) is not something that can necessarily merely be technically implemented; it needs an organic relationship with the particular polity or society and its history. Indeed, ten years ago the OECD's Development Assistance Committee's expert group on aid evaluation concluded that an adequate legal structure, equitable access and institutional capacity were essential for establishing the rule of law in recipient countries, but needed to be supported by political leadership (OECD/DAC 1997: 28). Without a concomitant political commitment to the norm itself, instituting legal structures would not deliver real progress toward the rule of law, and thus the (legal) professionalization of global politics complements technical assistance to deliver the political 'buy-in' that the process of neo-liberalization requires. This leads us back to the political project of the new constitutionalism and its relationship with the rule of law.

New constitutionalism and the rule of law

If we accept that the rule of law serves as the *Grundnorm* for the 'new constitutionalism', the foundation for a process of neo-liberalization, then we need also to understand how it has been established and, in times of political contestation and tension, is maintained and reproduced. I have suggested that in addition to a structural analysis of the 'new constitutionalism' that focuses on the neo-liberalization of capitalism, there is

---

[7] See Peerenboom (2004) for an extensive set of studies of the rule of law in Asia, both as rhetoric and as policy. On the question of whether an Asian rule of law might look different to a European conception, see Ghai (1999).

a need to attend to the agents that helped to produce the now widespread *pre-commitment* to the rule of law. There can be little doubt that the rule of law represents a powerful and important element of the common sense of contemporary global politics, but it is clearly insufficient to merely assume its place in the pantheon of global values as self-evident or without political origins. I have outlined briefly two processes that might contribute to the establishment of the rule of law qua *Grundnorm*: the professionalization of global politics; and the deployment of programmes of technical assistance that have sought to socialize elites and legislators into the rule of law mindset. Although there is considerable empirical work to be done to map the contours of these practices, from the account here, we can be confident that the 'new constitutionalism' is unlikely to be reliant only on the structural processes of agenda formation.

The focus adopted here also suggests the normalization of law is a process that allows spaces for contestation to be revealed. The process of (re-)producing the rule of law, and by extension maintaining the 'new constitutionalism', requires considerable resources (political and economic) precisely because the rule of law is contested, and is no longer entirely dependent on state authority (which is to say force). The (re-)construction of the rule of law within new constitutionalism involves a narrowing of its potential, focusing on those elements that foster and support the capitalist marketization of societies, while underplaying (or discounting) those elements of the rule of law that emphasize political values that are beside (or even contrary to) the requirements of economic development (linked to human rights or democracy for instance) (Ngugi 2005). The contested character of the rule of law suggests that its role as *Grundnorm* for new constitutionalism will involve a Sisyphean task of legitimation and socialization.

Therefore, as 'subversive' compliance with rule-of-law strictures suggests, the project of establishing the particular rule of law favoured by new constitutionalism will be a continuing practice of maintenance and (re-)production not a ratcheted political economic developmental trajectory. Indeed, perhaps the key question is whether the ever-more frequent invocation of the rule of law indicates the (relative) triumph of the *Grundnorm* or that its recitation is an ongoing attempt to defend the depoliticization of the new constitutionalism against forces of resistance that do not regard the rule of law as neutral or merely procedural? While neo-liberalization and the 'new constitutionalism' may be built on the foundations provided by the rule of law, the maintenance of this norm remains crucial for stability of the edifice.

Part II

Genealogy, origins and world order

Part II of the volume outlines some of the origins, purposes and forms of authority and power associated with liberal constitutions and world orders. The two chapters help illuminate what is 'old' and 'new' in the emerging new constitutional world order. They illustrate how historical struggles have forged dominant patterns of political authority and are now restructuring the global order. The main themes of Part II involve:

1. The genealogy of liberal constitutionalism, particularly that of the United States.
2. How liberal constitutionalism can be understood as a form of insurance on the part of dominant forces against threats to their power, privilege and property, stemming from popular and democratic forces.
3. The recent global convergence toward constitutional supremacy in light of the rapid spread of democratic politics.

Chapter 5 by Tim Di Muzio suggests that a deeper appreciation of historical struggles over the constitution of liberal political authority helps us to identify the links between what is 'old' and what is 'new' in the new constitutionalism. In mainstream political science, liberal constitutionalism is often deemed the most desirable framework for promoting material advancement and human freedom while circumscribing arbitrary, unjust and absolute rule. Di Muzio argues, however, that this conventional wisdom disregards how US constitutionalism was developed by a class-based political project that attempted to safeguard and legitimate an empire of liberty for an affluent minority and forms of domination for the rest. Di Muzio's genealogical enquiry focuses on key concepts in the political order of the West since at least the seventeenth century, and specifically how US colonial elites understood liberty, property and security during the American Revolutionary War and the subsequent constitutional settlement. He shows that the historical struggles for independence actually entailed two 'revolutions':

1. A popular insurgency against the British Empire; and
2. An internal upheaval – or a counter-revolution – whose ultimate goal was to secure the unequal distribution of property and liberty in

favour of the ruling classes against potential threats from democratic forces.

In the minds of wealthy colonialists, 'liberty was rooted in, and inseparable from, the security to accumulate money without limit'.

Even after victory in the war for independence, therefore, affluent patriots feared threats to their liberty and property, not from arbitrary royal power from above, but from social forces from below that were radicalized by the revolution and inspired by democracy. Given the potential for 'the violence of faction' under the '*various* and *unequal* distribution of property', the politico-strategic rationality of the elite Federalists centred on how to design a form of political rule in the interests of suppressing rebellious actions while protecting the minority of the propertied against the majority of property-less, both in the present and the future. This 'old' liberal constitutionalism did not bring an end to class and racial domination but rather fortified it in new forms, later allowing it to develop into a form of constituted power that could transform their 'direct power gained in war into a form of structural power that operates through juridico-political institutions, norms and rules'. Di Muzio underlines that 'new' constitutionalist initiatives designate the transnational continuation of this initial class-based project, seeking to secure the power of capital against possible democratic challenge.

Ran Hirschl in Chapter 6 also discusses the importance of returning to historical struggles over the constitution of the liberal social order for current debates on the new constitutionalism. His analysis of the political origins of constitutional trends mirrors Di Muzio's genealogical arguments: the establishment and maintenance of the new constitutionalism is mainly guided by the insurance logic of the risk-averse elite operating in a contractually insecure environment under the widespread norms and practices of representative democracy. Put differently, the new constitutionalism is defined as a 'hegemony-preserving' manoeuvre that aims to secure elite privileges, worldviews and policy preferences by insulating them from the vicissitudes of majoritarian decision-making processes and outcomes. Fear of democracy amongst the ruling elite is seen as a main driving force of the new constitutionalism; as such, the widespread adoption of judicial review stems from their endeavour to solve the problem of uncertainty in 'electoral market competitiveness' by a means of designing constitutional measures.

Hirschl explores the links between the 'old' and 'new' constitutionalism by drawing attention to the global convergence toward judicial empowerment and constitutional supremacy – a mechanism that has historically been a major pillar of the American state form – over the last few decades at both national and supranational levels. A review of transitions to democracy and constitutionalisation around the world sketches how the degrees of judicial independence vary depending on the ruling classes' time horizons and perceived threats to their governance. Despite variations, however, common to changes at the national level is that they have principally reduced risks to the governing elite while delegating to the courts the authority of translating constitutional provisions into guidelines for coping with 'foundational political questions that define the boundaries of the collective or cut through the heart of entire nations'.

This tendency at the national level, as Hirschl points out, parallels 'new' constitutional innovations at regional and continental levels that supervene over domestic constitutions. Thus legal integration within the European Union and the transfer of power to the European Court of Justice are hegemony-preserving responses by risk-averse power holders to the uncertainty and probable threats posed by EU enlargement. This 'constitutionalization-as-insurance' perspective informs the tremendous rise of quasi-constitutional economic treaties and institutions at the supranational level (e.g. the World Trade Organization) and other regional trade and monetary arrangements. They can be interpreted as attempts to secure the power of transnational capital through solidifying a business-friendly world order beyond the pressures of national political control and the vagaries of majoritarian decision-making processes. At issue is the fear of a possible 'tyranny of the majority'. This old fear on the part of the oligarchies of today therefore helps to explain both the 'old' and 'new' constitutionalism.

5 Toward a genealogy of the new constitutionalism: the empire of liberty and domination

Tim Di Muzio

Despite being the very legal and political framework of social order and the modern state, international relations and (international) political economy theorists have spent precious little time discussing constitutions or constitutionalism. Mainstream theorists, focused as they are at the level of the international, spend even less time considering the genealogy of these foundational politico-legal frameworks. In the discipline of political science, constitutionalism appears to be the purview of political theorists who largely approach the question of constitutionalism from ahistorical perspectives that rely on some variant of social contract theory and rational actors (Brennan and Buchanan 1985; Hayek 1960; Rawls 1971). In much of this literature, liberal constitutionalism is considered to be the most desirable form of government in so far as it is claimed that such frameworks enable material progress and human freedom by circumscribing governmental power.

However, beginning in the 1990s a new literature in IR and international law began to address an emerging juridico-political trend Gill called the 'new constitutionalism' (1992a). Far from employing the language of hypothetical social contract theory, these theorists offered a more critical and historically informed assessment of the new liberal constitutions being written and the trade and investment agreements that served to extend a previously circumscribed liberal world economic order. These critical scholars began to question the nature and purpose of these new legal frameworks from the point of view of class, power and global inequality at the very time when new constitutional developments were widely taken as a sign of liberal democratic capitalism's triumph over all other forms of political and economic rule.

Within this literature scholars situated the emergence of the 'new constitutionalism' in the 1980s and identified these initiatives with the increasing *transnational* power of capital. And while there is much to be learned in this literature, I want to suggest in this chapter that a deeper *genealogy* of liberal constitutions can help us link what is 'old' with what is 'new' in the new constitutionalism. Genealogy is an approach to social scientific enquiry and writing that seeks to problematize social relations of power that are taken as self-evident truths in the present. Typically, genealogies begin with an assessment and critical question about the present, moving on to problematize the 'inevitability', 'naturalness' or 'self-evidence' of current power relations through a historical investigation that moves back, rather than forward, in time. Genealogies can be considered 'effective histories' in so far as they aim to provide a counter-memory to dominant interpretations of history for use in the present (Di Muzio 2008; Vucetic 2011). The dominant narrative challenged here is that liberal constitutional measures – be they new or old – are impartial and universal rather than partial, and of particular benefit to one class over another.

I claim that when we use this historical mode of analysis we find that the first liberal constitutions were not born in hypothetical 'state of nature' scenarios but, in the words of Foucault, 'in real battles, victories, massacres, and conquests which can be dated' (Foucault 2003a: 50). And while we may celebrate the attempt to restrict arbitrary and/or absolute authority in any of its historical forms, this does not mean, contra liberal readings, that liberal constitutions have put an end to domination (Warren 1989; cf. Fukuyama 1992). In other words, I want to discard the method of ahistorical conjecture and imaginary scenarios – however useful some might claim them to be as heuristics – and consider earlier historical social struggles over the constitution of political order. To do so I use the case of the United States. In this context then, the main argument in this chapter is that the US Constitution did not secure any true, right or universal conceptualization of liberty and property, but a *particular* form of liberty and property connected to a class-based project of social reproduction with three major forms of domination: the master over the slave, predominantly in the south of the colonies, the capitalist over the worker, predominantly in northern colonies, and the colonialist over the native, primarily on the 'frontier' (Perelman 2000: 254ff.; Post 2011).

By returning to 'real battles' over the constitution of liberal political authority, critical spaces can be opened up for understanding the 'new' constitutionalism not simply as juridico-political initiatives that frame (inter-)national social action, but as the continuation of these initial wars to constitute and secure a particular interpretation of liberty and property that cements the right of a minority to accumulate wealth without limit. Put another way, the extension and deepening of 'new' constitutional mechanisms can be understood as the *transnational* continuation of an initial struggle to establish the political and legal foundations for private property and thus secure the interests of a minority of privileged owners (Foucault 2003a).

The chapter proceeds as follows. In the first section I offer a brief survey of the literature on the new constitutionalism and argue that a deeper appreciation of the emergence of liberal constitutions would contribute to current debates by demonstrating the historical links between the 'old' and 'new' constitutionalism. In the second section, I focus on the American Revolutionary War and how affluent colonialists conceptualized liberty, property and security in their political project for independence. The argument here is that colonial elites were not simply concerned with arbitrary authority from above, but also, and more importantly after independence had been gained, with democratic social forces from below (Holton 1999). With the revolutionary war in the background, I then take a closer look at the major concerns of the Federalists during the constitutional process. Here I argue that the constitutional process and settlement of 1787 can be interpreted as a political project by affluent owners to secure their class and racial power over workers, yeoman farmers, slaves and the indigenous population in perpetuity. In other words, the Constitution of the United States of America did not put an end to class and racial domination; its aim was to secure it against alternative political aspirations and forms of social organization. I conclude the chapter with some reflections on the link between the 'old' and the 'new' constitutionalism, noting that the security of unequal property ownership and liberty has been the constancy amidst historical change.

The new constitutionalism

To a number of theorists, juridico-political trends in the 1980s and 1990s suggested that the liberal world order largely constructed after the Second World War was being extended and deepened. A number of major events signalled this international transformation: the rise of structural adjustment programmes, the dissolution of the Soviet Union and the creation of new constitutions in Eastern Europe, the Maastricht Treaty of 1993, the ratification of NAFTA, new constitutions in Africa, the creation of the World Trade Organization, domestic legal reform initiatives spearheaded by the World Bank, and the failed attempt to forge a Multilateral Agreement on Investment. These, of course, were just some of the major developments that suggested that the constitution of world order was undergoing a profound period of liberal political and juridical change that favoured capital in general and the investor in particular.

In a seminal article, Gill called these juridico-political transformations the 'new constitutionalism' and subsequently elaborated on the concept (1992a, 1995a, 1998a, 2000, 2008; Bakker and Gill 2003). Soon afterwards, a literature blossomed that attempted to understand and to research in more detail these global political and legal developments. Unlike the literature that celebrates the laws, institutions and norms of a liberal world order, the 'new constitutionalism' literature was largely critical of these emerging juridico-political trends. For example, Gill argued that the 'new constitutionalism' was a class-based political project whose ultimate goal was to 'lock in' or cement 'liberal democratic capitalism as the sole model for future development' and thereby extend what he termed an international 'market civilization' where goods, services and life chances were ultimately mediated by market forces (Gill 1995a: 412). As a transnational political project, Gill argued that new constitutionalist initiatives privileged corporate capital over and above the rights of citizens and thereby served to constrain rather than enable struggles for representation and democratization. From the viewpoint of international law, Mandel's (1998) historically and theoretically sensitive analysis of judicial review's relationship to democracy substantiated Gill's earlier claim. Hirschl also made a major contribution to the debates by evaluating the political origins of the 'new constitutionalism', finding that the most convincing explanation for these developments was the effort to 'insulate [elite] policy-making from the vicissitudes of democratic politics' (Hirschl 2004a: 73, 2008 and Chapter 6, this volume). Hirschl called this process the rise of a juristocracy, by which he meant the unprecedented transfer of power 'from representative institutions to judiciaries' (Hirschl 2004b: 1).

For Gill, the chief beneficiary of the new constitutionalism was not the individual citizen, but the individual (institutional) investor (Harmes 1998). By securing 'disciplinary neo-liberal' patterns of economic and social development, the newly emerging juridico-political order at both domestic and international levels was largely designed to ensure the confidence of corporate executives and investors in government policy (Gill 2000). Adding to Gill's insights, Schneiderman (2008) probed deeper into multilateral and bilateral trade and investment agreements and came to similar conclusions: in the budding juridico-political order, the rights of investors appeared to be paramount over the democratic aspirations and concerns of everyday citizens.

So while some celebrated these juridico-political trends as furthering a liberal capitalist democratic world order, critical theorists have tried to focus attention on the fact that while there is an attempt to deepen and extend the rights of investors and corporations, there is an equal and greater effort to limit the potential of democratic social forces whose interests stretch beyond the accumulation of capital as a governing force for social action.

That the new constitutionalism is the juridico-political project of a global propertied minority, it could be said, is the critical conclusion of the new constitutionalist literature. However, I want to suggest that returning to the historical emergence of liberal constitutions can be rather instructive because such an analysis would serve to connect new constitutionalist initiatives with a deeper lineage of historical struggle over the constitution of social and juridical order. To do so, I offer a critical historical analysis of how elites understood liberty, property and security during the revolutionary period and constitutional settlement of the United States (1763–87).

Colonial elites and the American Revolutionary War

In order to trace a genealogy of the new constitutionalism through a consideration of the American Revolutionary War and constitutional settlement, my research is guided by three interrelated and historically contested concepts that appear throughout the political discourse of this period: liberty, security and property. Indeed, these concepts have been central to Western political tracts since at least the seventeenth century.

Now, in so far as these terms possess a *historical* rather than an essential or fixed meaning, when we connect them up with social struggles and the concept of social reproduction, they can serve to register the contested nature of political order. The concept of social reproduction has been defined in various ways, but what I mean by the concept here is the ways in which any class-divided society produces, consumes and reproduces its lives and lifestyles, how social forces within society conceptualize this mode of living, and how these same forces justify and defend their historically unique patterns of development both materially and discursively. And here I want to argue that if we start our analysis from the point of view of social reproduction we find that different social forces had different conceptualizations of liberty, property and security, depending on how they reproduced their lives and lifestyles. This focus immediately draws our attention to struggles over the constitution of political power. I argue that once we adopt this method of enquiry two key facts emerge: first, liberal constitutionalism does not put an end to domination but recodes it and reinforces it in new forms and, second, that liberal constitutionalism was, from its inception, rooted in a class-based project designed to transform the direct power gained in war into a form of structural power that operates through juridico-political institutions, norms and rules. While I cannot hope to canvass the entirety of the scholarly debates on the revolutionary period in the space provided here, highlighting how America's ruling elite reproduced their lives and how they conceptualized liberty, property and security throughout the struggle for independence will go a far way in demonstrating my main argument.

Broadly speaking, up until the twentieth century, the dominant historiography of the American Revolution was that it was 'another episode in the age-old struggle of liberty against tyranny, of colonial freedom fighters waging battle against the arbitrary and despotic forces of Imperial England' (Kirby 1970: 811). In this reading, the revolution was an overwhelmingly popular insurgency against the Crown and parliament by colonial subjects who believed that the British Empire was usurping their rights and encroaching upon their liberties. The goal of the revolution was not simply political independence from the British Empire, but also founding a republic where the liberty and property of settlers would be secure from arbitrary power and foreign-made laws. And up until the work of Charles Beard (1921/1941), the Constitution born out of this revolutionary struggle was largely celebrated as the product of an almost godlike genius of the so-called 'founding fathers' in the service of 'the people' of the 13 colonies.

However, if we move beyond celebratory accounts of the revolutionary war and the founding father fetish in American historiography to a critical genealogical enquiry, we find that there were in fact *two* revolutions – a popular one directed against the Empire and an internal revolution led by a minority of propertied men aimed at securing their unequal ownership of property and their liberty founded thereupon. The Constitution was not the product of united and harmonious social forces acting in concert for the equal benefit of an already cohesive polity, but the result of a conflict between the ruling class and their subordinates over future politico-economic possibilities. To illustrate this point I want to offer a sketch of how the affluent conceived of liberty, property and security, and reproduced their lifestyles. Doing so will shed light on the constitutional settlement of the United States.

At the apex of the class hierarchy in the 13 colonies was a tiny elite of large plantation owners, creditors, merchants and manufacturers. While earlier historical accounts believed there was a rough equality of property amongst colonialists, relatively recent research has found that the distribution of wealth in early America was radically uneven with only 10 per cent of the population claiming ownership over 50 per cent of all colonial net worth (Huston 1993: 1093). These men primarily derived their wealth from their political power, land speculation and the employment of slave, wage and indentured labour in small manufacturing, farming and external trade. While a number of characteristics distinguish this class from the rest of the colonial population, the most important factor in relation to social reproduction and property was their quest to amass vast fortunes well beyond their immediate physical needs. In other words, the aim of this class was not simply to reproduce their material livelihood through their own work or the direction and disciplining of the labour of others, but to accumulate money and the symbols of gentlemanly wealth without limit. This drive to accumulate for the sake of accumulating more social power crystallized as pecuniary worth existed only amongst a very small portion of the white male colonial population.

Against this background we can understand how the ruling elite understood liberty, security and property, a position that would largely go unchanged, but not unchallenged, once the revolutionary victory had been won and debates concerning the possibility of a national government began. In the minds of the ruling elite, it is fairly commonplace for historians to note that liberty was rooted in and inseparable from the security of property. However, a more accurate statement concerning the ruling-class relationship to liberty, property and security might be to say that liberty was rooted in, and inseparable from, the security to accumulate money without limit. This may be more accurate since, at least for the ruling elite, property was largely viewed as a means of accumulation and a leisurely aristocratic lifestyle, not as a means to a subsistence livelihood. Furthermore, in an era before fossil fuels, it was well understood that one's wealth and material comforts were largely derived from the control of others:

Human beings are the most powerful instruments of production, and therefore everyone becomes anxious to employ the services of his fellows in multiplying his own comforts. Hence the intense and universal thirst for power; the equally prevalent hatred of subjection. Each man therefore meets with an obstinate resistance to his own will, and this naturally engenders antipathy toward beings who thus baffle and contravene his wishes. (Bentham quoted in Perelman 2000: 21; and Nikiforuk 2012)

To see how this relates to ruling-class involvement in the revolution, it is important to note that for the ruling elite the concept of liberty largely occupied a middle ground on a continuum of threats that included arbitrary power without limits on the one end, and licentiousness or anarchy on the other. Both were understood as dangers to ruling-class liberty and the security of their rights to accumulate incessantly.

In their descriptions of arbitrary rule, the ruling elite consistently used the trope of enslavement as a metaphor for the loss of liberty. And here the ruling elite had one major grievance with their colonial parent that resonated with some colonials of lesser means and privilege. While this grievance is commonly expressed in the familiar format 'no taxation without representation', the principle the ruling elite were far more interested in advancing was the more encompassing proposition that *legislation* without consent was a species of tyranny (Reid 1988: 89). For wealthy colonists, above all, this meant, that any action not consented to by their class was illegitimate. Without a share in the exercise of sovereign power, affluent patriots considered themselves slaves. In this sense, the parliamentary enactments of the 1760s were viewed as little more than signs of an ongoing war to usurp their liberty to accumulate. In other words, imperial legislation had rendered the liberty, property and lifestyles of some of the wealthiest colonists insecure.

With reference to affluent patriots, I will single out only one major parliamentary enactment that served to convince them of their need to rebel against the Crown in parliament: the Proclamation of 1763 that was 'a royal decree forbidding settlement or the purchase of Indian lands west of a line drawn along the crest of the Appalachians' (Ferguson 1979: 32). The decree had been issued within the context of a massive debt accumulated by Britain in the French and Indian War (1754–63) – a war that had been fought by France and Britain over claims to the Ohio Valley. The Proclamation was intended to arrest any further costly wars with the Indians by guaranteeing them that no further settlement would take place beyond the boundary established by the royal decree. In effect, the Proclamation denied wealthy merchants, landowners and their companies access to vast tracts of land that could be resold to settlers or used in the production of cash crops. Having cheap and privileged access to land was of particular importance for the many large plantation owners who were deeply indebted to English merchants for their luxurious lifestyles. Land speculation seemed to provide the only easy way landed gentlemen could generate enough revenue to repay their creditors. Indeed, 'in 1766 a committee of Parliament obtained evidence that the American debt due English merchants amounted to £4,450,000. More than nine-tenths of this sum was the indebtedness of Southern planters' (Sosin quoted in Friedenberg 1992: 149). However, land speculation was also viewed as an important investment opportunity for colonial merchants as well. Thus, cutting off access from the means of accumulating more wealth was interpreted as a particular affront to colonial liberty. For instance, Thomas Jefferson vociferously argued that the king had no right to grant lands since this was the purview of local councils. In his study of land acquisition and ownership in early America, Friedenberg offered his own interpretation of what Jefferson's position entailed:

In effect, Jefferson was stating that the British government was unjust in its efforts to protect the Indians; but speculative grants and purchases of land based on wiping out the Indians were just. It was tyranny to protect the rights of the weak who had occupied the land for untold generations; it was liberty to seize this land, kill the natives, and then resell it at a profit to other white men who in many cases would then enslave blacks to farm it. (1992: 150–2)

This passage goes a far way in suggesting how liberty, property and security were understood by the land-hungry ruling elite – a principal source of wealth before the fossil-fuel revolution of the nineteenth century. According to some historians, the denial of capturing title to millions of acres of land gave wealthy colonists such as George Washington, Patrick Henry and George Mason more than sufficient reason to support revolutionary action against Britain (Bouton 2001: 669). Other historians, however, have downplayed the Proclamation as a primary cause for the revolution. Historians in this vein tend to stress that the Proclamation line was merely a 'paper blockade' that settlers could easily abrogate. According to Holton, however, these historians fail to make a distinction between settlers and speculators. Without garnering secure legal title to land beyond the Proclamation line, speculators could not resell this land to settlers at a profit. What made matters worse was the fear amongst land companies that once the ban on acquiring land was lifted, squatters or settlers could make a claim of pre-occupancy to the British parliament, thereby threatening the land companies' legal title (Holton 1999: 3–38). In this sense, affluent speculators not only feared that Indians would continue to have access to the land they had inhabited for 'untold generations', but that settlers would gain their own direct access to the means of livelihood without first having to purchase land from one of their companies. Given the threats to their freedom to accumulate, it is perhaps small wonder that Virginia's wealthy elite were at the forefront of declaring independence from Britain in 1776 and 'adopted a state constitution that nullified the Proclamation of 1763' (Holton 1999: 38). Nor should it come as a surprise that, after the war, James Madison and James Monroe 'formed a partnership to speculate on western land' (Holton 2009: 22).

For the affluent, however, liberty was not simply defined in relation to arbitrary power. It was also defined in relation to licentiousness or anarchy. While Reid has suggested that the revolutionary Whig leadership were more concerned with the threats to liberty/property from tyrannical power rather than licentiousness, by the end of the War of Independence, most affluent patriots agreed that democracy posed the greatest threat to the reproduction of their affluence (Main 1966; Reid 1988: 35). As Wood argued, 'where once the magistracy had seemed to be the sole source of tyranny, now the legislatures through the revolutionary state constitutions had become the institutions most to be feared'. Indeed, many argued that problems during the 1780s 'were not due to the drifting and unrepresentative character of the legislatures, but were rather due more to the legislatures' very representativeness' (Wood 1969: 409–10).

Nowhere in revolutionary America was this truer than in Philadelphia where representatives even went so far as to suggest that the legislature should have the power to confiscate or lessen property when it became too concentrated in the hands of the few (Wood 1969: 89). With the help of a broad-based movement, the colonial elites had won the war for independence only to find that their property and liberty remained insecure after victory – not because of arbitrary royal power but because of democratic practices. It should always be recalled that the aim of the founders was to create a republic, not a democracy.

The constitution of liberty and domination

If the revolution was primarily an armed struggle to cast off the Empire that threatened to usurp the liberties and property of colonial America from above, the question of political rule at home was largely left undecided until the 1780s. From the perspective of many affluent Americans, the decades of resistance and revolution generated new threats to the social order from below – threats that made Federalists realize that the Articles of Confederation were inadequate for the task of encoding their power in institutions after the revolution. The major fear here was that the people had become too involved in their own governance, and often initiated legislation that harmed the minority of affluent property owners. Debt and tax relief, as well as emissions of paper money, threatened the accumulation strategies of wealthy citizens. And where state legislatures were not responsive to popular demands for relief, aggrieved citizens often took up arms in open rebellion, regularly justifying their resistance by appealing to the language of liberation spawned by the revolution. What made matters worse, however, was the realization – articulated most forcefully by Madison – that an impending class war was perhaps inevitable.

In devising the national government of the United States, James Madison was careful to inform the delegates at the Constitutional Convention that they were not only deciding the design of republican government, but also its fate. While Madison identified a number of threats to republican government, he identified and stressed one ultimate danger: 'the violence of faction'. For Madison, factions were inevitable if liberty was to be preserved. He feared, however, that 'the superior force of an interested and overbearing majority' might ultimately threaten the rights of the minority. While he identified a number of sources of faction, he argued that 'the most common and durable source of factions has been the *various* and *unequal* distribution of property'. Here, Madison was certainly concerned with the diversity of property ownership and the possibility that there would be conflicts between men of property in regards to policy. What Madison was more concerned about, however, was the *unequal* distribution of property and the fact that 'those who hold and those who are without property have ever formed distinct interests in society' (Madison 1996 [1787]). In this context, we do well to recall that Madison and others not only had access to political theory, but also the historical experiences of other class-divided societies. In designing the Constitution, Madison realized that while the present distribution of property in the United States bore directly on the design of the national government, the future was perhaps more important. He remarked that while 'the United States have not reached the stage of Society in which conflicting feelings of the Class with, and the Class without property, have the operation natural to them in Countries fully peopled', the future would be different:

In future times a great majority of the people will not only be without landed, but any other sort of, property. These will either combine under the influence of their common situation; in which case, the rights of property and the public liberty, will not be secure in their hands: or which is more probable, they will become the tools of opulence and ambition, in which case there will be equal danger on another side. (Madison n.d.)

Thus, while the special circumstances in the 13 newly independent states served to suppress 'conflicting feelings' that were 'natural' to the propertied and property-less, Madison certainly anticipated a future when these conflicts would inevitably surface. However, in perhaps one of the most telling passages in the records of the Federal Convention – records that were not released for public scrutiny until 1840 – Madison admitted that the germs of class conflict were already blossoming in post-revolutionary America:

It ought finally to occur to a people deliberating on a Government for themselves that as different interests necessarily result from the liberty meant to be secured, the major interest might under sudden impulses be tempted to commit injustice on the minority. In all civilized Countries the people fall into different classes having a real or supposed difference of interests. There will be creditors and debtors, farmers merchants and manufacturers. There will be particularly the distinction of rich and poor. It was true as had been observed, by Mister Pinkney, we had not among us those hereditary distinctions, of rank which were a great source of the contests in the ancient Governments as well as the modern States of Europe, nor those extremes of wealth or poverty which characterize the latter. We cannot however be regarded even at this time, as one homogeneous mass, in which every thing that affects a part will affect in the same manner the whole. In framing a system which we wish to last for ages, we should not lose sight of the changes which ages will produce. An increase of population will of necessity increase the proportion of those who will labour under all the hardships of life, and secretly sigh for a more equal distribution of its blessings. These may in time outnumber those who are placed above the feelings of indigence. According to the equal laws of suffrage, the power will slide into the hands of the former. No agrarian attempts have yet been made in this Country, but symptoms, of a leveling spirit, as we have understood, have sufficiently appeared in a certain quarters to give notice of the future danger. How is this danger to be guarded against on republican principles? How is the danger in all cases of interested coalitions to oppress the minority to be guarded against? (Madison n.d.)

What this passage reveals is not only a concern to secure the minority against the majority in the present, but also in the future. In other words, the politico-strategic rationality that informed the Constitution was not a provisional consideration of the present but a going concern to be operationalized in the very design of the national government. Given the likelihood of a protracted class war and the possibility that more property-less people would be enfranchised over time, answering the question of how to guard the minority of property owners against the majority of property-less became the ultimate governmental security problematic. Indeed, as one student of the constitution has noted:

the original focus on property placed inequality at the center of American constitutionalism. For the Framers, the protection of property meant the protection of *unequal* property and thus the insulation of both property and inequality from democratic transformation ... Effective insulation, in their view, required wealth-based inequality of access to political power ... The inherent vulnerability of all individual rights became transformed into a fear of 'the people' as a threatening propertyless mass whose power must be contained. (Nedelsky 1990: 2)

The chief difficulty of designing a government to contain common people was the fact that the people had been radicalized by the revolution and politically inspired by its language of liberty and popular sovereignty to struggle for their own interests. For instance, from 1786–7, Daniel Shays and his band of Regulators took up arms and closed courthouses in Massachusetts. The Regulators argued that the high level of taxation imposed upon small farmers was a threat to their liberty and security of property since they could be dispossessed of their property if taxes went unpaid. Yet high levels of taxation were needed if financiers of the American Revolution were to be repaid. Since many of the state's militiamen were sympathetic with the Regulators, wealthy property owners had to finance their own private army to put down the insurrection (Brown 1983). This initial inability to control the rebellion helped convince Madison and others that a larger political union with the capacity to frustrate majority rule and suppress insurrection was needed.

Building on his theory of inevitable class conflict, Madison argued that only a larger political union could suppress majority rule and protect what he called the public liberty. As many Anti-Federalists recognized, this was a complete reversal of republican political theory, which argued that only small governmental units could protect the liberty of the people. With the experience of some of the state legislatures in mind, Madison, however, reasoned that small governmental units were vulnerable to majority rule and factious combination.

As Holton has suggested, Madison's strategy was to divide the population by extending the scale of government so that the minority, who could more effectively organize around issues and candidates, could rule it (Holton 2005). In this way, Madison argued, 'a rage for paper money, for an abolition of debts, for an equal division of property, or for any other improper or wicked project' would be frustrated by the electoral system spanning the entire voting population (Madison 1996 [1787]). However, the attempt to drown out popular voices was only one way of answering the question of how 'interested coalitions to oppress the minority' could be guarded against by a national government. Another mechanism, which proved to be of crucial importance, was the creation of a national army to suppress rebellious activity.

Thus, looking into the future and with the knowledge of these conflicts, many of the ruling elite set out to design a form of political rule in the interests of securing the reproduction of their own unequal liberties and strategies of accumulation – be they in trade, slavery, debt collection, or the control of wage or indentured labour. Put simply, the liberal Constitution of the United States did not secure any true, right or universal conceptualization of liberty and property, but a *particular* form of liberty and property connected to a class-based project of socially reproducing inequality and domination. That gross inequalities continue to persist in the US social formation can be taken as evidence of the Constitution's success at continuing an initial war by other means.

Conclusion

The problem for liberals is that their struggles against authority are typically read as being against arbitrary, unjust and absolute rule, and are therefore celebrated. They are read in only one direction: up. In actual history, these struggles were not simply directed at sovereign power, but perhaps more importantly, they were also directed against social forces from below – forces that struggled for more democratic forms of rule or different ways of organizing social life that did not entail the accumulation of capital as power. The Constitution of the United States of America sanctioned slavery and gave colonialists free reign over the indigenous population whose land was coveted and whose forms of social organization were deemed antiquated and therefore of little value. More centralized power and direction not only helped crush popular rebellions against heavy taxes (to pay down the debt of the revolutionary war) and to underpin the dispossession of farmers, but it would also assist in expropriating native land for white capitalist land speculators and an extension of the tax base. Like the sovereign project of the king, the emergent liberal constitutional project was the plan of a minority concerned not with livelihood, but with accumulation. This much was demonstrated in our genealogical account of US constitutionalism – popular forces had to be curtailed to preserve the unequal power, property and liberty of owners. This is the continuity amidst change and the genealogical relationship between the 'old' and 'new' constitutionalism. A major difference is that new constitutionalism involves politico-juridical mechanisms to constitute, extend and protect the rights of capitalist ownership more *transnationally*. They aim to broaden an empire of liberty for the wealthy few and forms of domination for the rest. Whether the legitimacy of this still-unfolding order can be effectively challenged by counter-hegemonic forces with an alternative agenda is an open question. But a start might be in imagining ways communities can reconstitute their social relations toward livelihood rather than accumulation. A concern for social justice as well as pressing environmental and resource problems could provide the needed incitement. In doing so, they may come to think and act beyond the exclusionary nature of capitalist private property.

6 The origins of the new constitutionalism: lessons from the 'old' constitutionalism

Ran Hirschl

Transformative changes have been taking place in the constitutional domain. Over the last few decades, the world has witnessed the rapid spread of constitutionalism and judicial review at both the domestic and supranational levels. Constitutional supremacy, a concept that has long been a major pillar of the American political order, is now shared, in one form or another, by over 160 countries and several supranational entities across the globe. Most of these polities can boast the recent adoption of a constitution or a constitutional revision that contains a bill of justiciable rights and enshrines some form of active judicial review. Consequently, constitutional courts and judges have emerged as the key translators of constitutional provisions into guidelines for public life, and as a main forum for articulating and dealing with foundational political questions that define the boundaries of the collective or cut through the heart of entire nations. Meanwhile, the international migration of constitutional ideas has grown exponentially (Choudhry 2006), accompanied by the rise of what may be termed 'generic' constitutional law – a supposedly universal, Esperanto-like discourse of constitutional adjudication and reasoning, primarily visible in the context of negative or 'first-generation' rights and liberties (Law 2005; Law and Versteeg 2011). In this new constitutional environment, even bastions of agnosticism toward American-style high-voltage constitutionalism and judicial review cannot entirely avoid some of the developments taking place internationally (Jackson 2010; Tushnet 2009).

Alongside this considerable expansion in the 'traditional' constitutional realm, a phenomenon that scholars have termed the 'new constitutionalism' has emerged (e.g. Gill 1995a, 2003). This phenomenon often refers to the largely pernicious spread of a set of quasi-constitutional supranational treaties and institutions that place global economic governance beyond democratic reach, and promote uneven development by

I thank A. Claire Cutler, Stephen Gill, the conference participants and an anonymous reviewer for their helpful suggestions.

privileging transnational corporations at the expense of the world's economic hinterlands. As Stephen Gill observes, '[n]ew constitutionalism is a macro-political dimension of the process whereby the nature and purpose of the public sphere has been redefined in a more privatized and commodified way ... it can be defined as the political project of attempting to make trans-national liberalism, and if possible liberal democratic capitalism, the sole model for future development. It is therefore intimately related to the rise of market civilization' (Gill 1995a: 412).

Although it lacks some core components of the classical understanding of constitutional law (e.g. formal separation of powers; a hierarchy of institutions; an amending formula; or an aspirational preamble ('we the people ...') that defines and constitutes the polity), the new constitutionalism does nonetheless feature several important elements of constitutionalism, ranging from forms of judicial review and quasi-constitutional structures that supervene over domestic constitutionalism, to an overarching aspirational commitment to progressive liberalization of the global economy. Most importantly, the new constitutionalism creates a de facto global constitution by erecting binding constraints on domestic politics, economic policies and social thought, so that any local contestation of its global mantra is either isolated and labelled as deviant, or is simply unfeasible and bound to fail.

That the new constitutionalism exists, and has potentially far-reaching implications on participatory democracy and global economic governance, is, at least among contributors to this forum, beyond dispute. Yet the reason for its emergence, indeed the precise causal story at its basis, remains somewhat fuzzy, and is often obscured by criticism of the new constitutionalism's dubious normative foundations and often disenfranchising consequences. To the extent that an analytically coherent explanation concerning the emergence of the new constitutionalism is advanced, it tends to portray it as driven by either an overpowering ideational project that strives to enshrine a market economy, individualism, the small state, efficiency and globalization as the ultimate organizing principles of public life (essentially an ideational story), or by a set of systemic or structural vectors that are inexorably linked to advanced capitalism and push it toward the adoption of transnational economic institutions (essentially, a variant of the structuralist neo-Marxian story).

In this short chapter, I suggest that turning our gaze to the political origins of constitutionalization trends at the national level provides another plausible explanation: the new constitutionalism is not driven merely or even primarily by a victorious ideological agenda or by organic pressures of an ever-expanding market civilization, but by the economic system's existential fear of, and response to credible threats posed by, the spread of democracy (at least as defined by universal suffrage leading to relatively open, procedurally fair and routinely held elections; see Huntington 1991; Przeworski 1999; see also Chapter 5, this volume). Akin to its close domestic relative, the new constitutionalism may be understood as an 'insurance' or 'hegemony-preserving' manoeuvre – an attempt to insulate a set of privileges, policy preferences, worldviews, and key decision-making junctures from the vicissitudes of democratic politics – driven by risk-averse agents operating in an insecure contractual environment.

The insurance logic of constitutionalization and judicial empowerment

The large-scale convergence toward constitutional supremacy worldwide is typically portrayed by constitutional theorists as stemming from modern democracies' post-Second World War acceptance of and commitment to the notion that democracy means more than mere adherence to the principle of majority rule. Not least, we are often reminded, it reflects every 'mature democracy's' (in Ronald Dworkin's terms) subscription to the view that democracy must protect itself against the tyranny of majority rule through constitutionalization and judicial review, most notably checks on government action and an entrenched, self-binding protection of the rights of vulnerable groups and individuals (Dworkin 1990). Even according to this prevalent narrative – resplendent as it is with myths about the liberalizing power of rights, the Herculean capacities of judges and a supposedly authentic 'we the people' quest for constitutional protection – fear is a main driving force of constitutionalization. The ineffectiveness of the Weimar Republic Constitution and horrors of the Third Reich and the Nazi era are commonly invoked as a stark illustration of why strong constitutions are necessary. In their pre-commitment guise constitutions are viewed (and justified) as self-binding precautions that responsible right-holders who are well aware of their weaknesses (e.g. at times of national panic or mass hysteria) have taken against their own imperfections. Fearful of succumbing to their own future desires, constitutional pre-commitments may reduce the probability that such harmful measures will be adopted and carried out.

Against this canonical, politics-light backdrop, an emerging body of social science literature attempts to go beyond the traditional focus on constitutionalization as emanating from broad demand-side pressures or an overly idealist self-binding pre-commitment story, to identify specific supply-side factors that are conducive to the establishment and maintenance of constitutional review, most notably the changing interests and incentives of pertinent political stakeholders. Here too fear is a main factor. Most importantly for our purposes, such a realist approach suggests that political power-holders' sense of threat, real or perceived, is a main driving force behind the timing, scope and nature of constitutionalization, and of judicial empowerment more generally.

Legal institutions – be they property rights, labour law or electoral rules – produce differential distributive effects: they privilege some groups, interests and policy preferences over others. This effect is further accentuated when it comes to constitutions, the *raison d'être* of which is to create, channel and monitor power. Given their entrenched status and relative difficulty to change or replace, constitutions provide an ideal platform for 'locking in' certain contested worldviews, policy preferences and institutional structures, while precluding the consideration of alternative perspectives.

A key notion here is that of constitutions as risk- or threat-reducing instruments. Think of the simple logic of insurance. Those who are absolutely confident do not buy it. Residents of California buy insurance against earthquake damage. Residents of the Netherlands or the Maldives buy insurance against flooding. By contrast, flood insurance is not common, it is safe to assume, in the Gobi Desert (one of the driest areas in the world) or in La Paz, Bolivia (the world's highest capital). Likewise, if, having bought an insurance policy against flooding, one happens to move from the Netherlands to the Gobi Desert, one would want to stop paying for the flooding insurance immediately, as the risk level would be deemed negligible. Or consider another example: a small private entity that seldom finds itself embroiled in legal disputes is unlikely to sign a retainer agreement with a law firm; a 'pay-as-you-go' arrangement is expected. But the risk of expensive litigation poses a major threat to those who face frequent legal challenges. Thus, the idea of retainer agreements was created to provide predictability of legal costs in an increasingly litigious environment. In short, it is the balance between the level of risk, real or perceived, and the insurance policy costs that is a main determinant of choices regarding insurance. A similar logic may be applied to conceptualize pertinent stakeholders' willingness to engage in constitutionalization as a type of insurance policy in an insecure political environment.

The basic premise that people tend to be risk-averse under conditions of systemic uncertainty or increased threat has been advanced by a wide array of thinkers in other scholarly domains, from John Rawls' 'principles of justice' agreed upon behind a veil of ignorance, to Marshall Sahlins' paradigm shifting explanation for the lack of food accumulation or storage amongst hunter-gatherer societies (a perception of unlimited resources and a pervasive belief in a 'giving environment'), and to

Tversky and Kahneman's seminal work on the psychology of choice (showing that people who are willing to take considerable risks when facing gains turn risk-averse when facing losses). Threat reduction and a quest for increased predictability and secured expectations as the main driving forces behind institutional change is also acknowledged in economic theory. Institutional economists, for example, have depicted constitutions as credible commitment instruments that foster predictability and enhance economic performance by establishing limits on erratic government action (e.g. North and Weingast 1989; Weingast 1993). Either way, it is the 'risk-aversion as a key pro-constitutionalization factor' point where the strategic approach to constitutions comes close to the generic 'constitutions as pre-commitments' metaphor, although the focus here is on strategic pre-commitment by concrete, self-interested actors, not on pre-commitment in its abstract, public-choice sense.

The idea of delegation as an effective risk-reduction measure first appeared in the mid 1980s in the literature on the political motivations behind the creation of independent administrative agencies (Fiorina 1982; McCubbins *et al.* 1987, 1989). From the politicians' point of view, delegating policy-making authority to administrative agencies or to courts may be an effective means of reducing decision-making costs as well as shifting responsibility thereby reducing the risks to themselves and to the institutional apparatus within which they operate. If delegation of powers can increase credit and/or reduce risk or blame attributed to the politician as a result of the policy decision of the delegated body, then such delegation can be beneficial to the politician (Voigt and Salzberger 2002). At the very least, the transfer to the courts of contested political 'hot potatoes' offers a convenient, 'blame deflection-like' retreat for politicians who are unwilling or unable to settle public disputes in the political sphere. Politicians may seek to gain public support for contentious views by relying on national high courts' public image as professional and apolitical decision-making bodies. Alternatively, when politicians are obstructed from fully implementing their own policy agenda, they may favour the active exercise of constitutional review by a sympathetic judiciary in order to overcome those obstructions (Whittington 2005).

Constitutionalization, and judicial empowerment more generally, may likewise reflect the competitiveness of a polity's electoral market or governing politicians' time horizons. So, for example, when a ruling party expects to win elections repeatedly, the likelihood of an independent and powerful judiciary is low (Ramseyer 1994). When a ruling party has a low expectation of remaining in power, it is more likely to support a powerful judiciary and attempt to staff courts with sympathetic judges to ensure that the next ruling party cannot use the judiciary to achieve its policy goals. In other words, under conditions of electoral uncertainty, the more independent courts (or other semi-autonomous regulatory agencies) are, the harder it will be for the successive government to reverse the policies of the incumbent government.

When it comes to constitutions, several complementary strategic motivations come to mind. First, constitutionalization may allow governments to impose a centralizing, 'one-rule-fits-all' policy upon enormous and diverse polities. (Consider the standardizing or centralizing effect of an overarching constitution and an apex court jurisprudence in exceptionally diverse polities such as the United States, India or the European Union.) Second, constitutions may be adopted so as to ease pressure in order to undertake comprehensive political change, or in order to signal a regime's acceptance, prima facie, of a set of international standards or expectations with respect to the openness of the political process and the rights of the polity's members. Third, as Tom Ginsburg and others have argued, the 'electoral market competitiveness' logic may be expanded to suggest that contractually insecure environments create a political setting that is highly conducive to the creation of constitutional review as an 'insurance' mechanism (Finkel 2008; Ginsburg 2003). During periods of political transition when no obvious winner is projected to emerge, the establishment of constitutional review may provide a safety net for all involved parties, thereby facilitating a transition to democracy. This in turn leads to a greater likelihood that a relatively powerful and independent constitutional court will emerge as insurance adopted by risk-averse participants in the constitutional negotiation game. Put differently, under conditions of electoral uncertainty, constitutional review may emerge as a 'form of insurance to prospective electoral losers during the constitutional bargain' (Ginsburg 2002: 54). In short, judicial review is a solution to the problem of uncertainty in constitutional design.

A fourth, related argument combines 'rational-strategic' impulses with elite-driven struggles over worldviews and policy preferences as the main driving forces behind constitutionalization. As I have argued elsewhere, the threat of losing control over pertinent policy-making processes and outcomes may be a significant driving force behind attempts to constitutionalize matters (Hirschl 2004b). Embattled elites and their political representatives are more likely to opt for constitutional reform when present or prospective transformations in the political system threaten their own political status, worldviews and policy preferences. Such threatened occupiers of a polity's symbolic 'centre' – these could be either old-timers on their way down or emerging hegemons who fear a comeback of their socio-political rivals – may favour constitutionalization as a hegemony-preserving manoeuvre when their grip over politics, cultural dominance, or the allocation of core perks and benefits are, or are likely to be, challenged in majoritarian decision-making arenas. In this fashion, threatened elites can achieve through the constitutional domain what they cannot get through the electoral market.

The time horizons and perceived threats to power-holders are key factors here. It is the arrival of credible political competition, or a new constellation of power, that makes those who operate in an insecure political environment – either politicians, parties or social groups – see the utility of constitutional protection and powerful courts. Those that have better control over and affinity with the constitutional arena are more likely to resort to it as a power-preserving measure when present or prospective transformations in the political system threaten their own political status, worldviews and policy preferences. In short, constitutionalization is not merely, or even mainly, a form of Ulysses-like self-binding against one's own desires, but rather a self-interested binding of other, credibly threatening political actors who advance rival worldviews and policy preferences.

And from theory to practice. The main assertions of the electoral market thesis – most notably, that the degrees of political uncertainty and competition facing politicians, either those on the decline or those insecure in their newly acquired power, are important predictors of whether or not a constitutional court will be established – have been supported in a variety of studies ranging from formal modelling or large-N statistical analyses to detailed comparative studies of constitutionalization (Ramos 2006; Stephenson 2003). Scholars within the latter camp have drawn on the insurance logic to explain the variance in choice of constitutional institutions amongst several polities in Eastern Europe (Magalhaes 1999); between different periods in the late nineteenth-century United States (Gillman 2002); and between two Argentine provinces (Chavez 2003).

Ginsburg (2003), to pick one example, turns to an exploration of the rarely discussed establishment of constitutional courts in three new Asian democracies: Taiwan, Mongolia and Korea. All three countries share a roughly similar cultural context. Each country underwent a transition to democracy in the late 1980s and early 1990s. And, the newly established constitutional courts in all three countries have struggled to maintain and enhance their stature within political environments that lack an established tradition of judicial independence and constitutional supremacy. Despite these commonalities, there has been a significant variance in judicial independence amongst the three countries. In Taiwan the democratization process was governed by a single dominant party (KMT) with an overwhelmingly powerful leader (Chiang Kai-shek). The result has been a very gradual constitutional reform and the evolution of a relatively weak and politically dependent court (the Council of Grand Justices). In Mongolia, the former Communist Party was in a strong position during the constitutional negotiation stage but was nonetheless unable to dictate outcomes unilaterally because of a newly emergent set of opposition parties. This has resulted in the 1992 creation of a 'middle-of-the-road', quasi-independent court (the Constitutional Tsets). On the other hand, in Korea, constitutional transformation took place amidst uncertainty stemming from political deadlock amongst three parties of roughly equal strength. As a result, in 1988, a strong and relatively independent constitutional court emerged as political insurance against electoral uncertainty.

Similarly, the transitions to democracy in Spain and Portugal in the mid 1970s were characterized by the lack of a single core of post-authoritarian political power, and the rapid adoption of strong constitutional review mechanisms (Magalhaes 2003). In Greece, by contrast, the post-authoritarian process was dominated by a single party (Constantine Karamanlis' New Democracy held over 70 per cent of assembly seats) that did not have to worry about elections following the approval of the new constitution. 'The result was that Greece, with similar authoritarian and civil law legacies as Spain and Portugal, and involved in an almost simultaneous democratic transition, remained the only Southern European democracy without constitutional review of legislation' (*ibid.*: 127).

The hegemonic preservation guise finds support in other notable examples of constitutionalization. Having opposed judicial review for most of the twentieth century, white elites in South Africa miraculously discovered the virtues of judicial review when it became clear that the days of Apartheid were numbered. Pierre Elliott Trudeau's drive to adopt the Canadian Charter of Rights and Freedoms came on the heels of his electoral defeat in 1979, the rise of the separatist Parti Québécois in 1976 and above all the credible threat of a Quebec secession as signalled by the 1980 secession referendum. In Mexico the ruling PRI, indifferent to judicial review for over 70 years, discovered its charms in the mid 1990s when credible political opposition emerged. For decades Israel's Labour Movement and its predominantly secular Ashkenazi constituencies were agnostic toward constitutional reform, but embraced constitutional supremacy and judicial review once their cultural and electoral dominance begun to erode, their historic grip over Israel's governing bodies faded, and 'new elites' and their policy preferences had gained considerable influence. The constitutional revolution of the mid 1990s then followed. In the years leading to the 1992–5 constitutional revolution, electoral support for the Labour Party and the old Ashkenazi establishment plummeted, while several other hitherto 'peripheral' groups and interests – very few of which have been represented, let alone proportionally, on the Supreme Court bench – gained momentum (Hirschl 2009). And there are more defensive moves, too. Having been in opposition for 44 years, and fearful of the return of the socialist establishment, the first thing the right-wing coalition in Sweden did when it finally ousted the Social Democrats in 1976 was to recognize the courts' authority to exercise judicial review. Conversely, little or no judicial empowerment has taken place in countries such as Japan or Singapore, where a single political force has controlled the policial system for most of the last half century.

In Thailand, the historically hegemonic yet electorally challenged coalition of monarchists, army generals and state bureaucracy resorted to a hitherto passive judiciary, to support a military coup, and later to carry out a massive constitutional overhaul to depose the anti-establishment Prime Minister Thaksin Shinawatra and his Thai Rak Thai Party, and later to topple Prime Minister Samak Sundaravej. The judiciary was also called upon to disband much of the People's Power Party (an offshoot of the formerly banned Thai Rak Thai), which had won the 2007 parliamentary election (see generally Dressel 2012). The Kemalist elite in Turkey discerned the benefits of a strong constitutional court in the last few decades, when religious parties seriously challenged its historical grip over Turkish politics. Having dissolved two pro-Islamist parties in 1998 and 2001, the Constitutional Court has become a bastion of Kemalist interests in their fight to curb the influence of the popular Justice and Development Party (AKP). In 2008, the Court came very close to banning the AKP; six of the 11 judges, one vote shy of the necessary seven votes, found the AKP platform unconstitutional. In so doing, the judges signalled that further Islamization would not be tolerated by the Court or by its secularist and military establishment backers. A few weeks later, the Court declared unconstitutional, a constitutional amendment that had been passed legally by the AKP-controlled parliament that would have directly challenged the official state policy of militant secularism. Little wonder why the AKP-led government reacted in 2010 by proposing a set of constitutional amendments that would, amongst other things, alter the composition of the Constitutional Court so as to better suit the interests of the ruling party. In early 2012, the Philippines' President Benigno Aquino III impeached through a senate hearing the Chief Justice of the Supreme Court, Renato Corona. The impeached Chief Justice was a last-minute appointment of the previous president, Gloria Macapagal Arroyo, named just two days after her electoral loss to Aquino.

And there are other variations on this uncertainty or perceived threat element. For 15 years (1996 to 2011), the constitution of Morocco remained unchanged. As the so-called 'Arab Spring' of 2011 began to gain momentum, the royal family introduced a new constitution aimed at pre-empting and staving off democratic demands while maintaing King Mohammed VI's grip on power. Having defeated President Musharraf in the February 2008 elections and in anticipation of a phoenix-like rise from the ashes of a military regime, the newly elected government of Pakistan led by the Pakistan People's Party (PPP) was quick to ratify the International Covenant on Economic, Social and Cultural Rights, and to sign the International Covenant on Civil and Political Rights in April 2008. A similar logic may explain the 1994 incorporation of ten international covenants into Argentine constitutional law. Scholars have identified many other examples of such strategic incorporation of international standards into domestic law so as to 'lock in', or signal commitment to, certain worldviews and policy preferences, in particlar at times of political transition or uncertainty (Ginsburg 2006; Moravcsik 2000).

While for many years Britain was unwilling to incorporate the provisions of the European Convention on Human Rights into its own legal system (let alone to enact a constitutional bill of rights of its own), it did promote enthusiastically the entrenchment of Convention rights in the 'independence constitutions' of newly self-governing African states as devices for protecting established interests from the 'whims' of independent majoritarian politics. The 1991 constitutionalization of rights in British-ruled Hong Kong took place shortly after the British parliament had ratified the Joint Declaration on the Question of Hong Kong, whereby Britain was to restore Hong Kong to China in July 1997. In fact, some scholars of British constitutional history even argue that the events known as the Glorious Revolution (1688–9), most notably the establishment of a constitutional monarchy and the adoption of the English Bill of Rights, were aimed at protecting the interests of the propertied classes against Dutch invasion and the ensuing political instability.

Back to the new constitutionalism

The constitutionalization-as-insurance argument has striking parallels in accounts of the empowerment of other semi-autonomous institutions. The literature on the political origins of central banks, for example, suggests that their autonomy in advanced industrial countries may be a function of government politicians' time horizons (e.g. Goodman 1992). The longer the horizon of their time in power, the more government politicians will desire the greatest possible control over economic policy. This implies a consequent loss of independence for the central bank.

By this logic, short horizons, forthcoming elections, or other threats to their governance or policy preferences can lead politicians who fear losing power to increase central bank independence in order to limit the future options of their political opponents. Central bank independence may also provide politicians with a 'blame deflection-like' retreat, enabling them to talk the talk of a certain populist policy, while assigning to central banks the 'bad cop' role.

A similar rationale may be applied to constitutionalization attempts at the regional or continental levels. The acceleration of EU constitutionalization processes in the last decade, including most recently the Treaty of Lisbon (2009), may be understood as a type of insurance scheme or hegemonic preservation measure undertaken by self-interested, risk-averse power-holders who, given the uncertainty and potential threats posed by EU enlargement from 15 to 25 members in 2004 and to 27 members in 2007, may seek to entrench their policy preferences through constitutionalization (Hirschl 2005). The 'intergovernmentalist' thesis concerning the evolution of the European Court of Justice (e.g. Garrett 1998) puts forth a similar argument. According to this thesis, member states choose to create (and selectively abide by the limits imposed by) supranational institutions primarily because these institutions help them to surmount challenges to their policy preferences at the national level. National governments of the EU member states have not been passive and unwilling victims of the process of European legal integration; they consciously transferred power to the Court so as to overcome oppositions from within. Moreover, the selective implementation of ECJ rulings by member states derives from domestic political considerations by national governments (such as a greater willingness to implement ECJ judgments that favour certain constituencies whose political support is essential for governments and ruling coalitions).

The same logic may be applied to explain the proliferation of quasi-constitutional economic arrangements at the supranational level (think WTO, NAFTA, MERCOSUR, ASEAN, and other regional trade and monetary agreements) as an attempt to solidify the foundations for a business-friendly global economic order that is largely beyond national political control and the vicissitudes of democratic politics more generally. As Stephen Gill observes, the new constitutionalism is intended to 'lock in commitments to liberal forms of development, frameworks of accumulation and of dispossession so that global governance is premised on the primacy of the world market' (2003: 132). David Schneiderman has likewise talked about the emergence of a global investment rules regime that places the interests of international corporations beyond the reach of domestic politics (Schneiderman 2008).

The lesson from all of these examples is that a sense of threat, not hubris (think 'the end of history') or uncontested hegemony, is the main driving force behind constitutionalization, old or new. The contemporaneous worldwide expansion of the ethos and practice of democracy and the global convergence to constitutionalism, old and new, is anything but coincidental. In fact, these phenomena are two sides of the same coin. The transfer of crucial policy-making prerogatives from majoritarian decision-making arenas to semi-autonomous domestic and transnational policy-making bodies has occurred alongside growing popular demands for political representation; the spread throughout the globe of universal suffrage (which has included breaking down the historical dependence of voting rights upon property ownership, gender, race or ethnic origin); a global decline in politically formalized group-based discrimination and segregation; a rapid growth in the level of education and political awareness amongst the general population; an unprecedented increase in immigration to prosperous Western countries over the past few decades, and which threatens to change the 'demographic balance' in these countries; increasing demands by ethnic and religious communities for greater self-government; and the growing presence of new or historically recessive interests and policy preferences (for example, environmentalism, disarmament, multiculturalism, non-traditional sexual preferences) in crucial majoritarian policy-making arenas. Consequently, the institutions of democratic governance now operate in a profoundly different environment than that in which they were founded. All these recent developments imply a potential threat to established interests. The expanded representation of such 'peripheral' interests has further emphasized the tension between powerful centripetal forces of convergence (such as formal democracy, economic neo-liberalism, global capitalism, an international stock-exchange culture, and media production and consumption controlled to a large extent by a handful of international mega-conglomerates) acting on the state from outside; and re-emerging centrifugal forces of divergence (such as regionalism, differentiated citizenship, and growing economic inequality) acting on it from inside.

In the face of such challenges, supporters of dominant but increasingly threatened interests may choose to limit the policy-making authority of majoritarian decision-making arenas by gradually transferring authority to relatively insulated, professional policy-making institutions. By keeping popular decision-making mechanisms at the forefront of the formal democratic political processes, while simultaneously shifting the power to formulate and promulgate certain policies from majoritarian policy-making arenas to semi-autonomous professional policy-making bodies, those who possess disproportionate access to, and have a decisive influence upon, such bodies, minimize the potential threat to their hegemony.

It would therefore suggest that the current global trend toward judicial empowerment through constitutionalization is part of a broader process, whereby self-interested political and economic elites, while they profess support for democracy and sustained development, attempt to insulate policy-making from the vagaries of democratic politics. Given the increasing presence of previously excluded groups and interests in majoritarian policy-making arenas, this large-scale insulation of policy-making is perhaps the least dangerous modus vivendi for threatened elites. Put bluntly, it can best be understood as an attempt to defend established interests from the potential threats posed by cultural divergence, growing economic inequality, regionalism and other centrifugal voices that have been given a public platform through the proliferation of representative democracy.

As Michael Mandel suggests, the recent history of constitutionalism, old and new, provides a perfect illustration of this logic (1998). As long as representative political decision-making institutions were kept safely in the hands of the established social circles (typically economic magnates, political aristocracy, professionals and the urban intelligentsia) parliamentary sovereignty was praised by politicians and constitutional theorists alike as the most sacred of democratic values. Accordingly, the delegation of policy-making to national high courts was relatively limited. As political representatives of the established interests started to lose control of these institutions (at different times in different polities), they started to worry about the 'tyranny of the majority' (*ibid.*). This led to high praise for and conversion to judicial review, and to the subsequent transfer of crucial policy-making functions to the courts. Thus, the new constitutionalism – the transformation in the relations between the people and policy-making institutions that has swept the world during the last few decades – appears from our present vantage point to be a fear-driven transformation that 'changes everything so that everything may remain the same' (*ibid.*: 251).

Part III

Multilevel governance and neo-liberalization

Part III highlights how the neo-liberal project of extending new constitutionalism has not simply resulted in the decline of the significance of the state but *rather* its transformation, a shift that is linked to a more general global redefinition of politics and multilevel governance. The main themes of Part III consist of:

1. The need to go beyond conventional understandings of the 'global' and the 'national' as reflecting opposed political logics under conditions of neo-liberal globalization and the new constitutionalism.
2. How this allows for an exploration of the shifting forms and roles of the state, including the privatization of norm-making authority, in 'new geographies of power'.
3. The 'variegated' development of neo-liberalizing market-disciplining 'rule-regimes'.
4. The centralization and decentralization of policy capabilities in the neo-liberal projects for federalism and multilateral governance, operating at local, national, regional and global levels.

Saskia Sassen in Chapter 7 seeks to problematize the common thesis of the demise of the state illuminating what is obscured by the conventional wisdom of accounts of neo-liberal globalization that are centred in a global–national dualism. She argues that a focus on new constitutionalism as the de facto political-juridical structure in the formation of the global capital market provides the basis for conceptually and normatively understanding the ways in which national states encounter and endogenize 'new geographies of power'. These geographies, according to Sassen, involve two sets of dynamics that profoundly transform the historically constituted form of liberal states, particularly their alleged separation between the public and private domains. On the one hand, the multiple negotiations between national states and global economic actors over the last few decades have generated a new normativity ushered in by the disciplinary logic of the capitalist market – in Sassen's words, the 'privatizing of capacities for making norms'. In this new normative order, certain types of economic policies, such as those that establish the autonomy of central banks and privilege anti-inflation measures over employment growth, are regarded as legitimate, while others, especially claims for general welfare expenditures, lose legitimacy because they are considered to render states 'less competitive' in the global capital market. Put differently, the increasing formalization of privatized norm-making capacities has imposed the criteria for 'proper' economic policy on national states, endorsing a 'convergence of diverse national regulations and law, so as to make the requisite conditions for corporate and financial globalization'. In so doing it has tightened restrictions on who might benefit, while weakening and even eliminating public accountability in the norm-making process.

On the other hand, Sassen directs attention to participation by the particular components of national states in producing and legitimating this new normative order, as another feature of new geographies of power. Sassen illuminates how the emergence of a distinct *assemblage* of territory, authority and rights as a strategic field for the operation of the global capital market entails the partial disembedding of specialized state operations from the broader public domain geared to national agendas. But, at the same time, it requires the states to continuously play a crucial role often as the institutional home for the enactment of the new legal regimes. Cross-border transactions amongst governmental agencies and business actors, as Sassen further notes, have facilitated realignments inside the states, characterized by not only constitutional supremacy (see also Chapter 6) but also a significant shift of power from the legislature to the executive. This structural trend toward greater executive power is part of the historical evolution/adaptation of liberal states in the context of economic globalization. She also links executive empowerment with the growing importance of supranational institutions (e.g. the IMF and the WTO) as key actors in the processes of making and implementing the rules of the neo-liberal project, which negotiate not with the legislatures but almost exclusively with the executive. As such, Sassen's discussion about the internal reconfigurations of national states highlights how the 'national' is one strategic site for creating some of the key political and institutional underpinnings that enable and legitimate the (re-)production of the new constitutionalism on a world scale.

Chapter 8 by Neil Brenner, Jamie Peck and Nik Theodore also focuses on the global/national relationship and its links to the new constitutionalism, which they interpret as a 'parameterizing' legal architecture oriented toward extended, accelerated capital accumulation since the 1970s. They draw on their concept of 'variegated neo-liberalization' to shed light on the uneven spatial and temporal spread of neo-liberalizing market-disciplinary 'rule-regimes' across territories, scales and places. Brenner et al. propose that an accurate understanding of the extension of neo-liberalization and, more specifically, the formations of the new constitutionalism, must take account methodologically of such systemically produced variegations in regulatory arrangements, forms and strategies. To explore these variegations, they argue, requires an investigation of the networks and processes associated with neo-liberalizing global rule-regimes, and how, although they may be designed through a complex of world-scale, multilateral and supranational institutions, they are nevertheless adapted and implemented in policy experimentation at both national and subnational scales.[1]

Brenner et al. seek to analyze the diverse forms of market-driven jurisdictional restructuring across differential contexts associated with three elements in the 'restless landscapes of neo-liberalization'. The first, *regulatory experiments*, captures the projects to initiate, consolidate or even reproduce politico-institutional infrastructures for market-disciplinary regulatory arrangements. *Systems of inter-jurisdictional policy transfer* refer to circulatory networks for the transnational promotion, legitimation and delivery of neo-liberal policy prototypes. *Transnational rule-regimes* designate large-scale jurisdictional-institutional frameworks to facilitate neo-liberal 'rules of the game' that shape policy experimentation and reforms across subordinate territories, scales and places, while confining the limits of possible practices within relatively circumscribed political parameters. Drawing on these interlinked dimensions of regulatory transformations, Brenner et al. sketch a stylized periodization of 'the creatively destructive trajectories and uneven development of neo-liberalization since the 1970s'. This period can be summarized as, in their words, a 'tendential, macrospatial shift from disarticulated to deepening forms of neo-liberalization'. This shift signifies how predominantly isolated context-specific experimentation of neo-liberalizing reform projects – e.g. financialization, liberalization and privatization – have circulated transnationally as policy prototypes, subsequently leading to their institutionalization and legitimation through the market-driven redesign of supranational institutions. Moreover, the global extension and consolidation of new constitutionalism has not eclipsed the specificity of contextually situated

---

[1] Editors' note: this perspective seems consistent with the following interpretation:

[Gill] noted the 'contingent and contested character' of [new constitutional] constraints (Gill 2002: 61) ... [and] 'that pressures and constraints that the new constitutionalism produces "vary according to the size, economic strength, form of state and civil society and prevailing national and regional institutional capabilities, and the degree of integration into global capital and money markets"' (Gill 2008: 142; cited in Dierckx 2012: 2–3).

regulatory experiments but qualitatively changed their politico-institutional and juridical canvas.

Thus, Brenner *et al*. underscore the importance of concentrating simultaneously on global regulatory transformations and their national and local ramifications. They also outline several scenarios for future pathways of regulatory restructuring as the consequences of the current global economic crisis. In their view, possibilities for forging 'progressive new constitutionalism' out of the struggles elicited by the contradictions of market-based regulation depend on *both* the creation of orchestrated counter-neo-liberalizing policy transfer networks that would interconnect market-restraining regulatory experimentation across territories, scales and places *and* the development of a credible image for an alternative global rule-regime as a transformative challenge to the hegemonic reign of neo-liberalization.

Chapter 9 by Adam Harmes critically examines the recent application of neo-liberal theories of federalism, and how this is understood across different jurisdictional scales: local, national, regional and global. Drawing on Karl Polanyi and largely consistent with Di Muzio's genealogical account in Chapter 5, Harmes emphasizes how new constitutionalism involves deliberate and self-conscious political projects to design institutional 'lock-in' mechanisms for separating economics from politics – or more precisely, for preserving property rights and guaranteeing capital mobility from the pressures of democratic control. From this viewpoint, he argues that neo-liberal projects for multilevel governance – in particular, the promotion of 'market-preserving federalism' – are part of a set of new constitutionalist initiatives, which seek to insulate the economic from the political in a distinctively vertical fashion.

As Harmes elaborates, the concept of market-preserving federalism originated in the work of neo-liberal intellectuals such as Friedrich von Hayek, Milton Friedman and James Buchanan. It involves two key principles for determining the assignment of specific powers to different levels of governments. The first principle is the centralization of policy capabilities regarding the protection of property rights, the enforcement of contracts and the creation/maintenance of markets. The second is decentralization of policy capabilities and control over issues that neo-liberals do not support, such as redistributive taxation, social welfare programmes, and environmental and labour regulations. Guided by these principles, neo-liberal federalism incorporates the mechanism of inter-jurisdictional policy competition to discipline governments. Governments are forced to compete for mobile capital and investment, since individuals and investors have an 'exit option': under a regime of free trade and capital mobility, individuals and firms can move themselves and/or their assets flexibly across subnational jurisdictions.

Harmes then directs attention to the consistency between market-preserving federalism and the neo-liberal visions for regionalization and globalization, that involve 'either a de facto or *de jure* centralization' of policy capabilities to promote and safeguard free markets, capital mobility and private property rights across political boundaries through various multilateral apparatuses and agreements. At the same time, to ensure policy competition and an exit option at the regional and global scales, neo-liberals argue for decentralization (to at least the national level) of policy capabilities related to redistributing wealth and correcting market failures. They also oppose 'any efforts to increase tax and regulatory burdens through multilateral harmonization'.

Therefore Harmes contends that neo-liberalism encompasses 'an explicit and self-conscious normative project for multilevel governance, which is fully consistent across the federal, regional and global levels'. He further suggests that for progressive social forces to realign the 'economy' with the 'polity' and to limit inter-jurisdictional competition can be possible in one of two ways:

1. 'Bringing the economy back down' to the level of the national 'polity' through re-imposing capital and exchange regulation, and withdrawing from multilateral trade agreements; or,
2. 'Bringing the polity up' to the level of the regional/global economy by means of promoting the internationally harmonized forms of social democratic governance.

7 When the global inhabits the national: fuzzy interactions

Saskia Sassen

In much of my work I have been keen on discovering what is obscured by the dominant vocabulary through which a major disciplinary subject is captured, described and researched. In the case of globalization and the neo-liberal project, the focus in this short piece, it is a vocabulary that emphasizes the global and the national as antagonists – what one wins the other loses. This holds whether the perspective on issues/events comes from the left or the right of the political spectrum. Such a dualism functions as a reasonable description and can be intuitively satisfying. Dominant explanations do explain and they are to be taken seriously. Yet their clarity rests partly on the selecting of some features and the discarding of others which wind up in the penumbra around the centre of light. It is in that penumbra around a powerful explanation where I do my research; it has been a key analytic tactic in my work (2007).

In the case of this essay, what I detect is that the global – whether an institution, a process, a discursive practice or an imaginary – is constituted inside the national to a far larger extent than is usually recognized in critical accounts. Far from antagonism I find that particular sectors of the national liberal state have been key makers of the global corporate economy, along with the more familiar makers. This entails a rejection of notions such as 'globalization weakens *the* state' or 'the rescue of our banks shows us the return of the strong national state'.

In contrast, I find that corporate globalization has sharpened the internal heterogeneity of the liberal state, with some components firmly planted in the new global corporate logics gaining power and others losing resources and influence. Similarly, the bank rescues of 2008 and onwards, whether in the United States or in the European Union, come down to the use of *national* law to access *national* taxpayers' money to rescue a *global* financial system. Both of these facts are in the shadow of the dominant account of a global–national dualism. They are partial and do not override dominant explanations. But by including key components of national states, we expand the analytic terrain for understanding and representing what we have come to name globalization.

This is also my way of engaging the 'new constitutionalism', even if my concepts do not necessarily correspond to those of Gill and Cutler. What matters from the perspective of my argument is that as a conceptual and descriptive framing, the 'new constitutionalism' (Gill 1998a, 2012) brings into plain sight many of the features that I think of as being in the shadows of today's more common or dominant explanations. Stephen Gill and A. Claire Cutler wrote in an earlier draft for the General Introduction to this volume 'both old and new juridical and regulatory forms have emerged and combined to constitute some of the key political and legal governance frameworks of "actually existing" capitalism'.[1] New constitutionalism both enables and is constituted through a range of often rather specific mechanisms, laws, rules and regulations for implementing neo-liberal frameworks of accumulation. I agree with this argument, and have argued (2008: Chapters 1 and 5; 2013b), with a narrower and more specific focus, that old capabilities (where capabilities refers to laws, norms, permissions, restrictions) can move or be moved to new organizing logics (e.g. from the protective national Keynesian policy frame to the global corporate frame); in such shifts these capabilities change their valence.

This brief chapter examines both the how – analytic tactics – and the what – the new constitutionalism – for understanding a few building blocks of the current global political economy, and the possibility of contestation and exit (see Sassen 2008 for a full account and bibliography). The first section discusses one of the strongest instantiations of the new constitutionalism, the global capital market and its norm-making capacities. The second section begins to move into what is obscured by the national–global duality: the focus is on the emergence of a strategic corporate field that entails a partial disembedding, not eliminating, of specific state operations from the institutional setting of national agendas. I find that the new constitutionalism brings this emergent operational field into the light, albeit through different language and conceptual tools. The third section moves even deeper into the shadows, and finds key instruments for the making of that global corporate order inside the executive branch of government, where it is dressed in the clothing of *national* policy.

---

[1] Editors' note: our view is that this reconfiguation of state institutions needs to be placed, as does Saskia Sassen in this chapter, within the context of a dialectic between national/localized and global/delocalized new constitutionalist disciplines. For somewhat different perspectives on this dialectic see also Chapter 9 by Neil Brenner *et al.* on the uneven and variegated nature of neo-liberalization processes and Adam Harmes in Chapter 10 on neo-liberal theories of federalism and their implications for relations between local and global forms of authority and power.

The global capital market: power and norm-making

In the multiple negotiations between national states and global economic actors we can see a new normativity derived from the operational logic of the capital market (Sassen 2008: Chapter 4). By the end of the 1990s it had succeeded in imposing itself on important aspects of national economic policy-making. Some of the more familiar elements of this new normativity are the importance attached to the autonomy of central banks and the privileging of anti-inflation aims over employment growth; other familiar components are exchange rate parity and the variety of items usually referred to as IMF conditionality. In this new normative order, certain claims and criteria for policy-making emerge as legitimate. In addition, other types of claims lose legitimacy – generally privileging job growth and expenditures concerning the wellbeing of people at large are now devalued and seen as making states 'less competitive' in a normative context where states are expected to become more so.

I try to capture this normative transformation with the notion of a privatizing of capacities for making norms that have long been centred in the liberal state. This brings with it strengthened possibilities for norm-making in the interests of the few rather than the majority. In itself this is not novel. What is novel is the formalization of these privatized norm-making capacities and the sharper restricting of who might benefit, two features that diverge from the prior Keynesian phase of many Western states. This process also brings with it a weakening and even elimination of public accountability in domains of norm-making, which when in the public sector were, at least in principle, so subject. Again, while in practice this might not appear to be much of a difference, it is the formalizing of this withdrawal from the sphere of public accountability that is important.

The formation of the global capital market that begins in the 1980s amounts to a concentration of power capable of systemically influencing national government economic policy and, by extension, other policies. The key concern here is the fact that the global financial markets are not only capable of deploying raw power but also have produced a logic that now is seen as setting the criteria for 'proper' economic policy, consistent with what Gill and Law (1988, 1989) have called the direct and structural power of capital. IMF conditionality has some of these features. In a way these markets can now exercise the accountability functions formally associated with citizenship in liberal democracies: they can vote governments' economic policies in or out; they can force governments to take certain measures and not others (Sassen 1996: Chapter 2, 2008: Chapter 5). The issue here is not so much that these markets have emerged as a powerful mechanism where those with capital can influence government policy. It is rather that the overall operation of these markets has an embedded logic that calls for certain types of public sector economic policy objectives. Given the properties of the systems through which these markets operate – speed, simultaneity and interconnectivity – they can generate high orders of magnitude and lead to a politico-economic situation where the outcome is much more than the sum of the parts. This influence and power can be exercised on any country integrated into the financial markets, which by now is most countries. In my reading, Gill and Cutler examine similar trends, even if they use a different conceptual lexicon (see Gill 2008 and Cutler 2003, 2012 on, respectively, the power of capital and private forms of power and authority).

The issue of the power of today's global market for capital, its features and its operational logics, raises two critical questions. One of these is whether today's global capital market is different from earlier ones; the other, whether it is in fact a larger market than that of earlier global eras. My answer to the first question is yes, and that this difference matters as we seek to understand the power of this market when it confronts states and national economic actors. My answer to the second question is that whether it is larger or smaller than previous world markets, as counted in value, is of secondary importance to the character of its globality – that is, under what conditions it is articulated with national states and economies.

The partial disembedding of specialized state operations and non-state actors

One outcome of these and other trends discussed elsewhere (Sassen 2008: Chapters 5, 7 and 8) is the emergence of a strategic field that entails a partial disembedding of specific state operations from the broader institutional settings of the state in good part geared to national agendas. It is a fairly rarified field of cross-border transactions amongst government agencies and business sectors aimed at addressing the new conditions produced and required by economic globalization. The transactions are strategic, cut across borders and entail specific interactions with private actors. One outcome is the making of what we might think of as global temporal frames that diverge sharply from the standardized bureaucratic time of the modern national state (2008: Chapter 8). Again, while I have decoded the making of an operational field with power to impose its norms on national states, Gill and Cutler have also focused more on the actual norms informing the legal and political mechanisms associated with the growing disciplines and mobility of capital.

I see here state operations that do not entail the state as such, in contrast to what is the case in international treaties. Nor are they confined to intergovernmental networks. Rather, these transactions consist of the operations and policies of specific subcomponents of the state (for instance, technical regulatory agencies, specialized sections of central banks, such as those in charge of setting particular monetary policies), components of the supranational system linked to the economy (IMF and WTO), and private non-state sectors.[2] These are transactions that cut across the private–public divide and across national borders in that they concern the standards and regulations imposed on firms and markets operating globally. In so doing these transactions push toward convergence of diverse national regulations and law, so as to make the requisite conditions for corporate and financial globalization.

There are two distinct features about this field of transactions that lead me to posit that we can conceive of it as a disembedded space in the process of becoming structured. The transactions take place in familiar settings: the state and inter-state system in the case of officials and agencies from governments and from the supranational system; the 'private sector' for non-state economic actors; and so on. But the practices of the agents involved contribute to the constitution of a distinct assemblage of bits of territory, authority and rights that function as a new type of operational field. It is a field that exceeds the institutional world of the inter-state system. In so far as interactions with private actors provide substantive public rationality, it is a field of practices within which denationalized state agendas get defined and enacted. This field of transactions entails a partial and often highly specialized unbundling of the condition of state bundling in the Keynesian period of the post-Second World War decades. This unbundling is also one element in the changed relation between state authority and national territory (Sassen 2013b).

The stickiness of multilateral agreements illustrates some of these issues. It produces a kind of disembedding from the context of national lawmaking; this effect is further strengthened if the multilateral agreement is constructed through top-down lawmaking. Stephan (2002) notes that the adoption of a general norm through multilateral agreements, if done consistently, leads to 'legal stickiness'. Once in place, these agreements typically require unanimity (or constitutional like-amendments) for their

---

[2] Editors' note: a key unifying element is the growing significance of experts, and decision-making by highly specialized and private sector technocrats, who are deemed to be authoritative and legitimate as apparently 'neutral' managers. On this see in particular, Cutler (2012) and Gill (2012).

modification or replacement, which according to Stephan functions as a barrier to adjustment and evolution of those agreements. We see at work here a kind of cumulative causation in a given direction within specialized domains, a dynamic I have found in several of these domains. Stephan further finds that '[w]idespread adherence to a difficult-to-change set of legal rules may produce an evolutionary dead end, rather than a clear and optimal regime' (2002: 311). He argues that given lawyers' built-in bias for harmonization in the context of multilateralism, and given the enormous diversity across national legal systems, supranational institutions are the ones legal analysts will see as preferable, further reinforcing 'legal stickiness'.

The other feature of this field of transactions is the proliferation of rules that begin to assemble into partial, specialized systems of law. Here we enter a whole new domain of private authorities – fragmented, specialized and increasingly formalized but not running through national law per se. The new constitutionalism captures this well (see Gill and Cutler in Chapter 1 of this volume; Gill 1998a, 2012).

My concern with unpacking this particular issue stems from the embeddedness of much of globalization in national territory, under conditions where national territory has been encased in an elaborate set of national laws and administrative capacities. The new geography of global economic processes and the strategic spaces for economic globalization had to be produced, both in terms of the practices of corporate actors and the requisite technical and institutional infrastructure, with global cities an acute instantiation. But it also required the work of the state in producing or legitimating new legal and institutional regimes. This signals a necessary participation by the state, including in the regulation of its own withdrawal. One question this raises is what specific type of authority/power this participation gives to the state or to particular state institutions, notably central banks and highly specialized technical regulatory agencies. This is the subject of the next section.

The state: one site for non-state actors

The particular combination of dynamics described in the two preceding sections is part of a larger organizing logic that includes specific components of national states – the executive branch of government, whether prime ministerial or presidential, central banks, ministries of finance and a few other specialized state agencies. This brings with it necessary and often foundational realignments inside the state.

These realignments are constitutive, which also means that the state is partly constitutive of the new organizing logic. In this context, then, I diverge from the scholarship that sees the state as merely evolving and adapting and losing power. The new constitutionalism does not necessarily emphasize this operational field where work gets done by specific state agencies. But it does capture the outcomes of this work, in my reading.

In positing foundational realignments inside the state, I do not preclude the presence of adaptive processes when it comes to other components of the state from those I focus on, but these need to be distinguished from constitutive ones. The distinction is critical for arguing that the above listed components of the state undergo specific, mostly partial, processes of denationalization. And this matters for a full specification of today's epochal transformation, to wit, that one strategic locus for globalization lies deep inside the national. Such an interpretation of what is epochal about the current transformation carries distinct policy implications for democratic participation and accountability in that it shows the national is one site for *global* politics and *global* claim-making (Sassen 2008: Chapters 4 and 5).

The US state is an illuminating case for apprehending the internal transformations of the national liberal state into a neo-liberal state beginning in the 1980s. In their aggregate the mix of policies we usually describe as privatization, deregulation and marketizing of public functions effected a significant shift of power to the executive, a loss of law-making capacities and political participation by Congress, and, partly as a result, a new critical role for the judiciary in public scrutiny of executive action and in lawmaking. Further, the globalization of a growing range of economic actors and processes brings with it an increased inequality in the power of different parts of the government, sharpening whatever inequalities may have long existed. Thus, in contrast to the common thesis of the decline of the state due to globalization, I have long argued that the executive branch of government, the US Treasury, the Federal Reserve and a few other specialized agencies gained significant powers precisely *because* of globalization (1996, 2008: Chapter 4).

While each state is different, the internal redistribution of power away from the legislature and toward the executive is becoming evident in a growing number of states worldwide. Further, through these changes a major realignment is effected in the historically constructed and highly formalized divide between the public and the private realms, with the latter increasingly absorbing forms of authority once exclusive to the state, a subject developed in some of the work on the new constitutionalism (Cutler 2003; Gill 1998a, 1998b; Mandel 1998). This privatizing of particular public authorities is also part of the tipping point that ushered the global age.

The growing power of the executive branch of government is, in my reading, a structural development that is part of the historical evolution/adaptation of the so-called liberal state. This structural development needs to be distinguished from the state of emergency or the state of exception – an anomalous condition that can return to 'normal' once the emergency is over. Today, when there is talk of the rise of executive power (whether presidential or prime ministerial) it focuses on the state of emergency (e.g. the Patriot Act in the United States or the new emergency anti-terrorist policies in the EU member states). Because of that focus it is easy to overlook this second, structural trend of greater executive power, which is not anomalous, but rather, I argue, the new norm of the liberal state (2008: Chapter 4).

The rise of a global corporate and financial economy has weakened large parts of the working class and of the liberal state, even as it has brought additional powers to the executive branch. These structural power shifts are not always visible – much of it happens in the often rather private executive branch. Thus the US $1.2 trillion extended by the Federal Reserve to just about all top banks in the global financial crisis, was a major allocation of taxpayers' money that never went through the legislature: it was handled exclusively within the executive branch of government. The US $700 billion bailout went through the legislature and hence a public debate, which resulted in multiple mini allocations to various legislative jurisdictions and to local governments.

Another key source of power for the executive branch is the fact that all key supranational institutions such as the IMF and the WTO, to mention but the best known, negotiate exclusively with the executive branch of government; they do not deal with legislatures. In the 1980 to 2000 period when most of the rules of the neo-liberal project were put in place, the IMF and other such rule-making bodies gained enormous importance as key actors in this process of implementing new rules. Most of these rules had to be adopted by national states. Thus, as the power of these supranational institutions grew so did the power of the executive branch of government, even as the rules weakened the state as a whole (for a detailed account see Sassen, 2008: Chapter 4). It also signals the structural realignment of a critical component of the national state: increasingly, the executive branch of government has one foot firmly planted in global corporate logics. In my research I find this to be a structural development and hence to transcend party politics.

At its most extreme, this structural shift may be signaling a new phase in the long history of liberal democracies, one where the executive branch gains power partly through its increasing role in helping make and in supporting the global corporate economy. We can see here a kind of internationalism. Pity it is being deployed for these and other not so attractive aims, such as the new type of 'international coalition wars'.

And yet, the fact of this emergent internationalism in the executive branch of government invites a question. Is it possible that these new international capabilities of the executive branch might be reoriented to more worthy aims – climate change, global hunger, global poverty and many others requiring new types of state internationalisms?

If the global is in good part constituted inside the national, as I argue, then globalization in its many different forms directly engages a key assumption in the social sciences: the implied correspondence of national territory and national institutions with the national, i.e. if a process or condition is located in a national institution or in national territory, it must be national. This assumption describes conditions that have held, albeit never fully, throughout much of the history of the modern state, especially since the First World War, and to a good extent continue to do so. But today these conditions are partly but actively being unbundled. Different also is the scope of this unbundling. This unbundling does not necessarily mean that they disappear. Rather, we see their partial reconstituting as denationalized processes that are part of the formation of the global.

We might reformulate this proposition as a research project (Sassen 2007). The fact that a process or entity is located within the territory of a sovereign state and encased in national policies and institutions does not necessarily mean it is a national process or entity. Today it is an empirical question. While most such entities and processes are likely to be national, there is a growing need for empirical research to establish this for what is in turn a growing range of localizations of the global and, perhaps more difficult to establish, components of the global that are endogenous to the national. Much of what we continue to code as national today may well be a sufficiently transformed condition to barely qualify as national – the national here understood as a historically constructed condition.

Conclusion

Today states confront and endogenize new geographies of power. One of these is internal to the state: the shift of power to the executive branch and away from the legislature. The other is external: a field of forces that includes a far broader array of non-state actors than ever before and the rise of new normative orders beyond that of the nation state. Both geographies entail a particular set of dynamics that profoundly alter the constituting of the private and public domains, a rupture in an old history that dates back to the origins of the liberal state. The 'new constitutionalism' is one way of framing the conceptual and normative components of this shift.

Here I briefly examined both of these geographies and argued that they point to a far more differentiated process and a more transformative process of the state than is indicated by notions of an overall decline in state significance. The global, largely electronic, capital market, precisely one of the most extreme instances of the ability to transcend the geographic jurisdictions of the national state, is simultaneously global and in need of multiple insertions in national territories. In this regard, it can be seen as an experiment that tests the limits of both the state's exclusive territoriality and global capital's transnational jurisdictions.

While the state participates in enabling the expansion of the global economy, it does so in a context increasingly dominated by deregulation, privatization and the growing authority of non-state actors, some of which assume new normative roles, as is the case with the global financial system. In many of these new dynamics and conditions, the state continues to play an important role, often as the institutional home for the enactment of the new policy regimes we associate with economic globalization. This institutional home within the state has evolved sharply over the last two decades and today consists largely of the executive branch, ministries of finance, central banks and a few specialized, often new, agencies. In the case of the private economic domain, it is the corporate economy and strategic spaces for global operation, notably global cities, where we can register the national as institutional home for global processes and actors.

The outcome is an emergent new spatio-temporal order that has considerable governance capabilities, as is well captured in the new constitutionalism. It also has a type of structural power that extends its base deep inside the executive branch of the liberal state. This institutional order strengthens the advantages and the claims of certain types of economic and political actors and weakens those of others. It is extremely partial rather than universal, but strategic in that it has undue influence over wide areas of the broader institutional world and the world of lived experience yet is not fully accountable to formal democratic political systems. While partially embedded in national public and private institutional settings, it is distinct from them. In so far as it is partly installed in national settings, its identification requires a decoding of what is national in that which has historically been constructed as the national.

These transformations are partial and incipient but strategic. The field of power within which national states now function is constituted not only by the community of states but also by the formation of a new private institutional order linked to the global economy and by the rise of institutional orders comprising NGOs and human rights organizations. Such significant, even if partial, transformations in the condition of the national generally, and the national state in particular, raise the possibility of profound shifts in the architecture of political membership. Citizenship, the foundational institution for membership in the modern state, has long been deeply articulated with the national state. A key element in the evolution of citizenship has been the will of the modern state to render national major institutions that might well have had a different trajectory and to some extent did for most of recorded Western history. The construction of political membership as a national category is today mostly experienced as an inherited condition. The degree of institutional formalization and socio-cultural thickness makes it difficult to experience the historicity of this construction. It is easily naturalized. And yet, for most of Western history territory was subject to multiple systems of rule – the king, the local lord, the church – and so was membership. The nationalizing of territory and allegiance entailed encasing geographic territory into an elaborate institutional system: territory became state territoriality, and identity became nation-based citizenship.

Some of the main dynamics at work today are destabilizing these particular arrangements and bringing their historical particularity to the fore – not necessarily producing their downfall but making legible the fact that other arrangements are possible. These developments have consequences for certain features of the state and the inter-state system, and in this regard inevitably perhaps for liberal democracy as well as for international law and the modes of accountability therein contained.

8 New constitutionalism and variegated neo-liberalization

Neil Brenner, Jamie Peck and Nik Theodore

Sparked by the pioneering interventions of Stephen Gill (1995a, 1998b, 2000, 2003), the literature on the new constitutionalism has provided an illuminating basis for conceptualizing the market-disciplinary regulatory reorganization of world capitalism since the 1980s. This work represents an important contribution to the ongoing debate on neo-liberalism, which has long been a lightning rod for discussions of contemporary capitalism, its regulatory dynamics, its crisis tendencies and its possible futures.

Studies of new constitutionalism have focused primarily on the worldwide legal architectures of market-disciplinary regulation, and have tended to emphasize the geopolitical institutionalization of marketizing, commodifying rules since the 1980s. Whereas the formation of global rule-regimes has been investigated in detail by analysts of new constitutionalism, less attention has been devoted to the role of inter-jurisdictional policy transfer networks and processes of regulatory experimentation at both the national and subnational scales. Building upon the concept of variegated neo-liberalization (Brenner *et al.* 2010), we argue that systematic attention to each of the latter dimensions of regulatory restructuring can strengthen the methodological apparatus for studies of new constitutionalism: it could provide the basis for analyzing the evolution of neo-liberalization tendencies, and of formations of new constitutionalism itself. Through such an approach, moreover, one can productively explore scenarios for counter-neo-liberalizing forms of regulatory restructuring within contemporary capitalism.

In our conception, neo-liberalization processes are variegated in so far as they systemically produce geo-institutional differentiation. We emphasize the systemically produced uneven development of neo-liberalizing projects across territories, scales and places, as well as the evolution of such projects over time and across space. In our view, a more sustained engagement with the problematic of variegated regulation can advance our understanding of new constitutionalism, its historical-geographical vicissitudes, its crisis tendencies and the possibility of its transcendence.

This chapter is thus a sympathetic critique of the extant literature on new constitutionalism, articulated from an allied methodological stance that aims more explicitly to explore the uneven geographical development of regulatory arrangements, forms and strategies under neo-liberalizing capitalism.

The global and the national in the new constitutionalism

According to Stephen Gill (2000), the new constitutionalism of the post-1980s period entails not only a rolling back of post-war restrictions on capitalist property rights, but the rolling forward of a new international juridical framework that systematically privileges the discretionary rights of capital on a world scale. Specifically, Gill argues, the new constitutionalism entails the construction of supranational institutional forms and the reconfiguration of existing state apparatuses in ways that 'lock in' the market-disciplinary agenda of globalized neo-liberalism. This process of neo-liberal institutional lock-in is composed, above all, of measures to promote maximal capital mobility, to extend capitalist markets into previously decommodified realms and to insulate economic relations from democratic control.

Gill's account of the evolution of modern constitutionalism since the late nineteenth century contains a suggestive theorization of the changing geo-historical construction of the global/national relationship (see Figure 8.1). Under both liberal and progressive constitutionalism, it is the national that appears actively to constitute the systemic features of the global capitalist order. In the case of liberal constitutionalism, it is the British state that attempts to institutionalize a self-regulating market on a world scale through the gold standard system; the resultant dislocations are then thought to ricochet back into Britain and other national societies in the form of wage volatility. Concomitantly, even though Britain aided in the construction of the Bretton Woods currency system after the Second World War, progressive constitutionalism was largely centred upon, and dominated by, the United States.

By contrast, the new constitutionalism appears to entail a direct inversion of the historically entrenched national/global relationship. The global is no longer seen as a product of nationally steered institutionalizations. Instead, it is now the global, institutionalized in the form of various multilateral apparatuses, that imposes market discipline upon national states. Whereas, under liberal constitutionalism, the global was only thinly institutionalized through the gold standard and incipient international free trade agreements, the new constitutionalism is composed of a relatively dense institutional web of market-disciplinary apparatuses at both global

	Liberal constitutionalism	Progressive constitutionalism	New constitutionalism
Historical context	Late nineteenth and early twentieth centuries	Post-Second World War period until the mid 1970s	Post-1980s period of 'disciplinary neo-liberalism'
Relation to market order	Market-constructing: goal is to create a self-regulating market on a world scale through the commodification of land, labour and capital	Market-restraining: goal is to 'embed' markets by tendentially restricting capitalist property rights	Market-disciplinary: goal is to institutionalize capitalist property rights on a world scale
Institutional expressions	Nineteenth-century national constitutions enshrining private property rights; gold standard system; high imperialism	Evolution of national constitutions enshrining private property rights in a context of mass labour movements; Bretton Woods monetary system; decolonization and post-colonial state formation	IMF, WTO, World Bank, World Economic Forum, EU, NAFTA
Global/national relationship	Global order constructed through the hegemonic project of Britain (see also Polanyi 1944/1957)	Global order constructed through multilateral and national institutions, but steered primarily by the United States (see also Ruggie 1983)	Global order constructed through a range of worldwide and supranational institutional apparatuses in close conjunction with the reorganization of national state structures (see also Sassen 2007)

Figure 8.1 Historical geographies of modern constitutionalism
Source: based on Gill 1998a, 1998b, 2000 and 2003.

and supranational scales, from the IMF, the World Bank and the WTO to the EU, NAFTA and other multilateral organizations. The disciplinary nature of this worldwide institutional web consists not only in its rigid orientation toward market rule, but also in its role in systematically narrowing the socioeconomic policy parameters available to national states.

The new constitutionalism establishes a worldwide institutional grid that offers transnational capital multiple exit options within putatively suboptimal regulatory environments. At the same time, it shrinks and weakens established relays of parliamentary-democratic control over capitalist investment activities. Consequently, the new constitutionalism can be understood as a means to discipline national states to create internal political-institutional spaces oriented toward extended, accelerated capital accumulation.

The distinctive contribution of new constitutionalist approaches is to foreground the global dimensions of contemporary market-oriented regulatory transformations and to excavate the quasi-disciplinary, undemocratic modalities through which market rule is being realized. As this work productively demonstrates, neo-liberalization is implemented, consolidated and reproduced through a complex of world-scale, multilateral and supranational juridical-institutional rearrangements that impose new, relatively circumscribed parameters – in effect, an encompassing 'rule-regime' (Peck 2002) – for regulatory experimentation across subordinate places, territories and scales. In our view, however, there remain several methodological and substantive blind spots that undercut the capacity of such approaches fully to illuminate these parameterizing rule-regimes, particularly at national and subnational scales.

Geographies of neo-liberalization

One side effect of the otherwise productive emphasis on the global institutionalization of market-disciplinary regulatory projects is a relative neglect of nationally and subnationally scaled processes of regulatory restructuring. For instance, Gill's model of the new constitutionalism appears to posit a unidirectional logic in which global and supranational institutions impose disciplinary constraints 'downwards' on national states. While there is no doubt that the devolutionary dumping of regulatory risks and the subnational canalization of 'appropriate' regulatory responses represent key dimensions of neo-liberal political strategy, the latter cannot entirely (pre-)programme the shape, timing or substantive content of national, regional and local institutional (re-)configurations. In fact, Gill (1995a: 412) acknowledges that 'discipline is both a transnational and a local dimension of power', but his accounts tend to focus almost exclusively on the former: he emphasizes the transnational construction of policy-making parameters, but he does not explore the possibility of differential strategies of (national and local) territorial adaptation to this globalizing disciplinary regime. Concomitantly, Gill does not fully consider the ways in which the process of global parameterization is reciprocally shaped and reshaped through sub-global forms of regulatory experimentation, interspatial policy transfer and institutional re-jigging.

Of course, given Gill's concern with frameworks of world order, reproaching this tradition for its underdeveloped analysis of sub-global regulatory transformations might appear to exemplify the category mistake of 'misplaced concreteness' – that is, expecting it to yield concrete descriptions when only an abstract portrayal is intended. However, the issue here is not merely one of abstraction versus concreteness; it is also methodological. In so far as market-disciplinary institutions and policies are implemented in different forms and degrees across places, scales and territories, the landscapes of neo-liberalization are constitutively and systemically uneven. Neo-liberalization projects build on, exploit, intensify and re-canalize inherited differences amongst (supranational, national and subnational) regulatory landscapes. Consideration of such systemically produced variegations should be more than an empirical addendum to the global portrait of parameterization. Such variegations are co-constitutive of the regulatory transformations under investigation, including those associated with the process of parameterization itself.

Modalities of neo-liberalization

On one reading Gill's analysis implies that the extension of neo-liberalization is basically a process of imposition, in which formerly market-restraining domestic political spaces are subjected to the disciplinary agendas of global institutions. This emphasis on 'downward' disciplinary imposition illuminates an important aspect of neo-liberalization processes: the undemocratic subjection of national populations to global or supranational forms of market rule. However, it is problematic to assume that neo-liberalization processes normally or necessarily move along a global-to-national vector, because this leaves unexamined other potentially significant interspatial circuits through which neo-liberalized regulatory programmes may be animated. For instance, attention must also be paid to 'upwards' relays within inter-scalar hierarchies; transversal manoeuvres across divergent institutional sites within a regulatory landscape; or still more elusive, promiscuous arcs of policy transfer that defy easy classification (Bockman and Eyal 2002; Dezalay and Garth 2002; Ferguson and Gupta 2002).

Furthermore, this super-ordinate gaze fails to take account of the strategic role of national, regional and local state apparatuses as active progenitors of neo-liberalizing institutional reforms and policy prototypes, and as arenas in which market-oriented regulatory experiments are initiated, consolidated and even extended. Thus understood, neo-liberal reform 'models' are not simply designed within multilateral institutions and then implemented *tout court* at national and subnational scales. More frequently, such models are polymorphic, inter-scalar constructions – born of transnational, national and (newly devolved) subnational institutional reform frameworks; honed, customized and proved through policy experimentation; revamped in light of unanticipated failures, conflicts and crisis tendencies; and then sometimes also purposefully (re-)circulated back into the interspatial networks of policy transfer from which they originated (Peck 2002).

Pathways of neo-liberalization

Gill's work offers a critical account of the broader, crisis-riven geoeconomic context in and through which contemporary and historical crisis tendencies are generated: he decisively rejects the assumption that processes of regulatory restructuring will preserve politico-institutional stability, emphasizing instead the polarizing, dysfunctional ramifications of disciplinary neo-liberalism. Here, a key analytical space is reserved for a Polanyian 'double-movement', implying that the disruptive effects of neo-liberalization may engender both progressive and reactionary responses. Thus, even when projects of market rule are imposed comprehensively upon a social formation – for instance, through the subjection of impoverished, politically weak nations to structural adjustment policies – the outcomes invariably include new forms of dislocation, conflict and political mobilization. The project of neo-liberalization is thus said not only to disrupt established regulatory practices and social conventions, but to open up new political spaces in which alternatives to transnational corporate power may be articulated.

Market-driven regulatory projects are indeed permeated by crisis tendencies, but it would be a mistake to focus one-sidedly on the 'response' side of the Polanyian double-movement – that is, on the oppositional social forces and political movements provoked by neo-liberalization projects. While this emphasis is certainly well justified, we would argue that it has led many analysts to bracket the ways in which neo-liberalization projects are iteratively reconstituted in conjunction with both emergent modes of resistance and their own crisis tendencies. The cooptation of market-constraining interests and institutions; the erection of flanking mechanisms to manage the polarizing consequences of intensified commodification; and the reinforcement or mutation of neo-liberal policies in the face of opposition or outright failure – all these are part of the extended dynamics of institutional creative destruction under conditions of deepening neo-liberalization.[1] Each 'round' of neo-liberalization reshapes the institutional landscapes through which subsequent neo-liberalization projects unfold. The substantive character of each round of neo-liberalization is forged through the contextually specific forms of friction, resistance and crisis that are engendered through this combative encounter. In effect, the interplay between neo-liberalization projects and inherited institutional landscapes produces a propulsive ricocheting of multiple, differentially spatialized yet interconnected double-movements across places, territories and scales. Whatever its spatial morphology and evolutionary pathway, each of these reactions represents a path-dependent expression of the regulatory incursions that preceded it. Each such reaction also opens up a determinate complex of politico-institutional spaces for subsequent double-movement dynamics. Given the extraordinary diversity of path-dependent double-movements involved in such regulatory transformations, their polymorphic spatial morphologies and their contextually specific evolutionary trajectories, a singular, world-scale application of the Polanyian double-movement scheme would seem to offer a relatively undifferentiated depiction of neo-liberalization processes. This is not simply a matter of movements in the global tides; currents, eddies and blockages in regulatory dynamics at all spatial scales make a (constitutive) difference.

The evolutionary pathways of neo-liberalization processes cannot be understood adequately either through an investigation of how nationally specific neo-liberal 'transitions' are guided 'from above', or alternatively, through a more contextually circumscribed periodization of nationally specific 'varieties of neo-liberalism' (Cerny *et al.* 2005). Rather, the mottled, striated and volatile dynamics of neo-liberalization across places, territories and scales have been co-evolving with the tendentially neo-liberalizing global, supranational and multilateral rule-regimes that have been explored so incisively within new constitutionalist scholarship. Through a mutually recursive process of institutional and spatial structuration, such rule-regimes variously collide with, parameterize and iteratively meld with these subordinate institutional landscapes. While the geographies and choreographies of such rule-regimes are at least partly forged through their combative interactions with subordinate institutional landscapes, the precise nature and implications of this co-evolution clearly require more systematic investigation.

---

[1] Editors' footnote: see Chapter 2 by Stephen Gill on measures for dealing with dislocations and contradictions, and associated mechanisms of incorporation.

Toward a moving map of neo-liberalization

Harvey has underscored the difficulties of constructing a 'moving map of the progress of neoliberalization on the world stage since 1970'. The challenge, Harvey (2005: 87) proposes, is 'to understand how local transformations relate to broader trends' by tracking the 'turbulent currents of uneven geographical development' that are produced through neo-liberalization processes.

How to confront this challenge, and how might studies of new constitutionalism contribute to it? What would a moving map of neo-liberalization processes during the last 30-plus years look like? With a few notable exceptions, the extant literatures on neo-liberalization have spawned no more than partial responses to this challenge, not least due to their underdeveloped conceptualizations of regulatory uneven development (Brenner *et al.* 2010). While they have identified any number of key features within the perpetually morphing landscapes of post-1970s market-disciplinary regulatory change, including the global rule-regimes analyzed by new constitutionalist scholars, most accounts have been less concerned with relating these elements to one another, and to the broader 'currents of uneven geographical development' to which Harvey (2005: 87) refers. In order to confront these tasks, we distinguish three core analytical dimensions of neo-liberalization processes.

Regulatory experiments

These are place-, territory- and scale-specific projects designed to impose, intensify or reproduce market-disciplinary modalities of governance. Such projects are necessarily path dependent, and generally entail both a destructive moment (efforts to roll back non-market, anti-market or market-restraining regulatory arrangements) and a creative moment (strategies to roll forward a new politico-institutional infrastructure for marketized regulatory forms).

Systems of inter-jurisdictional policy transfer

These are networks of knowledge sharing through which neo-liberal policy prototypes are circulated, generally transnationally, for redeployment elsewhere. By establishing certain types of regulatory strategies as 'prototypical', such networks enhance the ideological legitimacy of neo-liberal policy templates while extending their availability as readily accessible, all-purpose 'solutions' to contextually specific regulatory problems. At the same time, however, even the most apparently prototypical forms of neo-liberal policy are qualitatively transformed through their circulation through such networks. Although they may appear to be readily available for smooth transfer within a fast-moving circulatory network, and thus able to promote a homogenization of regulatory space, such policy mobilities remain embedded within politico-institutional contexts that shape their form, content, reception and evolution, leading to unintended and intensely variegated outcomes. In the context of neo-liberalization processes, therefore, inter-jurisdictional policy transfer is an important mechanism not only of spatial consolidation, but of institutional differentiation.

Transnational rule-regimes

These are large-scale institutional arrangements, regulatory frameworks, legal systems and policy relays that impose determinate 'rules of the game' on contextually specific forms of policy experimentation and regulatory reorganization, thereby framing the activities of actors within specific politico-institutional parameters.

Restless landscapes of neo-liberalization

Any mapping of neo-liberalization processes derived from these distinctions would contrast sharply with the diffusionist models that prevail in the orthodox literature, which are closely aligned with the anticipation of policy convergence and various forms of methodological nationalism. So too would it contrast markedly with the global-to-national models of neo-liberal imposition associated with some strands of new constitutionalist scholarship. But such a mapping could not, in itself, illuminate every concrete feature on the landscapes of neo-liberalization, across differential spatio-temporal contexts. Nonetheless, on a more abstract level, such an approach can serve as an analytical basis on which to interpret the creatively destructive trajectories and uneven development of neo-liberalization processes since the 1970s.

To this end, building on the above distinctions, Figure 8.2 outlines a stylized periodization of post-1970s neo-liberalization processes. In this figure, the three dimensions of regulatory restructuring no longer serve as ideal-typical categories, but are now mobilized to illuminate the historical-geographical evolution of neo-liberalization processes themselves. The top row delineates each of the three distinctions specified above, understood as interlinked dimensions of regulatory restructuring under conditions of ongoing neo-liberalization. The first column specifies a generic, decade-based timeline, from the 1970s through the 2000s. The

DIMENSIONS OF REGULATORY RESTRUCTURING			
	CONTEXT-SPECIFIC FORMS OF REGULATORY EXPERIMENTATION	SYSTEMS OF INTER-JURISDICTIONAL POLICY TRANSFER	RULE-REGIMES AND PARAMETERIZATION PROCESSES
1970s	**DISARTICULATED NEO-LIBERALIZATION** Neo-liberalization projects assume place-, territory- and scale-specific forms in a 'hostile' geo-economic context still defined by late Keynesian regulatory arrangements and emergent crisis tendencies	Intensification of neo-Keynesian forms of cross-jurisdictional policy transfer in response to pervasive geo-economic volatility, especially within the OECD zone Tendential emergence of neo-liberalizing forms of policy transfer across interstitial geopolitical vectors (e.g. Chicago to Santiago) Accelerating ideological critiques of Keynesian economic doctrines; increasing signs of systemic crisis within the international rule-regime of post-war embedded liberalism	
1980s	**ORCHESTRATED NEO-LIBERALIZATION** Continued intensification of market-driven forms of regulatory experimentation and institutional reform at various spatial scales and in strategic zones (e.g. United States, UK, Latin America) Tendential weakening/exhaustion of neo-Keynesian networks of policy transfer coupled with ongoing, intensely contested searches for new 'institutional fixes' to resolve persistent geo-regulatory crises Tendential thickening, transnationalization, mutual recursion, programmatic integration and co-evolution of policy networks oriented toward market-driven regulatory experiments and institutional reforms (e.g. monetarism, liberalization, privatization, urban entrepreneurialism, reinvented governance, etc.)		Tendential destruction of 'progressive constitutionalism' at global, supranational and national scales Tendential consolidation of a 'new constitutionalism' through the market-driven redefinition of various global, supranational and national regulatory institutions
1990s	**DEEP(ENING) NEO-LIBERALIZATION** Whether or not they are explicitly market-driven or market-constraining, contextually specific forms of regulatory experimentation and institutional reform are increasingly framed within broadly neo-liberalized parameters or 'rules of the game' Neo-liberalized systems of policy transfer are increasingly mobilized to address the crisis tendencies and contradictions engendered through earlier rounds of market-driven regulatory restructuring Macro-spatial institutional frameworks are now recast in neo-liberalized terms – market-based parameters are thus increasingly imposed upon subordinate scales of regulatory experimentation		

Figure 8.2 From disarticulated to deep(ening) neo-liberalization: a stylized outline

Note: Shaded cells denote the dimensions of regulatory restructuring in which neo-liberalization tendencies have been most pronounced. Even in the shaded cells, however, other forms of regulatory restructuring coexist alongside neo-liberalization tendencies.

shaded cells denote the dimensions of regulatory restructuring in which, on our reading, neo-liberalization has been most pronounced since its initial institutional elaboration in the 1970s. Concomitantly, the white cells in the upper quadrants denote zones of regulatory activity that, during the corresponding decade(s) specified in the first column, were largely configured according to market-restraining principles (Keynesianism, progressive constitutionalism). With each successive decade, the shaded zones in the figure are widened to include an additional column. This signifies what we view as a tendential, macro-spatial shift from disarticulated to deepening forms of neo-liberalization.

As depicted in the first main row of Figure 8.2, disarticulated neo-liberalization crystallized during the 1970s, and was based predominantly on place-, territory- and scale-specific forms of market-disciplinary regulatory experimentation. Of course, neo-liberal doctrine had emerged during the 1930s and 1940s, when it was mobilized as a critique of the consolidating Keynesian political-economic order. However, it was not until the early 1970s that real-time experiments in neo-liberalization were elaborated, albeit within a largely hostile geo-economic context defined by late Keynesian regulatory arrangements and strategies of crisis management.

During the 1980s, a new frontier of neo-liberalization was opened, as a repertoire of neo-liberal policy templates began to circulate transnationally and to acquire the status of all-purpose 'solutions' to diverse regulatory problems and crisis tendencies (Figure 8.2, row 2). While this occurred partly through a colonization of extant, neo-Keynesian policy transfer networks (for instance, within the Organisation for Economic Co-operation and Development (OECD), the World Bank and the IMF), it also involved the construction of new inter-jurisdictional circuits for the promotion, legitimation and delivery of neo-liberal policy templates, mediated through an increasingly influential cadre of experts and 'technopols' such as the infamous Chicago Boys. Through a series of trial-and-error manoeuvres, many of the core neo-liberalizing regulatory experiments of the 1970s – such as privatization, financialization, liberalization, workfare and urban entrepreneurialism – subsequently acquired prototypical status, and became key reference points for subsequent projects of neo-liberalization. Neo-liberalizing forms of regulatory restructuring were mobilized in diverse policy arenas by national, regional and local institutions not only in North America and Western Europe, but also within an uneven, globally dispersed patchwork of post-developmental states and post-communist zones from Latin America and Sub-Saharan Africa to Eastern Europe and Asia. In order to facilitate the circulation and legitimation of market-based reform strategies, new extra-jurisdictional relays were constructed. Such fast policy networks were thickened by the late 1980s following the Latin American debt crisis and, subsequently, the collapse of the Soviet bloc. The previous formation of disarticulated neo-liberalization was thus transformed into a more tightly networked, transnationally orchestrated formation of mutually recursive, inter-referential policy reform strategies. Under these circumstances, neo-liberalization projects no longer appeared as relatively isolated instances of market-disciplinary regulatory experimentation lodged within a hostile political-economic environment. Instead, patterns of reciprocal influence, coordination and exchange were established amongst neo-liberalizing reform programmes across diverse jurisdictional contexts and scales. Increasingly, such programmes were recursively interconnected in order to accelerate, deepen and intensify their transnational circulation and implementation.

This deepening formation of neo-liberalization was further consolidated during the 1990s, as market-disciplinary reform agendas were institutionalized on a world scale through an array of multilateral, multilevel and supranational juridico-institutional rearrangements. This tendency is depicted in the lowest, fully shaded row of Figure 8.2. Prior to this period, post-war regulatory institutions such as the IMF, the World Bank, the General Agreement on Tariffs and Trade (GATT) and, until the early 1970s, the Bretton Woods agreement had established a broadly Keynesian framework for worldwide production and trade. While these arrangements were destabilized during the 1970s and 1980s, it was not until the 1990s that a genuinely post-Keynesian, neo-liberalized global rule-regime was consolidated. Through the market-disciplinary redesign of supranational institutional arrangements, from the OECD, the World Bank and the IMF to the WTO, the post-Maastricht EU and NAFTA, neo-liberalization now came to restructure the very geo-institutional frameworks governing national and subnational regulatory experimentation. This neo-liberalized geo-institutional configuration is frequently referred to as the 'Washington Consensus', but its regulatory elements and political-economic geographies cannot be reduced to a purely US-based hegemonic project. Rather, the new constitutionalism associated with the ascendant neo-liberalized global rule-regime has also hinged upon forms of regulation and enforcement produced and administered by the WTO; supranational regulatory bodies, multinational organizations and regional free trade zones; as well as quasi-independent global economic bodies such as the Bank for International Settlements (Gill 2003). The consolidation of such neo-liberalized rule-regimes, which are designed to impose market-disciplinary parameters upon national and subnational institutions, is arguably one of the most far-reaching consequences of the last three decades of neo-liberalizing political-economic reform.

As the bottom row of Figure 8.2 indicates, neo-liberalization processes have also transformed the very geo-institutional frameworks within which regulatory uneven development unfolds, causing otherwise contextually specific forms of regulatory experimentation and interjurisdictional policy transfer to be canalized along market-disciplinary pathways. This rule-regime has certainly not dissolved the path dependency and contextual specificity of neo-liberalizing reform projects. But it has qualitatively transformed what might be termed the 'context of context' – the political, institutional and juridical terrain within which locally, regionally and nationally specific pathways of regulatory restructuring are forged. No moving map of neo-liberalization can be complete, we would argue, without attention to such macro-spatial frameworks and politico-institutional parameters, for they have crucial implications for contextually situated processes of regulatory experimentation, whether market-disciplinary or market-restraining.

Scenarios of counter-neo-liberalization: toward a progressive new constitutionalism?

The medium- and long-term trajectories of regulatory restructuring are inherently unpredictable; they remain to be fought out through the conjuncturally embedded struggles provoked by the contradictions of earlier rounds of neo-liberalization. Nonetheless, the preceding considerations suggest an approach for confronting such questions – one that attends simultaneously to global regulatory shocks and their place-, territory- and scale-specific ramifications, while avoiding dualistic transition models and associated declarations of neo-liberalism's demise. Here we sketch several possible scenarios for future trajectories of regulatory restructuring (Figure 8.2; for a more detailed discussion of contemporary pathways of crisis-driven regulatory restructuring, see Peck *et al.* 2010, 2012, 2013).

The upper row of Figure 8.2 presents each of the three dimensions of neo-liberalization; the far left column lists four scenarios for future pathways of regulatory restructuring. As indicated by the shaded pattern in the figure, each of the four scenarios entails a different degree of neo-liberalization, defined with reference to some combination amongst the three dimensions listed in the top row.

The scenario of zombie neo-liberalization is depicted in the first row. In this scenario, despite its disruptive, destructive consequences, the global economic crisis of 2008–12 does not significantly undermine

	DIMENSIONS OF REGULATORY RESTRUCTURING		
	CONTEXT-SPECIFIC FORMS OF REGULATORY EXPERIMENTATION	SYSTEMS OF INTER-JURISDICTIONAL POLICY TRANSFER	RULE-REGIMES AND PARAMETERIZATION PROCESSES
Scenario 1: zombie neo-liberalization	Orthodox neo-liberal ideology is severely undermined, but there is a continued neo-liberalization of each of the three dimensions of regulatory restructuring, often through technocratic means Crisis tendencies and failures of market-driven regulatory arrangements contribute to a further entrenchment of neo-liberalization projects as putative 'solutions' to persistent regulatory dilemmas across scales, territories and contexts		
Scenario 2: disarticulated counter-neo-liberalization	Tendential mobilization of market-constraining, redistributive and/or 'push-back' regulatory experiments across dispersed, disarticulated contexts at local, regional and national scales	Continued neo-liberalization of transnational policy transfer systems and rule-regimes Counter-liberalization projects remain relatively fragmented, disconnected and poorly coordinated – they have not significantly infiltrated multilateral, supranational or global institutional arenas Macro-spatial rule-regimes continue to be dominated by market logics, despite persistent critiques from extra-institutional locations and 'from below' (e.g. the global justice movement)	
Scenario 3: orchestrated counter-neo-liberalization	Intensified orchestration, mutual recursion and tendential co-evolution of market-constraining, redistributive regulatory experiments across increasingly interlinked contexts Thickening, intensification and extension of networks of policy transfer based upon (progressive or regressive) alternatives to market rule		Continued neo-liberalization of rule-regimes: counter-liberalization projects may now begin to infiltrate macro-spatial rule-making institutions (e.g. the World Bank, the European Union) but do not succeed in reorienting their basic market-driven orientations
Scenario 4: progressive, communal or socialist neo-constitutionalism	Continued intensification of (progressive or reactionary forms of) market-constraining, redistributive, re-embedding and socializing regulatory experimentation Continued elaboration and transnational consolidation of market-constraining, redistributive and socializing forms of cross-jurisdictional policy transfer Destabilization/dismantling of neo-liberalized rule-regimes; construction of alternative, market-constraining, redistributive and socializing frameworks for macro-spatial regulatory organization		

Figure 8.3 Counter-neo-liberalization: future pathways and scenarios
Note: Shaded cells denote the spheres of regulatory restructuring in which neo-liberalization is most pronounced.

the neo-liberalization tendencies of the last three decades (Peck *et al.* 2010). The new constitutionalist, neo-liberalized rule-regime that had been consolidated during the 1990s and early 2000s may be recalibrated to restrain certain forms of financial speculation, but its basic orientation toward imposing market-disciplinary parameters on supranational, national, regional and local economies remains dominant. Orthodox neo-liberal ideology is now increasingly called into question, but the political machinery of state-imposed market discipline remains essentially intact; policy agendas continue to be subordinated to the priority of maintaining investor confidence and a 'good business climate'; and policy agendas such as free trade, privatization, flexible labour markets and urban territorial competitiveness continue to be taken for granted. In this scenario, as Bond (2009: 193) argues, the most likely outcome of the current geo-economic crisis is a 'relegitimised neo-liberalism and imperialism'. Consequently, there is a further entrenchment of market-disciplinary regulatory arrangements, lubrication of neo-liberalized systems of interjurisdictional policy transfer, and entrenchment of neo-liberalized forms of regulatory experimentation.

In a second scenario, disarticulated counter-neo-liberalization, a new constitutionalist, neo-liberalized rule-regime and associated systems of policy transfer persist, but meanwhile the global economic crisis offers new strategic opportunities, albeit within relatively dispersed politico-institutional arenas, for social forces concerned to promote market-restraining or market-transcending regulatory strategies. Even prior to the 2008–12 global financial crisis, there had been plenty of organized opposition to neo-liberal policies by workers' movements, peasant movements, urban movements, various strands of the anti-globalization movement and, in some cases, by official social democratic, communist and populist political parties. There will be new strategic openings for such social movements and political organizations to pursue market-restraining agendas in the future. In this scenario, however, such counter-neo-liberalizing projects remain disarticulated – they are largely confined to localized or nationalized parameters while still being embedded within geo-institutional contexts that are dominated by market-disciplinary regulatory arrangements and policy-transfer networks. Clearly, the experiments associated with disarticulated forms of counter-neo-liberalization are a strategically essential frontier for exploring alternatives to a neo-liberalized geo-economic order. But, unless they are interconnected across places, territories and scales, and linked to institutional recalibrations, such initiatives confront systemic constraints that may undermine their medium-to-long-term reproducibility, their capacity for interspatial generalization will be circumscribed.

Under a third scenario, orchestrated counter-neo-liberalization, market-restraining regulatory experimentation no longer occurs in isolation, as relatively self-enclosed 'outposts' of dissent, but is recursively interconnected across places, territories and scales. Under these conditions, there are sustained efforts to create anti-systemic networks of knowledge sharing, policy transfer and institution building amongst diverse sites of counter-neo-liberal mobilization. This scenario may assume a statist form – for instance, a coalition of neo-Keynesian, social democratic or eco-socialist governments. It may also assume a movement-based form – for instance, that of the World Social Forum, with its project of creating an alternative network of progressive policy transfer. Whether state-driven or movement-led, such networks gain significance and become increasingly well coordinated in this scenario, possibly leading to the development of new, solidaristic and ecologically sane visions for global economic regulation and interspatial relations. The creation of transnational networks for policy transfer was essential to the consolidation, reproduction and evolution of neo-liberalization, and such networks will be equally essential to any project(s) that aspire to destabilize market-disciplinary geo-regulatory arrangements. In the scenario of orchestrated counter-neo-liberalization, however, the increasingly coordinated counter-neo-liberalizing policy transfer networks still lack the capacity to infiltrate the echelons of global political-economic power, such as multilateral agencies, supranational trading blocs and powerful national governments. Consequently, even though the neo-liberalized global rule-regime may be destabilized, it survives intact.

Can an alternative global rule-regime be forged? Under a fourth scenario, progressive (or solidaristic, or socialist) new constitutionalism, the neo-liberalized global rule-regime is subjected to greater public scrutiny and popular critique. Subsequently, the inherited institutional frameworks of new constitutionalism are infiltrated by social forces and political alliances oriented toward market-restraining agendas. These might include capital and exchange controls; debt forgiveness; progressive tax regimes; non-profit-based, cooperatively run, de-globalized credit schemes; intensified global redistribution; public works investments; and the de-commodification of basic social needs such as shelter, water, transportation, healthcare and utilities. Out of the ashes of the neo-liberalized, new constitutionalist global rule-regime emerges an alternative, social democratic, solidaristic and/or eco-socialist model of global regulation. The substantive political content of such a rule-regime is – indeed, has long been – a matter of intense debate within the global left (see, for example, Amin 2009; Gorz 1989; Holloway 2002). But one of its core elements would be a radical democratization of decision-making and allocation capacities – a prospect that stands in stark contrast to the principles of market discipline and corporate rule on which neo-liberalization has been based.

Conclusions

The new constitutionalist/neo-liberalized rule-regime has been more than three decades in the making, and throughout this period, it has been in a perpetual state of contestation and reconstruction. What has not killed it, one might say, has made it stronger. Certainly, counter-neo-liberalizing regulatory experiments remain strategically crucial. But in the absence of orchestrated networks of counter-neo-liberalizing policy transfer, they are likely to remain confined within particular places and scales. Just as importantly, the construction of counter-neo-liberalizing systems of policy transfer, whether amongst social movements, cities, regions or states, represents a major step forward for progressive activists and policymakers. But, in the absence of a plausible vision for an alternative global rule-regime, such networks are likely to remain interstitial, mere irritants to the global machinery of neo-liberalization, rather than transformative threats to its hegemonic influence.

Our reading of the near-term prospects suggests that the neo-liberal power grid is already becoming markedly more multipolar than in the past, with ascendant global powers – from Beijing to Moscow – asserting their own (market) interests within enlarged regulatory arenas such as the Group of 20. This raises the question of whether the worldwide rules of financial transactions, monetary exchange and trade, as currently regulated through such international fora and through the multilateral financial institutions, will be qualitatively reformed in ways that contest their earlier, pro-market orientation, or whether they will merely be adjusted or reconstituted in ways that perpetuate such an orientation (Bond 2009). How far the rules will change when new players join the game cannot be predicted at this point, though some form of adaptive change (at least) seems certain. The moment of systemic crisis now having passed, it may be that the prospects of transformative regulatory change are likewise receding. Soberingly, this must be confronted as a failure of alternative visions and movements – as well as testimony to the doggedness of neo-liberal rule and its alignment with prevailing power structures. The contradictions and limits of market-based regulation persist, however, even if the regulatory landscape is, for the moment at least, destabilized. The challenging question that remains, then, concerns not only what progressive alternatives to neo-liberalism and new constitutionalism might look like but also what it will take for alternatives to bite?

9 New constitutionalism and multilevel governance

Adam Harmes

Introduction

Stephen Gill has argued that a key component of the contemporary neo-liberal project is the growing use of legal-juridical mechanisms designed to separate economics from politics in order to 'lock in' neo liberal policies over the long term. The intent of this process, which he terms the 'new constitutionalism', is to insulate economic policies from democratic influence in a way that privileges mobile investors and firms (1995a, 1998b). Moreover, by drawing on the work of neo-liberal intellectuals such as Friedrich von Hayek, Milton Friedman and James Buchanan, Gill has demonstrated that the concept of new constitutionalism is a valuable tool for theorizing a central and self-conscious element of the contemporary neo-liberal project. However, one aspect of new constitutionalism that is under-explored in Gill's work is the neo-liberal approach to federalism, known as 'market-preserving federalism', and its more recent application to the regional and global levels.

Reflecting this gap, this chapter examines the neo-liberal approach to multilevel governance. In doing so, it makes three arguments. The first is that neo-liberalism contains an explicit and self-conscious normative project for multilevel governance, which is fully consistent across the federal, regional and global levels. The second argument made is that the neo-liberal project for multilevel governance can be understood as a distinct subset of new constitutionalist initiatives in so far as it seeks, through legal-juridical mechanisms and intergovernmental bargaining, to separate the economic and the political across a uniquely vertical axis. The third argument is that the neo-liberal project for multilevel governance is being actively promoted by neo-liberal social forces, and opposed by progressive social forces, and can thus provide a model for explaining the policies they advocate on a wide variety of issues related to federal, regional and global governance.

What is not examined in this chapter is the extent to which the neo-liberal project for multilevel governance has actually influenced governance outcomes. As noted in the conclusion, the broad and ongoing trend toward 'glocalization' (globalization and localization), and the specific patterns of centralization and decentralization contained within it, do seem to reflect the neo-liberal project for multilevel governance. However, to the extent that specific governance outcomes reflect the competition between neo-liberal and progressive social forces, as well as the role of other social forces, determining a direct link would require a case-by-case analysis that is beyond the scope of this short chapter.

New constitutionalism and the neo-liberal separation of the economic and the political

In *The Great Transformation*, Karl Polanyi argues that it was democracy that created the need for an institutional separation of the 'economic' and the 'political' within liberal capitalism. As Polanyi observes: 'When the Chartist Movement demanded entrance for the disinherited into the precincts of the state, the separation of economics and politics ceased to be an academic issue and became the irrefragable condition of the existing system of society' (1944/1957: 225). Moreover, while there were a number of institutions that limited democratic control over economic policy, one of the most effective methods was the creation of (liberal) constitutions.

Important here, for Polanyi, was the creation of the American Constitution under conditions of intensified democratic pressures. 'Under these conditions', he writes, 'constitutionalism gained an entirely new meaning. Until then constitutional safeguards against unlawful interference with the rights of property were directed only against arbitrary acts from above' *(ibid.)*. In other words, prior to the American Constitution, constitutional provisions for the protection of property were designed to protect merchants from monarchs. In the American Constitution, however, the legal separation of politics and economics was directed at democratic forces that might seek to interfere with property rights from below. As Polanyi notes:

The American Constitution ... isolated the economic sphere entirely from the jurisdiction of the Constitution, put private property thereby under the highest conceivable protection, and created the only legally grounded market society in the world. In spite of universal suffrage, American voters were powerless against owners. *(ibid.: 225–6)*

While Polanyi may overstate the case, both in terms of intention and impact, he does usefully highlight the way that constitutionalism became a key institutional lock-in mechanism for separating politics and economics and, thus, for insulating economic policy from popular forces.[1]

This need for institutional lock-in mechanisms to separate the economic and the political under conditions of democracy forms the basis for Gill's analysis of the contemporary neo-liberal project and its efforts to re-intensify the commodification of land, labour and capital. Specifically, through the return to capital mobility and the liberalization of economic policy inherent in contemporary economic globalization, proponents of neo-liberalism have sought to create a disembedded economic order reminiscent of the nineteenth-century self-regulating market analyzed by Polanyi. But as in the nineteenth century, Gill sees increasing commodification today as producing similar dislocations and demands for more democratic control over economic forces. To prevent such developments from occurring, Gill argues that the contemporary neo-liberal project has also sought to promote various institutional lock-in mechanisms to insulate economic policy from democratic influence; a process that he terms the 'new constitutionalism' (1995a, 1998b). Thus, for Gill, '[t]he aim of new constitutionalism is to allow dominant economic forces to be increasingly insulated from democratic rule and popular accountability. Indeed, in neo-liberal discourse ... private forms of power and authority are only fully stabilized when questions of economic rule ... are removed from politics' (1998b: 23).

In making his argument, Gill identifies a number of new institutional lock-in mechanisms, in addition to formal constitutional provisions, which have been developed and promoted by contemporary neo-liberals. First and foremost is the return of international capital mobility and the disciplinary effect that it has on states. As Gill notes: 'What is new, then, about the present situation is that capital mobility has re-emerged in ways that force states to provide price and exchange rate stability [and other neo-liberal policies] ... in order to be credible in the eyes of investors' (1998b: 25). The well-known logic here is that capital mobility (through liberalized financial markets and free trade) forces states to compete for transnationally mobile capital by providing the types of neo-liberal policies that investors and corporations demand. Moreover, while Gill views capital mobility as helping to lock in a neo-liberal policy bias at the domestic level, he argues that neo-liberals have also sought to lock in capital mobility itself. This has been done through measures such as the International Monetary Fund (IMF) making capital market liberalization a condition of both membership and loans, as well as international

---

[1] Editors' note: for a contrasting interpretation see Chapter 5 by Tim Di Muzio in this volume.

trade agreements such as the World Trade Organization (WTO) and the North American Free Trade Agreement (NAFTA), both of which lock in the mobility of transnational direct investment (on the role of taxation in relation to international capital mobility see Chapter 12, this volume).

Other examples of new constitutionalist lock-in mechanisms that go beyond formal constitutions are the intellectual and investor property rights provisions contained within various trade agreements. The agreement on Trade-Related Aspects of Intellectual Property Rights (TRIPS) within the WTO and Chapter 11 of the NAFTA are just two examples where provisions have been created to allow for investor-to-state lawsuits in cases where firms feel that government policies have infringed on their property rights (see also Chapters 10 and 11, this volume). At the more domestic level, Gill points to additional lock-in mechanisms such as balanced-budget amendments, referendum requirements for tax increases, independent central banks and fixed exchange rate regimes, all of which work to further lock in a neo-liberal policy bias in macroeconomic policy. In terms of social forces, Gill argues that the 'new constitutionalism operates in practice to confer privileged rights of citizenship and representation to corporate capital and large investors. What is being attempted is the creation of a political economy and social order where public policy is premised upon the dominance of the investor, and reinforcing the protection of his or her property rights. The mobile investor becomes the sovereign political subject' (Gill 1998b: 23).

In addition to its practical implications, what is interesting about Gill's discussion of new constitutionalism is his demonstration that it represents a deliberate and self-conscious element of the broader neo-liberal project. To make this point, Gill draws on the work of neo-liberal intellectuals (and Nobel laureates) such as Friedrich von Hayek, Milton Friedman and James Buchanan, as well as on the World Bank's *World Development Report 1997* (World Bank 1997). In the former case, he cites the importance that these thinkers attach to both capital mobility and institutional lock-in mechanisms for preserving the small government and near-absolute property rights that they associate with economic and social freedom. As Gill notes, 'Hayek singled out exchange controls as particularly oppressive for individual freedom. As Friedman put it in *Capitalism and Freedom*, exchange controls are "the most effective way to convert a market economy into an authoritarian economic society"' (1998b: 24). This is the case as exchange controls limit the 'exit' options of capital and thus prevent capital mobility from exercising a disciplinary effect on governments. In terms of institutional lock-in mechanisms for preserving property rights, Gill notes that 'neoliberals argue for the redefinition of the political to construct a "protected domain" to secure individual freedom against encroachments of the power of the state and pressures of the "tyranny of the majority" in democratic systems' (Gill 2002: 52). Cited specifically here is Hayek's laudatory work on the entrenchment of property rights in the American Constitution as well as James Buchanan's more recent work on 'constitutional economics' with its advocacy of 'fiscal and monetary constitutions' (*ibid.*). As Gill argues, 'what is crucial for neoliberals is the strong protection of liberty and property rights, with particular emphasis on the power of the state to protect capital from expropriation and seizure' (*ibid.*: 56).

Thus, for Gill, the explicit desire of Hayek, Friedman and Buchanan to separate politics and economics through capital mobility and institutional lock-in mechanisms helps to highlight the self-conscious underpinnings of contemporary new constitutionalism. To further demonstrate this point, he cites the similar and similarly self-conscious arguments put forth in the *World Development Report 1997*. As Gill reports, 'much attention is given in the report to "locking in good policies" through the disciplinary effects of capital mobility as well as through various institutional "mechanisms of restraint"' (1998b: 34). The purpose of such restraints, according to the World Bank, is to ensure that the neo-liberal policy commitments of governments are credible in the eyes of investors (World Bank 1997: 99). For Gill, these '"mechanisms of restraint" in macroeconomic policy involve the clear separation of the economic and the political in ways that lessen the possibility for democratic accountability' (1998b: 35).

Based on these arguments, Gill has demonstrated that the concept of new constitutionalism is a valuable tool for theorizing a central and self-conscious element of the contemporary neo-liberal project and for recognizing the constitutionalist implications of a variety of new institutional mechanisms. However, one feature of new constitutionalism that is under-explored in Gill's work is its more multilevel aspects. As will be argued below, these aspects are important in that they point to an equally self-conscious strategy associated with the contemporary neo-liberal project, one that is uniquely directed toward the issue of multilevel governance.

Neo-liberalism and 'market-preserving federalism'

The argument outlined over the next two sections is that neo-liberalism contains an explicit and self-conscious normative project for multilevel governance, which is consistent across the federal, regional and global levels. The origins of this project are found in the work of neo-liberal intellectuals on 'competitive federalism' and 'market-preserving federalism'. Moreover, as with new constitutionalism more generally, ideas on market-preserving federalism use the American constitutional model as their starting point. The *World Development Report 1997*, for example, describes the horizontal and vertical separation of powers in the American Constitution as 'the classic constitutional mechanism' (World Bank 1997: 100). The horizontal aspect refers to the separation of powers between the executive, legislature and judiciary, while the vertical aspect refers to centralization/decentralization and federalism. In both cases, the separation of powers in the American Constitution reflects James Madison's assertion in the *Federalist Papers* (No. 51) that 'ambition must be made to counteract ambition' (cited in Aranson 1990). Therefore, as with constitutionalism more generally, federalism was seen by the American founding fathers as a further institutional lock-in mechanism for limiting the arbitrary powers of government.

Competitive or market-preserving federalism, however, goes a step further by advocating a specific *type* of federalism based on two key principles for determining which policy capabilities should be assigned to which level of government. The first principle is to centralize those policy capabilities that relate to protecting property rights, enforcing contracts and creating/maintaining markets. Of particular importance here is that subnational governments should not have the ability to limit the right to exit (or enter) their jurisdictions. This ensures a national economy based on internal free trade and capital mobility and, in turn, that individuals and firms have the ability to move themselves and/or their assets across subnational jurisdictions. The second principle of neo-liberal federalism is to decentralize the policy capabilities that neo-liberals do not support, including those that relate to wealth redistribution and the correction of many market failures. This includes the assignment of redistributive taxing powers related to income, capital gains and corporate taxes to the subnational level, along with jurisdiction over redistributive social programmes such as public education, healthcare and social security. It also includes a similar decentralization of regulatory powers related to, for example, environmental and labour policy.

In each case, the intent is to prevent national policies on issues related to wealth redistribution and market failures and to confine as many of the undesired tax and regulatory powers as possible to the subnational level, where they will be constrained by inter-jurisdictional policy competition and the need of governments to compete for mobile citizens and firms. Thus, neo-liberal federalism seeks to reinforce neo-liberal constitutionalism by creating an 'exit option' in the realm of politics that will subject social democratic policies to the constraint of policy competition. The well-known logic here, as outlined in the classical fiscal federalism literature, is that local policies designed to redistribute wealth and correct market failures can be constrained by the outmigration of wealthy individuals and firms seeking lower taxes and regulatory burdens (Oates 1972).

The neo-liberal approach to federalism finds its most prominent origins in the work of Hayek who, in the Great Depression context of growing limits on trade and capital mobility, viewed federalism as a mechanism for creating an exit option and policy competition within individual countries. Moreover, he is explicit that the purpose of such policy competition was to impose constraints on social democratic forms of government intervention. As Hayek notes: 'Not only would the greater mobility between the states make it necessary to avoid all sorts of taxation that would drive capital or labour elsewhere, but there would also be considerable difficulties with many kinds of indirect taxation [i.e. regulation]' (1939: 270). Further, Hayek believes that excessive government intervention in the economy would become 'altogether impracticable under a federal organization' owing to the ability of firms to move to other jurisdictions (1939: 270). In his 1960 work, *The Constitution of Liberty*, expanded on this view by explaining that:

> The reason why a division of powers between different authorities always reduces the power that anybody can exercise is not always well understood. It is not merely that the separate authorities will, through mutual jealousy, prevent one another from exceeding their authority. More important is the fact that certain types of coercion require the joint and coordinated use of different powers or the employment of several means, and, if these means are in separate hands, nobody can exercise those types of coercion. The most familiar illustration is provided by many kinds of economic control which can be effective only if the authority exercising them can also control the movement of men and goods across the frontiers of its territory. If it lacks that power, though it has the power to control internal events, it cannot pursue policies that require the joint use of both. Federal government is thus in a very definite sense limited government. (1960: 184–5)

In this sense, Hayek's argument draws on both the traditional separation of powers argument as well as the need for this separation to be specifically designed to promote an exit option and policy competition.

A similar argument in favour of using decentralization to create an exit option is made by Milton Friedman in his seminal *Capitalism and Freedom*:

> If government is to exercise power, better in the county than in the state, better in the state than in Washington. If I do not like what my local community does, be it in sewage disposal, or zoning, or schools, I can move to another local community, and though few may take this step, the mere possibility acts as a check.

If I do not like what my state does, I can move to another. If I do not like what Washington imposes, I have few alternatives in this world of jealous nations … The preservation of freedom is the protective reason for limiting and decentralizing government power. (1962: 3)

Thus, as with Hayek, Friedman highlights the importance of political decentralization within a national economy and the need for an exit option to act as a check on government intervention. More recently, Barry Weingast (1995) has sought to formalize this neo-liberal approach to federalism by developing the notion of 'market-preserving federalism'. Specifically, Weingast views federal systems as having two main characteristics: '(F1) a *hierarchy* of governments, that is, at least "two levels of government rule the same land and people", each with a *delineated scope of authority* so that each level of government is autonomous in its own, well-defined sphere of political authority; and (F2) the *autonomy* of each government is institutionalized in a manner that makes federalism's restrictions self-enforcing' (1995: 4).

In addition to these general characteristics, Weingast argues that:

A federal system is market-preserving if it ha[s] three additional characteristics: (F3) subnational governments have primary regulatory responsibility over the economy; (F4) a common market is ensured, preventing the lower governments from using their regulatory authority to erect trade barriers against the goods and services from other political units; and (F5) the lower governments face a hard budget constraint, that is, they have neither the ability to print money nor access to unlimited credit. This condition is not met if the central government bails out the lower one whenever the latter faces fiscal problems. (1995: 4)

Emphasized in Weingast's version, therefore, is the need to have the private economy, in the form of free trade and capital mobility, operate at a level *above* that of tax and regulatory capabilities related to wealth redistribution and the correction of market failures. This, he believes, will have the effect of constraining the ability of governments to implement policies that negatively affect the interests of mobile firms and individuals.

Beyond Weingast, one of the strongest and most explicitly normative arguments in favour of market-preserving federalism (what he calls 'competitive federalism') comes from James Buchanan. In his 1995 article on 'Federalism as an Ideal Political Order and an Objective for Constitutional Reform', Buchanan builds on his earlier work on constitutional economics and the need for institutional lock-in mechanisms to preserve property rights and markets. For example, he argues in favour of constitutional protections for property rights and free markets based on his belief that the market, unlike the political process, is free from economic coercion and exploitation. He argues:

> The *categorical difference between market and political interaction* ... lies in the continuing presence of *an effective exit option in market relationships* and in its absence in politics. To the extent that the individual participant in market exchange has available effective alternatives that may be chosen at relatively low cost, any exchange is necessarily voluntary. In its stylized form, the market involves no coercion, no extraction of value from any participant without consent. (1995: 20, emphasis added)

From this perspective, therefore, constitutional limits on government intervention are seen as necessary to promote a society that is free from coercion and (political) exploitation.

For Buchanan, however, constitutional provisions may not be enough:

> Enforceable constitutional restrictions ... may constrain the domain of politics to some extent, but these restrictions may not offer sufficient protection against the exploitation of citizens through the agencies of governance. (1995: 20)

To solve this problem, Buchanan favours a political system that incorporates the *self-enforcing* principles of the market, particularly the principle of maintaining an exit option through the construction of a federal system. As he notes:

> The principle of federalism emerges directly from the market analogy. The politicized sphere of activity, in itself, may be arranged or organized so as to allow for the workings of competition, which is the flip side of the availability of exit, to become operative. The domain of authority for the central government, which we assume here is coincident in territory and membership with the economic exchange nexus, may be severely limited, while remaining political authority is residually assigned to the several 'state' units, each of which is smaller in territory and membership than the economy. Under such a federalized political structure, persons, singly and/or in groups, would be guaranteed the liberties of trade, investment, and migration across the inclusive area of the economy. Analogously to the market, persons retain an exit option. (1995: 21)

Buchanan's point about the necessity of federalism as a self-enforcing back-up to constitutional provisions is a significant one. It serves to demonstrate the coherence of neo-liberal thought on federalism and to emphasize the importance of multilevel governance within the broader neo-liberal approach.

The neo-liberal approach to federalism has been most recently and explicitly promoted in the policy sphere by the American Enterprise Institute (AEI), one of the most influential neo-liberal think tanks in the United States. In early 2000, the Institute set up its AEI Federalism Project, which:

> [C]onducts and sponsors original research on American federalism, with particular emphasis on federal and state business regulation, legal developments

and the role of the courts, and the prospects for rehabilitating a constitutional federalism that puts states in competition for productive citizens and businesses. (AEI 2000)

The Project publishes various books and commentaries, runs a website, and holds numerous conferences attended by business and political leaders. Its explicit aim is to promote a 'competitive federalism' that, in the view of project director Michael Greve, 'does not seek to empower states; rather, it *seeks to discipline governments by forcing them to compete for citizens' business*' (2000, emphasis added). The AEI Project is thus fully consistent with the market-preserving federalism advocated by Hayek, Weingast and Buchanan, and it helps to highlight the overall coherence of neo-liberal thought in this area. Further demonstrating this coherence is the fact that the AEI has also sought to make links between market-preserving federalism and the need to ensure an exit option at both the regional and global levels. As Greve observes:

The benefits of jurisdictional choice and competition are visible at all levels of government ... At the international level, the free flow of capital (and to some extent labour) has rewarded America's comparatively freewheeling economy, while punishing countries whose governments insist on pursuing collectivist experiments. (2000)

Market-preserving regionalism and globalism

At this point, we should already be able to discern a number of clear similarities between market-preserving federalism and the neo-liberal project as it relates to regionalism and globalism. In both cases, the neo-liberal projects for regionalism and globalism are consistent with Weingast's key criteria for market-preserving federalism. Most important here is the criterion that: '(F4) a *common market* is ensured, preventing the lower governments from using their regulatory authority to erect trade barriers against the goods and services from other political units' (Weingast 1995: 4, emphasis added). In practical terms, this implies either a de facto or *de jure centralization of those policy capabilities related to the promotion of free markets, capital mobility and property rights*. It is for this reason that neo-liberal social forces have supported free trade agreements such as the WTO, NAFTA and the Single European Act, as well as the incorporation of various investor and intellectual property rights regimes within them. Noting this consistency between market-preserving federalism and the neo-liberal case for internationalism, Buchanan argues that 'the relationship between federalism, as an organizing principle for political structure, and the freedom of trade across political boundaries must be noted. An inclusive political territory, say, the United States or Western

Europe, necessarily places limits on its own ability to interfere politically with its own internal market structure to the extent that this structure is, itself, opened up to the free workings of international trade, including the movement of capital' (Buchanan 1995: 27).

While free trade and capital mobility ensure an exit option, they do not – on their own – ensure policy competition. This is why the neo-liberal visions for regionalization and globalization are also consistent with the further criterion of market-preserving federalism that '(F3) subnational governments have primary regulatory responsibility over the economy' (*ibid.*: 4). In general terms, this implies the *decentralization* (to at least the national level) of those *policy capabilities that relate to wealth redistribution and the correction of market failures*. At the regional and global levels, this requires more than simply avoiding the creation of supranational institutions with these policy capabilities. It also requires that governments avoid entering into multilateral agreements – such as the OECD Initiative on Harmful Tax Competition and the Kyoto Protocol – that would aim to increase tax and regulatory burdens through cross-national harmonization. Such harmonization would effectively reduce the disciplinary effect of policy competition by creating a tax or regulatory 'floor' below which no country would be allowed to go. It is for this reason that neo-liberals have opposed the centralization of many policy capabilities in supranational institutions as well as any efforts to increase tax and regulatory burdens through multilateral harmonization.

Making this point in the case of European regionalization, Buchanan has argued that:

> The opportunity has existed, and still exists, to organize European politics so as to put in place a genuine federal structure with many elements of the ideal set out earlier. The Europe-wide economy has been substantially integrated, with historically unprecedented liberties of resources flows and trade across traditional national boundaries. *Reform requires the establishment of a strong but limited central authority, empowered to enforce the openness of the economy, along with other minimal state functions.* In this way, and only in this way, can the vulnerability of the individual European to exploitation by national political units be reduced. At the same time, however, the extension of the central authority's powers beyond such minimal limits must be rigidly opposed. The separated nation-states, as members of the federal union, must zealously protect the whole range of subminimal political activities. (1995/1996: 266, emphasis added).

Therefore, based on this desire to ensure policy competition, we can expect neo-liberal social forces to oppose many international regimes and, instead, to advocate in favour of national fiscal and regulatory sovereignty (Rabkin 1998).

Taken as a whole, it would seem that the neo-liberal project for multi-level governance can be usefully theorized through Gill's concept of 'new constitutionalism'. Thus, just as the World Bank identifies both horizontal and vertical aspects within the constitutional separation of powers, so too can we analytically disaggregate Gill's concept of new constitutionalism. For example, some of the new constitutional lock-in mechanisms identified by Gill – such as balanced-budget and property rights amendments in national constitutions, and investor and intellectual property rights provisions in trade agreements – work to separate the economic and the political in a 'horizontal' fashion in that they must be enforced in a deliberate and organized way through a legal challenge. In contrast, the lock-in mechanisms connected to market-preserving federalism separate the economic and the political in a more 'vertical' fashion that is 'self-enforced' through spontaneous capital flight. Put differently, the horizontal aspects of new constitutionalism are enforced by 'direct power', while the vertical aspects are enforced by the 'structural power' of market forces (Gill and Law 1989). As noted earlier, to the extent that the latter are automatic, neo-liberals prefer policy competition over legal challenges as the most effective way to lock in free market policies.

Social forces and multilevel governance

This chapter has argued that neo-liberal theory contains an explicit and self-conscious normative project for multilevel governance that is fully consistent across the federal, regional and global levels. This project was shown to be evident in the normative work of neo-liberal intellectuals on 'market-preserving federalism' and the more recent extrapolation of these ideas to the regional and global levels. In all cases, the aim of market-preserving federalism (or regionalism or globalism) is to impose constraints on social democratic forms of government intervention through the creation of an exit option and inter-jurisdictional policy competition. This means that, at all levels, neo-liberals seek to have the private economy, in the form of free trade and capital mobility, operate at least one level above that of tax and regulatory capabilities related to wealth redistribution and the correction of market failures. This is achieved by centralizing policy capabilities related to protecting property rights, enforcing contracts and creating markets, and decentralizing those that relate to redistributing wealth and correcting market failures. Moreover, when we recognize that neo-liberal theory contains this explicit and self-conscious project for multilevel governance, it can provide us with a model for explaining the policies advocated by neo-liberal and progressive social forces on a wide variety of issues related to federal, regional and global governance.

In particular, it can help us to understand why neo-liberal social forces, such as transnational corporations, cannot be accurately described as either 'pro-globalization' or 'pro-decentralization'. Instead, they are best described as being pro-policy competition based on a vertical separation of the economic and the political. This means that, while we can expect neo-liberal social forces to support economic globalization, we can also expect them to oppose any forms of political globalization that undermine policy competition by internationally harmonizing social democratic forms of intervention (Harmes 2012). As Levy and Prakash argue, multinational corporations 'tend to support the creation of market enabling regimes at the international level, and prefer to keep social or environmental regulation under national or private authority' (2003: 131). We can also expect neo-liberal social forces to be in favour of a more decentralized form of federalism, except on issues related to protecting property rights, enforcing contracts and maintaining markets (Harmes 2007).

In a similar fashion, for all the reasons that transnational capital is likely to favour policy competition, labour and social activist groups are likely to oppose it (Harmes 2006). For these groups, policy competition limits the ability of governments to levy the taxes they deem necessary for funding redistributive social programmes, as well as the regulations that they believe are required to improve labour, environmental and other social standards. In fact, many progressive social forces decry inter-jurisdictional competition for creating a 'race to the bottom' in terms of these programmes and standards (Barlow and Clarke 2001). It is based on this opposition to capital mobility and policy competition that many commentators have described these groups as being inherently 'anti-globalization'. Again, however, the neo-liberal approach to multilevel governance may help to explain why 'anti-globalization' – like 'pro-globalization' – is not an accurate term. Rather than being anti-globalization (or anti-regionalization), we can expect progressive social forces to advocate policies that seek to realign the 'economic' and 'political' in ways that work to limit policy competition. Important to note here, however, is that this realignment can occur in one of two distinct ways.

The first is by 'bringing the economy back down' to the level of national democratic control through 'economic nationalism' and an end to capital mobility. In practical terms, this implies the re-imposition of capital and exchange controls and a withdrawal from international trade agreements. The second way is by 'bringing the polity up' to the level of the regional or global economy through multilateral harmonization and progressive forms of regional and global governance, such as the proposal for a Social Charter in Europe. (Within states, it implies a re-centralization of the taxes and regulations needed to redistribute wealth and correct market failures.) Moreover, this recognition that there are two paths to limiting policy competition can help to explain some of the policy differences amongst progressives themselves. Within the global protest movement, for example, 'nationalist' groups tend to favour the 'bringing the economy down' approach while 'reformists' tend to favour the 'bringing the polity up' approach (Green and Griffith 2002). Thus, while appearing to advocate the fundamentally different programmes of economic nationalism vs. progressive global governance, what unites both groups is the desire to have the 'economy' operate at the same level as the 'polity' in order to prevent policy competition and any subsequent constraints on government policy.

Conclusion: prospects for progressive multilevel governance

Both between and within states, the rise of neo-liberal policies has led to, and been facilitated by, a greater vertical separation of the 'economic' and the 'political' and the resulting growth of policy competition. This is most evident in the broad and ongoing trend toward 'glocalization' (globalization and localization), where specific patterns of centralization and decentralization do seem to reflect the neo-liberal project for multilevel governance (Brenner 2004). Thus globalization and regionalization have been primarily characterized by free trade, capital mobility and investor property rights rather than by effective multilateral agreements related to harmful tax competition or labour, environmental and social standards. Similarly, localization is primarily characterized by the downloading of tax and regulatory powers as well as responsibility for social programmes. This is evident in the rise of 'entrepreneurial cities' (Jessop 2000), the municipal counterparts to Cerny's 'competition states' (1997), where policy is oriented toward competing for mobile investment.

However, while many observers view these trends as a seemingly natural and inevitable side effect of globalization and the information revolution (Courchene 1995), the neo-liberal project for multilevel governance helps to highlight the agency behind these trends and, thus, the potential for change. Also highlighting the potential for change is the historical fact that a shift from a free market to a more progressive form of multilevel governance has occurred once before. In the time of Polanyi's self-regulating market, the Anglo-American countries were characterized by economic globalization and political decentralization. Following the Great Depression and the Second World War, Keynesian opposition to capital mobility and the new public finance approach to fiscal federalism (Oates 1972) sought to reduce policy competition by vertically integrating the economic and the political at the national level. They did so through a progressive form of multilevel governance based on capital controls and more centralized welfare states. Today, social democrats are increasingly returning to the insights of fiscal federalism theory and are again seeking to integrate the economic and the political to limit policy competition. The difference today, as noted earlier, is a growing emphasis on integrating the economic and the political at the international level through various forms of social democratic multilateralism.

Part IV

Trade, investment and taxation

Part IV seeks to explore how the new constitutionalism of disciplinary neo-liberalism has reshaped the global regimes on investment, trade and taxation. It outlines how neo-liberal restructuring of these regimes – despite contradictions and crises – is intensifying in ways that are driven by, and that tend to reinforce, the direct and structural power of capital. The five main themes in Part IV are:

1. The globalization of capital-exporting legal norms.
2. The expansion of market-based investment disciplines and agreements.
3. Challenges for public service provision and environmental regulation in light of these neo-liberal arrangements.
4. Prospects for the post-global economic crisis political economy of taxation.
5. Prospects for alternative forms of governance of the investment, trade and tax regimes.

In Chapter 10, David Schneiderman bridges the themes of Parts III and IV by linking the question of multilevel governance with the global investment regime. He draws on Foucault's genealogical account of (neo-)liberal political economy to underline the crucial significance of 'facilitative' states and the role of law in providing an infrastructure for the development of free markets. This account provides a backdrop for understanding 'the globalization of capital-exporting legal norms associated with the new constitutionalism'. Contrary to the dominant rhetoric and conventional wisdom that neo-liberalism requires states that govern minimally in the context of economic globalization, Schneiderman argues that neo-liberalism requires the ongoing complicity of states to actively structure and regulate globalized markets. This shows 'how neo-liberalism is not a fixed blueprint but a fluid concoction with no real consensus about the appropriate limits to state action'.

Schneiderman sheds light on two dimensions of the facilitative role of states:

1. The 'mobilization and extension of markets (and market logics)'; and
2. The 'disciplining and containment of those marginalized or dispossessed by the neo-liberalization of the 1980s'.

He then outlines how construction of the legal regime aimed at protecting and promoting international investments long advocated by capital exporting states emerged, noting 'it is only in the 1990s that the international investment regime began to secure foreign investments in legally sophisticated ways associated with new constitutionalism'. This regime involves numerous Bilateral Investment Treaties (BITs) and some bilateral and regional trade agreements. Its principal objectives are to limit what had hitherto been recognized as legitimate exercises of public authority to achieve the highest possible standards of legal protection for (foreign) investment interests. Schneiderman underscores how the international investment regime reflects the disciplining features of the new constitutionalist initiatives that endorse the insulation of markets from the control of democratic politics while providing transnational investors with extraordinary citizenship rights. This regime, promoted by international financial institutions such as the IMF and World Bank is constructed and managed through states' internalization of its restraints and disciplines. For instance, under the North American Free Trade Agreement (NAFTA), Philip Morris International and R. J. Reynolds threatened to seek damages for hundreds of millions of dollars against a potential loss of profits if the Canadian government went ahead with its proposal to legislate mandatory plain packaging for cigarettes sold in Canada. This appeared to force a swift abandonment of this plan by Canada.

For Schneiderman, however, given the necessity of states' active engagement in implementing and enforcing global legal rules, it is possible that challenges to new constitutionalism can also emerge via the authority of states, effectively opening up the potential of 'governing differently'. Noting the growing disenchantment with the current global investment regime, several states have resisted its juridical strictures, such as Ecuador, South Africa and Australia. In contrast to Canada, the Australian government enacted its new tobacco plain packaging legislation (this came into operation in December 2012).

While Schneiderman is concerned with the domestic adoption of new constitutionalism and the emergent resistance of national states against it, Scott Sinclair in Chapter 11 scrutinizes how the proliferation of the neo-liberal trade and investment treaties has increased both the direct and structural power of transnational capital. Sinclair concentrates on the NAFTA and the WTO's General Agreement on Trade in Services (GATS), which, according to him, are distinct from the previous multilateral trade and investment regime under the General Agreement on Trade and Tariffs (GATT). This is because:

1. The NAFTA and the GATS are much broader in scope;
2. They promote a shift from relative to absolute standards of protection for property rights and investor freedoms; and
3. They have much stronger enforcement mechanisms.

These are thus not simply to be understood as trade agreements but rather as groundbreaking initiatives for disciplining government authority in regulating the actions of global firms and investors in order to extend global markets. Such rule-based new constitutionalism has also accelerated the commodification of production and social reproduction.[1] Sinclair investigates the implications of these developments for the balance of power in regulating public service provision.

Sinclair encapsulates the impacts of the neo-liberal trade and investment rules on public services as mainly structural and constitutional. They include:

1. The confinement of public services within existing boundaries through making the creation or expansion of services more difficult and expensive;
2. The rise of global corporations' bargaining power when new public services are proposed or contemplated;
3. The application of 'pro-competitive' rules to the regulation of previously socialized services; and
4. The creation of a 'ratchet effect' that 'locks in' commitment to future privatization, by constraining 'the ability of governments to restore, revitalize or expand public services' by establishment of legal means for foreign investors and commercial service providers to claim compensation or impose retaliatory sanctions.

Building upon these discussions and drawing on Robert W. Cox's (1987) notion of the 'internationalization of the state', Sinclair demonstrates how the state is not a passive but an active participant in the construction of the neo-liberal trade and investment regime.

Sinclair notes, however, that the efforts to expand the GATS and the NAFTA-driven investment and services liberalization on a global scale have provoked resistance since the mid 1990s and permitted international

---

[1] See Glossary on social reproduction as well as Chapters 13–15 in this volume.

networks of progressive social forces to revive more fundamental critiques about its legitimacy. More strikingly, during the 2008 global economic crisis, the major developed countries largely ignored key rules and principles of the neo-liberal trade and investment regime to secure dominant and systemic interests. In this light, Sinclair concludes by positing: 'The need to bypass trade rules in order to deal with the aftermath of the financial crisis' suggests that such new constitutional frameworks will be not only unsustainable but also 'incapable of responding to other emerging crises in relation to energy, climate change and food security, which will also require extraordinary levels of state intervention and regulation'.

Chapter 12 discusses the structural power of transnational capital from a different viewpoint: the connection between new constitutionalism and the global tax regime. Here Dries Lesage, Mattias Vermeiren and Sacha Dierckx explore how far and in what ways the current global financial crisis has shaped the new constitutionalism of disciplinary neo-liberalism by focusing on its implications for the global political economy of taxation. They argue that the crisis has in a certain sense raised the possibilities of higher taxation of transnational capital, but the lack of a general critique of international capital mobility continues to lend stability to financial globalization and, more specifically, to the taxation policies associated with the neo-liberal economic order.

For Lesage *et al.*, there are two interrelated dimensions of the new constitutionalism that are crucial in the realm of tax policy. The first dimension involves legal restrictions on taxation of certain individuals, corporations and transactions via the domestic and international mechanisms that firmly safeguard the protection of private property rights. The second dimension entails a political-geographical configuration of different scales at which particular economic, social and political activities are situated in ways that constrain public authorities' capacities to tax internationally mobile capital. These two dimensions of the new constitutionalism, according to Lesage *et al.*, have hindered 'the implementation of progressive tax policies' as alternatives to the project designed to 'lock in' neo-liberal policies to national and international legal frameworks. Moreover, Lesage *et al.* underline that the material and ideological consequences of the global financial crisis do not fundamentally contest the hegemony of the neo-liberal notion of the free movement of capital, i.e. recent developments can be understood as bringing about a 'crisis *in* neo-liberalism' rather than a 'crisis *of* neo-liberalism'. In this light, they provide an overview of the impacts of the crisis on the global tax regime by examining the post-crisis developments and obstacles to more progressive taxation of:

1. The financial sector;
2. Wealthy individuals; and
3. Multinational corporations.

Lesage *et al.* illustrate how the complex and multidimensional dynamics in the post-crisis global political economy of taxation have made it even tougher to enhance 'mutual understanding in the domain of international tax policies' for the development of the globally coordinated action that aims 'to defeat the international logic of competitive deregulation and tax competition'. For instance, in the realm of the taxation of the financial sector, the global crisis prompted Germany and France to float the idea of introducing a global financial transaction tax (FTT) as a new way of compelling the banking sector to share in the burden of the recession. Nevertheless, this proposal was never included in the priority list of the G20 agenda on the global financial reform process. What is vital to note here is that an FTT is strongly opposed by some countries from the emerging market economies, such as China and India, which have felt far less need to subject their financial sectors to new taxation. With other emerging markets' unwillingness to participate in the global implementation of an FTT as well as a backlash from a number of key players (e.g. the United States and the UK) against its proposal, other G20 members feared the problem of tax arbitrage stemming from its unilateral or regional adoption in a particular jurisdiction. Nonetheless, reflecting a very recent agreement among 11 European Union (EU) member states to proceed with an FTT through the formula of 'enhanced cooperation', Lesage *et al.* note that 'both the material and ... institutional constraints that have held back the introduction of an FTT within the EU will in the end be overcome, although the geographically very limited tax remains far removed from a global tax on the financial sector'. Indeed, Lesage *et al.* observe that despite the global economic turmoil, international tax competition, numerous hurdles to intergovernmental tax cooperation and other obstacles have made it difficult for national states to tax the capital of individuals and companies. In sum, they conclude that although multilateral cooperation – similar to the idea of the upward harmonization of taxation policies noted in Chapter 9 by Harmes – is the only way to move beyond the new constitutionalism of taxation policies that secure and enhance the structural power of transnational capital, political majorities needed to achieve this do not currently exist.

10 How to govern differently: neo-liberalism, new constitutionalism and international investment law

David Schneiderman

Neo-liberalism has evinced an impressive ability to structure political possibilities and constrain the discursive space for political alternatives on a global scale. This is not only a truly impressive cultural and political achievement, but also an important institutional one. As the neo-liberal imaginary has been internalized, it has turned 'into other things', namely, 'neo-liberal political economy, new practices of various sorts, new identities, new material realities' (Fairclough 2006: 30). These achievements include the institutions and practices associated with the new constitutionalism. The continuing power of neo-liberalism to structure a 'universal common sense' (Bourdieu and Wacquant 2005), even in the face of an ongoing global recession, bespeaks of a discursive and institutional vigour that is difficult to overcome.

But neo-liberal agents could not have secured this kind of supremacy without the ongoing complicity of states. Institutionalizing neo-liberalism requires a great deal of 'work by a large number of distinct institutions ... and thereby partly shapes the actual work of states' (Sassen 2008: 232). State actors, indeed, have been energetically working to maintain neo-liberalism's supremacy.[1] Much of this is achieved through the vehicle of legal reform. For a couple of decades, the United Nations Conference on Trade and Development (UNCTAD) has been tracking national regulatory changes having an impact on the entry and establishment of foreign investment. Taking the ten-year period 2000–10, there were a total of 1,944 regulatory changes introduced by 1,417 countries. This represents a vast amount of activity on the part of differing states (though a number of states will have been counted more than once). Amongst these changes, about 85 per cent had the effect of 'liberalizing' investment policy while only 15 per cent were investment restrictive (UNCTAD 2011). The number of restrictive changes has increased proportionately

---

[1] On the distinction between hegemony and supremacy, see the Introduction to this volume by the editors and the Glossary.

throughout the 2000s, precipitated in part by disenchantment with legal rules to promote and protect investment.

Neo-liberalism's proponents largely elide the extent to which states are implicated in the structuration of neo-liberal globalization. This is particularly the case for those inspired by the 'Chicago School' who proffer the illusion that, in the age of economic globalization, states govern minimally. Yet neo-liberalism, offers Peck (2008: 25), 'can live neither with, nor without the state'. As a consequence, neo-liberalism is perpetually in flux, if not crisis, never quite being able to live up to its rhetorically impossible premises. It is in 'constant jeopardy', Corrigan and Sayer (1985: 195) write in another context, 'from the very facts of material difference'. In contrast to Chicago-School rhetoric, state complicity in the structuration of markets was something that German neo-liberals (or 'ordo-liberals') earlier in the twentieth century readily admitted. The activity of states is necessary, they theorized, to establish the institutional framework in which markets can be expected to do their work.

Foucault's 1979 lectures at the Collège de France presciently contrasted these two variants of neo-liberal thought. In the first part of this chapter I draw on Foucault's genealogical and conceptual account in order to underscore the reality of neo-liberal practices, better represented by the German ordo version, despite the overwhelming noise of the Chicago variant.[2] I turn, in the second part, to the legal regime to protect and promote foreign investment. It is this regime, I argue, that evinces well the features of the new constitutionalism at work that is elided by dominant neo-liberal rhetoric. Rather than governing minimally, we should expect state law to be ever present in new constitutionalist legal projects. If state power is ever present, we then can appropriately turn to a critical question, formulated by Foucault, of how to govern differently: 'how not to be governed like that, by that, in the name of those principles, with such and such an objective in mind and by means of such procedures, not like that, not for that, not by them' (Foucault 1978/2003: 265). The last section of the chapter begins to address this task, one that includes not only unmasking neo-liberalism's false premises but also rolling back its strictures, opening up the possibility of governing differently.

---

[2] Drawing on Foucault, Gill argued that institutions associated with economic globalization perform a panoptic function by imposing discipline on political actors and institutions, reinforced by 'new constitutionalism' (1995a, 1995b, 2008: 138ff.). The idea being advanced here is that globalized markets also need states; see also Harcourt (2011).

Neo-liberalism under construction

In his 1978 lectures entitled 'Security, Territory and Population' Foucault (2007: 102) traced the origins of early liberal political economy via the rise of state 'police powers' – regulation of such things as health, safety and morals – with a view to ensuring a populace's productivity in the service of the successful sovereign (what Foucault associates with *raison d'état*). The deployment of technical knowledge, having to do with 'statistics' (i.e. mortality rates, taxes and duties, and the current balance of payments), would further secure the sovereign's success (*ibid.*: 274). A state of a different order is presaged in the mid-eighteenth century by English utilitarians and French *économistes*. The natural processes associated with the economy were to be released and, though not entirely autonomous, allowed to bear fruit (Gordon 1991: 11). Positive law could be expected to do no more than 'instantiate' natural economic laws and punish those who deviated from these fundamental precepts (Harcourt 2011: 93). Foucault's lectures describe the rise of a facilitative state in this context whose 'essential function [is that] of ensuring the security of the natural phenomena of economic processes or processes intrinsic to the population' (2007: 353).

Foucault enquired into the origins of US neo-liberalism in the next year's set of lectures. He was prompted to do so because neo-liberalism, Foucault observed, was becoming 'a pet theme in France' (2008: 215, 234, fn. 1). The lectures anticipate the rise of economical-liberal orthodoxy in North Atlantic economies on the eve of Prime Minister Thatcher's and then President Reagan's coming to power. Moving from *raison d'état* in 1978 to 'reason of the least state' in his 1979 lectures, the marketization of all relations emerges as the pre-eminent technique of government. A permanent critique of government operates internal to state processes so as to ensure that government is not rendered too 'costly' to economic processes. This is the measure by which state success now will be tested, one we typically associate with the political project of neo-liberalism.

Foucault, as mentioned, traces the origins of political economy as an internal limit on governmental reason by contrasting two versions of neo-liberalism: the German post-war variant (associated with the Freiburg School and the journal *Ordo*, hence, ordo-liberalism) and the neo-liberal workings of political reason in the United States, associated with Professors Becker and Friedman at the University of Chicago (Burchell 1996; Foucault 2008).[3] Whereas, for German ordo-liberals,

---

[3] Vanberg translates the usage of the Latin word *Ordo*, associated with Thomist scholasticism (Friedrich 1955: 509), by Freiburg School economists as a normatively desirable economic order (Vanberg 1998: 173–4).

the state was legitimate to the extent that it actively created space for market freedoms (Foucault 2008: 84–5), for American neo-liberals (or what Foucault labelled 'anarcho-capitalists') the state and most everything else was legitimate to the extent it was subsumed under the rubric of economic rationality (Lemke 2001). Foucault anticipates a move by which the public domain is 'eradicated' and political life legible only in terms of economic rationality (Tribe 2009: 694).

Ordo-liberalism, however, imagines a role for the state fundamentally at odds with the American variant, which makes it a particularly apt model for apprehending the new constitutionalism. The ordo-liberal target was the totalitarian state, represented by Nazism on the one hand and communism on the other (the first 'third way', one might say). If the state, and not markets, was intrinsically defective then constitutional statecraft should be harnessed so as to free up competition by which market success is secured. Rather than imposing external limits on state functions as does classical liberalism, the ordo variant sought to organize the state around the necessity of markets. This, however, inverted the early liberal formulation so that, in effect, the state was supervised by the market. If competition was central to the maintenance of markets, this was not the natural outcome of market processes, ordo-liberals maintained, instead, it required the 'incessant and active' intervention of states (Lemke 2001: 193). Hence the paradoxical slogan of the West German model that put ordo-liberalism into practice: 'as much competition as possible and as much planning as necessary' (Foucault 2008: 91). Ordo-liberals therefore called for new institutional solutions to the generation of market freedoms, via the idea of *Rechtsstaat* for example.[4] Law, according to this account, had a special role to play in the structuration of free markets by laying down the rules of the game via an 'economic constitutional order' (Vanberg 1998). This was underscored at the Walter Lippmann Symposium of 1939, which is considered a signal moment in the development of post-war German neo-liberalism (Denord 2009).[5] In his introduction to the Lippmann Symposium, Rougier observed that the 'liberal regime is not just the result of a spontaneous natural order … [rather it presupposes] a juridical framework which fixes the regime of property, contracts, patents, bankruptcy, the status of professional associations and commercial societies, the currency, and banking, none of which are given by nature … but are contingent creations of legislation' (Foucault 2008:

---

[4] *Rechtsstaat* is the complex German legal concept roughly corresponding to the idea of the 'rule of law'. See Kommers (1997: 36–7).
[5] The proceedings were published in *Travaux du centre international d'études pour la rénovation du libéralisme, Le colloque Lippmann* (Paris: Librairie de Médicis, 1939).

161). Liberalism of this sort was not about preserving the status quo, rather it was about adapting legal forms to fit economic ordering, which itself was continually evolving via a 'plebiscite of prices', namely, properly constituted free markets (*ibid.*: 162).[6] Ordo-liberals would call this programmatic framing the *Ordnungsrahmen* or legal-institutional framework (Vanberg 1998: 174–5). In order to secure this economic constitution, legal and economic rationalities are conjoined. Lawyers must make themselves open 'to the findings of economic research', Böhm *et al.* declared in their *Ordo* programmatic statement (Böhm *et al.* 1936: 24).[7]

The state here is no mere passive bystander but the producer of an 'active governmentality … Government must accompany the market from start to finish', observes Foucault (2008: 212). He asks, for instance, how can we institute free trade 'if we do not control and limit a number of things' including the establishment of barriers to trade in order to protect nascent industry or, in the case of internal trade, establishing mechanisms to block anti-competitive behaviour? (2008: 64). One of the great merits of Foucault's resurrection of the ordo-liberal variant of neo-liberalism, then, is to underscore the prevalent role of law and states in the construction and maintenance of markets (and without any reference to Polanyi).[8] It provides us with a backdrop with which to understand the globalization of capital-exporting legal norms associated with the new constitutionalism.

Foucault's lectures subsequently turn to the Chicago School, where a positive role for the state ceases to be a major preoccupation. It was not sufficient to have states merely facilitate market freedoms, argued American neo-liberals such as Becker and Friedman. Market logic is generalized into all of the domains of human activity, and all public policy is limited internally and subject to constant critical evaluation by the criterion of efficiency, flexibility and individuality – a sort of 'permanent economic tribunal confronting government' (Foucault 2008: 247) – associated with the 'reason of the least state'. The market is the appropriate frame by which citizens are expected to govern themselves, in which case, all social relations are subsumed under the market paradigm. This is a 'politics of economic activism', in which the state is expected to retreat in

---

[6] As Hayek (1944: 74), who was present at the Lippmann Symposium, would famously proclaim, states are limited to laying down the rules of the road – they should not order people where to go.
[7] This sort of framework legislation in the advance of markets anticipates the EU common market policy (Foucault 2008: 141; Joerges 2005; Streit and Mussler 1995) and debates about its subsequent constitutionalization (Joerges 2008).
[8] Polanyi's book was only translated into French in 1983 as *La Grande Transformation: aux origines politiques et économiques de notre temps*, by Catherine Malamoud and Maurice Angeno (Paris: Gallimard, 1983).

the performance of certain social functions, and individuals are expected to self-actualize the capacity to pursue economic wellbeing (Rose 1999). State law, according to this account, is expected to get out of the way. Irrespective of the transaction costs, free markets, rather than governments, are likely to produce the most efficient outcomes (*ibid.*).

Even if ordo accounts more faithfully represent neo-liberal institutional design, as I argue below, ordo-liberalism turns out not to be as homogeneous as Foucault intimates; nor did it remain static over time. There were at least two significant groupings, one of lawyers and economists based in Freiburg, and another influenced by sociology, and so emphasizing the 'social', based in Cologne and elsewhere (Dardot and Laval 2009: 191; Streit and Wohlgemuth 2000: 225). Early on, there were affinities between ordo-liberal conceptions of the strong state and Schmittian critiques of parliamentary democracy (Schmitt 1985),[9] together with an economic programme that would be put into service by the National Socialist state (Joerges 2003: 179, fn. 65; Ptak 2009: 111, 117). Not only did ordo-liberals exhibit scepticism of democracy, they were not very enthusiastic about the redistributive state (Streit and Wohlgemuth 2000). The Keynesian social-welfare state, for many of them, was anathema to freedom.[10]

Only later, as ordo-liberals gained hegemony in post-war German intellectual life (socialists and communists, after all, were either killed or in exile) did the idea of 'social market economy' gain intellectual traction within the group, even if hesitantly, as means of generating cross-class alliances in support of the Bonn government's economic programme. 'Every social system', admitted Under-Secretary of State in the Economics Ministry Müller-Armack (an ordo-liberal who also was attracted to Mussolini's fascism in the 1930s), 'needs a simple expression with which it can make its will visible' (Joerges 2003: 178–9). This was strategic behaviour intended to secure the success of a programme that was intended to promote free competition and consumer choice. It went 'much, much further', however, than would have the social policy of other German neo-liberals (Sally 1996: 248).[11]

---

[9] Schmitt advocated the primacy of politics over the economy. For ordo-liberals, the converse would have been true (Joerges 2003: 179).

[10] Foucault reports that Röpke described the Beveridge plan for social welfare in the UK as 'quite simply Nazism' (2008: 110). This penchant for limited government is better understood in light of the close relationship between Hayek and the founders of the Freiburg School (Peacock and Willgerodt 1989: 6; Streit and Wohlgemuth 2000). We might understand Hayek, then, as the intellectual hinge between the ordo and US variants of neo-liberalism (Chang 2002: 540).

[11] Producing messages that are 'simple, readily identifiable, and easy to diffuse' has been the largely successful public relations strategy of 'conservative policy entrepreneurs' (Dezalay and Garth 2002: 80–1).

It would have been impossible, in other words, for 'pure ordo-liberalism' to have successfully gained lift-off in postwar Germany without a more pragmatic approach to the social question (Ptak 2009: 103). In practice, of course, it has not been possible for neo-liberal states elsewhere to sustain economic life without state complicity. Foucault rightly remarked that markets are not spontaneous but actively constructed and managed by states. They require, he wrote, 'a permanent vigilance, activity, and intervention' (2008: 132). Freedom, Foucault pithily declares, 'is something which is constantly produced' (2008: 65).

The undeniable persistence of states in this age of economic globalization reveals how neo-liberalism is not a fixed blueprint but a fluid concoction with no real consensus about the appropriate limits to state action. We might understand neo-liberalism following Peck and Tickell (2002), not as having stood still but as having passed through various stages (see also Chapter 8, this volume). The initial, highly experimental version promulgated by Hayek and Freidman they associate with 'proto neo-liberalism'; the version associated with the deregulation and downsizing of the Reagan and Thatcher 1980s they label 'roll-back neo-liberalism' (the 'Washington Consensus'), which since has been followed by a stage where states are no longer discredited but reconstructed along certain lines, what is called 'roll-out neo-liberalism', which proactively reconstructs state functions along preferred lines, epitomized by 'third-way' approaches. No longer concerned narrowly with the mobilization and extension of markets (and market logics), neo-liberalism, according to this account, is increasingly associated with the political foregrounding of new modes of 'social' and penal policy-making, concerned specifically with the aggressive reregulation, and disciplining and containment of those marginalized or dispossessed by the neo-liberalization of the 1980s (Peck and Tickell 2002: 389).[12] This will require more state work than neo-liberals prefer to admit. The paradox is made evident by investigating state operations within a particular juridical framework. I next turn to a discussion of international investment law as an exemplar of this state role.

International investment law under construction

The disciplinary mechanisms of global surveillance encapsulate the roll-out phase of neo-liberal policy evolution. Though the protection of alien investments under international law has long been the project of

---

[12] In some respects, this is reminiscent of the 'new law and economic development' paradigm, which recommends 'appropriate regulation' and law reform. See Trubek and Santos (2006).

capital- exporting states, it was only in the 1990s that the international investment regime began to secure foreign investments in legally sophisticated ways we associate with the new constitutionalism (Wälde 2009: 725). This represents well the institutional re-engineering element of neo-liberalism. In what follows, I relate this development to important aspects of the new constitutionalism.

I have argued elsewhere that the international investment regime mimics functions performed by the national constitutional systems of capital-exporting states (Schneiderman 2008). Constituted by over 2,800 Bilateral Investment Treaties (BITs) and some bilateral and regional trade agreements, international investment rules prohibit a wide range of state behaviour having the effect of substantially depriving investors of the value of their investment interest. Measures equivalent to an expropriation (in whole or in part), measures preferring local nationals over foreign ones or measures that deny investors 'fair and equitable treatment', amongst other disciplines, can provide ground for an investor to seek damages against a host state for hundreds of millions of dollars. Significantly departing from international law practice – which was exclusively a law for states – investment disciplines entitle individual investors to enforce treaty terms before investment arbitration tribunals. The regime has the effect of removing disputes from local courts and 'elevating' them to what is considered a 'depoliticized' form of dispute resolution peopled by lawyers almost exclusively with expertise in commercial and investment arbitration.

The regime has as its object the placing of legal limits on the authority of government, isolating economic from political power and assigning to investment interests the highest possible protections (Polanyi 1944/1957). Like constitutions, they are difficult to amend, include binding enforcement mechanisms together with judicial review and oftentimes are drawn from the language of national constitutions (Schneiderman 2008: 4). For these reasons, the regime exhibits features associated with the new constitutionalism, further separating out markets from ordinary politics and entitling investors to extraordinary citizenship rights (Gill 2008: 139). Constitutionalism, according to this account, is about generating a structure of normative expectations about that which can be changed and that which is a 'non-agenda' (Foucault 2008: 12, citing Bentham) generating a form of 'deliberate deadlock' intended to hinder opportunities for innovation and redress (Christodoulidis 2009: 10).

There are innumerable remarkable features of this regime. Though its disciplines are drawn from the legal traditions of dominant capital-exporting states, the regime imposes restraints that do not represent whatsoever the historical experiences of capital-exporting states. That is, the paths to development that are being promoted by the investment regime, and touted by international financial institutions such as the IMF and World Bank, largely are mythical ones that these states, in the course of developing their economic infrastructures, never themselves encountered (Chang 2004; Schneiderman 2008: 225–30). Nor would these sorts of disciplines have been tolerated then or even now – they go much further in breadth and depth than do the current national legal systems of many capital-exporting states (Been and Beauvais 2003). Even in early twentieth-century debates over the minimum standard of treatment expected of aliens that would have been demanded by the 'standards of civilized justice', it was admitted that accepting standards promoted by only one side of that dispute 'condemns as contrary to civilization legislation which *ex hypothesi* has been accepted for its own citizens by a state hitherto recognized as being a member of international society' (Williams 1928: 21). Put differently, the disciplines associated with the regime are intended to establish thresholds beyond which states and citizens are expected never to step beyond what would reasonably, prior to the ascendance of neo-liberalism, have been construed as legitimate exercises of public authority. Let us turn to some examples.

Early on in the life of the North American Free Trade Agreement (NAFTA), having its own investment chapter (Chapter 11), the US tobacco giants Philip Morris International and R. J. Reynolds threatened to sue for hundreds of millions of dollars should the government of Canada proceed with a plan to legislate the plain packaging of cigarettes sold in Canada. The legislation, they claimed, was tantamount to the expropriation (or, to use the US legal term, the 'taking') of big tobacco's trademarks and goodwill (part of their intellectual property rights), resulting in a significant drop in future profits. The proposal was swiftly abandoned. There are similar disputes now pending before the International Centre for the Settlement of Investment Disputes (ICSID, the World Bank facility that hosts such disputes). They concern cases brought by Philip Morris International against Uruguay and Australia for having introduced similar packaging measures intended to dampen cigarette consumption.

There exist not only threatened and pending claims but claims that have been successfully pursued against, for instance, the Republic of Argentina. These concern extraordinary measures taken in the face of an economic meltdown in Argentina that can be likened to the Great Depression of the 1930s. Unilateral state measures – such as converting contractual commitments from US dollars to Argentinian pesos – were treated by an arbitration tribunal in one of the first of such disputes (there were, at one point, 40 such disputes pending) as amounting to a denial of fair and equitable treatment. There could be little doubt, the CMS tribunal unanimously wrote, that 'a stable legal and business environment is an essential element of fair and equitable treatment' (CMS Gas Transmission Company c. República Argentina 2005: paras. 274, 284).

States are expected to internalize these limitations on their capacity for action as part of their 'good governance' learning curve. Such 'best practices' provide cover for states that otherwise might be compelled to behave otherwise. Paraguay, for instance, has refused to repatriate indigenous land taken from the Sawhoyamaxa Indigenous Community presently in the hands of German investors, though ordered to do so by the Inter-American Court of Human Rights (Lehavi 2010). Paraguay maintained that, in so far as the indigenous land claim requires the state to 'take' land out of the hands of productive German investors, they are constrained in their capacity to expropriate by the terms of a German–Paraguayan BIT that also has been incorporated into the law of Paraguay (Inter-American Court of Human Rights 2006: para. 137).

Latitudinal interpretation of investment treaty disciplines (though, admittedly, not all investors win) helps to explain the response of the US Congress to George W. Bush seeking trade promotion authority in 2001. As the experience under NAFTA's investment chapter revealed, arbitration tribunals were interpreting disciplines expansively, in ways that exceeded the rights available to US citizens under the US Constitution (though the United States has yet to lose an investment dispute as a respondent in contemporary times). Congress instructed the executive branch to alter the model investment treaty being touted globally so as to ensure that rights available to foreign investors were no greater than those available to US citizens.[13]

Not all states, however, find dissonance between national constitutional disciplines and transnational ones intolerable. To the extent that the German model is amenable to social-democratic aspirations, there is no evidence that its model treaty will be modified in the near future. Nor is there any expectation that the EU, which has obtained European-wide competence to negotiate investment treaties under the Lisbon Treaty, will alter this pattern of behaviour. Embracing the European Commission's recommendations that the 'best available standards' together with 'binding commitments' represented by investor–state dispute settlement be adopted, in 2010 the Council of the European Union agreed that EU policy 'should increase the current level of protection and legal security

---

[13] This turns out to be have been impossible to do given the breadth of investment interests protected under modern investment treaties (see, for example, the definition section of the model treaty).

for the European investor abroad' (EU 2010: para. 9). New investment agreements should be as 'equally effective' as existing European country BITs with high standards of investor protection acting as the 'main pillars of future EU investment agreements' (*ibid.*: para. 14).

Thus the Canada–EU Comprehensive Economic and Trade Agreement (CETA), near completion at the time of writing will likely to include an investment chapter that, in many respects, replicates disciplines already in place in Canadian agreements with European countries and, in some instances, further tightens those disciplines (Van Harten and Schneiderman 2010). A 'sustainability impact assessment' of CETA bluntly concluded that the 'Investment Chapter in CETA will create reductions in regulatory flexibility that on the one hand will likely have positive economic effects, while on the other hand … may also constitute a reduction in economic policy space' (EU/Canada 2011: 44). Nevertheless, the executive arm of the EU confirmed in secret proceedings that the Union should aspire to achieve 'the highest possible level of legal protection and certainty for European investors' abroad (EU General Affairs Council 2011). European negotiators are directed to secure these high standards of protection as part of free trade negotiations with not only Canada but also with Singapore and India (*Inside U. S. Trade* 2011). Though the EU views its development policy as more 'enlightened' than that of the United States, the most recent evidence suggests an embrace of the disciplining effects of the new constitutionalism over alternative policy paths that might challenge dominant orthodoxy.

Rolling back the new constitutionalism

The task now facing critics of the new constitutionalism is one that is perhaps as much diagnostic as it is emancipatory. It is to identify and act upon fissures in transnational norms and forms in ways that will liberate states and citizens from the binding constraints of such transnational legal strictures.

If it is correct to say that the investment rules regime represents a victory of sorts for capital-exporting states, we should expect expressions of resistance to originate in national locales that have not been promoting investment strictures on a global scale. We might find counter-narratives, in other words, more likely emanating from capital-importing states. It may be that social movement activism, even originating in capital-exporting states, will help to generate alternatives to the contemporary common sense of neo-liberalism. The Occupy Wall Street movement, for instance, has had some success in diffusing its contentious repertoire to various capitals (both national and subnational) in the developed world.

Whether this coordinated movement, rooted within distinct national spaces in the global North, can channel political demands either via existing political processes or exterior to them but so as to alter them (as in Cairo's Tahrir Square) remains in doubt. I would argue, however, that it is principally via the authority of national states – those authorities with legal jurisdiction to alter global legal rules – that change at transnational levels effectively can occur (Schneiderman 2013).

There is evident disenchantment with the investment rules regime that is precipitating state work in selected locales. The government of Ecuador, for instance, has withdrawn from the convention that grants jurisdiction to the International Centre for the Settlement of Investment Disputes (ICSID 2009). Ecuador also has denounced 11 BITs that have proven less than fruitful to the Ecuadorian economy (UNCTAD 2009: 32) and may denounce a further 13 BITs with countries such as the United States, Germany, France, the United Kingdom and Canada (Alvaro 2009). Throwing a wrench into the workings of investment rules more generally, the new Ecuadorean Constitution provides that no jurisdiction will be ceded to international arbitration concerning commercial and contractual disputes (Art. 422). South Africa also has reconsidered its place in the international investment regime. The Department of Trade and Industry undertook a wholesale review of the BIT framework, observing that the current model of investment treaty, borrowed from the United Kingdom, disserved South Africa's constitutional project of societal reconciliation in the face of stubbornly persistent economic inequality. The cabinet largely agreed with this assessment and concluded that South Africa should 'refrain from entering into BITs in future, except in cases of compelling economic and political circumstances' (Davies 2012). Cabinet also decided that South Africa would 'codify typical BIT provisions into domestic law', ensuring their compliance with South African constitutional commitments (*ibid.*). The UNCTAD has declared that the regime 'is at a crossroads' (2011: 93). Professor Sornarajah, only a few years earlier, described investment arbitration as 'in crisis' (2008: 73). However one describes the current conjuncture, critique of the new constitutionalism has gained ground, generating the conditions for change of unprecedented proportions in some locales.

The legitimation problems being experienced by the international investment regime is resulting in rollback in less likely places. As mentioned, the United States modified investment treaty language in its model BIT, motivated as much by ensuring that international standards did not depart significantly from US constitutional ones as by conserving policy space from investor claims. The Canadian government followed suit in its own model BIT, modifying Canadian treaty text along almost identical lines. The government of Canada presumably was less preoccupied with promoting US constitutional law doctrine abroad than about limiting the scope of investor rights, though Canada long has served as a conduit for the promotion of US trade and investment policy abroad (Clarkson and Mildenberger 2011). The government of Australia resisted the incorporation of an investor–state dispute mechanism in its 2004 free trade and investment treaty with the United States. This was a significant departure from the standard norm as most states with capital-exporting sectors typically would insist on removing disputes from local courts to international investment tribunals. Indeed, the United States has been intent, as has the EU, on securing the highest standards for US investors abroad enforced by investor–state dispute mechanisms (Vandevelde 1992). Even China, which promoted a model treaty without an investor–state dispute mechanism, now seeks adherence to a new model of investment treaty that looks almost identical to the model issuing out of most every other capital-exporting state (Schill 2007). The Australian Department of Foreign Affairs and Trade justified this initial departure from standard treaty text on the 'confidence of investors in the fairness and integrity of their respective legal systems' (Schneiderman 2008: 220). The suspicion was, however, that Australia was able to extract this concession from standard US practice because of Australia's participation in the US-led invasion of Iraq as part of the 'coalition of the willing' the year before.

This turns out, however, not to have been an aberration. Hesitantly embracing the new constitutionalist critique, the Australian Gillard government announced in April 2011 that it 'does not support provisions that would confer greater legal rights on foreign businesses than those available to domestic businesses'. Nor would the government 'support provisions that would constrain the ability of Australian governments to make laws on social, environmental and economic matters where those laws do not discriminate between domestic and foreign businesses' (Australia 2011: 14). The government had, in the past, sought to include investor–state dispute settlement provisions in its trade and investment agreements 'at the behest of Australian business' (*ibid.*), the 2004 US–Australia free trade agreement being the exception. This practice, however, now would be discontinued: 'If Australian businesses are concerned about sovereign risk in Australian trading partner countries, they will need to make their own assessments about whether they want to commit to investing in those countries' (*ibid.*).

This shift in Australian policy cuts significantly against the grain of neo-liberal orthodoxy although it could be reversed with a change in government. It appears to have been the product of a coordinated campaign by critics of investment rules within Australian academic, trade union and civil society movements, with little corresponding engagement by Australian business and industry associations (Australia 2010: 270). What seems to have particularly peeved the new Gillard government were threats by large tobacco interests that a new Australian plain packaging initiative would run afoul of both the Australian Constitution's property guarantees and international economic disciplines, including a Hong Kong–Australia BIT. The Bill, requiring that cigarettes sold in Australia be wrapped in plain brown paper wrapping without logos and trademarks, was endorsed by both houses of the Australian parliament and took effect in December 2012. It is claimed by Philip Morris Asia Limited that the legislation runs afoul of Hong Kong–Australia investment treaty obligations by amounting to the expropriation of its intellectual property and goodwill without the provision of just compensation.[14] The legislation, Philip Morris International (Asia) argues, substantially deprives the company of the commercial value of its investments in Australia including brands that have reached iconic status, such as 'Marlboro' and 'Peter Jackson' (Robinson 2011: para. 32). The Australian case suggests that this sort of misfiring on the part of transnational capital, in combination with critics exploiting contradictions endemic to international investment law, might in future help to dislodge aspects of the new constitutionalism. Citizens and states might be prompted to learn anew how to govern differently.

---

[14] Philip Morris made representations to the US Trade Representative's Office (USTR) that the United States insist on an investor–state dispute settlement mechanism in the course of negotiating a proposed Trans-Pacific Partnership Trade Agreement (Philip Morris International 2010).

11 Trade agreements, the new constitutionalism and public services

Scott Sinclair

Trade and investment agreements are a key feature of the emerging 'de facto constitutional governance structure for the global economy' that Stephen Gill refers to as 'the new constitutionalism'. This theoretical approach reveals the coercive and anti-democratic character of disciplinary neo-liberalism in general, and of trade and investment agreements in particular. It contrasts with the mainstream discourse, which portrays such agreements, and their increasing reach and complexity, as inevitable and irresistible steps in the creation of a single global economy. Fundamentally, 'the aim of the new constitutionalism is to allow dominant economic forces to be insulated from democratic rule and popular accountability' (Gill 1998b: 23).[1]

As Stephen Clarkson and David Schneiderman have both argued, trade and investment agreements serve as external, quasi-constitutions that protect and privilege the interests of corporate capital and transnational investors (Clarkson 2002; Schneiderman 2005). Much like domestic constitutions, they bind governments over long periods of time to legally enforceable disciplines that are difficult to change. Yet these agreements lack the legitimacy and normative power of domestic constitutions (Van Harten 2010: 9–10).

Through binding a broad range of government measures, the latest generation of trade and investment agreements consciously limit or even foreclose key options for more progressive governance. This is true across a wide range of matters, often only peripherally related to trade, such as intellectual property rights, investment protection, government purchasing, health and food safety standards, and environmental regulation. This chapter will discuss the impacts of these new treaties on public services.

---

[1] I wish to thank Stephen Gill, A. Claire Cutler and Isabella Bakker for inviting me to the Workshop on New Constitutionalism and World Order at York University in May 2011. I also wish to thank the other participants in the conference, particularly Janine Brodie, Adam Harmes, Sol Picciotto and Teivo Tevainen. Thanks are also due to Gary Schneider who edited this chapter and to Rana Arbabian who provided invaluable assistance with references and sources.

The GATS and the NAFTA

The adoption in the mid 1990s of the investment and services chapters of the North American Free Trade Agreement (NAFTA) and the World Trade Organization's (WTO) General Agreement on Trade in Services (GATS) was a significant breakthrough for transnational corporations attempting to 'secure protection for property rights and investor freedoms on a world scale' (Gill 2000: 9). At first glance, these are simply trade agreements. On closer inspection, however, they clearly are broader governance agreements designed to both prescribe and to restrict the role of the state in regulating the activities of international corporations.

These groundbreaking agreements created a new legal and conceptual framework that redefined services – which had previously fallen largely beyond the scope of international trade rules – in terms of their potential for commercial exploitation by global firms and capital. In addition, their broader scope and more powerful enforcement mechanisms significantly shifted the balance of power in regulatory matters in favour of international investors and commercial service providers.

There are key differences between these new trade and investment treaties and the previous multilateral regime – the General Agreement on Tariffs and Trade (GATT), which was forged and developed in the period following the Second World War – particularly in terms of their much broader scope, the shift from relative to absolute standards of protection, and stronger enforcement mechanisms. Together, these changes amount to a constitutional shift – a fundamental reworking of the trade and investment regime and its role in the international system, that is a shift in the governance structures that constitute the global political economy.

The GATS and the NAFTA were negotiated concurrently and both were adopted at the mid-point of the 'roaring nineties', when market fundamentalism – the belief in the virtues of liberalized market forces – was arguably at its most ascendant (Stiglitz 2003). The new constitutional agreements are not concerned, however, with regulating the actions of global firms or investors other than guaranteeing them protections from expropriation or for the inviolability of investor freedoms (Griffin Cohen 2004: 41). Instead, they focus exclusively on restricting government actions. And since almost any government measure can be argued to affect cross-border trade in services or foreign investment, their reach is far broader than the earlier GATT, which was mainly concerned with reducing tariffs and other border measures affecting trade in goods. These new agreements are a key aspect of a broader ideological project to reregulate society, to shift away from social protections and limitations on capital toward a neo-liberal model that tends to treat services purely as commodities.

The NAFTA was the first agreement to combine investment protection guarantees with comprehensive rules on cross-border trade in services. Its investment and services rules included *relative* standards to ensure non-discriminatory treatment of foreign investors and service suppliers. In principle, a relative restriction permits governments to adopt the policies they choose, even if those differ from other signatory governments, so long as they are not discriminatory in law or in effect. At the same time, its investment chapter also established *absolute* standards of protection, such as expropriation-compensation provisions, minimum standards of treatment and performance requirements prohibitions. Absolute standards of treatment preclude certain types of policies, whether they are discriminatory or not. It was also the first comprehensive trade agreement to include investor–state dispute settlement.

The GATS brought services under the domain of multilateral trade rules for the first time. The scope of the GATS is, in principle, universal. It applies to all services (no service is excluded a priori) and all means of providing a service internationally. It has been aptly described by the WTO secretariat as 'the first multilateral agreement on investment' since it covers not just cross-border trade but every possible means of supplying a service, including the right to set up a commercial presence in the export market (quoted in Sinclair 2000: 35).

The NAFTA's services and investment obligations are 'top down', meaning they apply automatically to all measures and sectors unless governments explicitly exclude them by negotiating exceptions, called 'reservations'. By contrast, the GATS is a 'bottom-up' agreement. This means that the strongest GATS obligations only apply to those sectors that governments explicitly agree to cover by listing them under the agreement. Once a government agrees to commit a sector under the GATS, however, it can only protect non-conforming policy measures within that sector by explicitly excluding them through exceptions, called 'limitations'.

The GATS provides for non-discriminatory treatment of foreign services and service suppliers, including national treatment and most-favoured-nation treatment rules. Under the national treatment rules, governments must extend the best treatment given to domestic services or service providers to like foreign services or service providers. The most-favoured-nation treatment rules dictate that governments must extend the best treatment given to any foreign services or service providers to all like foreign services or service providers. But similarly to the NAFTA, the GATS also includes certain absolute standards of protection, which restrict even non-discriminatory measures. The most important of these is the prohibition in committed sectors of six specific types of 'market access' restrictions, including public monopolies.[2]

The enforcement mechanisms of both agreements are far stronger than under the previous international trade regime. Dispute settlement under the GATT was essentially diplomatic. Panel rulings had to be adopted by consensus, including the agreement of the defendant government. Under the WTO, dispute settlement is legally binding. The adoption of panel rulings can only be blocked by consensus, including the agreement of the complaining government. Rulings are enforced through trade sanctions. The NAFTA investor–state dispute settlement mechanism went even further, transforming a relatively obscure commercial arbitration procedure designed to settle international disputes between consenting parties into a powerful, compulsory device that allows foreign investors to challenge and constrain public policy measures (Clarkson 2002). Rulings are enforced through monetary damage awards.[3]

Impacts on public services

In recent decades, the basic principles guiding the provision of public services have changed dramatically in many countries. The shift has been from social protection to social inclusion, from universal coverage to targeted benefits, from rights of citizenship to privileges of membership and from direct state provision to subsidized private delivery (Gilbert 2004). Large-scale programmes of privatization, the fire sale of state assets and accompanying deregulation have also been widespread.

Ironically, the high levels of public debt incurred to stabilize banks and insurers during the 2008 financial crisis, and to weather the ensuing economic downturn, are now being used to justify a new wave of global restructuring of public services. This strategy ignores the mounting evidence that previous neo-liberal reforms did not result in the presumed positive impacts on overall economic growth and efficiency, and actually had substantial regressive impacts on the distribution of wealth and income (Florio 2004: 341–2).

[2] World Trade Organization, 1994. General Agreement on Trade in Services, Article XVI, Market Access.
[3] By the end of 2010 there had been 66 NAFTA investor–state claims against the three NAFTA signatory governments, challenging a very broad range of policy measures. Mexico had lost or settled five claims, paying damages of over US $187 million. Canada had lost or settled five claims, paying damages of CA $157 million. The United States has yet to lose an investor–state arbitration. All three parties have incurred tens of millions of dollars in legal costs defending against investor–state claims (Sinclair 2010a).

In developing countries, these trends have been driven primarily through structural adjustment programmes enforced by international financial institutions. In developed countries, the justification for privatization and weaker social protection has usually been fiscal pressure, despite the fact that much of this pressure is the result of lowering tax rates. Neo-liberal trade and investment treaties, such as the GATS and NAFTA, have also played an important structural role.

The latest generation of trade and investment agreements limit key options for more progressive governance, including public services. By requiring that foreign commercial interests be compensated when public services are expanded or when a privatization is reversed, these agreements limit existing public services and attempt to lock in privatization initiatives.

The negative impacts of these new trade and investment agreements on public services include: confining public services within existing boundaries, increasing the bargaining power of multinational corporations, applying 'pro-competitive' regulation to previously socialized services, and locking in future privatization.

Confining public services within existing boundaries

The first impact of the new trade and investment regimes is to fix the boundaries of public services by raising the costs of expanding existing services or creating new ones. The NAFTA's investment chapter and the GATS both codify, in different ways, the deeply regressive concept that foreign commercial service exporters and investors must be 'compensated' when new public services are created or existing ones are expanded. While governments retain the formal right to expand public services, the treaties make doing so far more difficult and expensive.

The GATS prohibition of monopolies and exclusive service suppliers in committed sectors (Article XVI) significantly constrains governments' ability to expand existing public services, such as public health insurance or universal childcare, into new areas. Under WTO rules, governments would either have to withdraw their GATS commitments in the affected sectors and negotiate compensation in the form of trade concessions with other WTO members, or face possible retaliatory trade sanctions. For example, in situations where full commitments covering environmental services have been made by the national government, the decision of a municipal government to deliver currently privatized recycling, waste management or water distribution services through a public utility could trigger an international trade dispute and possible trade sanctions.

Though the NAFTA's services rules do not explicitly prohibit monopolies, its investment rules nevertheless constrain the expansion of public services. Governments expanding public monopolies into new areas face the prospect of investor–state claims for compensation from foreign investors whose economic interests are allegedly expropriated. This hurdle is not part of domestic law and norms on investment regulation in most countries, where expropriation usually means the taking of property for the state's own use or benefit.

In a study for a Royal Commission examining the future of the Canadian healthcare system, one of the country's leading trade lawyers concluded that if the NAFTA's expropriation/compensation provisions and investor–state dispute settlement 'had existed in the 1960s, the public healthcare system in its present form would never have come into existence' (Johnson 2002: 29). This observation could be similarly applied to a range of other public services, from a national postal system to municipal utilities (such as drinking water, waste management or public transit) that traditionally rely on public monopolies. Furthermore, the costs of compensating foreign corporations under trade and investment treaties can be prohibitive, undermining both the financial viability and the political feasibility of creating or re-establishing public services in privatized markets.

Increasing the bargaining power of global corporations

A second impact of the new regimes is to increase the bargaining leverage of private economic interests, specifically foreign investors and commercial service providers, when new public services are proposed or implemented.

The threat of corporate retaliation creates a 'chilling effect'. While policy chill is difficult to prove conclusively in specific cases, the real, although uncertain, risk of trade and investment treaty penalties will deter some governments from acting in the public interest by distorting policy choices toward options that are less injurious to private commercial interests. This underlines how governance is often as much about what does not happen, or is not even contemplated as an option for policy, as it is about the specific policy initiatives that are actually taken.

Examples of this policy chill include the fate of proposals for public automobile insurance in the Canadian provinces of Ontario and New Brunswick (Schneiderman 2005: 848–50).When it made its GATS commitments covering financial services, the Canadian federal government exempted existing programmes of public auto insurance in four provinces.

These not-for-profit public insurance systems provided superior coverage, lower administration costs and more affordable premiums (particularly for youth, seniors and rural drivers), than the private, for-profit insurance systems operating in most provinces (Legislative Assembly of New Brunswick 2004). But Canada's GATS limitations did not provide future policy flexibility to adopt similar programmes in other provinces and territories. The private insurance industry, which vigorously opposed the public insurance plans, threatened to take action under the NAFTA's investor–state dispute settle mechanism to gain compensation for lost profits. Despite widespread political and public support, the proposed policies never went ahead in either Ontario or New Brunswick.

While global corporations are the primary beneficiaries of this shift in the balance of power between private and public interests, the process is more complex than a mere lessening of state sovereignty. The state is not a passive participant, and the reshaping of state sovereignty through trade and investment agreements has actually been effected by commercial and trade ministries acting on behalf of corporate interests.

This seeming paradox can be understood as an instance of what Robert Cox termed the 'internationalizing of the state', namely "the global process whereby national policies and practices have been adjusted to the exigencies of the world economy of international production (Cox 1987: 253). From this perspective, the latest generation of trade and investment agreements can be viewed as codifying an elite global policy consensus on 'restricting regulatory actions by government, and harmonizing regulations across borders to the greatest extent possible, in order to facilitate trade and investment by global corporations' (Lee and Campbell 2006: 27).

Trade agreements provide a means to punish policies or government regulatory measures that stray from a shared neo-liberal ideological framework. The latest generation of trade and investment treaties have not simply reduced state sovereignty; they have weakened democratic authority and local control over the economy while obstructing alternative paths of development.

Trade and investment agreements have also contributed to a realignment within national state structures, with power 'concentrated in those agencies in closest touch with the global economy' (Cox 1992: 31). For example, within Canada, a key feature of a Cabinet Directive on Streamlining Regulation (CDSR), adopted in 2007 and revised in 2010, 'is to bring Canada's regulatory regime into line with the government's international commitments as reflected in the NAFTA and WTO Agreements. Departments contemplating new regulations are obliged to consult with International Trade Canada to ensure compliance with these agreements' (Lee 2010: 8).

Similar dynamics are also at work in relations between federal and subnational governments in federal states such as Canada. International trade and investment agreements are negotiated by the federal executive (which has exclusive treaty-making authority), but most provisions bind subnational governments. The prospect that a provincial regulatory measure might incur damages or trade retaliation that must be borne by the national government gives the latter a strong interest in ensuring provincial compliance.

The settlement in the recent *AbitibiBowater* v. *Canada* (NAFTA 2010) case illustrates this constitutional issue. In 2009 the multinational forestry company declared bankruptcy and closed its last remaining mill in Newfoundland and Labrador. The provincial government expropriated the company's assets, offering to pay for its land, buildings and equipment. The provincial legislation, however, appropriately denied compensation for the company's loss of timber and water rights. Access to publicly owned natural resources is based on the understanding that the resource rights holder will develop the resources productively, in a manner that benefits the public. AbitibiBowater could no longer fulfil its part of that social contract.

The Canadian federal government responded to the company's investor–state challenge by agreeing to the largest NAFTA payout to date (CAD $130 million). The settlement compensated the investor for the loss of water and timber rights on public lands, while the provincial government was left to cover the costs of severance and pensions for workers, as well as environmental remediation.

This troubling case sets the stage for more direct federal intrusion into provincial jurisdiction. While the federal Conservative government has stated it will not seek to recover costs of the AbitibiBowater settlement from the provincial government in this instance, it has put provincial and territorial governments on notice that, in future, it intends to hold them liable for any NAFTA-related damages resulting from subnational government measures.

Applying pro-competitive regulation to previously socialized services

Even where public services remain intact, the agreements' provisions governing monopolies and anti-competitive practices can make it more difficult to maintain viable public services by hampering public monopolies' ability to operate in committed sectors falling outside their exclusive privileges. Furthermore, such rules usually oblige state entities to act strictly in accordance with commercial considerations, undercutting their *raison d'être* as instruments of public policy or social redistribution.

These so-called 'pro-competitive' rules on government regulation were pioneered in the 1997 GATS Telecommunications Reference Paper and have since been proposed for a range of other service sectors. These suites of rules are primarily designed to facilitate the entry of foreign commercial providers into formerly monopolized sectors and to curb the power of incumbents, including privatized public entities.

Such rules generally acknowledge the right of governments to apply universal service obligations (USOs) in privatized sectors, but even these vestiges of public service values are subjected to necessity tests and other pro-market requirements biased toward global service providers. For example, fees for access to public networks must be 'cost based'. This obligation was a key point of contention in a 2004 GATS case brought by the United States against Mexico (Panel Report 2004). Mexico, like most developing countries, charged a premium for telecommunications companies to complete their international long-distance calls to Mexico. Mexico, however, lost the case and as a result, US-based long-distance firms can no longer be required to contribute to the development of Mexico's telecommunications infrastructure as a condition for gaining access to the Mexican system.

The ruling denied Mexico an important source of revenue that should be used to expand basic telephone service to poor customers and into rural areas, many of which do not have any access to phone services. All governments that have made or will make GATS Telecommunications Reference Paper commitments are thus forbidden to include the costs of expanding telecommunications infrastructure or improving universal access when setting rates for interconnection. This prohibition will hit developing countries the hardest and deprive governments of a proven regulatory method and source of revenues for improving their citizens' access to basic telecommunications services.

Furthermore, in sectors where public providers continue to coexist with commercial providers, the rules prohibit cross-subsidization. They also require legal separation between regulators and service providers, and guarantee commercial service providers non-discriminatory access to networks, such as telecommunications infrastructure, postal delivery networks or electrical transmission systems, which were typically built through public investment.

Public service providers, such as public post offices or degree-granting educational institutions, often compete with commercial operators in sectors outside their core monopolies. The revenue from these competitive services helps to cross-subsidize costly universal service obligations (USOs).

Where public and commercial service providers coexist, the public entities are handicapped. Any advantage given to the public provider, including subsidies in the case of the GATS, must be extended to the commercial provider. These constraints pave the way for future privatization by both strengthening private competition and eroding public support for public service providers.

Locking in future privatization

The agreements also bolster the momentum toward further privatization by making it more difficult for subsequent governments, disillusioned with its results, to change course. Once foreign investors or service providers become established in a previously socialized sector, efforts to resocialize it can result in claims for compensation. The resulting 'ratchet effect' permits future reforms that move in one direction only. This structural bias interferes with the usual ebb and flow of policy-making in a democratic society. This is reflected, for example, in the electoral rotation between socialist and conservative forces, each of which is normally associated with different concepts of regulation. The former tend to prefer socialized forms of regulation, the latter more liberalized forms.

Examples can be drawn from investor–state challenges under Bilateral Investment Treaties, which are similar to the NAFTA's investment chapter. One clear instance involves investor claims for compensation following reversals in health insurance policy reforms by the Slovakian government. As David Hall of the Public Services International Research Unit explains, 'Private health insurance schemes were first introduced in Slovakia in 2004. A number of private companies set up to take advantage of this new market. In 2007, a new government changed the law to reduce the role of the private sector. Part of this law states that health insurance companies can only use their profits to reinvest in the health insurance business' (Hall 2010: 85).

Following this policy change, a foreign holding company that owned two of the Slovakian insurance companies took action under a Bilateral Investment Treaty between the former Czechoslovakia and the Netherlands. In December 2012, the Dutch insurance company, Achmea, announced that it had prevailed in its challenge and been awarded 22 million euros in compensation by the investor–state tribunal. Similar challenges have occurred as a result of reversals in health policy in Poland (Hall 2010), a reversed water privatization in the Bolivian city of Cochabamba (Vandevelde 2007) and a raft of investor–state claims against Argentina stemming from the failed privatization of municipal public utilities in the aftermath of that country's financial crisis (Peterson 2004: 16–19).

The case of Cochabamba is notable because it demonstrates that popular mobilization and resistance can, in certain circumstances, successfully contest these formal external constitutional constraints. In 1999, Bolivia attempted to privatize the municipal water system in Cochabamba, the country's third-largest city, by granting a 40-year contract to a firm controlled by Bechtel, a US-based multinational corporation. After large local protests, the contract was terminated and the water system returned to public hands. Subsequently, Bechtel sued for compensation under a Bilateral Investment Treaty between Bolivia and the Netherlands. The popular movement in Bolivia, however, waged a highly effective, international public relations campaign against Bechtel. In 2006 the company settled its claim for a token amount.

When trade and investment agreements are negotiated, governments have a one-time opportunity to insulate existing services from the full force of the agreements and, to some extent, preserve future policy autonomy. Such protections are often partial or temporary.[4] Moreover, once the agreement is in place, any future government can unilaterally eliminate country-specific protections, permanently exposing previously excluded sectors or measures to the full force of the treaties. A closely related issue is that country-specific reservations exempting otherwise non-conforming measures simply highlight them as targets to be eliminated in subsequent negotiations. Within the WTO's logic of 'progressive liberalization' exclusions are temporary, while commitments are permanent.

Shifting the balance against public services

From the vantage point of the NAFTA and the GATS, public services are viewed, at best, as missed commercial opportunities or, at worst, as illegitimate market access barriers (Sinclair 2011). Both agreements constrain the ability of governments to restore, revitalize or expand public services. In such cases, governments must negotiate compensation or face retaliatory sanctions. When a state must pay to govern, its authority has clearly been diminished.

In practice, the adverse impacts on public services are often attenuated through the application of reservations, limitations and other country-specific exemptions. But the existence of contingent or temporary protections should not obscure the basic thrust of the agreements.

---

[4] Under the NAFTA, for example, parties are not permitted to take any reservations against the expropriation-compensation clause (NAFTA Article 1110).

Indeed, the legal redefinition of public services as exceptions to be justified, rather than norms to be emulated, is in itself a crucial ideological, political and legal achievement for global capital. The breakdown of the post-war consensus regarding the role of public services and the welfare state is now embedded in international trade and investment rules.

Dynamism of the agreements

Since the mid 1990s, the efforts to construct these new trade and investment regimes on a truly global scale have encountered major obstacles and resistance. But the momentum to create more favourable conditions for global business interests through new agreements is not a spent force.

The WTO's Doha Round of negotiations, launched in Qatar in 2001, is currently teetering on the brink of failure. The main points of contention involve industrial goods and agriculture, but differences over services – the third pillar in the negotiations – have also contributed to the stalemate. Many developing countries, both large and small, are disinclined to accept the ambitious package of services liberalization that developed countries insist upon as part of an overall agreement.

Investment and services liberalization has not, however, completely stalled. Frustrated with the Doha Round impasse on services, a self-selected group of WTO member governments (calling themselves the 'Really (*sic*) Good Friends of Services') began talks in 2012 towards a Trade in Services Agreement (TISA). The real targets of this EU and US-led initiative are the so-called BRICs (e.g. Brazil, China, India and other major developing countries), although no BRIC governments except China have yet shown any inclination either to join the TISA talks or to accept any eventual agreement as part of the WTO framework.

Nonetheless, there have also been over 200 Regional Trade Agreements (RTAs) negotiated since the mid 1990s. Most of these include services and investment coverage that can be categorized as following either a 'GATS-inspired' or 'NAFTA-inspired' template (Houde *et al.* 2008: 4). Despite this momentum, however, even RTAs have encountered limits. Most are North–South deals, that is, between developed and developing countries. Moreover, developing countries that already have an agreement with a major developed country account for a disproportionate share of RTAs, as they replicate the original treaty with other countries. There have been only a limited number of South–South RTAs that have included extensive services and investment coverage.

Importantly, there are very few RTAs between developed countries – the US–Australia Free Trade Agreement is an exception – even though such relationships still account for the bulk of global investment and trade in services. The largest newly industrializing countries have also not jumped on the RTA bandwagon or, in the case of Brazil and South Africa, have focused their energies on less-intrusive pacts with their closest neighbours. China and India have also remained aloof, although there are signs that this attitude may be changing.

Yet despite major setbacks, a new momentum is building behind a new wave of binding services and investment treaty expansion being driven by global corporations and their political allies. The action has shifted from broader multilateral or regional groupings to bilateral or regional negotiations between more ideologically like-minded partners, seen as 'coalitions of the willing'.

In this context, there are important new regional negotiations underway that involve both developed and developing countries, most notably the nine-country Trans-Pacific Partnership (TPP) talks, which have broken off from Asia-Pacific Economic Cooperation forum (APEC). There are also now examples of bilateral Free Trade Agreements (FTAs) between developed and the major newly industrializing nations (New Zealand–China and India–Japan), which for the first time include full-fledged investment protection chapters and investor–state dispute settlement. India, in particular, has an active negotiating strategy with major developed countries, including the European Union (EU) and Canada. While the US bilateral negotiating agenda stalled during the early years of the Obama administration, the president, with Republican support, subsequently secured congressional approval for several bilateral FTAs negotiated by the Bush administration and is now driving an ambitious trade and investment negotiating agenda focused primarily on the TPP. Other developed countries – notably Canada – have taken a hyperactive approach to negotiating comprehensive trade and investment agreements, e.g. with the European Union and China. Finally, as a result of recent constitutional reforms, the European Commission (EC) has gained new authority to negotiate full investment protection, including investor–state dispute settlement.

On the other hand, there have been push-backs against these changes. While mass protests such as those in Seattle in 1999 and Quebec City in 2003 have diminished, international networks of activists, non-governmental organizations and progressive academics are coalescing around the issue of *just investment regimes*. The Australian government's recent decision to reject investor–state arbitration (Peterson 2011) in future agreements was an important victory for such forces. India has reportedly rejected European pressure to include an investor–state arbitration mechanism in the EU–India FTA currently under negotiation (Mishra

2011). Ecuador has terminated several Bilateral Investment Treaties, and both Ecuador and Bolivia have withdrawn from the arm of the World Bank that adjudicates such arbitrations (UNCTAD 2010). South Africa is also refraining from entering into new Bilateral Investment Treaties (BITs), working to terminate existing BITs that include investor–state arbitration and developing national legislation that would provide the security of investment that foreign investors should legitimately expect (Carim 2012). Within South America, there are also new regional initiatives to construct alternatives for regulating investment that are more deferential to state authority and democratic choice (Leathley 2011). In each of these examples, governments have reversed their previous support for investor–state arbitration when confronted with controversial investor–state claims and pressure from below by social movements and civil society networks.

Trade negotiations between the EU and Canada

The dynamics and interaction between the GATS and the NAFTA frameworks, and the agreements' implications for public services, can be explored through one of the current sets of negotiations, the Canada–European Union Comprehensive Economic and Trade Agreement (CETA). The CETA is the EU's first negotiation with a country that has a fully developed economy. It is also the first in which the EC has had the authority to negotiate full investment protection, including an investor–state dispute settlement mechanism similar to that in the NAFTA Chapter 11.

The talks, which began in 2009, aptly illustrate the pressures that can be brought to bear on initial exemptions for public services in subsequent negotiations. In the GATS and its subsequent RTAs, the EU lodged a 'public utilities' horizontal limitation that permitted services at the national and local level within the EU to continue to be provided by public authorities or through government contracts with exclusive service suppliers. Public monopolies and exclusive supplier arrangements would otherwise have been inconsistent with the GATS Article XVI and its equivalents in the EU's Free Trade Agreements. As a direct result of pressures applied in the CETA negotiations, the EC proposed to dispense with the 'public utilities' limitation.

In February 2011, the EC issued a confidential 'reflections paper' proposing to revamp its treatment of public services in international trade and investment agreements (European Commission 2011). The paper addressed 'services of general interest', which are composed of 'services covering such essential daily realities as energy, telecommunications, transport, radio and television, postal services, schools, health and social services, etc'. In the paper, such services are divided into:

1. Non-economic services of general interest, such as the police and judiciary, prisons and border security; and
2. Services of general economic interest, which are further subdivided into:
   (i) network industries; and
   (ii) services other than network industries.

Only the 'non-economic services of general interest' category would be fully excluded from the scope of the CETA's services and investment commitments. Since these services are provided on neither a commercial nor competitive basis, they are, the paper notes, 'essentially equivalent to GATS definition of services carried out in the exercise of governmental authority'. This restrictive characterization of the GATS governmental authority exclusion is remarkable in light of the assertions by the WTO and developed country government officials that public services were excluded from the GATS by Article I:3.[5] In effect, the European Commission (EC) now admits that critics of the GATS were correct in their analysis that the exclusion would be interpreted very narrowly.

It is worth noting that the proposed exclusion, like the GATS governmental authority exclusion, operates by virtue of the fact that such services are currently of 'no commercial interest for either party' rather than due to any principled position that these core activities should be reserved to the public sector. This means that if and when services such as prisons, border security or social security schemes attract commercial interest or competition from private commercial providers (as in the United States), the purported exclusion would no longer be operative, and the services and investment provisions of international treaties would apply.

The 'network industries' within the services of general interest category refers to telecommunications, energy, transport, postal and environmental services (such as waste and water). While the EU's current public utilities *exemption* generally excludes such network industries where publicly provided, under the proposed new approach, such services would be almost fully committed and thus potentially liable to liberalization.

---

[5] For example, in 2001 then Director-General Moore of the WTO publicly responded to concerns regarding the potentially corrosive impacts of the GATS on public services by asserting that 'GATS explicitly excludes services supplied by governments' (see Moore 2001). Similarly, an influential Organisation for Economic Co-operation and Development 'advocacy piece' asserted that 'the GATS governmental authority exclusion "carves out" a potentially wide category of services from the scope of GATS rules' (OECD 2001: 42).

As the EC paper acknowledges, this proposed change reflects both the extensive degree of commercialization of these services in the EU's internal market and the priority given to the export interests of EU-based global service corporations. The current exemption for such services should be discarded, the Commission notes, because it allows EU's negotiating partners 'a broader policy space which could be abused'. In the CETA negotiations, the EC is seeking full coverage of subnational (provincial and municipal) procurement, an area where Canada had, until recently, not made any commitments to liberalization under international trade treaties, including the NAFTA.[6] In Canada, as in Europe, many important public services, such as waste, water and public transit, are delivered by local authorities. The exclusion of such services from the procurement restrictions of trade treaties has provided policy flexibility to use such procurement as a tool for local economic development. It has also reduced the risk of litigation and demands for compensation from foreign investors and services providers when privatization schemes are halted or reversed.

The bargaining dynamics of the CETA negotiations pit the private interests of global service corporations against the broader public interest in so far as this involves preserving the policy space for public service provision at the local level, both in Canada and Europe. Under the EC's preferred approach to the CETA, instead of the blanket protection provided by the EU's current public utilities exemption, any remaining national or regional public monopoly would have to be explicitly listed or lost. Existing network industry monopolies at the local or regional level (for example, public transit systems or municipal water utilities) would be 'grandfathered', but subject to 'standstill' and a 'ratchet' (broadly, that no new impediments to trade should be introduced). This would mean that if, in future, a local service was privatized, renationalization would be inconsistent with the EU's international trade treaty commitments.

On the one hand, 'non-network industries of general interest', including health or education, would receive somewhat stronger protection, for example, reserving the right to renationalize a service once privatized. On the other hand, the inclusion of NAFTA-style expropriation compensation provisions in the CETA, as the document briefly acknowledges, would undercut this policy flexibility, by requiring compensation for expropriation when renationalization occurs. Again, it is likely that as a result of this provision, and given the 'chill effects' noted above, the commercial interests of EU firms are likely to be given disproportionate

---

[6] Canada made its first commitments covering subnational procurement as part of the 2010 Canada–US Government Procurement Agreement (see Sinclair 2010b).

weight. As one critical analysis of the reflections paper observes, these 'shifting boundaries' are contrived to favour 'one-sided commercial interests' at the expense of 'comprehensive protection of public services' (Prausmueller and Wagner 2011: 5–6).

The privatization of municipal services, especially water, is one of the most contested and politicized issues in the EC's internal drive to commercialize services of general interest. Here there are clearly contending interests at play. European-based global service corporations seek to employ trade and investment agreements to gain access to foreign markets (Corporate Europe Observatory 2009). However, there are also many local governments who insist on preserving their authority to reverse failed privatizations and who have in many instances already moved to re-municipalize water and other basic local services. As the CETA negotiations draw to a close, it appears as if enough EU member states have sided with local governments, public sector unions and civil society groups to rebuff the Commission's proposal to weaken the EU's public utilities exemption.

It is equally likely, nonetheless, that the CETA will contain strong investment protection provisions, including expropriation-compensation obligations and an investor–state dispute settlement mechanism. This would be the first time that investor–state arbitration has been included in an EU bilateral trade agreement. Based on the NAFTA record and the experience of developing countries under similar provisions in Bilateral Investment Treaties, such a step can be expected to lead to a growing number of investor–state challenges against the EU and Canada in the areas of public utilities and essential services.

Conclusion

The impacts of the latest generation of new, more far-reaching trade and investment agreements on public services are primarily structural and constitutional. By requiring that foreign commercial interests be compensated when public services are expanded into new areas or when a privatization is reversed, such agreements limit existing public services and attempt to lock in unpopular, and even unworkable, privatization initiatives.

Global services corporations and their allies in government commercial ministries championed these agreements in order to check the expansion of existing public services, to open previously socialized sectors to commercial exploitation and to augment their ability to frustrate public interest regulation. The agreements were designed to lock in future reforms and to facilitate ever-increasing coverage when conditions were favourable. But each effort to broaden or deepen these agreements provokes resistance and permits progressive social forces to revive fundamental critiques about their legitimacy.

Key rules and precepts of the investment and services regime were largely ignored during the 2008 financial crisis, in order to protect dominant and systemic interests in the core developed countries. The bailout of financial institutions, extraordinary levels of subsidy to national auto makers and the local content requirements of the stimulus measures all violated the spirit, if not the letter, of existing trade agreements.

The unfairness of this double standard has not been lost on the many subordinate groups and peripheral countries that have been compelled to abide by these rules at great social cost. The need to bypass trade rules in order to deal with the aftermath of the financial crisis also suggests that these regimes will be incapable of responding to other emerging crises in relation to energy, climate change and food security, which will also require extraordinary levels of state intervention and regulation.

The persistent, and probably insurmountable, impasse in the WTO talks in Geneva signals that the multilateral agenda of ever-deeper and more intrusive trade and investment rules has foundered due to deep scepticism in the global South and rising public unease about the uneven social impacts of globalization in the North. While a significant group of governments continues to pursue a deep liberalization agenda bilaterally and regionally, many others are standing aside, opening up the possibility of more heterodox and progressive approaches to public interest regulation, economic development and public services.

12 New constitutionalism, international taxation and crisis

Dries Lesage, Mattias Vermeiren and Sacha Dierckx

Introduction: new constitutionalism and taxation

This chapter explores how the global financial crisis of 2008–9 has affected the stability of the 'new constitutionalism of disciplinary neo-liberalism' in the realm of international tax policy. New constitutionalism forms a principal institutional component of neo-liberal hegemony. In neo-Gramscian international political economy, neo-liberalism is understood as a political project aimed at restoring capitalist class power after the economic and social crisis of the 1970s (Harvey 2005; van Apeldoorn and Overbeek 2012). This project is undergirded by dialectically intertwined material, ideational and institutional components. In the material realm, the structural power of transnational capital is manifested by the predominance of international finance and transnational corporations in the global political economy. The cross-border mobility of these fractions and the associated 'exit option' discipline governments, parliaments and national trade unions to introduce and accept neo-liberal economic policies. Ideationally, neo-liberalism is characterized by the hegemony of pro-market, supply-side and monetarist discourses (van Apeldoorn and Overbeek 2012). However, militant neo-liberalism has to a certain extent been succeeded by the seemingly more politically 'neutral' globalization discourse, which pretends that states have lost a considerable deal of their actual sovereignty and that for nations there is no alternative (TINA) to adjusting to the exigencies of internationally mobile capital.

In the institutional sphere, new constitutionalism firmly institutionalizes neo-liberal globalization. Stephen Gill (2008) defines new constitutionalism as the political project designed to anchor neo-liberal policies into national and international legal frameworks, insulating these policies from normal, day-to-day democratic debate and decision-making. As Gill has stated, the central goal of new constitutionalism is to firmly secure the protection of private property rights, and as such to transform public policy in the interests of mobile capital. What is emerging is a social order in which holders of that capital are conferred privileged rights of citizenship and representation, and in which these rights are 'locked in'. In effect, 'the mobile investor becomes the sovereign political subject' (1998b: 25). Consequently, dominant economic forces, in particular wealthy individuals, transnational corporations and financial institutions, are 'increasingly insulated from democratic rule and popular accountability' (*ibid*: 23), and, in the case examined here, from taxation.

In the realm of tax policy, there are two, interrelated dimensions to the new constitutionalism. The first dimension entails legal and constitutional constraints on taxing certain transactions or holders of mobile capital, via two mechanisms. First, there are domestic and international legal frameworks that safeguard property rights in ways that limit taxation. The obvious example is the laws of bank secrecy that enable tax evasion or tax avoidance. In this way, limits to transparency are also limits to taxation. Second, taxing certain transactions (e.g. international capital transfers) is prohibited by international agreements such as Bilateral Investment Treaties (BITs), Free Trade Agreements (FTAs) and international treaties (e.g. the EU Treaty). Via these two mechanisms, new constitutionalism legally encodes the regulatory dimension of disciplinary neo-liberalism, both at the domestic and international levels. Moreover, these frameworks can only be modified in extraordinary circumstances and through burdensome procedures, often requiring special majorities or unanimity.

Having said that, it is useful to see the concept of new constitutionalism, being the *legal* anchoring of neo-liberal globalization, in relation to the latter's *economic* anchoring. Both are narrowly intertwined. For individual states and even groups of states it has become extremely difficult to withdraw from certain neo-liberal policies. For their long-term prosperity, states need, for example, investments from transnational corporations and capital from wealthy individuals or financial institutions to finance government debts. In this context, countries have been more or less obliged to provide an attractive investment climate on a permanent basis, generating a transition of the era of the (Keynesian) welfare state to that of the competition state (Cerny 1997). Values such as business confidence, policy credibility, discipline and competitiveness are crucial in this regard (Gill 1998b, 2008; Grabel 2000).

In this light, new constitutionalism contains an important political-geographical dimension (see Harmes 2006 and Chapter 9 in this volume). This second dimension of new constitutionalism is crucial in the domain of tax policy. It legally anchors the free movement of capital, goods and services as one of the main drivers of neo-liberal globalization. In the meantime, however, policies of market correction (such as taxation) most of the time still reside at the national level. In this way, new constitutionalism more or less freezes a political-geographical mismatch between market promotion and market correction. It codifies a certain 'Gestalt of scales' (Swyngedouw 2004), a specific configuration of different political scales at which respective economic, social and political activities are located. In this way, internationally mobile capital is capable of playing off one political-regulatory jurisdiction against another by the possibility of 'regime shopping' or 'regulatory arbitrage'. As such, new constitutionalism has induced national governments to embrace neo-liberal-oriented policy regimes in order to thwart off potential investment strikes and/or capital flight (Gill and Law 1989). Neo-liberal thinkers have consciously promoted this 'market-preserving federalism' to constrain government intervention by anchoring inter-jurisdictional competition (Harmes 2006). This phenomenon demonstrates that organization of human activity at certain political-geographical scales is far from a power-neutral process (see also Macartney and Shields 2011).

Thus, to sum up, two dimensions of the new constitutionalism obstruct the implementation of progressive tax policies 'in ways that seek to subordinate the universal to the particular interests of large capital' (Gill 2008: 175). First, taxation of certain individuals, corporations and transactions is hindered by legal restrictions. Second, the political-geographical dimension of new constitutionalism limits states' abilities to tax internationally mobile capital. Consequently, new constitutionalism, itself the product of transnational capitalist interests and neo-liberal ideas, has increased the structural power of transnational capital and feeds the disempowering globalization discourse.

The political economy of global taxation after the crisis

The crisis in/of neo-liberalism and taxation

The global financial and economic crisis has, however, started to produce cracks in the neo-liberal project, although in a complex and often contradictory way. These cracks are very relevant to the new constitutionalism of taxation policies. First, the economic crisis has to a certain extent brought about an ideological crisis. While it could be argued that the neo-liberal project was never about 'state withdrawal', it is certainly true that neo-liberalism in the public debate is associated with the notion that free markets are efficient and self-regulating. Because of the crisis and the bailouts of insolvent banks this notion has been strongly delegitimized, especially with respect to the operation of financial markets and institutions. Thus, the case for state intervention, and for taxing certain financial transactions or institutions, has been much stronger after the crisis. Second, as Thirkell-White (2009) points out, public anger over the credit crisis and large-scale protests have increased the politicization of the global financial reform process to a considerable degree, 'triggering the rise of a populist politics seeking punishment for the banking sector' (2009: 689). As a result, governments seem to have gained the self-confidence to keep the bankers in check and to search for measures that will force the financial sector (and possibly the speculators) to pay, for instance by curbing and/or taxing excessive remuneration of cadres and traders.

Finally, the budgetary crises, especially in the United States and the Eurozone, have led to a vigorous search for new means to cut the fiscal deficits and reduce public debt: bank bailouts and fiscal stabilization policies in the aftermath of the global crisis have produced huge fiscal deficits that need to be pushed back in the near future. While until now the austerity measures have largely attacked the lower and middle classes, public debates have been growing on higher and/or new taxes on financial markets and institutions, wealthy individuals and multinational corporations as a way to spread the burden of fiscal consolidation more evenly across society. This also brought the issue of international tax competition and the abuse by these players of 'unfair' international tax arbitrage opportunities again into the picture: some governments raised objections about bailing out banks with public money at the same time that some of those banks were still in the business of helping citizens and companies to avoid and evade taxes, including through their own branches in tax havens.

Thus, the material and ideological consequences of the crisis have in a certain sense increased the possibilities of higher taxation of transnational capital. However, there are indications that the global financial turmoil is yet to become a crisis *of* neo-liberalism instead of a crisis *in* neo-liberalism (Saad-Filho 2010). This is also clear in the domain of taxation. While the crisis has delivered a blow to the legitimacy of neo-liberal ideas, this does certainly not imply that the whole neo-liberal legacy will be swept away altogether. The self-regulating market is to a certain extent delegitimized, yet other pillars of neo-liberal hegemony remain deeply embedded in commonsense assumptions. For instance, there is still a lot of wariness on state intervention in the economy, which is often considered to be inefficient and the result of 'rent-seeking'. Moreover, the fiscal crisis has produced and reinforced the notion that states have been living beyond their means for a long time. Reports by the ECB and the IMF have argued that the focus of fiscal consolidation should be on cuts in public spending instead of new taxes, which are believed to hamper urgently needed economic growth. Thus, neo-liberal policymakers believe states should not search for extra tax revenues but should instead cut back spending.

Importantly, the structural power of transnational capital remains largely intact. While the dependence on state support and bailouts during the crisis to some extent weakened the material power of the banking sector, its importance should not be overstated. The social purpose of state intervention in the financial sector was more about the need to restore the stability of financial markets than it was about seizing the opportunity to reclaim control over the financial sector. Watson (2009), for instance, has shown that the British bailout plan defended the underlying deregulatory logic of the existing financial regime instead of restoring state capacities in the banking sector to improve societal welfare. The need by public authorities to restore financial stability and economic growth is also exploited by both financial and productive corporations, whose investments remain crucial for the economic health of nations, in an efficient way to prevent a backlash against capital in terms of more stringent regulation and/or higher taxation (cf. Blyth 2010). Lastly and most importantly, the neo-liberal norm of the free movement of capital has not been seriously contested, especially in the West (Helleiner 2009). Internationally mobile capital is still able to play different jurisdictions off against one another by means of regulatory arbitrage. Therefore, in cases where wealthy individuals and multinational corporations have attracted criticism because of their low contributions to tax revenues in the context of fiscal crises, the argument that they can easily exit a particular jurisdiction remains very powerful. As such, because the free cross-border movement of capital has not been affected by the crisis, the neo-liberal hegemonic proposition that 'there is no alternative' remains very influential (Macartney 2009).

On top of these complex and multidimensional dynamics, the rise of emerging markets complicates matters even more. Whereas before, the United States and EU were to a large extent able to define and impose international tax policies, this ability is starting to fade. In the future, international tax policies and coordination will require the consent of more countries, with very different political-economic, cultural, social and historical backgrounds. Moreover, the crisis has played out very differently in emerging markets: their banks have not invested as much in complex financial derivatives and were less affected by the crisis. As a result, emerging market economies have experienced a far less dramatic deterioration of their fiscal position and feel far less need to subject their financial sector to new regulation or taxation. The different dynamic after the crisis thus deepens the global collective action problem to defeat the international logic of competitive deregulation and tax competition by making it even harder to achieve mutual understanding in the domain of international tax policies.

How have these dynamics played out in the post-crisis global political economy of taxation? In what follows, we give an overview of the post-crisis developments and hurdles in international tax policy by focusing on three key dimensions:

1. The taxation of the financial sector;
2. The taxation of wealthy individuals; and
3. The taxation of multinational corporations.

Taxing the financial sector

The first key dimension of international tax policy ensuing from the global crisis is the search for new ways of taxing the financial sector. The formulation and implementation of a new tax on the transnational banking sector quickly became an important yet contentious issue of the G20 agenda on global financial reform. Germany and France were the two forerunners in the campaign to introduce a tax on international financial transactions as a means to force the banking sector to share in the costs of the crisis. As Peer Steinbrück, Germany's minister of finance at the time, argued:

> The Group of 20 nations' average support for the financial sector is more than 30 per cent of gross domestic product (including capital injections, guarantees, treasury lending and asset purchases, liquidity provision and other central bank support). In our political response to this crisis, new forms of fiscal burden-sharing will be needed. One of these is a global Financial Transaction Tax (FTT).
> (Steinbrück 2009)

Proponents proposed to introduce a tax of 0.05 per cent on all trades of financial products to be applied across all the G20 countries, which according to some estimates could yield up to US $690 billion per year. While the FTT is frequently compared to the age-old Tobin Tax proposal, the Tobin Tax proposed a much bigger tax of 0.1 to 1 per cent on international currency transactions in order to reduce international financial speculation by discouraging cross-border capital flows. As such, it is important to note that the FTT – in contrast to the Tobin Tax – would not have the effect of 'deglobalizing' global finance by slowing down the international mobility of financial capital. While former French President Sarkozy, the UN administration and global civil society wanted to dedicate at least part of the FTT proceeds to development and climate finance, the key purpose of the FTT would be to boost fiscal revenues for the state.

Nevertheless, despite being quite modest, the financial transaction tax proposal never reached the priority list of the G20. After Gordon Brown, then prime minister of the UK, floated the idea of introducing an FTT before a G20 meeting, Timothy Geithner, the US Treasury secretary, responded that 'A day-by-day financial transactions tax is not something we are prepared to support' (Giles 2009). Several other G20 members joined the US backlash against the FTT. Importantly, some emerging market economies are strongly opposed. Emphasizing that Indian banks have not suffered any threat of collapse nor earned a reputation for excessive risks or returns, the Indian minister of finance argued that Western policymakers needed to consider 'better regulation instead of taxation' (Lamont 2010). One important reason for countries such as China and India not to support the FTT – or any other bank levy for that matter – is their desire to minimize the tax burden on their largely state-owned banking systems. But with a number of key players not willing to jump on the FTT train, other G20 members worried about the problem of tax arbitrage arising from unilateral or regional implementation. Lord Turner, chairman of the UK Financial Services Authority and self-proclaimed defender of a global tax to curb the 'swollen' financial sector, underlined that it would be 'ridiculous' to erode the competitiveness of the City of London by imposing the tax unilaterally (Pickard 2009). An editorial of *The Times* went even further in this concern:

[Even if] all the main financial centers signed up for a tax ... that still leaves the offshore financial centers. It is difficult to see what possible incentive they would have to implement a tax when it would plainly be in their financial interest to attract business from international banks. (Editorial 2009)

The position of the UK is highly important for the European approach to the financial transaction tax. Indeed, even though Jean-Claude Trichet – president of the ECB at that time – urged European policymakers to ditch plans for an FTT by calling for 'great prudence in introducing something which is not done at the global level' (Pignal 2011), France and Germany were unwilling to abandon the plan and ordered the European Commission (EC) to propose a plan to introduce the tax unilaterally at the EU level. In September 2011, in the midst of the Eurozone debt crisis, the EC publicized the first official proposal for an EU-wide – rather than global – FTT that went further than the original FTT idea: arguing that a comprehensive FTT is both feasible and desirable, the EC proposed a tax of 0.1 per cent (instead of 0.01 per cent) on transactions of stocks and bonds, and a tax of 0.01 per cent on transactions of derivatives (European Commission 2011). Moreover, the taxes would have to be paid by both partners in the transaction, the buyer and the seller. Although the EC wants to use the revenues of the tax – which it estimates to be about €57 billion per year – to build an independent EU budget, it is interesting to note that 'limiting the undesirable market behaviour and thereby stabilizing markets' is one of the key objectives of the tax (European Commission 2011: 4). This shows that the EC is now distancing itself from the 'efficient market hypothesis' that has shaped the neo-liberal policies of the EU over the past three decades.

There are, nevertheless, two crucial caveats that are highly pertinent from a new constitutionalism perspective. First, spot currency transactions are excluded from the proposed FTT with the justification that these financial transactions are important for citizens and non-financial corporations. But the most important reason to exclude these transactions is the need to make the FTT compatible with the quasi-constitutional EU principle of free capital mobility. In accordance with the concern of the ECB about the legality of a currency transaction tax, the EC thus specified in its proposal that 'currency transactions on spot markets are outside the scope [of the] FTT, which preserves the free movement of capital' (2011: 8). Therefore, 'the Commission is adopting the standard central bank and financial sector interpretation, which questions the compatibility of a currency transaction tax with the EU Treaty freedoms' (Patomäki 2012). Second, the principle of unanimity in EU decision-making grants member states an effective veto power to block proposals of positive integration such as the FTT, making it very hard for EU policy-making to go beyond the lowest-common-denominator level of the British variant of Anglo-Saxon neo-liberalism (Hay et al. 1999). The UK has fiercely resisted the EC proposal and wants by all means to prevent an EU-wide tax from undermining the global competitiveness of the City. The UK minister of finance dubbed the FTT proposal 'a bullet aimed at the heart of London' (Barker 2011). Unsurprisingly, an alliance of City bankers stirred up this British concern:

> The UK has the largest financial derivatives market in the world, with an average daily turnover in interest rate derivatives of just over US$1.4 trillion, equivalent to 45.8 percent of the total. It is hard to comprehend how such a reduction of this business would not significantly affect the UK economy. (Knight et al. 2012)

At the time of writing (November 2012) it seems that 11 countries within the Eurozone will proceed with the FTT without – amongst others – the UK (European Commission 2012). The 11 expressed their will to introduce the FTT, as it was proposed by the EC in September 2011, through the formula of 'enhanced cooperation'. This formula allows a group of at least nine EU member states to move ahead with an initiative on which it proves impossible to reach unanimity. To do so, they must have the consent of both the European Parliament and a qualified majority of the European Council (which includes all EU member states). After these two bodies have authorized the procedure of enhanced cooperation, the road to the FTT lies open. As such, the hurdle of the principle of unanimity might be overcome through a geographically more restricted FTT.

As for the problem of tax arbitrage with (amongst others) the FTT-excluded City of London, this might be addressed – according to the EC – by the obligation of both parties of a financial transaction to pay the tax, which would force British banks to pay the tax for their London-based trades with continental European banks. Thus, the EC believes 'London will lose out' because 'the tax is designed in such a way that it does not matter where the transactions are taking place' (Barker 2011). To sum up, it seems that both the material and – importantly for the purpose of this chapter – institutional constraints that have held back the introduction of an FTT within the EU may in the end be overcome, although the geographically very limited tax remains far removed from a global tax on the financial sector.

Taxing the capital of wealthy citizens

Financial globalization has also made it much harder for national states to tax the capital of individuals. There is evidence of widespread tax-inspired capital flight, to which governments have responded by tax competition. An alternative approach for states reluctant to reduce their taxes on capital income is enforcing the residence principle on an extraterritorial basis. This principle, which most countries in the world seek to apply, means that a national citizen is taxed upon his/her worldwide income (Genschel and Schwarz 2011). The crisis has visibly strengthened governments' determination to target and pull back taxable cross-border capital income and to strengthen international cooperation for this purpose. Nevertheless, a set of institutional factors at various levels continue to impede a full restoration of states' tax authority. At the heart of the matter is the institution of banking secrecy in dozens of countries and dependent territories, the so-called 'tax havens' in particular. Bank secrecy laws should be conceptualized as an important element of the project of new constitutionalism. In most cases bank secrecy is so deeply entrenched as an institution that it is qualitatively different from, for example, laws setting the tax rates. In most tax havens secrecy is the core around which a large financial industry has developed to become a dominant sector in the national economy. Given this strategic importance, a political consensus vehemently protects the institution of secrecy against internal subversion and external attacks. This also explains its long-term stability: Swiss banking secrecy, for instance, has been enshrined in criminal law since 1934 (Palan *et al.* 2010).

In a globalized world, banking secrecy in particular countries is an institutional factor foreign states need to reckon with, yet several forms of cooperation and strategies are employed to protect the latter's tax bases. The most far-reaching international arrangement is the EU Savings Tax Directive (EUSTD), which since 2005 provides for a system of automatic exchange of information amongst, the member states with regard to interest income of EU citizens. By exception, two EU tax havens, Austria and Luxembourg, are allowed to levy a withholding tax and transfer the revenue to the respective resident states, while preserving the anonymity of the investor. The EU managed to exact a similar withholding tax system from third countries, notably Switzerland, Liechtenstein, Andorra, Monaco and San Marino. The EUSTD required 14 years of struggle to become a reality. The idea was put on the agenda at the end of the 1980s to address fears of massive tax arbitrage and competition at the time the European Community decided to liberalize the movement of capital in the internal market. The difficulty of international tax cooperation in the context of the principle of unanimity in the EU Council in order to address tax competition amongst member states is a clear example of 'market-preserving federalism' as discussed by Adam Harmes in Chapter 9 of this volume: a regulatory and politico-institutional mismatch between national systems of taxation and a fully liberalized regional capital market. One might argue that the EUSTD could only get unanimous approval because of its inherent flaws: trusts and various kinds of bonds, which are equivalent to interest income, are exempted whereas dividends and capital gains are not covered at all (for an account of the decision-making process, see Sharman 2008). In 2008 the EC submitted a legislative proposal to amend the EUSTD in order to address a few important loopholes concerning equivalents of interest income, yet Austria and Luxembourg have effectively stalled the revision process. Furthermore, the EC also reports capital flight toward financial centres such as Hong Kong and Singapore, with which agreement is unlikely. As such, significant deficiencies have undermined the effectiveness of the EUSTD.

Another problem is that the EU-regional effort is not supported at the global level by similar arrangements to curb tax competition and evasion. While since the end of the 1990s the Organisation for Economic Co-operation and Development (OECD) has attempted to bring overseas tax havens in line with its standard for information exchange *upon request*, it is required for national tax inspectors to have at least strong suspicion of tax evasion by the individual taxpayer on whom information is requested; random requests or 'fishing expeditions' are ruled out by the OECD standard. This makes it a much weaker standard than the EU norm of *automatic* information exchange. Although the OECD initially envisaged a globally coordinated action against non-cooperative jurisdictions, it was eventually forced – under various pressures – to launch a much watered-down initiative: the 'Global Forum on Taxation', in which OECD members and tax havens discuss on an equal basis how to evolve toward a 'level playing field' (Sharman 2006).

However, the simultaneous occurrence of tax scandals pitting Switzerland and Liechtenstein against the United States and Germany, and the global financial crisis, induced a radicalization of the positions of Berlin, Paris and Washington. A clampdown on tax havens – now again with a threat of concerted sanctions – became a priority of the G20 summitry that started in 2008. Because the G20 fully adopted the OECD standard for the renewed blacklisting exercise, most tax havens swiftly consented to the standard and engaged in bilateral agreements for tax information exchange with other countries. The Global Forum was expanded with all members of the G20 and a few other countries. But at the same time, the endorsement of the OECD norm by the G20 clearly underscored the limited effectiveness of the approach: non-universal application of the standard has caused relocation of capital between havens, whereas tax havens have raised legal and administrative barriers to genuine information exchange (Johannesen and Zucman 2012; Meinzer 2012). Despite these problems, the OECD secretariat and various member states refuse to consider the more effective norm of automatic information exchange. Overhauling the existing consensus in the OECD, Global Forum and G20 requires an extraordinary and powerful majority. From the perspective of new constitutionalism, this status quo can be viewed as a path dependency in favour of the long-standing yet suboptimal norm of the predominant multilateral institution in this domain. Yet, at its 2012 summit in Los Cabos, Mexico, the G20 spoke out in favour of automatic information exchange (G20 2012). It remains to be seen, though, whether and to what extent this norm will be implemented in the G20 and OECD zones, and how it will be enforced vis-à-vis tax havens.

Financial globalization, banking secrecy and the numerous obstacles to intergovernmental tax cooperation are not insurmountable, however. Because tax evasion cannot be legitimized on ideational grounds and only a few wealthy citizens will emigrate for tax reasons, the residence principle remains a powerful asset for extraterritorial tax enforcement. In past years, (former) employees of financial firms in Luxembourg, Switzerland and Liechtenstein leaked data concerning thousands of wealthy taxpayers to their respective home country authorities. Countries such as Germany even paid for this kind of information. Furthermore, the United States puts pressure on individual banks in Switzerland, such as UBS, to provide financial details on US citizens, threatening those banks with sanctions. With the Foreign Account Tax Compliance Act (FATCA), the United States is standardizing its approach of putting the onus on individual banks at a global scale (Anonymous 2012). But the United States can only achieve this because of its market power. Theoretically, the EU could follow suit, but countries such as Luxembourg and Austria will presumably not agree. The sanction part of the policy, which would probably raise legal internal market issues in the EU, prevents individual EU members from going it alone. A FATCA-like approach is not an option to smaller and developing countries at all. For the latter, effective taxation depends indeed on a robust multilateral framework based on automatic information exchange.

Corporate taxation

Change in the realm of corporate taxation is even more difficult to achieve. The residence principle is harder to enforce in this domain, even after the legitimate taxing rights of the host countries of foreign direct investment – i.e. the source principle – are taken into account by means of bilateral treaties to avoid double taxation. Just like individuals, companies can shift taxable income to lower-tax jurisdictions. But the threat to move their residence as well is more realistic and consequential. The exit option is supported by a powerful discourse in favour of maintaining national competitiveness. States have responded by designing more favourable tax regimes and by engaging in tax competition. Unilateral policies to curb tax arbitrage by companies obviously face significant competitive limits in a world of free capital mobility and free trade (Genschel and Schwarz 2011).

Multilateral harmonization setting a minimum level of corporate taxation is the only solution to reverse the trend. But tax havens and countries with particular economic disadvantages disproportionally benefit from tax competition, whereas other governments reject multilateral efforts on interest-related and ideological grounds. New constitutionalism supports them by having codified neo-liberal regional integration and globalization without any multilateral arrangement to diminish tax competition. In the EU, tax harmonization of this type requires unanimity. For several member states it remains out of the question. Without rate harmonization, the proposed Common Consolidated Corporate Tax Base (CCCTB) directive to enable multinationals to submit only one tax file in the EU (still subject to 27 national rates according to the location of activities) is a mere exercise in internal market completion. Existing tools of the EC, such as rules to combat special tax regimes for multinationals, have been circumvented by non-discriminatory, economy-wide corporate tax reduction.

At the global level, the international community is stuck with a suboptimal regime to avoid double- and under-taxation on multinational profits between their income's residence and source countries. This regime is again largely governed by the OECD, based on its model bilateral tax treaty. In this domain, the OECD enjoys a historical first-mover advantage (Rixen 2011a). The rich countries have prevented the United Nations from playing a larger role in international tax cooperation (Lesage *et al.* 2010). Critics argue that the OECD standard favours residence countries (mostly advanced countries) over source states (mostly developing countries) (Government of India 2012). Furthermore, the OECD issues authoritative guidelines to governments concerning the valuation for tax purposes of cross-border trade between entities of the same multinational group. The complicated 'transfer pricing' guidelines follow the so-called 'at arm's length' principle, which means that the branches and subsidiaries of the company should be dealt with separately, as if the transactions occurred between unrelated parties. According to opponents, this approach provides ample opportunities for tax evasion and avoidance, because companies are still able to manipulate certain transfer prices, in particular for intangibles such as intellectual property rights, trademarks and marketing studies, which are hard to compare to regular market transactions. This enables them to artificially shift profits to tax havens.

An alternative approach would be 'unitary taxation' with apportionment per country through a formula that reflects genuine economic activity. This would facilitate tax enforcement by more adequately acknowledging the economic reality of a transnational corporation (Rixen 2011b). But here as well it seems politically hard to relinquish a well-entrenched and globally adopted OECD standard. The strong international adherence to the OECD standards in tax, backed by business interests in various countries, is an indication of the 'paradoxical strength of soft law'. It demonstrates 'that the challenge of globalization to the nation state, which is often conceptualized as an exogenous pressure, is (often) endogenously produced by prior institutional choices on the international level' (Rixen 2011a: 220–1). In sum, forces of international tax competition, and the interest configurations, ideational constructs and institutional environments that support them, have thus far proven more powerful than the indignation and the budgetary degeneration created by the global financial crisis. Public pressure against under-taxation of transnational business is building up, however. In 2012, the UK and Germany put the issue on the agenda of the G20 (Houlder 2012). It remains to be seen how seriously leaders and ministers will take the issue, and to what extent international collective action problems will be overcome.

Conclusion

At the level of discourse, the idea has gained ground that the financial sector should contribute more to the post-crisis clean-up and to global public goods. Tax havens are now fiercely criticized by both governments and international organizations such as the OECD. However, change on the ideational front is poorly translated into substantial policy change. The main reason is that change is blocked within institutions, while this is the only route to transformative policies given the fact that the crisis has not undermined the power of capital in a fundamental way. In spite of the global financial crisis, both new constitutionalism and the absence of a general ideational backlash against free capital mobility continue to lend political stability to financial and economic globalization. In such a context, multilateral cooperation through the EU, OECD, G20 and/or UN is the only way to break the status quo on taxation. But also in these bodies new constitutionalist elements provide for stability. While a consensus in the G20 is far away, introducing an FTT in the EU requires unanimity. This hurdle may be overcome through the formula of enhanced cooperation, but this implies that a small and arguably suboptimal group of only 11 EU member states will introduce the FTT. The revision process of the EUSTD is equally crippled by unanimity requirements. The G20 and OECD, in their turn, are stuck to a path dependency revolving around a suboptimal standard of information exchange upon request. As a result, a domestic component of new constitutionalism, that is the very deeply entrenched banking secrecy laws in Switzerland and other tax havens, survives despite external attacks; only unilateral US policy seems able to erode it in a partial way. In the realm of corporate taxation, the OECD-centred regimes against double taxation and transfer price manipulation do not allow for an effective response against tax arbitrage by companies and tax competition between states. For the time being, the political majorities needed to overhaul these conditions do not exist.

Part V

Social reproduction, welfare and ecology

Part V addresses the general question: how far and in what ways has the emergent global extension of neo-liberal market civilization, locked in by new constitutional mechanisms, reconstituted some of our basic socioeconomic and ecological conditions of existence? The contributions explore how restructuring of these conditions amidst ongoing crises has deepened contradictions, inequalities and insecurities, and raised fundamental concerns over social reproduction and ecological sustainability, provoking new patterns of resistance and challenges to disciplinary neo-liberalism. The principal themes of Part V are:

1. How – in the context of global organic crisis and the intensification of social inequalities – the restructuring of systems of social reproduction is linked to more 'regressive' and unjust tax systems in ways that are generating significant constraints on expenditures for health and care, welfare and education ('fiscal squeeze'), developments that are partly the result of the global extension of new constitutional measures.
2. How the proliferation of private debt in the United States relates to the erosion of welfare and transformations in social reproduction, and how in response the US legal apparatus has strengthened coercive governance via criminalization and incarceration of debtors.
3. How, nevertheless, new 'constitutions' of the social emerge in complex, variegated and uneven ways through neo-liberalization processes.
4. How the current global financial crisis impacts on social policy regimes.
5. How the tension between neo-liberal new constitutionalism and the ethical-normative principles required for sustainable and just ecological governance, especially in light of climate change, is posing urgent threats to humanity.

Chapter 13 by Isabella Bakker advances the book's discussions about the interconnection between new constitutionalism and social reproduction, linking it with neo-liberal reform of global tax regimes (see also

Chapter 12 by Lesage *et al.*). Bakker argues that neo-liberal fiscal policy is highly regressive (it redistributes income upwards) and indeed, it reflects key aspects of 'the deep organic crisis of capital accumulation and social reproduction' today. The recent reform of global tax regimes has also gone with the tendency toward privatization of social programmes while heightening inequalities, although perhaps paradoxically, the deep crisis of accumulation may have opened 'spaces of resistance to neo-liberal policies' that can be linked to the pursuit of more just and democratically accountable tax and expenditure regimes and the democratic remaking of the 'real constitution', a term used by Harry Arthurs (2007: 56) to capture the mechanisms that constitute 'the steep gradient of wealth and power that determines so much in our society'.

In this context, Bakker draws attention to the changing conditions of social reproduction which she defines as follows: 'Feminist political economists see social reproduction as involving fundamental social processes and institutions that are part of the intergenerational mechanisms and activities through which communities are reproduced and develop over time – and upon which all production and exchange ultimately rest.' Bakker then draws our attention to the broader and changing conditions of social reproduction and their links to new constitutional measures associated with governmental and juridical shifts to promote both the expansion of markets and greater market disciplines. These shifts – as well as the development of offshore tax havens and other mechanisms that allow capital to escape taxes – have tended to go with more regressive systems of taxation in ways that have resulted in fiscal squeezes – states' tax revenues tend to be reduced by international capital mobility. Fiscal squeeze in both global North and South thus tends to constrain states' capacities for social redistribution and welfare. Related developments concern:

1. Attempts by states and capital to create and expand liberal capitalist markets, a process that has gone with the transformation of traditional livelihoods and the replacement of collective rights with private property rights; and
2. Formation of new markets through active strategies of continuous enclosure (currently exemplified by the practices of 'land grabs', often involving the sale of public lands to private investors as a result of fiscal squeeze). (See also Chapter 3 in this volume).

These developments extend and deepen the penetration of capitalist private property relations and commodification into social activities heretofore protected from the capitalist market.

Such developments have tended to (re-)privatize key aspects of social reproduction in a complex set of shifts that include:

1. The *naturalization* of social reproduction, e.g. care work is treated as if it is natural for it to occur within the household. (This development is also accompanied by the commodification of care work and the rising transnational migration of female careworkers.)
2. *Informalization*, that is 'normalizing the informal modes of social reproduction' in the household and reconstituting responsibility for social reproduction on an individualized rather than on a collective basis.
3. *Commercialization*, e.g. treating life forms as private intellectual property that can be bought and sold by corporations; the buying and selling of human body parts as commodities; the growth of commercial surrogacy.

Many of these developments are deeply controversial, and it is partly in this context that Bakker discusses potentials for new spaces of resistance and for the remaking of the 'real constitution' of power and potentials in our societies. Growing and extreme inequality in the OECD countries has mobilized movements such as Occupy Wall Street (OWS), which aims to challenge 'the richest 1% of people that are writing the rules of an unfair global economy'. OWS is but one of many such movements worldwide that share similar concerns. For Bakker, what is crucial is that such forces focus their challenges on key aspects of public policy, for example to challenge regressive tax systems and to ameliorate 'the most immediate crises of social reproduction' by removal of the fiscal squeeze on expenditures for health, education and care. What is needed is to make systems of public finance and taxation 'more democratically accountable through popular participation in budget formulation and auditing'. This requires binding means by which states will be held responsible for 'directing financial resources toward the realization of human rights and gender equity'.

In Chapter 14, Adrienne Roberts looks in detail into the reconfiguration of both the state and social reproduction in the case of the United States. She argues that the new constitutionalist project has reconstituted US legal architectures to underpin market-based frameworks of power and accumulation. Similar to Isabella Bakker, she considers this to have undergirded a shift toward the (re-)privatization of social reproduction and the individualization of welfare provisioning, a development particularly associated with the rise of private debt amongst American households over the past several decades.

Roberts highlights how the acceleration in (private) debt in the United States has stemmed, in part, from the neo-liberal drive to reprivatize the means of financing social reproduction – given the erosion of its national welfare programmes for housing, education and particularly healthcare. The debt problem is inextricably linked to inequality: growing individual and household debt has not only disproportionately impacted low-income debtors across US society but also deepened economic and social inequalities and insecurity along lines of class, gender and race.

Roberts then outlines how the US state's legal and criminal apparatuses endorse fundamentally private debt relations by compelling debtors to discipline and regulate themselves under credit obligations, in ways that strengthen the power of capital. Significant changes were made to US bankruptcy laws in 2005 as a response to the upsurge of default on debt in ways that transferred the burden of bankruptcy from creditors to borrowers (debtors). The measures:

1. Abolished the rights of debtors to choose their bankruptcy and repayment options;
2. Mandated a procedure to specify the amount of future earnings to be used for repayment;
3. Significantly increased the cost of declaring bankruptcy; and
4. Extended the period that individuals must wait between tax filings, making it much more difficult to file for bankruptcy.

The pro-creditor orientation of the legislation perpetuates the 'ideology that views unsustainable levels of debt and bankruptcy as a result of the irresponsible behaviour of borrowers'. Furthermore, this ideology is firmly rooted in the intensified criminalization and incarceration of low-income debtors who fail to comply with the individualized norms of self-discipline.

Nevertheless the coercive debt collection practices that have stemmed from these changes have been subject to various forms of contestation and resistance, in ways that raise critical questions about the sustainability of the debt mechanism as a principal means of mediating the ongoing tensions between capitalist accumulation and social reproduction. This has generated new spaces to challenge the (re-)privatization and individualization of welfare provisioning under new constitutionalism and disciplinary neo-liberalism.

Janine Brodie, in Chapter 15, also emphasizes the importance of growing inequality and she sheds light on some of the complex, uneven and still unfolding linkages between new constitutionalism, neo-liberalism and social policy in the contemporary global era. Brodie underlines how neo-liberalism should be understood as not 'a monolithic governing formula' but as various '*processes of neo-liberalization*, which have unfolded in "sporadic wave-like non-linear sequences" in the past three decades and more'. She argues that neo-liberalization processes have therefore brought about the new 'constitutions' of the social, as a consequence of a flurry of policy experiments that, though mediated by national histories and path dependencies, bear strong cross-national resemblances.

Indeed, Brodie demonstrates how prevailing theoretical predictions about the impact of economic globalization on social policy regimes, including the dominant race-to-the-bottom thesis, are inconsistent with mixed evidence drawn from comprehensive studies of public social expenditures in the metropolitan capitalist countries over the recent decades of neo-liberal governance. Indeed, her review of the empirical evidence concerning aggregate data pertaining to social spending shows their insufficiencies in capturing accurately how the neo-liberalization processes diminish post-war welfare states and reinvent new social initiatives or programmes. She maintains, following the argument put forward in Chapter 8 by Brenner *et al.*, that the neo-liberalization processes can therefore be characterized as 'uneven, variegated and reactive forms of regulation' while at the same time they generate many similarities in the reconstitution of social policy. Neo-liberal resemblances not only often interlock with administrative mechanisms but also undermine the core ideals of 'the citizen–state bargain of post-war social liberalism', thereby 'transform[ing], amongst other things, individual subjectivities, the prerogatives of citizenship, and social wellbeing, broadly defined'. The permeation of the neo-liberalization processes into social policy reforms includes erasing, subjugating, privatizing and, most importantly, 'fiscalizing' what were formerly public goods and services.

Brodie then reflects on interconnections between social policy and neo-liberalism in the aftermath of the 2008 global financial crisis. Since mid 2010, most G20 governments have attempted to achieve deficit and debt reduction by relying on what appears to be an oxymoron: 'expansionary austerity ... a strategy that effectively obliges citizens to pay for the Great Recession's massive bailouts of financial institutions and unprecedented stimulus packages *with* their social programmes and public services'. Social policies and social wellbeing are thus threatened as much by the outright failures of neo-liberalism as its successes. Nonetheless, the rapid spread of public austerity programmes and the resulting protests have 'moved social policy from the footnotes to the front page of contemporary neo-liberal governance'. This has prompted international networks and financial institutions to 'rethink the role of social policy in sustaining economic growth and social stability'. Paradoxically, as Brodie suggests, it may be the revival of robust social regimes that emerge as a result of new patterns of resistance and political organization pressing for greater social protection that may permit neo-liberal globalism to reinvent itself in the wake of the current Great Recession.

In Chapter 16, Hilal Elver looks at relationships between social reproduction and the environment, and specifically explores the contentious relationship between the new constitutionalism and the ethical-normative principles that are required for the sustainable and just governance of the environment. Her chapter complements and advances the analyses presented by Cutler and Sinclair in Chapters 3 and 11 respectively.

While, on the one hand, ecological problems, such as biological diversity and climate change, have been widely recognized as urgent trans-border concerns within the contemporary context of neo-liberal economic globalization, on the other, the global expansion of new constitutionalism since the 1980s has strengthened multinational corporations' access to markets, labour and resources by progressively eliminating 'impediments', i.e. the very legal measures created by states for the purpose of environmental and health protection. Neo-liberal new constitutionalism therefore locks in this situation, while simultaneously promoting the widening of market-based solutions to environmental and ecological challenges.

Elver shows how market-based legal reforms, which aim to secure and legitimate the transitional mobility of capital and investment, have resulted in a deterioration in the management of natural resources and brought about serious damages or risks to human health, especially in the developing countries that have 'very little manoeuvring space' because of their dependency on the global financial institutions. This 'new environmental colonialism' involves how developing countries have been targeted as places for 'the export of hazardous wastes and the relocation of the most polluted industries such as chemical factories'. She elaborates the increasing power and influence of multinational corporations on ecological governance by drawing attention to:

1. The corporate lobby's promotion of 'soft law' associated with 'voluntary codes of conduct' for business practices;
2. The replacement of the traditional 'command and control' mechanisms with market-based policy instruments to regulate environmental protection; and
3. The creation of 'hybrid institutions' through public–private partnerships as the new governing bodies for resource management, whose primary aim is 'to control and dominate the regulatory framework in favour of international business'.

Nevertheless, recently emerging ecological challenges against humanity and, in particular, the adverse impacts of climate change on people's everyday lives across the globe have made clear the ineffectiveness and/or dysfunction of the neo-liberal governing strategies of voluntary self-regulation and market-based solutions. As Elver notes, the United Nations cannot provide the global legal remedies to address these urgent issues because of its state-centric orientation and subordination to geopolitical and geo-economic pressures. However, by identifying possible options to combat climate change, she underlines that to protect the present and future ecology of the world requires a new global environmental law – consistent with Richard Falk's concept of a 'just new constitutionalism' outlined in Chapter 18. The new law should be based upon cosmopolitan and humanitarian norms of justice and equity, and go beyond narrowly defined national interests. It would be administered and constituted through political processes involving 'transparent, democratic and participatory institutional frameworks'.

13 Social reproduction, fiscal space and remaking the real constitution

Isabella Bakker

This chapter explores links between new constitutionalist frameworks, neo-liberal market rationality and changing conditions of social reproduction, with particular reference to the role of fiscal policy. It also argues that in an era of heightened inequality involving greater privatization of social provisioning, neo-liberal new constitutionalism is meeting growing forms of resistance that can be related to contemporary struggles over the remaking of economic policy and constitutional forms.

Introduction

A key aspect of the *longue durée* of capitalism involves externalizing the costs of social reproduction through offloading them to households, especially onto the unpaid labour of women (Picchio 1991). In the OECD region (Organisation for Economic Co-operation and Development), this process has been marked by resistance to privatization of social reproduction, often resulting in its greater socialization through the public sector.

Thus the Keynesian period represented a political effort to create greater public provisioning of social reproduction through a broad-based, progressive tax regime and rising wages (see Chapter 15 by Janine Brodie). However, recent neo-liberal public policies have reversed this commitment, with uneven erasure and privatization of social programmes, public goods and services. New constitutional forms of governance, e.g. balanced-budget laws that constrain types of government economic intervention ('fiscal space'), limit capacities for social redistribution and welfare, and tend to promote more privatized systems.

These changes have been compounded by a shift in the governing 'common sense' away from the social liberalism of the Keynesian period toward a more neo-liberal sensibility (Brodie 2007a). As Brown observes, neo-liberalism involves a distinct form of political rationality and a (radical) cultural/ideological project: it aims not only at reconfiguring the human being as *homo œconomicus* but at ensuring that 'all dimensions of human life are cast in terms of a market rationality' (2005: 40).

This recasting of not only everyday life but also political reforms in terms of market rationality means states' capacities to support social reproduction are being squeezed ideologically and literally: loss of state revenues due to internal tax shifts toward more regressive tax regimes and by trade and investment liberalization (allowing for greater mobility of capital, which becomes harder to tax). The significance of linking new constitutionalist measures to social reproduction becomes more evident:

> The significance of new constitutionalism for social reproduction becomes highlighted when one considers the relationship between on the one hand, mobile capital (e.g. the investment and disinvestment power of multinational corporations) and, on the other, the nature of production and reproduction of territorially based communities. Capital relies on the state and the legal order to ensure its conditions of existence and potential for accumulation. But when it is fully mobile between jurisdictions, capital may exercise social power relatively independently of particular communities. (Bakker and Gill 2008: 22)

Indeed, evidence on reforms of national tax regimes suggests that they have responded to, and reinforced the structural power of capital, paradoxically, often to forestall investment strikes and capital flights (see also Chapter 12, this volume). This fiscal squeeze on governments has heightened inequality and emphasized privatization of social reproduction.

So what is social reproduction? And what is its significance for political economy? Feminist political economists see social reproduction as involving fundamental social processes and institutions that are part of the intergenerational mechanisms and activities through which communities are reproduced and develop over time – and upon which all production and exchange ultimately rest. Outside of subsistence economies and in the context of ever-expanding neo-liberal global markets, social reproduction depends on some form of incomes which may be in the form of wages, transfers by governments, access to arable lands for small-scale farming or informal sector activities (Picchio 1991). Thus many of the insecurities that are inherent in capitalist labour markets, and other forms of access to money, are absorbed, mediated and managed at the household level. At the same time, labour power as a produced input of labour processes is constituted, reproduced and socialized in the household. In this sense, the lens of social reproduction offers a more holistic view of political economy – shifting the concept of 'the economy' away from merely market forces, relations or measures toward a more ample and dynamic understanding. This includes institutions (and social relations) that provide for socialization of risk, healthcare, education – indeed, many of the key elements of what Marx referred to as 'species being': social institutions that distinguish the life of human beings from that of animals (Bakker and Gill 2003: 18).

Discussions of social reproduction in the 1970s and 1980s focused on women's domestic labour as subsidizing capitalist reproduction under Fordism. Today, concepts reflect the increasingly privatized and marketized forms of social provisioning and risk that characterize the neo-liberal moment where everyday activities of maintaining life and reproducing the next generation are increasingly being realized through the unpaid and paid resources of (largely) women – as states withdraw or reduce their support for public provisioning. The Organisation for Economic Co-operation and Development (OECD) governments spend about 13 per cent of gross domestic product (GDP) on public social services, which is the same as all cash benefits (entitlements/transfers) taken together (OECD 2011b). These public social services and entitlements are at risk in the new politics of fiscal austerity that has followed from the global financial crisis that started in 2008.[1] Hence, the renewed focus on social reproduction seeks to place its costs at the centre of an analysis of the capitalist system of accumulation, relating it to questions of how economic surplus is produced, distributed and consumed (Bakker 2007; Elson 1997). The lens of social reproduction also clarifies questions of material living standards and wellbeing in the context of how neo-liberal disciplines are radically reordering social life and relations. Here, we see a further paradox: on the one hand, market wages increasingly reflect people's access to income as government transfers and services are reduced through fiscal austerity. On the other hand, time taken for producing for one's own consumption and that of others is a significant contributor to overall material living standards. The OECD's *Society at a Glance 2011: OECD Social Indicators* devotes a chapter to unpaid work inside and outside of households. The study finds that the value of unpaid work is considerable, amounting to about one-third of GDP in OECD countries. In all countries, women were found to do more unpaid work than men to the tune of an average 2.5 hours per day, although this was partly offset, varying across countries, by the fact that women do less market work (OECD 2011b: 24). This trend has implications for overall tax revenues collected, women's lifetime income security, pensions and more broadly, for the extent to which the work of care and social reproduction shapes choices and opportunities.

---

[1] A striking indicator of this is *The Financial Times* site devoted to 'Austerity Europe' with the header: 'Europeans are braced for a new age of austerity as governments across the region take action to eliminate unsustainable budget deficits' (www.ft.com/indepth/austerity-in-europe).

With these considerations in mind, this chapter begins with attention to two sets of new constitutionalist measures related to social reproduction:

1. Measures that reconfigure governments and constitutional forms to operate under greater market discipline; and
2. Measures by governments and capital to construct and extend liberal capitalist markets, promoting commodification and capital accumulation.

The final section of this chapter provides examples of how the deep organic crisis of capital accumulation and social reproduction is provoking new spaces of resistance to neo-liberal policies.

New constitutionalism, social reproduction and fiscal squeeze

Here I discuss measures noted above relating to not only internal governmental and juridical shifts within states but also to external mechanisms, such as investment and trade treaties that have constitutional status for their signatories (e.g. those that created the World Trade Organization and the North American Free Trade Agreement). Such institutional and legal innovations 'provide not only rights of entry and establishment to capital in foreign jurisdiction, that is to new markets and territories, but also to the provision of exit options' (Gill 2000: 12). Other key mechanisms are laws mandating balanced budgets and independent central banks. The latter are now committed to publicly specified inflation targeting as the centrepiece of monetary policy (as opposed to the promotion of full employment as was the case in the Keynesian social liberal era). In many cases they have locked in the anti-inflation bias by statute. In practice, this has served to insulate the making of much of economic policy from legislative or popular accountability and control.

Several implications for social reproduction can be drawn from these governance shifts. The first relates to *fiscal squeeze*, a direct result of shifts in global tax regimes and the declining contribution of corporate taxes to public goods and collective social provisioning. Thus the prevailing trend toward increasing liberalization of trade and finance makes mobile capital much more difficult to tax; offshore mechanisms allow many corporations and wealthy investors to avoid taxes, undermining the tax base of governments. Transnational corporations also have a long history of evading taxes through complex accounting measures, such as transfer pricing, which locate the losses and profits of their activities in the most favourable jurisdictions where taxes are lowest. At the same time, there has been intense tax competition between different jurisdictions as capital has become more mobile. To attract such capital, countries must provide a favourable investment climate, which inevitably means lower corporate tax rates as well as enormous subsidies and tax holidays for new investments. As a means of broadening the tax base under these circumstances, many governments throughout the world have shifted to indirect taxes, such as value added taxes, which are 'regressive' in so far as they exact the same amount of tax per transaction on each consumer irrespective of that person's income level, whether that person is a low-income worker or a billionaire. These taxes are also regressive since poorer people spend a greater proportion of their income on everyday necessities such as food, fuel and housing (Gill and Bakker 2011).

These more global trends can be directly linked to developments in the United States. Grunberg notes that the 1986 US Tax Reform influenced all OECD countries in a number of significant ways:

1. The US tax base was broadened to simultaneously remove many tax privileges and exemptions but also to include low-income families in the tax base;
2. A dramatic reduction of the very top direct tax rates ensued; and
3. Fewer tax brackets were established in contrast to the old system.

The result was the income tax structure overall became much less progressive (Grunberg 1998: 595–6). The change toward more regressive systems of taxation can be described as a 'double shift': on the one hand, a reduction in the highest corporate income tax rates and less direct taxes for upper income earners and, on the other, an increasing reliance on broad-based indirect taxes such as value added taxes (VAT), which are regressive: people must pay these taxes on daily goods and services irrespective of their income level.[2] In reality, this means that those at the lower end of the income scale pay a greater proportion of their total income in taxes than does a well-off person. More than 125 countries now rely on some form of VAT and it is the backbone of revenue systems in most of the world (Bickley 2011; Grown 2010). This double shift in tax regimes is a key contributor to rising income inequalities. Furthermore, in low-income countries, from 1970 to 1998, import and export taxes as a share of total taxes decreased on average from 40 per cent to 35 per cent.

---

[2] I want to thank Stephen Gill for this insight. In future work I will link this double shift in taxation to the intensification of the double burden of many women in paid and unpaid work.

In sum, fiscal squeeze both in the global North and South has reduced governments' revenues, and states have tended to cut capital expenditures on infrastructure. This is also in the context of debt servicing to bond holders being treated as sacrosanct so that social expenditures are cut rather than interest payments on government debts. Currently, 75 per cent of the global population does not have access to social guarantees that allow them to cope with livelihood risks. Some recent statistical findings from the International Labour Organization (ILO) illustrate the coverage gaps in social security systems (defined by the ILO as income security plus availability of medical care). On average, 17.2 per cent of global gross domestic product (GDP) is allocated to social security but these expenditures are largely concentrated in high-income countries (ILO 2011: 3). Nearly one-third of the world has no access to any health facilities or services at all, while for many others, personal expenditure on health may cause financial catastrophe since they have no adequate social health protection; worldwide nearly 40 per cent of the working-age population is legally covered by old-age pension schemes, but effective coverage versus legal coverage is significantly lower – in high-income countries 75 per cent of persons over 65 years of age are receiving some kind of pension versus 20 per cent in low-income countries (*ibid.*: 2).

As noted, governments appear to have less manoeuvrability in their public finances and often prioritize international debt repayment or deficit reduction over the social spending that supports some of the work of social reproduction. In many poor developing countries, there is a lack of institutional and/or fiscal capacity to pursue effective stimulus and welfare measures (for example, in response to the 2008 global financial crisis) and often they are dependent on aid or remittances to fill shortfalls in education, health and other social programmes. The United Nations Educational, Scientific and Cultural Organization (UNESCO) estimates that there is a $16 billion annual shortfall in funding needed to meet internationally agreed development goals. As a result, social reproduction is absorbed into the unpaid sphere of (largely) women's work or, in the case of more affluent women, becomes commodified and often linked to migrant women's labour and the 'global survival circuits' that have pushed them to seek employment in the North to secure remittances for their own and their families' social reproduction (Bakker and Silvey 2008; Sassen 2002).

Monetary policies, operating in tandem with financial liberalization reforms in an effort to draw in foreign capital, also help frame the conditions for social reproduction. For example, as noted, monetary policy as exercised by central banks was, until the current crisis of accumulation, focused on price stability rather than aiming for full employment as in earlier periods (Osberg 2011). Maintaining price stability affects interest rates and exchange rates, which can have ramifications for social reproduction. Interest rates can, for instance, affect access to and affordability of housing; exchange rates can impact on the prices of food, fuel and on employment outcomes through trade effects (Balakrishnan *et al.* 2011: 19).

Expropriating the commons and extended commodification

A *second set of new constitutionalist measures* relates to efforts by states and capital to construct and extend liberal capitalist markets and to extend the potential scale and scope of commodification. There are two broad dimensions involved here that also are significant for social reproduction:

1. 'Original' or 'primitive' accumulation, which involves a range of processes whereby capitalist forms of accumulation and law (e.g. property rights) replace other systems of livelihood and property relations; and
2. Creation of new markets through the extension of private property rights and commodification (Bakker and Gill 2008).

Primitive accumulation replaces collective rights and systems of livelihood with a system of control based on the primacy of private property. As Marx and more recent critical thinkers have noted, such processes do not emerge spontaneously but are rather made possible through active strategies of enclosure of commons and the means of livelihood; in turn this increases people's dependence on capitalist markets for their social reproduction and subsistence (De Angelis 2007: 133). Rather than this being a moment in the development of capitalism, enclosures are a continuous characteristic of capital logic that makes the world through commodification. It fragments and destroys the 'commons' which are the social spheres of life affording protections from the pressures of the capitalist market. This is why the fight for 'commons' has been a historical and continuous struggle for direct access to the means of reproduction and for the self-governance of communities (Linebaugh 2008).

One current example is the 'land grabs' triggered by speculators that have intensified in the last decade.[3] This process creates new dynamics of property including the 'dispossession of land, water, forests and other common property resources; their concentration, privatization and

---

[3] A double issue of the *Journal of Peasant Studies* defines land grabbing as 'the large-scale acquisition of land or land-related rights and resources by corporate (business, non-profit or public) entities' (White *et al.* 2012: 619).

transaction as corporate (owned or leased) property; and in turn the transformation of agrarian labour regimes' (White *et al.* 2012: 620).

There are many aspects to 'land grabbing' but the focus here is on the parallel development of financialization and 'land grabs' in a conjuncture in which, according to McMichael, 'investors [generally] prefer to hold capital in liquid (rather than illiquid/asset) forms' (McMichael 2012: 688). In this context there are deepening links between investment in land and the financial markets. McMichael notes that trade in agricultural futures and other derivatives increased in 2007 by 32 per cent, and the number of futures increased by 65 per cent on the Chicago Mercantile Exchange between October 2007 and March 2008, generating the food crisis of 2007–8 and 'deepen[ing] investor attention to offshore crop-land' (2012: 689).

Far from representing a response to food riots and the need to grow food for hungry people, this land rush signals land speculation based on anticipated price increases due to increasing populations – a practice known as 'land banking'. Also, many developing countries are 'under pressure from the IMF, the World Bank and other regional banks to put farmland on the international market to increase economic development and improve the balance of payments' (Vidal 2011). In Africa, most of the land deals have been to grow crops for export and these 'unrestricted export clauses in contracts, together with small-scale food producers losing their key productive asset, may well worsen rather than improve food security' (*ibid.*). Saskia Sassen has recently documented how the expulsing of people and the destruction of traditional livelihoods are intended 'to feed the needs of high finance and the needs of natural resources' (Sassen 2010). She links her analysis to the debt burdens of the global South from the 1980s that have favoured debt repayment over basic health, education and welfare needs. She points to how financial adjustment crises lead to 'a savage sorting of winners and losers' that heighten people's expulsion from jobs and livelihoods.

As De Angelis notes, all strategies and types of enclosure share the common character of forcibly separating people from whatever access to social wealth they have, thus leaving them only with access to livelihoods mediated by capitalist markets and money as capital (De Angelis 2007: 144). The enclosing represents an immanent drive of capital that is common to different historical periods rather than representing the incorporation of pre-capitalist modes of production into capitalist relations.[4] Furthermore, enclosures can be seen as 'central to understanding the

---

[4] This discussion of enclosure and the social commons is elaborated in Gill and Bakker (2011).

dynamic flux between capitalist social relations and the household since this concept highlights contested processes that seek to channel human activity into forms compatible with the priorities of capital accumulation' (LeBaron 2011: 890).[5]

In terms of *social reproduction*, three broad shifts that signal a (re-)privatization process can be identified:

1. *Naturalization*: this involves a combination of the naturalizing of care labour within the family (represented as if it is its 'natural home') (Brodie 2003) and the increasing commodification of care work, often through transnational networks of migrant women (Folbre and Nelson 2000; Onuki 2009);
2. *Informalization*: normalizing the informal modes of social reproduction by reconstituting individual responsibility; and
3. *Commercialization*: heightened commercialization of life forms develops, for example through markets (and private property rights) for human body parts and babies.

The first shift relates to how, under neo-liberal restructuring, public provisioning of care work has been attacked and partly reprivatized thereby reducing the socialization of risk for the majority and privatizing risk at the level of the individual (Gill 1995a; Pijl 1998). The second, related shift, involves normalizing private solutions as part of a discursive shift from social citizenship to market citizenship. At the micro level, this involves a reconstitution of the self and the subject at the deepest level: this is 'the way in which bourgeois individuals are constituted; in their interaction they produce market-constructed rationality and therewith themselves' (Altvater 1993: 61). The neo-liberal approach, partly based on Hayek and Buchanan, rests on the strong protection of liberty and property rights: each person is his/her proprietor and does not owe society; civil society protects individuals from expropriation of private property through constitutional 'lock-in' mechanisms (Gill 1998b, 2000).

The third aspect of social reproduction relates to the heightened commercialization of life forms and the market for human body parts and babies: examples of the extension of private property rights by corporation and legal forms into the biological bases of social reproduction. However, the law fails to protect specialized local communal practices related to, for example, indigenous seeds and herbal potions, as forms

---

[5] There are many forms of commons unfolding outside the money/market economy led by women, the primary subjects of reproductive work, e.g. urban gardens, common kitchens and women-made banking systems, which are quite distinct from the microcredit systems promoted through the World Bank.

of both common knowledge and communal property. At the same time, the WTO's Agreement on Trade-Related Aspects of Intellectual Property Rights (TRIPS) privileges capitalized inputs and consequently the interests of large transnational corporations, allowing for such knowledge to be treated as private intellectual property. I have argued elsewhere that commercial surrogacy is a more recent example of 'new enclosure' (Benatar *et al.* 2009): it commodifies for the first time the most fundamental biological aspect of social reproduction. A woman's womb becomes the commodity that is temporarily 'rented' to yield, in this case, a child. Commercial surrogacy represents a more extreme example of what is a general condition of capitalism: that human beings become increasingly dependent on the market to satisfy human needs – and now to secure their self-reproduction (Wood 1995). Separated from the means of production through a series of new enclosures (Federici 2004; Harvey 2003: 63–88) they are increasingly tied to the commodity form and money to realize their survival and reproduction. And yet, a significant amount of care work remains outside of capitalism in the realm of unpaid work.

All these unfolding processes represent a simultaneous commodification and dispossession of common property and rights, and redefinition of social provisioning through markets or through informal, unpaid labour. While feminists critiqued the post-war male breadwinner model for its patriarchal foundations, it did partly subsidize social reproduction and by assuming a limited collective social responsibility for social reproduction through welfare states (Braedley and Luxton 2010: 15). Neo-liberal restructuring and new constitutional mechanisms as discussed above are dramatically restructuring gender, class, and social relations and forces, restructuring social reproduction away from public and collective action toward private and individual responsibility (Broomhill and Sharpe 2009).

Enlarging spaces of resistance

New constitutionalism involves mechanisms through which contestation and challenges to the neo-liberal capitalist order can be channelled to within the confines of what James Buchanan (1991) called 'ordinary politics'. Nevertheless, it is clear that the deep crisis of capital accumulation that now engages the very solvency of many states is provoking new spaces of resistance, e.g. with reference to fiscal policy.

Creating fiscal space

As implied above, the gradual erosion of the nation state as the pre-eminent space of politics has in part been a reflection of the increasing permeability of national boundaries and the constraints imposed on governments through the power of capital and new constitutionalism. These disciplinary measures constrain modes of government economic intervention ('fiscal space'), limit capacities for social redistribution and welfare, and tend to promote more privatized systems. According to the OECD (OECD 2011a), the shift in income taxes and social security contributions due to neo-liberal measures has played a major role in exacerbating income inequality in the OECD region over the last three decades, beginning first in the late 1970s and early 1980s in some Anglophone countries (e.g. the UK and the United States), followed by a more widespread increase in income inequality in other OECD countries from the late 1980s.

I have noted then that much of the recent rise in income inequality can be attributed to changes in the structural power of capital. Indeed, capital does not involve the accumulation of goods for livelihood and social wellbeing; rather it pursues profits and seeks to further its power over society, which allows it to extract social surplus. One indicator of the increased power of capital is evidence that rising inequality is associated with the rise in the 'capital share' of total income, with corresponding falls in the 'labour share' and the 'transfer share'. As the former Director of the UN University World Institute of Development Economics Research (UN-WIDER) notes:

This shift was caused by the effects of liberalization and globalization policies that weakened labour institutions, raised interest rates and interest spreads, led to insider privatization as well as rising asset concentration and rents in the financial and real estate sector, reduced progressive redistribution via the budget, and exacerbated regional disparities. (Cornia 2005: 2)

Cornia points to a number of cases where the rise in capital share has been very pronounced: e.g. in the UK and Northern Ireland (pre-2007 crisis), the income share of the top 1 per cent of the population rose from 21 per cent to 34 per cent over the period 1979–2001 (*ibid.*: 2–3). In a large majority of countries, for example, household incomes of the top 10 per cent grew faster than those of the poorest 10 per cent (OECD 2011a: 5). In fact, the average income of the richest 10 per cent in the OECD region at present is about nine times that of the poorest 10 per cent.

These trends all point to the political importance of re-examining the notion of equity in taxation and addressing the sustainability of the tax base through more progressive income redistribution, amelioration of the most immediate crises of social reproduction, and fulfilment of substantive economic and social rights commitments. This indeed has been a major focus of the Occupy Wall Street Movement and its depiction of 99 per cent vs. 1 per cent – the movement 'aims to fight back against the richest 1% of people that are writing the rules of an unfair global economy that is foreclosing on our future'.[6] A more targeted effort focused directly on socially re-embedding the tax system has been the Robin Hood Tax movement, which proposes a tax on the financial sector similar to the Tobin Tax.[7] Both movements have spread to many countries and are receiving healthy public support in favour of wealth redistribution. Support for the Robin Hood Tax came from a growing number of G20 countries at Cannes in 2011 and from the Stiglitz Commission in the United Nations.[8] The Commission suggested that certain international taxes could be earmarked for global objectives, including a carbon tax and a tax on financial transactions (UN 2009). Proposals for a global currency tax – the so-called Tobin Tax – are designed to prevent speculative manipulation of currency transactions for short-term profit and to help to sustain consistent flows of capital to less-developed countries. Revenue from such a tax could be used globally as a source for universal public provisioning of basic social services and to create a fund to realize gender equality goals. It has been suggested that a portion of the revenues could be awarded to governments for the design of gender-equitable social protection systems. The European Commission has recently called for such a Tobin-style tax on the European Union's financial sector to generate direct revenue for its first trillion-euro budget (see Chapter 12, this volume, for more detailed discussion of this proposal). Feminists also point out that a more progressive and equitable tax system needs to not only be inclusive, involving tax compliance for all, it also needs to be gender-sensitive, particularly since different taxation regimes affect men and women across the social spectrum in very different ways.[9]

Enhancing fiscal space requires systems of public finance to be made more democratically accountable through popular participation in budget formulation and auditing. Participatory budgeting initiatives, such as those originating in Porto Alegre, Brazil, connect budget analysis to advocacy work consistent with social justice and widening prosperity. This means recognizing that macroeconomic policies related to questions such as deficit repayment are also social policies that redistribute income, risk, time use and opportunity between different segments of the population. Gender budget initiatives have been particularly prominent

---

[6] http://occupywallst.org/about/ (accessed 10 June 2012).
[7] http://robinhoodtax.org/ (accessed 10 June 2012).
[8] www.salon.com/2011/10/31/how_ows_has_transformed_public_opinion/; http://robinhoodtax.org/latest/g20-verdict (accessed 10 June 2012).
[9] The latter requires support for expanding existing efforts to improve the collection of sex-disaggregated data and data on the gender bias in indirect taxes such as VAT, consumption and trade taxes.

having been launched in over 60 countries to link expressed commitments to gender equality with decisions on how governments raise and spend public monies (Bakker 2002).

Remaking the real constitution

Harry Arthurs (2007: 56) has coined the term 'the "real" constitution' by which he means 'the steep gradient of wealth and power that determines so much in our society'. He proposes that labour and other social interests (who argue for equity) will have their interests determined largely through the 'real' constitution, that is, the structure of its economy. A characteristic feature of neo-liberalism in North America has been the deeper continental integration of the Canadian economic space dominated by the United States, which has steered restructuring of economic sectors and promoted changes in the balance of power between employers and workers and in the conditions of social reproduction (*ibid.*). This has led to a mismatch of scales: a disjuncture between trade and macroeconomic policy on the one hand, and labour market and social policies on the other. Consequently, social policies and rights become secondary to the achievement of 'sound' macroeconomics as a first-order principle (Elson and Cagatay 2000). This mismatch can be found in many parts of the world and it needs to be addressed in ways that are accountable and made binding.

This need for binding forms of democratic accountability raises the issue of how '*soft law*' global regimes of human rights can be translated into *substantive and binding economic and social rights* that can be made to govern economic policies and commitments (on corresponding issues of soft and hard law with respect to ecology see Chapter 16 by Hilal Elver). Human rights have often been characterized as a form of soft power, often not taken seriously by political leaders. Richard Falk (see Chapter 18 in this volume) has consistently argued for a counter-hegemonic perspective on human rights that can take political advantage of the intergovernmental normative architecture of international human rights law. This corpus of norms he suggests can be 'ethically helpful in challenging prevailing forms of oppression and exploitation'. I wish to argue that a counter-hegemonic form of the power of rights necessarily entails the harnessing of national resources (e.g. via fiscal policies) to rights commitments. My argument suggests we need binding means by which governments will be held accountable for their obligations to fulfil economic and social rights under the United Nations Charter and international human rights covenants. These are obligations they are required to meet under international law. They are obliged to use 'maximum available resources' to deliver on economic and social rights commitments as outlined in the International Covenant on Economic, Social and Cultural Rights (UN 1966). The remaking of the real constitution should therefore be linked to not only budget expenditures but also other key economic tools that can advance the realization of human rights – monetary policy, financial sector policy, taxation and deficit financing. Such a focus relies less on the legal architecture of human rights than on the architecture of governments and central banks as the key sites for directing financial resources toward the realization of human rights and gender equity, in ways 'that are in compliance with human rights principles, such as non-discrimination, progressive realization, participation, transparency and accountability' (Balakrishnan *et al.* 2011: 4).

14 New constitutionalism, disciplinary neo-liberalism and the locking in of indebtedness in America

Adrienne Roberts

Introduction

As Stephen Gill and other critical political economists have argued, over the past three to four decades, various quasi-legal mechanisms of the 'new constitutionalism' have been used to 'lock in' political and economic reforms designed to promote fiscal discipline, a reduction of public expenditures, the privatization of state-owned enterprises, free trade, financial liberalization and other reforms associated with 'disciplinary neo liberalism' (Gill 1995a, 2008). The latter term refers to a politico-economic project that combines the direct and structural power of capital with more diffuse forms of 'capillary power' and 'panopticism' in order to compel states, social forces and individuals to conform to certain norms of behaviour. The locking in of disciplinary neo-liberalism at various sites and scales through these quasi-legal mechanisms secures the formal separation of politics and economics by limiting the policy space available to governments and progressive social forces, and by restricting the ability of governments to generate revenue (Gill 2008: 137–42).

Rather than entailing the retreat of the state, the new constitutionalism is part of the neo-liberal *restructuring* of state forms, partially through constitutional and legal means, in ways that support and extend market-based frameworks of power and accumulation. The new constitutionalism has also supported the reconstitution of the nature of social welfare and the governance of social reproduction more generally. This chapter seeks to further elucidate the ways in which the nature of social welfare has shifted under the broader frameworks of the new constitutionalism and disciplinary neo-liberalism. It also seeks to draw attention to the ways in which the state's legal apparatus, including its criminal and penal institutions, underpins market-based frameworks of power and accumulation.

Specifically, focusing on transformations taking place within the United States, this chapter makes three interrelated arguments about the nature of social change under the new constitutionalism. First, it is argued that one countervailing trend to the erosion of the welfare state has been the rise of private debt. That is, one aspect of what feminists have termed the '(re)privatization of social reproduction' (Bakker 2003) is the rise of personal debt as a privatized form of social provisioning. Second, it is argued that the state has restructured domestic legal policies in ways that lock in private debt obligations and compel individuals to discipline and regulate themselves in the interests of capital. The third overlapping argument is that when individuals fail to adhere to the norms of self-discipline, specifically, when they attempt to default on debts owed to creditors, the coercive legal and penal arms of the state are used to enforce private credit obligations. While these trends have a longer historical lineage than can be discussed here, it will be argued that they have intensified over the past decade and in the wake of the most recent global financial and economic crisis.

Rather than retaining a primary analytical focus on the specific *mechanisms* of the new constitutionalism that have been adopted by states over the past several decades, this chapter explores the ways in which contemporary forms of global governance have led to the restructuring of relations of social reproduction in ways that render them more individualized, privatized, precarious and disciplinary. This chapter then contributes to the broader political economy literature by:

1. Highlighting the tensions between capitalist accumulation and social reproduction;
2. Shedding light on the *artificial* nature of the separation of economics and politics, and the disciplinary and coercive nature of actually existing capitalism; and
3. Outlining the ways in which these processes draw upon and reproduce social insecurities and inequalities, including those based on the lines of class, gender and race.

While much of the political economy literature on the new constitutionalism and neo-liberalism more broadly tends to focus on global transformations, this chapter focuses primarily on transformations taking place within the United States. This is not to suggest that they can be understood in isolation from broader processes taking place at the global level. Rather, as will be noted below, the proliferation of private debt in the United States, the majority of which has taken the form of mortgage debt, is intricately linked to the restructuring of global macroeconomic policies. However, the social relations of debt vary considerably between countries and they are conditioned by a certain amount of path dependency. As such, it is difficult to draw generalizations from the US experience, though comparative studies have noted similarities between the rise of debt in the United States and other countries such as the UK and Canada that have relatively liberalized social welfare regimes, open financial systems and have displayed strong commitments to anti-inflationary policies (Castles 1998; Schwartz and Seabrooke 2009).

The arguments presented in this chapter are laid out in three sections. The first section argues that the rise of indebtedness in the United States is part of the broader process of the (re-)privatization of social reproduction and the individualization of forms of social provisioning. The second section focuses on the Bankruptcy Abuse Prevention and Consumer Protection Act (BAPCPA) of 2005, arguing that this legislation shares some of the features of other mechanisms of the new constitutionalism as it has strengthened the power of creditors vis-à-vis debtors and intensified the disciplinary power of capital. The third section argues that there has been an intensification of the criminalization and incarceration of debtors and a rise of coercive debt collection practices over the past decade and particularly in the years following the global financial crisis.

Debt and the reprivatization of social reproduction

As a number of critical political economists have argued in this volume (see Chapter 15 by Janine Brodie and Chapter 13 by Isabella Bakker; Bakker 2003; Bakker and Gill 2006), the new constitutionalism project has conditioned the reconstitution of the nature of social welfare and has undergirded a shift toward more market-based, privatized and individualized forms of social reproduction. Laws that require governments to maintain balanced budgets, commitments that limit a government's ability to borrow from external sources and conditions placed on loans by the international financial institutions (IFIs) that limit public spending, are just a few examples of new constitutionalist mechanisms that condition this shift toward the individualization and (re-)privatization of social reproduction. There is further evidence to suggest that some of these mechanisms have been strengthened in recent years as countries in both the global North and the global South have turned to loans from the IFIs in order to address the economic and social costs of the global financial crisis. For example, by May 2009, the International Monetary Fund (IMF) had already extended loans to nearly 50 countries seeking to stabilize their exchange rates and prevent a collapse of their banking systems. However, while many countries in the global North were pursuing counter-cyclical policies and injecting large sums of money into the economy, many of the IMF lending arrangements continued to impose pro-cyclical macroeconomic tightening, which included requirements to reduce public spending and to increase interest rates (UNCTAD 2009: vi–vii).

This is not to suggest that austerity measures and cuts to forms of social provisioning are limited to the global South, as many countries in the global North (including Spain, Portugal, Greece and Ireland) have also agreed to reduce levels of public spending in exchange for loans from the IFIs and other OECD countries. Similarly, various social forces in the United States, particularly those associated with the Republican Party, have argued that the debt incurred by the massive bailout of the global financial system will require cuts to many of the nation's social programmes. Rather than increase revenue through taxation, it has been argued that the best, if not the only way to reduce the US deficit is through cuts to programmes such as Medicare, Medicaid and Social Security, all of which assist some of the poorest members of the population.

The paradox, which Janine Brodie (2003) has termed the 'paradox of necessity', is that these quasi-constitutional requirements to reduce social spending have come at a time when three to four decades of neo-liberal restructuring have rendered social reproduction increasingly precarious for much of the global population whose risks have been privatized and who have been compelled to depend on capitalist markets to meet their daily and long-term needs. In the United States, one of the ways in which this paradox has been addressed is through the deepening of debt as a means of financing aspects of social reproduction, including access to housing, healthcare, education and consumption (LeBaron and Roberts 2012; Montgomerie 2013; Roberts 2013).

Indeed, between 2000 and 2008, the median household income in the United States fell from $52,400 to $49,800. Real household wealth also fell, dropping from $503,500 to $486,600 between 1999 and 2009 (Montgomerie 2013). During the same period, consumer lending was rising. While in 1992, the ratio of average household debt to income was 100.1 per cent, by 1998, this rose to 122 per cent and by 2007, debt had reached 171 per cent of total income (Montgomerie 2013).

The main driving force behind this change was debt secured by residential real estate, which accounts for over 80 per cent of household liabilities, though other forms of consumer debt, such as credit card debt, auto loans and student loans, also rose sharply during this period (Brown *et al.* 2010: 2). Rather than helping to build up financial assets, borrowing and debt have largely been used to fuel consumption and to support the social reproduction of particular sectors of the population, leading some political economists to argue that, in the United States, debt has operated as a 'privately led social innovation' (Froud *et al.* 2010; see also Crouch 2009). This shift is underpinned by the discursive linking of the

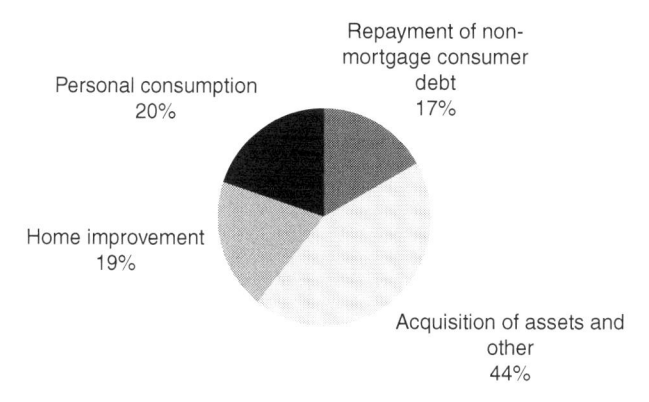

Figure 14.1 Uses of home equity extraction 2001–8
Exhibit from 'Will US Consumer Debt Reduction Cripple the Recovery?' March 2009, McKinsey Global Institute, www.mckinsey.com/mgi. McKinsey & Company. Reprinted by permission.

Pie chart segments:
- Repayment of non-mortgage consumer debt 17%
- Personal consumption 20%
- Home improvement 19%
- Acquisition of assets and other 44%

extension of credit to the so-called 'democratization of finance' and the benefits of participation in the so-called Ownership Society (Froud *et al.* 2010; Soederberg 2007, 2013).

Others have argued that the proliferation of private mortgage debt represents a 'welfare trade-off' or a form of 'privatized Keynesianism', as citizens in the United States and elsewhere have supported lower levels of taxation, and subsequently lower levels of public provisioning, in exchange for the so-called 'opportunity' to store and accumulate capital in their homes (Castles 1998; Crouch 2009). In this context, fiscal and monetary policies that subsidize home ownership (such as taxation policies that allow for the deduction of mortgage interest and the maintenance of low interest rates) operate as a privatized form of welfare and are part of the broader trend toward the (re-)privatization of social reproduction (Roberts 2013).

This trend is confirmed by recent studies that have shown that rather than leading to a growth in home equity, over the past several years, a significantly large proportion of mortgage loans have been in the form of second mortgages, cash-out refinancing loans and home equity lines of credit that have been used to pay down personal debt, to fund consumption and to pay for other necessities such as healthcare and education.

Credit cards have also become an increasingly important means of financing social reproduction, including the costs associated with healthcare in the largely privatized US system. One survey found that close to 30 per cent of low- and middle-income households with credit card debt linked this debt to medical expenses. The average credit card debt for these 'medically indebted' households without private health insurance was $14,512 in 2005. For those with health insurance, the average debt was $10,973. Sixty per cent of all households with medical debt that refinanced their homes in 2005 then used this money to pay down credit card debt, pointing to an important correlation between mortgage and other forms of debt (LeBaron and Roberts 2012; Zeldin and Rukavina 2005: 1, 8).

In so far as the deepening of debt has been driven by these and other demand-side dynamics, as numerous critical political economists have argued, the dramatic proliferation of mortgage and other forms of debt in the United States cannot be separated from transformations taking place at the global level that have created the conditions for a glut of cheap credit to be available to US consumers (see for instance Dymski 2009; McNally 2011; Schwartz 2009). Essentially, the supply of cheap credit was conditioned by the growth of securitization processes as loans were sold to investment bankers who pooled them into asset-backed securities (ABSs), which include mortgage-backed securities (MBSs). These were then sold to a variety of foreign and domestic investors, including many governments and sovereign wealth funds. As part of this process, a massive market in credit derivatives emerged and, by 2009, a notional $610 trillion – approximately 11 times the total *global* gross domestic product (GDP) – rested in financial derivatives markets (Wigan 2010).

This global financial regime, which has allowed for the massive accumulation of wealth based on the trade in ABS and related instruments and derivatives, has been secured through a range of legislative processes and new constitutionalist mechanisms. For example, in the United States, the 1999 Gramm–Leach–Bliley Act repealed the law separating commercial and investment banking and was central to the deregulation of the derivatives market. This act ultimately allowed mortgage originators to move loans off of balance sheets, thereby transferring the risk associated with lending onto banks and investors. In other words, it allowed originators to avoid the market discipline imposed by holding direct assets and created an incentive to lend to lower-income borrowers. The new constitutionalist mechanisms involved in securing the free movement of finance across borders have also been central in shaping this macroeconomic framework of financial accumulation.

On the one hand, this framework has facilitated the accumulation of capital. On the other, it has intensified inequalities between countries as well as between social classes, between men and women, and along racial lines. Indeed, while the deepening of debt has been ubiquitous across US society, some of the most dramatic increases in borrowing have occurred amongst the lower classes, women, blacks and Hispanics. This is partly the result of the proliferation of subprime mortgage lending over the

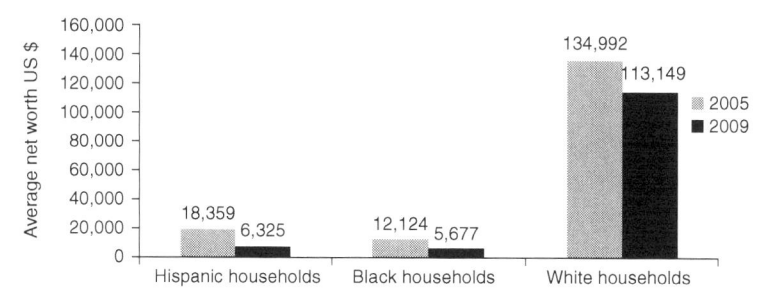

Figure 14.2 Average net worth of US households by race, 2005 and 2009
Source: Taylor *et al.* (2011: 5).

past decade. The high cost and predatory nature of many of these loans have led to an accumulation of debt (but not assets) amongst borrowers, a disproportionate number of whom are women, black and Latino, thereby intensifying inequalities in wealth (Dymski 2009; Froud *et al.* 2010; Montgomerie and Young 2011). At the same time, social reproduction has been rendered increasingly insecure for these sectors of the population. For example, it has been estimated that the foreclosure crisis in the United States will likely result in 10 to 13 million foreclosures by the time it abates. These foreclosures, combined with the loss of home equity that has resulted from the collapse of the housing bubble and rising levels of unsecured debt, have led to a 66 per cent fall in the average net worth of Hispanic households, a 53 per cent fall in the net worth of black households and a 16 per cent fall in the net worth of white households between 2005 and 2009 (Figure 14.2).

Class divisions have also intensified within racial groups as the wealthiest 10 per cent of households in each group increased their share of wealth relative to the bottom 90 per cent (Taylor *et al.* 2011: 32). Though the gendered dimensions of housing debt are somewhat less well documented, foreclosure and the loss of home equity in the face of falling housing prices may also intensify gender-based inequalities since women tend to have higher debt levels than men and their assets are concentrated in home equity to a much greater extent (Ginty 2010).

Whereas socialized forms of provisioning tend to be oriented toward some progressive redistribution of resources, the operation of debt as an individualized and privatized form of provisioning has integrated, embodied and socially embedded individuals into markets in ways that reproduce and at times intensify inequalities and hierarchical power relations between classes and along racial, gendered and other lines. It has also intensified the structural power of capital relative to that of labour, as debt operates as a disciplinary social relation that compels individuals to adhere to certain norms of behaviour, for instance, to conform to the norms of wage labour and to maintain a good credit rating by dutifully paying creditors each month (Gill 2008; McNally 2011).

Though this discussion has primarily focused on the micro scale, debt clearly operates as a disciplinary force at various sites and scales, including at the macroeconomic scale through lending conditionalities and other means. However, whereas much of the critical literature on debt retains an analytical focus on the ways in which debt operates through the market, as a structural power relation, it is important to emphasize that disciplinary debt relations are fundamentally underpinned by state power. The following section focuses on bankruptcy legislation in order to argue that the US state's legal and criminal justice apparatuses have been used to lock in the interests of capital by compelling debtors to commit assets and future earnings to pay back debts and to criminalize and even incarcerate those who are unwilling and/or unable to do so.

The new constitutionalism and bankruptcy protection

As noted above, the rise of debt as a privatized form of social provisioning is a highly contradictory trend that has actually served to intensify social insecurities and inequalities and is ultimately unsustainable. One manifestation of the unsustainable nature of this project is the explosion of personal bankruptcies that has occurred over the past several decades. By 2004, 'more Americans were filing for bankruptcy each year than were graduating from college, getting divorced, or being diagnosed with cancer' (White 2007: 175). In an effort to curtail the default on debt through bankruptcy, the lending industry launched a major lobbying campaign for bankruptcy reform that cost more than $100 million and resulted in the Bankruptcy Abuse Prevention and Consumer Protection Act (BAPCPA) of 2005. Ultimately, the BAPCPA made bankruptcy laws much more pro-creditor (see also Soederberg 2013). It also led to a sharp reduction of bankruptcy filings in its immediate aftermath though, in recent years, personal bankruptcies in the United States have begun to rise again, with approximately two million people filing for bankruptcy in 2009 (Brown *et al.* 2010).

Specifically, the BAPCPA shifted the burden of debt and bankruptcy from capital to individuals in at least four ways. First, it abolished the right of debtors to choose between Chapter 7 and Chapter 13 bankruptcy. Whereas under Chapter 7, those filing for bankruptcy are required to pay debts with their assets, Chapter 13 allows them to keep their assets but requires them to repay a certain proportion of their debts from future incomes. Since most debtors, and particularly lower-income debtors, have fewer assets, they are generally better off filing for Chapter 7. However, the new reforms subject those seeking to file under Chapter 7 to a 'means test', limiting this outlet to those with an income lower than the median income in their state (White 2007). Second, the BAPCPA abolished the ability of debtors to propose their own Chapter 13 repayment plans and introduced a new procedure that determines the amount of future income that must be used for repayment.

Third, the law greatly increased the cost of filing for bankruptcy through new requirements that compel debtors to provide detailed financial information, including the past four years of tax returns. Since many of those filing for bankruptcy have not kept up to date with their tax returns, they incur the cost of filing taxes prior to filing for bankruptcy (Elias 2006). The new law also requires debtors to take a credit counselling course prior to filing for bankruptcy as well as a financial management course after filing. Finally, the BAPCPA increased the amount of time that individuals must wait between filings. For Chapter 7, the time increased from six to eight years, and for Chapter 13, from six months to two years.

The revised bankruptcy code disproportionately impacts the lowest-income debtors and does little to curb the incentive for lenders to continue to extend credit to low-income borrowers on highly inequitable terms. There are also important gender dimensions to bankruptcy reform, as the BAPCPA has made it more difficult to discharge credit card debt, thereby putting women seeking domestic support from debtors in bankruptcy in direct competition with credit card companies that have much more extensive resources available to compel payment (Warren 2009). Thus, while the BAPCPA privileges the rights of capital above workers in general, it also specifically disadvantages women and families dependent on support from debtors in bankruptcy.

With its pro-creditor (and pro-capital) orientation, the reform of bankruptcy through the BAPCPA has ultimately failed to address the demand for credit that has been shaped by falling or stagnating real wages, rising costs of living, and the individualization and privatization of social provisioning. Rather, it raises a number of material barriers to bankruptcy while simultaneously perpetuating an ideology that views unsustainable levels of debt and bankruptcy as a result of the irresponsible behaviour of borrowers. This ideology is well captured in the writings of Charles Murray, a social scientist at the American Enterprise Institute (a conservative think tank), who is described on the back of his most recent book as '[a]rguably the most consequential social scientist alive'. In *Coming Apart* (2012), Murray argues that there is a growing cultural rift between the upper and lower classes in the United States, which threatens to bring about the destruction of American society. Murray argues that while the rich are enclosing themselves in private enclaves, in poor communities, the core virtues of industriousness, honesty, marriage and religion are being eroded. As evidence of the erosion of honesty and integrity, Murray points to rising personal bankruptcies, arguing that the choice to declare bankruptcy (in the wake of revisions to the Bankruptcy Code in 1978 that made it slightly more attractive to debtors) 'is akin to deciding to shoplift if the criminal justice system becomes more lenient' (2012: 198). Brushing aside arguments that creditors are also to blame for unsustainable debt loads, Murray goes on to say that '[s]omeone for whom integrity is paramount is scared of incurring debts that can't be repaid, and doesn't take out the loan' for such 'imprudent expenditures' as houses, automobiles and consumer goods (2012: 198).

In blaming individual borrowers, this discourse leaves little room for considering the irresponsible, and at times illegal, lending practices on the part of credit card companies, banks and mortgage originators who have been found to have targeted particular individuals, and particularly women, blacks, Hispanics and the elderly, for higher-cost loans regardless of their actual credit scores (Dymski 2009; Fishbein and Woodall 2006). Indeed, Murray overlooks the corporate bankruptcies and bailouts post-2008 and argues that though accusations of 'corporate and financial wrongdoing are real ... it is not clear whether they reflect a growing loss of integrity within the business community as a whole' (2012: 196). This ideology is firmly rooted in material practices and power relations, as, while the poor are treated as morally (if not criminally) suspect, the number of cases referred to the Justice Department by bank regulators, who are ultimately responsible for policing the banking sector, fell from 1,837 cases per year in 1995 to 72 by 2010 (Morgenson and Story 2011; see also Taibbi 2011).

The state, the law and the coercive relations of debt

The BAPCPA shares many of the features of the new constitutionalism identified by Gill and others, as it operates as part of a broader framework of structural and legal power that supports the interests of capital by compelling debtors to commit assets and future earnings to pay back debts. However, more directly coercive forms of state power further underpin this, as debtors have increasingly been subjected to coercive debt collection practices and have been criminalized and incarcerated for their inability and/or unwillingness to pay consumer and other forms of debt (LeBaron and Roberts 2012).

The criminalization and incarceration of debtors – which amounts to the use of the legal arm of the state to coercively enforce private credit obligations – has intensified in the wake of the global financial crisis. According to a recent investigative report in the *Wall Street Journal*, for instance, between the beginning of 2010 and March 2011, more than 5,000 warrants had been issued by judges in nine US counties (with a total population of 13.6 million) (Silver-Greenberg 2011).[1] This surge has been conditioned by a combination of slow economic growth, high levels of unemployment, high consumer debt and the steady growth of the debt-collection industry (LeBaron and Roberts 2012; Serres and Howatt 2011). The latter trend is particularly important, as debt-collection firms have grown considerably over the past two decades. Essentially, these firms buy old debt portfolios from credit card companies, utilities, phone companies, banks and other lenders for pennies on the dollar and then aggressively pursue individuals for payment of the underlying debts, often through the use of lawsuits (Fox 2012; Holland 2011). While this phenomenon is under-explored in much of the political economy literature, a number of investigative journalism reports have highlighted the role of debt collectors in criminalizing growing segments of the poor population. An investigation by *The Boston Globe* into debt collection in Massachusetts found that professional debt collectors had filed an estimated 575,000 lawsuits between 2000 and 2005, amounting to about one lawsuit for every 11 residents (*The Boston Globe* 2006).

This strategy has proven to be quite profitable for this burgeoning industry, particularly in the aftermath of the global financial crisis (Serres and Howatt 2011). In 2010, Encore Capital Group, the largest publicly traded debt-buying firm in the United States, filed 425,000 lawsuits against debtors, up 27 per cent from 334,000 in 2009, and collected $266.7 million through lawsuits. The estimated total revenue for that year was $381.3 million, up 21 per cent from $316.4 million a year earlier.[2] Another major player in the debt-collection industry is Portfolio Recovery Associates (PRA). Since their initial public offering in 2002, PRA has increased their debt portfolio more than tenfold, from $5.1 billion (in face value) to over $54.8 billion. According to their annual report,

---

[1] While it is actually illegal to incarcerate people for debts they cannot pay, in many instances, warrants are issued for the failure to appear in court on the behest of creditors and other means.

[2] 'Encore Capital Group Announces Fourth Quarter and Full Year 2010 Financial Results, Increased Revolving Credit Facility and Second Tranche of Seven-Year Notes', Press Release, 14 February 2010.

2010 was 'an exceptional period' for the company, which 'shattered previous milestones for cash collections, revenue and net income, setting new records' (PRA 2010: 2). A large part of this growth resulted from investment in the bankruptcy market from 2004 onward. Collections for bankrupt accounts represented an estimated 35 per cent of total cash collections in 2010 (PRA 2010: 6), while 34 per cent of their revenue (amounting to $91.5 million) was generated through lawsuits (Silver-Greenberg 2011).

Many of the nation's largest banks are also intricately involved in promoting the aggressive pursuit of debtors through strategies of harassment, coercion, criminalization and incarceration. For instance, Encore currently has a $410 million revolving credit line with a number of large banks, including JPMorgan Chase, Bank of America and Citibank. This line of credit is then used to buy consumer debt from these same banks, which are also the top three credit card issuers in the United States. This suggests that rather than operating on the margins of the ballooning debt industry, coercive debt-collection practices are a constitutive element of the industry itself.

This industry is only anticipated to grow over the coming years, as the global financial crisis has led to a rise in delinquencies, and banks are now charging off bad debts at historical levels, with charge-off rates for credit cards growing from 4.24 per cent in 2008 to 10.96 per cent in 2010 (Fox 2012: 361). According to the Bureau of Labor Statistics, in the coming decade, employment in the debt-collection industry is expected to grow more rapidly than any other occupation (Fox 2012: 357).

As with other aspects of the disciplinary neo-liberal project, the coercive practices that underpin credit relations are subject to various forms of contestation and resistance. Over the past several years, class action lawsuits have been filed against Encore in Ohio, Minnesota, California and Texas, and against PRA in Florida, Georgia, New York and Colorado. Allegations are based on the violation of a number of laws designed to protect consumers, including the Fair Debt Collection Practices Act (by 'robo-signing' thousands of affidavits without reading or verifying the accuracy of the material, failing to have collectors properly identify themselves, attempting to collect on debts that fall out of the statute of limitations, etc.) and the Telephone Consumer Protection Act (by calling debtors' cellular phones without their prior express consent, using automatic dialling systems or prerecorded messages, etc.).[3]

---

[3] 'Attorney General Lori Swanson Charges One of Nation's Largest "Debt Buyers" with Defrauding Minnesota Courts and Citizens by Filing "Robo-Signed" Affidavits', Press Release, 28 March 2011.

The police and certain elements of the collection industry have also expressed the need to strengthen the regulation of the industry and to limit the incarceration of debtors. While the police have taken issue with the dedication of limited resources to debt-related arrests, industry proponents are concerned with maintaining the legitimacy of practices that critical observers are likening to a modern version of nineteenth-century debtors' prisons (LeBaron and Roberts 2012). However, consistent with broader trends in so-called 'good corporate governance', the preferred regulation takes the form of self-imposed and self-regulated 'codes of conduct' rather than firm and enforceable regulation by the state. In other words, consistent with trends noted by other contributors to this volume, the preferred form of governance takes the form of 'soft' versus 'hard' law. Encore, for instance, has sought to pre-empt state regulation of the debt-collection industry and to present a positive corporate image by developing a Consumer Bill of Rights and advocating its adoption by other firms.[4]

The criminalization and incarceration of debtors and the reliance upon the legal force of the state to enforce private credit obligations highlights the assemblage of public and private mechanisms and forms of authority involved in supporting the extension of capitalist markets (Cutler 2003). It further points to the *supremacist* nature of contemporary forms of capitalist accumulation, as directly coercive techniques are used to compel low-income debtors to repay debts. In contrast, there has been a notable shift away from the surveillance, investigation and prosecution of those in charge of the major banks and investment firms that engaged in the lending and trading practices, many of which were illegal, that ultimately led to the most recent global financial crisis (Taibbi 2011).

Conclusion

This chapter touched on a number of overlapping processes that are generally left out of the analyses of global capitalism presented by mainstream and critical political economists. In so doing, it has drawn attention to the way in which the accumulation of capital involves more than economic processes and market-based structural forms of discipline. While these forms of power are central features of the disciplinary neo-liberal project, they are further underpinned by more directly coercive forms of

---

[4] Article 6, section H of the Bill of Rights states that Encore will refrain from requesting bench warrants except in those instances when the defendant fails to respond to a direct order from the court. The complete Bill of Rights is available online from www.encore-capital.com/.

power and discipline, including the use of the state's legal and penal arm to compel adherence to capitalist norms and behaviours. These disciplinary and coercive processes further serve to perpetuate divisions, inequalities and insecurities within the poor and working classes.

The deepening of disciplinary and coercive practices noted in this chapter is part of the broader reconstitution of the nature of social reproduction in ways that have rendered it more market-based, privatized and individualized. This shift has been conditioned by various mechanisms of the new constitutionalism that have constrained the ability of many governments to pursue more progressive and redistributive social welfare policies. However, despite these structural constraints, the rise of debt as a privatized form of social provisioning in the United States was not an inevitable outcome of the new constitutionalist project but was rather promoted by those domestic and transnational social forces (including those associated with Wall Street) that stood to profit from this process.

The contradictions of indebtedness have become apparent on numerous fronts, extending from the foreclosure crisis in the United States to the near-collapse of the global financial system in 2008. While the immediate response in the United States has included an intensification of the criminalization and incarceration of debtors, this overtly supremacist politics creates the space to challenge such directly coercive practices and to call upon the state to redirect resources away from the criminalization of poverty and toward the active surveillance and disciplining of capital (on the need for this see Gill 1995b). Looking beyond the state, various social movements have put forth alternative solutions to the crisis of indebtedness in the United States. For instance, Strike Debt, which is an offshoot of Occupy Wall Street, has launched a campaign to raise money in order to buy and forgive the bad debt that is generally sold by banks to collection firms. The aim of Strike Debt is to have 'a jubilee for the 99 percent'.[5] Given these ongoing tensions, contradictions and resistances, it is by no means clear that debt will continue to operate as a primary means of mediating the tensions between capitalist accumulation and social reproduction, and to support the new constitutionalist project more broadly.

---

[5] http://rollingjubilee.org/.

15 New constitutionalism, neo-liberalism and social policy

Janine Brodie

Introduction

In the early 1990s Stephen Gill introduced the terms 'new constitutionalism', 'disciplinary neo-liberalism' and 'market civilization' into the lexicon of international political economy. These conceptual benchmarks have occupied persuasive ground in an ongoing debate about the character, coherence and consequences of neo-liberal governing ideas in contemporary international and national politics. An early and influential participant in this debate, Gill's conceptual troika helped to demystify and denaturalize economic globalization, depicting it instead as a resolutely political project aimed at establishing 'transnational liberalism, and if possible liberal democratic capitalism, [as] the sole model for future development' (2003: 132; see also 1995a). Gill's portrayal of the new constitutionalism projected a new transnational governing order enforced through the binding decrees of transnational legal instruments, trade agreements and international financial institutions. This new constitutional order disciplined national states to protect and extend property rights and to insulate key aspects of national economies from democratic accountability (2003: 132). Although the new constitutionalism was transnational in scope, Gill also understood disciplinary neo-liberalism as having micro dimensions because its capillaries stretched down into organizational and individual behaviour, progressively imposing the imperatives of the global market on everyday life (Griffiths *et al.* 2009: 181).

Although principally focused on the global and the economic, the concept of new constitutionalism also drew suggestive links between this ascendant global regulatory regime and the potential erosion of national

---

This research was funded by both the Canada Research Chairs programme, in which I hold a Tier 1 Chair in Political Economy and Social Governance, and the Pierre Elliott Trudeau Foundation, which awarded me a Fellowship in 2010. Thanks to Brent Epperson for providing background research.

welfare states, of embedded liberalism, and with it the post-war social compromise. Other political economists similarly identified the bundle of governing instruments most commonly associated with the new constitutionalism, notably, liberalization, deregulation, privatization and commodification, as constraints on the capacity of governments to sustain robust social policy regimes (Brodie 2004). For the most part, however, mainstream social policy analysts have not drawn explicitly on the idea of the new constitutionalism to explain either the attrition of social welfare policies, or the cultivation of new social governance strategies in the contemporary global era. There are several reasons for this. First, the weight of social policy research remains firmly in the grip of methodological nationalism and thus assumes that the relevant forces shaping social policy are contained within national boundaries and shaped by historically and institutionally generated path dependencies. If the global enters the social policy equation, it is assumed to be mediated by the national and local rather than the reverse. As a consequence, contemporary social policy change is frequently attributed to domestic demographic pressures or to so-called 'new social risks', amongst them precarious employment, long-term unemployment, working poverty and work–life balance constraints, without connecting these new social realities to transformations, disciplinary or otherwise, in the global economy. Second, when social policy research does look beyond national boundaries, it situates social policy and the welfare state in opposition to underspecified conceptions of globalization, which are often devoid of any appreciation of neo-liberal globalism as a governing template and a political project. Financial liberalization, for example, is treated as one amongst many competing explanatory variables rather than as a governing instrument that redistributes income, wellbeing and life chances. Finally, although there is now a critical literature examining the ways in which neo-liberal rationalities reframe the assumptions underlying social policy reform, these studies emphasize the *constitutive* power of neo-liberal political rationalities rather than the *impositional force* of disciplinary neo-liberalism (Brown 2003, 2005).

The interplay between the new constitutionalism, neo-liberalism and social policy is complex, uneven and, as this chapter underlines, still unfolding. In order to better demonstrate these interconnections, this chapter casts the net more widely, focusing on neo-liberal globalism broadly rather than on the new constitutionalism exclusively. The chapter reviews predictions, spanning three decades of neo-liberal governance, about the ways in which social policies and the welfare state might be affected by global economic forces, as well as empirical studies that have tested these propositions. Next, the chapter examines less quantifiable experiments in the delivery and content of social policies, which both help shape new 'constitutions' of the social and attest to the instability and variability of the neo-liberal governing project. The social sector has defied a one-size-fits-all formula for restructuring, although clearly there are many cross-national resemblances in play. Finally, the chapter explores the fate of social policy in the aftermath of the 2008 global financial crisis. The unfolding of this crisis suggests that social policy regimes are threatened as much by the failures of neo-liberalism as by its successes. In many countries, the financial crisis has precipitated austerity policies that are aimed directly at the social field. Paradoxically, the capacity of neo-liberal globalism to reinvent itself in the wake of the longest and deepest economic contraction since the 1930s may very well depend on the revival of robust social regimes.

Globalization and social policy

Predictions

Predictions about the effects of economic globalization on social policy and the welfare state are as numerous as they are contradictory, and have shifted in emphasis as neo-liberalism has matured. Broadly these conjectures can be grouped into three distinct arguments; first, globalization necessitates an expansion of the social welfare; second, globalization erodes social welfare policies as national states are forced to engage in a competitive race to the bottom; and, third, neo-liberal globalism prompts a flurry of policy experimentation in the social field, which, although mediated by national legacies, presents strong cross-national similarities (Brady et al. 2005: 922–3; Brenner et al. 2010: 202).

The prediction that globalization prompts the expansion of social protection has been a minority view, most often encountered during neo-liberal globalism's formative years but rarely after its ascendancy. This school understood globalization largely as economic liberalization and the growth of international trade, and predicted that trade openness increased risks of social dislocations. It drew support from social policy research of earlier times, which found that 'historically countries with the most international exposure had more generous welfare states' (Brady et al. 2005: 922; Katzenstein 1985). Finally, this view was informed by that part of the Keynesian mindset, which understood social policy as a necessary state response to inevitable market fluctuations and the insecurities and inequalities that they generated. These studies, moreover, assumed that governments would pay a price for failing to deal with the social fallout emanating from trade openness, either at the ballot box or in deeper challenges to political authority and legitimacy.

The weight of literature on globalization and social policy, however, predicted precisely the opposite, notably that economic globalization threatened to devour post-war welfare states. According to this second perspective, the social policy infrastructures of advanced capitalist states were vulnerable to erosion and displacement because economic globalization forced governments to compete for increasingly mobile transnational corporations and capital. Globalization, this second group argued, forced downward convergence in social spending and social policy interventions. The idea of convergence has a long history in the social policy field. Earlier studies assumed that industrialized societies would experience upward convergence in the form of robust social policy regimes. Advanced economies ratcheted up their social policy architectures because they shared similar internal pressures and opportunities, amongst them, strong economic growth, extensive trade unionism, the expansion of social citizenship rights and the expectation that governments should underwrite the male breadwinner model of social reproduction (Barberis *et al.* 2010b). In contrast, economic globalization, it is argued, exerts external pressures on advanced economies to ratchet downward, to 'roll back' the post-war social architecture, and to set in motion a race to the bottom in the social policy field (Tickell and Peck 2003). Two assumptions framed this view: first, largely reproducing the rhetoric of the purveyors of neo-liberalism, social policy was assumed, almost by definition, to be an impediment to international competitiveness; and, second, it was assumed that all governments would necessarily have to respond in the same way to neo-liberal imperatives. Economic globalization, in other words, dictated that 'there was no alternative' (neo-liberalism's TINA principle) to eliminating universal social entitlements and social programmes and to dramatically reducing social spending.

Many early proponents of this vision drew inspiration from Karl Polanyi's (1944/1957) powerful account of the dystopias of market governance. Writing in the aftermath of the Great Depression of the 1930s, Polanyi disparaged laissez-faire's 'uncritical reliance on the alleged self-healing virtues of unconscious growth', arguing instead that societies, foolhardy enough to enable 'the market mechanism to be the sole director of the fate of human beings and their environment' invited 'the demolition of society' (*ibid.*: 33, 173). Polanyi's insights about an earlier experiment with market governance thus prompted later social commentators such as John Gray to conclude that neo-liberal governments had embraced a script whose finale was already written: to wit, 'we are at present in the midst of an experiment in utopian social engineering whose outcome we *can* know in advance' (1999: 16, emphasis in the original). Polanyi's dystopia also echoed through Gill's vision of market civilization and Bakker and Gill's account of the growing antagonisms between disciplinary neo-liberalism's model of accumulation and the maintenance of stable conditions for social reproduction and social security, broadly defined, on a global scale (Bakker and Gill 2003).

There are actually strong and soft versions of this 'globalization as antagonistic to social' argument. The so-called 'strong globalization thesis' is exemplified by Ulrich Beck's 2000 pronouncement that 'the premises of the welfare state ... melt under the withering sun of globalization' (2000: 1). This thesis points to the unprecedented capacities of capital to move around the world, thereby forcing national governments to adhere to neo-liberal fundamentals, to deregulate, to open new markets and to cut corporate taxes (Gill 1995a: 402–5; Hirst *et al.* 1999: 4–5). These policies, in turn, placed pronounced downward pressures on social spending and programme development. Instead of envisioning a new social infrastructure and new social investment that might enhance social wellbeing, economic efficiencies and international competitiveness, social programmes and spending were reduced or eliminated and public goods and services were put on the market (Larner 2000: 8–9).

In many ways, this somewhat deterministic account has been undermined by the experience of the past three decades. Although post-war welfare states and the promises of universalism and social citizenship have been diminished, hollowing out has been accompanied by filling-in processes at national and subnational scales. This third and softer perspective thus characterizes social policy development in a globalizing era as a double movement, a rolling back of the old and a rolling out of the new, which is characteristically experimental and uneven (Tickell and Peck 2003: 166). In many advanced economies, for example, social policy reforms have focused on active labour force participation, tax measures to subsidize the increasing prevalence of low-wage jobs, and policies aimed at shoring up the disappearing family wage. This softer version thus allows for a measure of coexistence between economic globalization and social protection but continues to imagine social policy as subservient, and functioning to advance the neo-liberal project rather than operating as a buffer for the social citizen against the social insecurities and disparities generated by the global market (Jessop 2002: 461–2). Social policy, so the argument goes, has been reinvented to advance neo-liberal assumptions about and prescriptions for global economic competitiveness (Birch and Mykhnenko 2010: 7).

Outcomes

The evidence pertaining to erosion or reinvention of social policy in affluent democracies is decidedly mixed. The OECD social expenditure database, for example, shows remarkable consistency in public social spending over the past 30 years. During this time, overall social spending has increased in most OECD countries, although still reflecting pronounced national variations. Countries with a strong legacy of comprehensive social policies such as Sweden, Denmark and Norway continue to outspend, as measured by percentage of GDP, characteristically less generous regimes such as Canada and the United States (OECD 2012). Public social expenditure data thus do not appear to support the claim that economic globalization has forced a race to the bottom in the social field. As noteworthy, many emergent economies have introduced significant social policy initiatives that provide social protection for both workers and vulnerable populations; a few notable examples will suffice: Indonesia, the Philippines, Brazil and Thailand have or are near to achieving universal public healthcare; China and India have launched massive healthcare initiatives for the poor; South Korea has introduced a universal basic pension, long-term care insurance for the elderly and a minimum wage; and Thailand has established a pension plan for the informal sector. These nascent social policy regimes are admittedly lean compared to those of advanced economies. These emergent economies, however, are at about the same level of development as the United States was when it passed its 1935 Social Security Act (*The Economist* 2012).

Several comprehensive comparative studies have attempted to measure the impact of economic globalization on advanced welfare states in recent decades, but they too provide few definitive answers. Duane Swank's frequently cited study found little evidence to support the convergence-at-the-bottom thesis, indeed any thesis. He concluded that the domestic impacts of international capital mobility are complex, variable and strongly mediated by national histories and path dependencies (Swank 2002: 5). Brady *et al.* similarly found that aggregate indicators of economic globalization are poor statistical predictors of either social expenditures or social transfers amongst affluent democracies. The few statistically significant globalization effects that were observed in this study were inconsistent, neither moving in the same direction nor supporting the predictions of existing theories (2005: 921). Brady *et al.* concluded nevertheless that globalization has some impact on the welfare state 'even if the exact relationship remains unclear' (2005: 921).

Conflicting evidence, drawn from aggregate data, however, does not solve the puzzle about economic globalization and social policy, or support hastily drawn conclusions that there is no discernible relationship (Loughlin 2007: 391). Aggregate public expenditure data paint policy landscapes with broad quantitative strokes, but are decidedly too blunt to discern complex and multifaceted processes such as substantive policy change or institutional realignments achieved through funding priorities, regulatory frameworks, delivery mechanisms and scales of governance (Barberis et al. 2010b: 367). Moreover, as Loughlin appropriately argues, evidence of a continuing rise in public expenditures fails to capture changes in the 'role and functions of the state at the level of aspirations and values much less commitment to old ideas of the social and to the positive role of the state in achieving these ideals' (2007: 391). Put differently, these data do not address central questions about whether and how neo-liberal governing strategies eliminate established social programmes, reinvent others or inform new initiatives, thereby reshaping citizen choices, subjectivities, and the constraints and possibilities of daily life.

There is another methodological issue at play here. The first wave of research on globalization, neo-liberalism and social policy, and I include my own work here (Brodie 2003, 2004), was perhaps too eager to read the fundamentals of neo-liberal governance from neo-classical economic theory, lending it more disciplinary power in our theoretical imaginations than it could achieve in the face of either domestic political constraints or its own policy failures. In addition, social policy research may have focused too narrowly on the impacts of neo-liberalism's macro governing instruments such as liberalization, deregulation and privatization, while ignoring the many different policy experiments that now populate the social field of advanced democracies.

An unsettled policy field

By most indicators, the social policy field of advanced democracies is unsettled, often eluding the projected path dependencies of regime theory, or the expectations of globalization theorists (Brenner et al. 2010; Esping-Andersen 1990). This instability has led some to argue that we should abandon the 'neo-liberal' template altogether (Clarke 2008), while others regard the introduction of new social initiatives or an infusion of new social spending as evidence that the neo-liberal moment has been surpassed by a social investment or post-neo-liberal state form (Jenson 2008; Mahon 2008; Porter and Craig 2004).

To be sure, neo-liberalism is not a monolithic governing formula, not least because of variations in national and local institutional histories, policy responses and capacities, and the legacies of counter 'discourses, projects, practices, and imaginaries' (Clarke 2008: 138). These qualities of unevenness, instability and reflexivity, however, less detract from *than define* the contemporary neo-liberal governing experiment in the social policy field (Brenner *et al.* 2010; Brodie 2010). Building on this perspective, Peck *et al.* (2010) and Brenner *et al.* (2010) argue persuasively that neo-liberalism has yielded 'a bewildering array of local trajectories', 'contingent forms' and 'hybrid assemblages', not only in the social field, but across the spectrum of contemporary governance. Rather than conceptualizing neo-liberalism as a coherent ideology, a bundle of favoured policies or as a unique state form, they contend that neo-liberalism is more productively parsed into *processes of neo-liberalization*, which have unfolded in 'sporadic wave-like non-linear sequences' in the past three decades and more (Brenner *et al.* 2010: 187, 207; Larner 2000; see also Chapter 8, this volume).

Effectively experiments in governance, Brenner *et al.* understand neo-liberalization processes as necessarily uneven, variegated and reactive forms of regulation. They are increasingly shaped and reshaped by transnational and translocal circuits of policy diffusion, as well as by neo-liberalism's own policy failures. The chronic underperformance of neo-liberalism, they argue, has not prompted abandonment of this grand project or movement toward some kind of post-neo-liberal order. Instead, 'policy failure is central to the exploratory and experimental *modus operandi* of neo-liberalization' and 'the source of forward momentum for the project as a whole'. Unanticipated outcomes and policy failures spur 'continual reinvention' and 'further rounds of reform' (Brenner *et al.* 2010: 209–10). This said, these researchers maintain that these waves of policy reform also bear cross-national and cross-jurisdictional 'family resemblances, interdependencies, and interconnections' (Brenner *et al.* 2010: 195; Peck *et al.* 2010: 104). 'Experiments *are* the process but these experiments *are* patterned' (Brenner *et al.* 2010: 210).

New 'constitutions' of the social

Social policy research has identified a handful of 'family resemblances' in the social policy reforms of advanced democracies in recent decades. These family resemblances, however, are often in the form of administrative rather than programmatic similarities, although the two are often interrelated. While post-war welfare states adopted similar programmes related to, for example, social security, welfare assistance, healthcare and education, neo-liberal family resemblances often reflect shared preferences for administrative mechanisms such as decentralization and subsidiarity, block funding, fiscalization and active welfare policies (Kazepov

2010: 35–7). Yet, upon closer inspection, these family resemblances house important substantive differences: family similarities in administrative orientations may be only distant cousins in goals and outcomes. For example, decentralization simply shifts responsibility for social policy to lower levels of government or authorities, but it is often dressed up in the soothing rhetoric of subsidiarity. This principle holds that policies are most effective when they are designed and administered by the smallest and least centralized unit of administration. However, as Michael Keating has argued, the subsidiarity principle also can enforce the 'decentralization of penury' (1998). Decentralization begs the question of whether subnational states and less centralized authorities have sufficient financial resources or expertise to fill the gap left when central governments abdicate responsibility for social policies. At the very least, subnational social policy experimentation requires active subsidiarity, a downward shift in responsibility, capacity and especially resources (Kazepov 2010: 50). Passive subsidiarity, the downloading of responsibility without resources, promises only the barest forms of market discipline or the externalization of social responsibilities to non-state actors, or both.

Similarly, active welfare or labour activation policies can affect quite different experiences and possibilities depending on both degrees of conditionality and what is being activated (e.g. labour power or individual and family capacities) (Sabatinelli 2010: 86). Workfare, labour activation in its crudest and most coercive form, imposes the obligation to work as a condition for the receipt of social welfare benefits. It does not enhance the skill sets of those previously excluded from the paid labour force and frequently it does not appreciably improve material conditions or security for those forced into these programmes. In contrast, labour activation policies that underwrite skills development, retraining and modest income security build capacities, resilience and potential for a successful transition from social welfare to financial self-sufficiency. The former model enforces vulnerability to market imperatives, while the latter can provide citizens with requisite capacities to negotiate contemporary labour markets. These distinctions thus underscore the many ways in which even family resemblances can result in uneven and asymmetric social landscapes and outcomes. Although changes in delivery strategies and conditionality have important consequences, they are ultimately only second-order changes in the new constitution of social policy in neo-liberal times. As Wendy Brown reminds us, 'neo-liberalism is not simply a set of economic policies', it also carries a social analysis. 'Neo-liberal rationality', she continues, 'while foregrounding the market, is not only or even primarily focused on the economy; it involves extending and disseminating market values to all institutions and social action, even as the market itself remains a distinctive player' (2005: 39–40). Neoliberalization processes in the social field are informed by a cluster of core assumptions, which do not so much borrow from the lexicon of classical economics as undermine the premises of the citizen–state bargain of post-war social liberalism. These core assumptions interlock, more or less coherently, with the administrative innovations noted above and reach down into and help transform, amongst other things, individual subjectivities, the prerogatives of citizenship and social wellbeing, broadly defined (Brodie 2007b, 2008: 39–42; Clarke 2008: 141).

Twentieth-century social liberalism, while accommodating pronounced cross-jurisdictional differences in the scope and design of social policy regimes, operationalized two core ideals: first, the state was responsible for the just distribution of social resources; and second, the market could and should be regulated in order to maximize economic and political stability and the collective wellbeing of all citizens. These ideals prescribed that certain goods – for example, education, social security and healthcare – should not be entrusted to capitalist markets because they were incapable of ensuring fair distribution or achieving collective goals. Social liberalism also provided spaces for citizens to make claims to a measure of equality and collective provision as a right of citizenship, independent of their status in the market or individual capabilities and character. This model thus required positive obligations on the part of the state to underwrite the welfare of individuals and families, through progressive taxation, the pooling of resources and risk, social welfare policies and social insurance (Brodie 2008; Young 1990: 67). The 'social' in social insurance embodied the idea of 'shared fate' and a widespread social consensus that inevitable threats to social wellbeing such as sickness, unemployment and old age were not the responsibility of individuals alone (Brodie 2012; Somers 2008: 34).

John Clarke argues that, in contrast to social liberalism, neo-liberal public policy is invariably grounded in the combination of four foundational orientations: an unequivocal commitment to market rationalities; individualization; preoccupation with calculating economic efficiencies; and the celebration of multiple forms of authority beyond the national state (2008: 140–1). Clarke goes on to enumerate a repertory of strategies that operationalize these orientations and undermine previous instantiations of the social in public policy. Using Brenner *et al.*'s terminology, these neo-liberalization processes include: *erasing* or the simple elimination of many post-war social programmes, *privatizing* formerly public goods and services to market providers; *subjugating* by imposing market logics of private profit and supply and demand on previously decommodified public goods; *narrowing* and targeting social programmes to specific groups; *functionalizing* by redesigning social programmes so that they primarily address the needs of neo-liberal labour markets rather than social wellbeing; and *fiscalizing* (Brodie 2007b). The latter transforms social intervention strategies, which once required social policy expertise, planning and expert service providers, into cash transfers, tax credits and tax deductions (Brodie 2010; Brodie and Bakker 2008).

Over the span of a generation, these neo-liberalization processes have been written into social policy reforms, alone or in combination, displacing the vision and practices of post-war social liberalism and creating uneven and variegated social fields both within and across affluent democracies. The permeations of these processes are countless but the evolution of childcare policy in Canada provides an illustration of the new constitution of social policy in recent decades. Childcare emerged relatively recently in Canadian social policy debates. Post-war family policy was premised on the male breadwinner model and the expectation that women would take up the full-time unpaid work of homemaker and caregiver. This model was underwritten by a raft of social policies that together comprised the family wage. Amongst these policies, the family allowance, also called the 'baby bonus', was introduced in the 1940s as Canada's first universal social programme. It provided a monthly allowance, paid directly to mothers, for every child under the age of 16.

The family allowance was one of the first targets of neo-liberal social policy reform. In the mid 1980s, it was stripped of its universality and increasingly targeted at low-income families. Within a few years, it was replaced with a tax credit. During these same years, women entered the labour force with increasing frequency, often to supplement the eroding family wage, and the number of female-led single families began to rise. Women's groups and progressive non-governmental organizations began to demand of the federal government a comprehensive and universal publicly provided childcare programme, which, after a few false starts, began to take shape in the early 2000s. Representing the first major federal social policy initiative in decades, the federal government, in collaboration with the provinces, introduced a plan to fund regulated and accessible childcare centres, preschools and nursery schools. However, the plan was abruptly cancelled by a newly elected Conservative government in 2006 and replaced with a universal childcare benefit – a modest and taxable monthly benefit ($100) for all children under six years of age to assist in paying for childcare (Makarenko 2007).

Also termed the 'choice in childcare benefit', this initiative represented a significant new social expenditure but, reflecting the new constitution of social policy, it also replaced a publicly funded and regulated early child development programme (a collective goal) with a fiscalized formula, which subsidizes private care providers, whether multinational corporations or self-employed entrepreneurs. This fiscalized formula also downloads responsibility onto parents to find individual solutions for their childcare needs and, because the benefit is inadequate to cover the cost of quality childcare and early education, many parents are forced to rely on private and informal arrangements such as paid care provided by a neighbour or the unpaid care offered by friends and relatives, often aging parents. The policy thus underwrites both market providers and the precarious or unpaid work of women.

This neo-liberal social policy reform illustrates the neo-liberalization processes of erasing, subjugating, privatizing and, most important, fiscalization, a strategy that pursues social goals through cash payments, tax credits, tax benefits and tax deductions. This neo-liberalization strategy, however, rests on two questionable assumptions: first, social needs will be met through choices configured in the market; and second, recipients will use relatively small increments in income provided through fiscalized programmes for the designated policy goal (Brodie 2010; Brodie and Bakker 2008). Fiscalization is also the strategic glove that fits on the discursive hand of individualization. It effectively assigns responsibility for systemic changes such as the decline of the family wage and the rise of dual-earner families onto individuals and families (Brodie and Bakker 2008: 3). It demands that people find personal causes and responses, what Beck and Beck-Gernsheim term as 'biographic solutions', to what are in effect shared social challenges in a globalizing era (Beck and Beck-Gernsheim 2002: 22–6; Brodie 2007b). The problem with this formulation is not that individuals, both inside and outside of families, do not try to seek solutions to their particular needs, or comply with individualized solutions when forced upon them (Bauman 2001: 105–6). People do seek out help for their caring needs from neighbours and relatives. Rather, the problem, as Bauman explains, is 'the subjects of contemporary states are individuals by fate: the factors that constitute their individuality – confinement to individual resources and individual responsibility for the results of life choices – are not themselves matters of choice' (Bauman 2002: 69). The choices available to us are neither equitable nor universal. As the case of the Canadian childcare benefit demonstrates, those who do not have sufficient money to buy market services have little choice in childcare.

Epilogue: social policy and the Great Recession

The Great Recession, which took flight in the American financial sector in 2008, stands as the deepest and longest economic contraction since the Great Depression of the 1930s. The crisis spread beyond North American borders, unravelled European financial markets and public finances, stalled emergent economies and continues to threaten even deeper waves of global economic instability. Contrary to predictions that the 2008 financial crisis sounded the death knell for neo-liberal globalism, responses to the Great Recession to date have put flesh on Brenner *et al.*'s observation that the chronic underperformance and outright failures of neo-liberal governance are a source of forward momentum for the project as a whole. Recurring economic crises have prompted frenzied searches for next-stage reforms, which, in time, spiral into even deeper crises and more extreme responses (Brenner *et al.* 2010: 207). G20 countries first responded to the Great Recession with restoration strategies and then turned to public austerity. The former relied on unprecedented levels of public borrowing to stabilize financial institutions, stimulate production and employment, and get on with business as usual (Peck *et al.* 2010: 101). Although it is widely agreed that the bailout and stimulus packages forestalled an even bleaker future, they neither contained the financial crisis nor reignited a stalled and fragile global economy. Then, in mid 2010, G20 governments agreed to cut their deficits and contain public debt with public austerity programmes aimed directly at social programmes, public services and public sector jobs. The rationale for contemporary public austerity measures represents yet another innovation in the neo-liberal toolkit. The doctrine of 'expansionary austerity', also known as 'expansionary fiscal contraction' (EFC), contends that reducing the size and scope of government, even in recessionary times, generates economic growth. 'Expansionary fiscal contraction' advances the idea that cutbacks in the public sector revive entrepreneurial confidence in the private sector and that pains of austerity will be quickly erased by economic growth (Krugman 2012: 147). Public austerity, however, also promises to further erode the social state and flexibilize the public sector workforce – each an enduring goal of neo-liberal governance (Brodie 2014). More cynically perhaps, public austerity represents a strategy that effectively obliges citizens to pay for the Great Recession's massive bailouts of financial institutions and unprecedented stimulus packages *with* their social programmes and public services. Thus, contrary to the race-to-the-bottom thesis discussed earlier in this chapter, the failures of neo-liberalism appear as a more virulent threat to social policies and social wellbeing than its successes, at least in this post-crisis moment. Public austerity represents an extreme articulation of neo-liberal fundamentals, a next stage of reform as Brenner *et al.* put it, which potentially threatens to spiral into even deeper crises. Only two years after it was introduced in the UK and across Europe, many countries find themselves once again mired in or teetering on the brink of another economic recession. Not only have these contracting economies dealt harsh blows to regular citizens, especially youth and the vulnerable, and dampened global demand, they find themselves with larger debt-to-GDP ratios than they had before public austerity was implemented. Yet, austerity has not ignited entrepreneurial zeal in the private sector. The newly fabricated doctrine of expansionary austerity, in other words, has proved to be a decided failure, and the IMF has warned austerity-prone governments to ease up on their aspirations of achieving deficit and debt reduction by further eroding social policies and the public sector. Other international policy networks such as the OECD (2011b) recommend that advanced economies reverse course and reinvest in social programmes.

Paradoxically, the Great Recession and public austerity have moved social policy from the footnotes to the front page of contemporary neo-liberal governance. Escalating protests on the streets of Athens, Madrid and London as well as the growth of social movements such as the Indignados and Occupy Wall Street telegraph a crisis in legitimacy for neo-liberalism: a growing number of people simply no longer accept the core tenets of neo-liberal governance. This crisis is increasingly reflected in national partisan politics, such as the 2012 presidential campaigns in France and the United States, which drew clear faultlines between champions of the market and proponents of state intervention, income redistribution and social protection. International policy networks and international financial institutions, once ardent advocates of neo-liberal globalism, moreover, have begun to rethink the role of social policy in sustaining economic growth and social stability. Economic inequality, for example, has been identified as a key driver of the 2008 financial crisis and an ongoing impediment to a robust economic recovery. Policy ideas, such as increased taxation for upper income earners and renewed social investments (once anathema to the neo-liberal mindset) have climbed to the top of national and international policy agendas. These unlikely conversions to a social way of thinking, it should be underlined, are focused as much on breathing life back into the global economy as on improving the lives of the legions of the insecure that have paid dearly for economic globalization and the Great Recession. This story, like neo-liberalism itself, is still unfolding.

16 New constitutionalism and the environment: a quest for global law

Hilal Elver

Introduction

In this chapter I interrogate the relationship between the legal and institutional frameworks of economic globalization associated with the concept of 'new constitutionalism' (e.g. the liberalization of trade and capital movements) and their impact on ecological principles. There is a constant tension between new constitutionalism of disciplinary neo-liberalism and the ethical, normative principles of environmental law. My analysis implies the necessity for a new global environmental law to protect our common future, to overcome major environmental and human crises. This new legal order must be based on cosmopolitan ethical principles, respect for human rights, justice and equity; it should supervene over the national interests and sovereignty concerns of individual states in order to protect the global commons; and finally it should follow transparent, democratic, participatory institutional frameworks. In this proposed order, previously excluded groups that are victims of adverse effects of climate change and other environmental degradation must be included in decision-making mechanisms. Global environmental law should provide an ethical foundation and permit action on behalf of the whole of humanity rather than powerful, hegemonic states, international organizations and the interests of multinational corporations. International environmental law in the 1970s brought innovative principles, such as the precautionary principle, the concept of common but differentiated responsibility, of intergenerational justice, of limited sovereignty and of sustainable development, and in so doing, extended the horizons of traditional international law. However, by internalizing these principles, states are experiencing competing regulatory options. These options involve the protection of the environment, but they also require the safeguarding of free enterprise principles. Such principles aim to protect the free movement of international capital and investment, to remove protectionism, and, to a greater or lesser extent, to limit social and environmental services that were previously the responsibility of state or local governments. These principles provide easy access to resources for foreign capital and limit governmental powers, shifting regulation to the private sector and promoting pro-market reforms.

Stephen Gill defines such legal and political frameworks and their institutions as forming a neo-liberal 'market civilization' (see Chapter 2, this volume). The contradictions of market civilization have a profound impact on transitional economies and developing countries that do not have the freedom to choose whether to implement neo-liberal rules because of their economic dependency on the global financial institutions. Neo-liberal policies that include free trade and less government have altered the environmental management of natural resources such as fresh water, forests, agricultural land and fisheries in developing countries. Case studies of developing countries show how the privatization and pricing of environmental services plus the impact of free trade and neo-liberal policies have had profound though varying degrees of influence on the environment and its management.[1]

Evolution of environmental law and constitutionalism

Environmental pollution is increasingly transcending national borders, and global problems, including declining biological diversity and climate change, are considered to pose significant risks to the health of the planet. Worldwide population growth, excessive consumerism and the expansion of global trade have all contributed to alarming environmental problems.

Internationalization of the concern over the environment emerged in the early 1970s in the aftermath of the UN Conference on the Human Environment held in Stockholm, June 1972. The development of international environmental law principles in the post-Stockholm Conference period is considered a turning point amongst environmental law scholars. Soon after, the first UN institution on environment, the United Nations Environmental Programme (UNEP) was established. Afterwards, several countries founded national environmental institutions, and environmental principles were placed in various forms in new constitutions of many developing countries. This was the initial stage of environmental constitutionalism, 'in which certain needs and interests of present and future generations, the global community, and other forms of life are given foundational legal importance' (Kysar 2012:1). Approximately 130

---

[1] For Latin America see Liverman and Vilas (2006).

countries now have constitutions that include environmental protection, 70 of which provide individuals with some degree of what might be called 'fundamental' rights to a 'clean', 'healthful' or 'favourable' environment. The intersection of constitutional and environmental law has also influenced other areas of law, such as real estate, land use, administrative, torts, civil procedure, workplace safety, tax and international law.

Besides constitutionally based environmental protection at the domestic level, states continued to negotiate and sign major global environmental treaties. Besides UNEP's activities, some important scientific discoveries and accidents also helped to keep up the initiatives. Amongst those, depletion of the ozone layer and disasters such as the nuclear accident at Three Mile Island in 1979, the Union Carbide chemical leak in Bhopal in 1984 and the Chernobyl nuclear meltdown in 1986 added a sense of urgency.

In 1987, focusing on economic and ecological connections and the compromise of developed and developing countries' interests, the concept of *sustainable development* became a new motto of global environmental policy. However, the earlier glorious period of environmental principles gradually faded away because of the rising power of the free market – or more precisely free enterprise – principally in the 1980s, and especially in the post-Cold War era.

The Rio Summit of 1992, the largest UN conference in history, put the environment and development on the global agenda. However, corporate lobbying captured the agenda at Rio and, in the decades following, global environmental issues slipped down the list of state priorities, as they turned to the threat of terrorism and security after 9/11, and most recently to addressing the global financial crisis in 2008.

Globalization, environment and inequality

Economic globalization has been associated with free enterprise, trade liberalization, deregulation of corporate activity, and privatization of many (common) resources and public services. The Bretton Wood institutions (WTO, IMF and World Bank) assist these policies by creating rules that require nations to eliminate 'impediments' that might restrict corporate access to markets, labour and resources. Most of these so-called 'impediments' are laws created by governments to protect the environment, labour rights and public health. All of these laws, many created by governments through democratic processes, are viewed by the advocates of free enterprise as 'nontariff barriers to trade' subject to WTO challenges (Mander 2003). Calling this system 'free trade' is misleading: what is 'free' is only freedom for global corporations, and it entails the suppression of freedom for communities or nations to regulate or otherwise maintain their primary values, such as the environment, health or labour standards.

The WTO has an enormous track record for challenging countries that have strict national environmental laws, such as the United States, Japan and the European Union.[2] The WTO is a forum that gives opportunities to corporations to take legal action against other countries by means of their parent countries instigating disputes. As a result, corporations (and their parent governments) can attack foreign countries' environmental or public health standards. It is a kind of 'cross-deregulation': corporations press their own governments to destroy laws in other countries, just as they push for deregulation domestically. Under the pressure of the WTO not only have many developing countries had to change their environmental laws but also developed countries such as the United States and Canada have been influenced by regional trade rules, such as those of NAFTA.

One of the main objectives of economic globalization is pushing countries to export-oriented production. This means cheaper goods can come to the marketplace from anywhere, without any consideration of environmental or social costs. Creating a mono-cultural export system encourages countries not to be self-reliant, but to open their borders to private investments. Any country that is not willing to do so is labelled 'isolationist' or 'protectionist'. Developing countries have very little manoeuvring space in resisting such pressure because of their dependence on financial aid from the World Bank or the IMF for much-needed national development projects.

The advocates of economic globalization argue that as countries globalize, often by exploiting resources such as forests, minerals, oil, coal, fish, wildlife and water, their increased wealth will enable them to use technical devices to mitigate the negative environmental impacts of increased production. There is ample evidence, however, that when countries increase their apparent receipts in a global economy, most of the benefits go to global corporations who have little incentive to put their profits back into environmental protection or local development. Indeed, critics of globalization note that it encourages excessive economic growth and production with no real concern for unequal or unsustainable patterns of consumption, since, it is argued, globalization exacerbates ecological inequality within and between countries and marginalizes women, indigenous peoples and the poor. One point two billion people live on less than US $1 per day and 2.8 billion people live on less than US $2 per

---

[2] The most well-known cases the WTO fought against are the US Clean Air Act, Marine Mammal Protection Act and the Endangered Species Act.

day, over a billion people do not have access to clean water, and nearly 800 million people in the South suffer from chronic *under*nutrition: the global economy is not working for all.

Moreover the gap between the rich and poor is getting wider and deeper (OECD 2008). According to the UN, a group of 48 of the world's poorest countries have a per capita GDP of under US $900 and they have very low levels of capital, human and technological development. They include just over 10 per cent of the world's population, but their share of the world GDP is less than 1 per cent (UNCTAD 2010). The GDP of the 41 heavily indebted poor countries (567 million people) is less than the wealth of the world's seven richest people combined.

These statistics show that the argument that the global economy is 'good for the poor' is totally unwarranted. Environmental vulnerability of the least developed countries (LDCs), especially in relation to climate change, is officially recognized in the United Nations Framework Convention on Climate Change (UNFCCC). LDCs are supposed to be the beneficiaries of the special climate fund for adaptation, as they have no role in producing greenhouse gas (GHG) emissions, but because of their geographical conditions, they are already subject to the most burdensome effects of climate change (UN LDC 2003).

Moreover, while new environmental standards became globally applicable, poor countries gradually became home to the major pollution activities. The export of hazardous wastes and the relocation of the most polluted industries such as chemical factories to the developing world is one of the major indications of this new environmental colonialism. The Bhopal incident is a monumental example of such wrongdoing; after 25 years, second-generation children are still suffering from the effects of the Union Carbide gas disaster of 1984. The worst industrial disaster in history, and subsequent contamination of groundwater by Union Carbide (a US company now owned by Dow Chemical, the second-largest chemical company in the world), shocked the world and changed the town of Bhopal forever. Yet, the victims still continue to fight for justice over the ongoing medical and social disaster, despite their memories of the traumatizing experience.

The environmental impacts of corporate mining activities have extensive effects that go beyond damage to the natural environment and extend to the severe impact on the social and cultural wellbeing of mining communities. Ignorance of such impacts was prevalent during the colonial period, but even today, despite the inclusion of environmental and social commitments in recent mining policy, corporate environmental abuses still exist, and no individual or corporate entity has been found legally culpable for environmental atrocities (Schwartz 2009: 430).

Nigeria and Sierra Leone provide examples of the devastating impact of multinational corporations in mining, oil and mineral exploitation in poor countries. Even though in recent years what was happening in Sierra Leone gained prominence on the international arena as a result of long civil war, it is remarkable how multinational corporations maintained very few links with the domestic economy. Mobile investors and financiers benefited from weak local jurisdictions and escaped environmental responsibility, accountability and appropriate enforcement mechanisms (Ebbesson and Okowa 2009: 270–93).

While environmental regulations have been constitutionalized and internalized by developed states, activities dangerous to human health and the environment that are banned in developed countries find ways of locating in developing countries. Environmental regulations migrate slowly to developing countries. For instance, it took three decades to ban the import of asbestos in developing countries by the WTO.[3] The doctrine of free trade is based on the premise that products should be able to circulate freely without hindrance from technical obstacles erected by states. It is therefore diametrically opposed to domestic regulations in the areas of public health or environmental protection. The philosophy of the WTO directly conflicts with environmental and health protection. Ideally, free trade rules, human health and the environment should be equally important and protected. However, until now, efforts to reconcile these two goals have been rather unsuccessful even in the developed world (De Sadeleer 2009).

Environmentalism versus corporate governance?

Voluntary codes of conduct

The environmental and human rights impacts of corporate-led globalization in the form of large dams, mining, industrial agriculture and, most recently, market-oriented climate mitigation policies such as Clean Development Mechanisms (CDMs) and reducing emissions from deforestation and degradation (REDD) are visible impacts of disciplinary neoliberalism and new constitutionalism. Against the emerging power and influence of corporations on environmental destruction, environmentalists, human rights activists and anti-globalization forces have initiated large-scale resistance movements against multinational corporations to

---

[3] See 'European Communities — Measures Affecting Asbestos and Asbestos-Containing Products'. WTO case No. 135. Ruling adopted on 5 April 2001, available online at: www.wto.org/english/tratop_e/envir_e/edis00_e.htm (accessed 4 September 2013).

combat operations harmful to people and the environment.[4] The 1999 Battle of Seattle and the establishment of the World Social Forum are indicators of global civil society mobilization and signify an important turning point. The voice of civil society has become a voice of globalization from below against market forces and globalization from above (see also Chapter 18, this volume).

In response to the pressure of regulatory demands initiated by the environmental NGOs, the corporate lobby has proposed 'voluntary codes of conduct' and 'corporate social responsibility' to divert attention away from such demands (Assadourian 2005). These policies sought to divert attention from the need for 'hard law' to enforce environmental controls backed by state apparatuses, instead promoting 'soft law' associated with voluntary self-regulation of business practices. These principles are 'soft' in that they are not legally binding and voluntary in the sense that they are not required by law, nor enforceable. Agenda 21, the official outcome of the 1992 Rio Summit, Chapter 30 encouraged such soft rules of environmental practices. More positive proposals came from socially responsible investors that have pressured corporations by threatening to divest their holdings in companies that do not develop policies to improve their environmental practices.

Market-based regulations

Driven by successful corporate lobbyists, environmentalists and governments have begun to explore market-based, performance-related initiatives to regulate environmental protection. Market-based instruments encourage behaviour through market signals, rather than through explicit directives. These policy instruments, such as tradable permits, cap and trade, or pollution charges, according to Robert Stavins, 'can be described as "harnessing market forces", because if they are well-designed and properly implemented, they encourage firms or individuals to undertake pollution control efforts' (Stavins 2003; see also Chapter 3 by Cutler). In recent years, this perspective of free market environmentalism, following the American experience, gained an international platform amongst the OECD countries. Traditional environmental principles such as 'polluter pays' and other command and control mechanisms were considered

---

[4] See *Doe* v. *Unocal Corp.*, 395 F. 3d 932 (9th Cir.2–2): this was a class action filed against a US oil company for complicity in the forced labour, murder, rape and torture of natives of Burma by the country's military in the course of constructing an oil pipeline. See also *Doe* v. *Exxon Mobil Corp.*, 393 F. Supp. 2d 20 (D.D.C 2005): this was a lawsuit by Indonesian villagers against a US oil company, charging human rights abuses by Indonesian military guarding oil facilities.

ineffective. Thus market-based regulatory systems are preferred options in many countries outside of the United States and Europe. The Kyoto Protocol, the regulatory legal document of the UNFCCC, introduced three market-based mechanisms for greenhouse gas (GHG) emissions reductions. Two mechanisms generate project-based offsets: the Clean Development Mechanism (CDM) aims to mobilize emission-reduction projects in countries without legally binding emission commitments, whereas Joint Implementation (JI) is limited to projects in countries with such commitments. International Emission Trading (IET) allows countries with emissions commitments to trade parts of their emissions budgets. There are ample discussions amongst environmentalists and economists about the success or failure of the system (Michaelowa 2012). Whether the main target of reduction of the greenhouse gas emissions will be reached in order to reverse or stop the adverse impact of climate change is yet to be seen.

Public–private partnerships

At the beginning of the twenty-first century, the United Nations introduced the Millennium Development Goals to work toward eliminating poverty and providing access to vital resources and services to poor communities. One of the ways to deal with these goals was by introducing the privatization of public services. After some failed projects of the 1980s and 1990s, the IMF and the World Bank proposed public–private initiatives or partnerships to promote privatization. Considering the political resentment against the word 'privatization', eventually this term was dropped and 'partnerships' replaced it, allowing multinational companies to access development projects such as large dams. Large dam projects had been largely abandoned in the developed world due to the adverse impact on the environment and social destruction of local communities.

Public–private partnership initiatives gave birth to new 'hybrid institutions'. Partnerships amongst corporations, international institutions and established NGOs created new policy-making bodies for resource management. For instance, the partnership between the CEO Water Mandate and the UN; the Alliance for Water Stewardship with the Nature Conservancy; the Water Stewardship Initiative, World Water Council and the cooperation with several UN agencies, and many others are examples of these new hybrid institutions. While they provide global policies for vital resources, they actually participate in rule-making processes as equal partners to states and international institutions. The aim of such intrusion is to control and dominate the regulatory framework in favour of international business (Elver 2012). The major aim behind this is not only taking over lucrative services that traditionally were part of state responsibility, but also clearing away regulatory hurdles for corporate operations. Sadly, many environmental NGOs have started to work with such institutions in order to be part of the new governing process.[5]

A new global challenge: climate change

Despite significant environmental injustices in relation to pollution, disastrous accidents and resource exploitations at national, international and global levels, earlier environmental challenges, including transboundary air and water pollution and ozone depletion, were largely manageable. Intergovernmental cooperation proved to be sufficient in addressing problems through norm-constraining behaviour. In those cases, either interests were shared in achieving regulatory effectiveness or, as was the case with ozone depletion, the availability of commercial substitutes and the small number of actors responsible for disseminating the ozone-depleting chlorofluorocarbons (CFCs) meant governments more responsible for the harm should accept a disproportionate share of the adjustment costs, which were not too burdensome. This cooperation and relative success indicates that states are willing to promote global wellbeing by reliance on legal regimes when there are not large economic or security interests at stake.

While the rules of new constitutionalism are dismantling some environmental regulations, promoting voluntary compliance and pushing countries to privatize major public services, new challenges are facing humanity where needed solutions go far beyond these alternatives. Most significantly, challenges associated with global-scale concerns cannot be entrusted to the rationality or strategic priorities of a particular country or to the logic of market forces. Climate change is perhaps the most challenging single problem that humanity faces as a whole. In dealing with the adverse impact of climate change, drastic mitigation and adaptation policies are necessary. Yet, the shortcomings and limitations of even progressive new environmental law principles are dramatic. This is because climate change is filled with uncertainties and controversies, and likely requires major economic adjustments that will burden certain kinds of societal activities in a major way. Moreover, climate change policies are against the interests of energy companies (coal, oil and gas), one of the most powerful and lucrative industries worldwide. It is now a scientifically known and widely accepted reality that greenhouse gas emissions are

---

[5] See, for example, Pacific Institute Globalization Program. Available online at: www.pacinst.org/about-us/mission-and-vision.

the most significant causes of planetary warming. Ironically, the way in which the free market economy operates is exacerbating GHG production because of greater storage and handling processes for various goods and, more importantly, the need for increased carbon-based energy resources for production. Export-oriented production goes with long-distance, often excessive, transportation. Ocean transportation carries nearly 80 per cent of the world's international trade in goods, and container ships generally use the most polluting diesel engines in the world. However, the jurisdiction of the UNFCCC excludes the mandate to control GHG emissions associated with the shipping industry. Global warming pollution from shipping is significant and virtually unregulated.[6]

The impact of global warming is geographically diverse. For instance, it has particularly raised earth temperatures in Sub-Saharan Africa, producing severe drops in rainfall and droughts in ways that have generated intense competition for water and land use. Several African countries have experienced internal conflict as we have seen in Sudan. Climate change, as the US naval forces rightly confirmed, is becoming a security concern not only for African countries, but also developed countries by way of forced immigration and other spillover impacts.[7]

While Africa is the most vulnerable continent in relation to the adverse impact of climate change, its relative contribution to the accumulation of CO_2 in the atmosphere is minimal. Already home to many of the world's poor, the region has very little capacity to respond to the dramatic effects of climate change, which include water and food scarcity, famine and infectious diseases. Only a global community orientation could generate the political will to give serious implementation to forms of obligatory responsibility that would provide relief to the victims of global warming that are located well beyond the borders of rich countries with enough resources available to address the problem.

Without a global solidarity norm reinforced by global institutions it will not be possible to deal humanely with the tens of millions of environmental refugees likely to flee across borders to escape from coastal flooding, drought, and shortages of food and water (Laczko and Aghazarm 2009). However, the United Nations cannot consistently provide the legal remedy in the twenty-first century, although its efforts have been notable in establishing a normative architecture with a global orientation in several areas, especially in relation to human rights. In the 1970s, a

---

[6] 'Shipping Impacts on Climate: A Source with Solutions', July 2008. Available online at: http://oceana.org/sites/default/files/o/fileadmin/oceana/uploads/Climate_Change/Oceana_Shipping_Report.pdf.
[7] See 'National Security Implications of Climate Change for U.S. Naval Forces', 2011. Available online at: www.nap.edu/catalog.php?record_id=12914#toc.

series of global conferences organized by the United Nations on human rights, population, women's rights and the environment were a step in the right direction. Its positive impact on global policy-making and the establishment of a network amongst transnational civil society organizations were of enormous significance. However, in the late 1990s, such initiatives were completely hijacked by powerful global economic forces, and the role of the UN shifted from a global policy-making institution to a project-proposing institution. The Millennium Development Goals of 2000 are a vital example of this shift.

The UN is too state-centric and subordinate to geopolitical and geoeconomic pressures to provide the sort of global legal order that the most pressing challenges of our time demand. The yearly conference of the member parties of the UNFCCC (1992) clearly indicates this failure. It revealed that a UN-sponsored effort to provide a voluntary framework for the reduction of greenhouse gas emissions responsible for climate change failed because individual states were unwilling to cast aside their special interests and priorities connected to their economic success or developmental preoccupations to support goals beneficial for all. This makes global criteria and long-term adaptation almost impossible to achieve.

Considering the failures of the last few years to reach consensus amongst the parties of the UNFCCC to reduce greenhouse gas emissions, it is not even clear whether there has been extension of the Kyoto Protocol or the creation of new legally binding commitments for all. Even though the members of the Kyoto Protocol only constitute 60 per cent of the GHG producers, it is so far the only mandatory regulatory regime to reduce GHG emissions. As noted, the Kyoto Protocol embraced market-based principles to promote so-called 'Clean Development Mechanisms' and to pressure countries to reduce GHG emissions by way of technological exchange or other means by doing business with developing countries. However, China receives the biggest portion of help through Clean Development Mechanisms instead of the LDCs because transnational corporations have big production platforms and markets for their goods in China.

As of 2007, China became the biggest CO_2 emitter, bypassing the United States. Yet, as a developing country, China currently is not subject to any mandatory reduction according to the existing legal system. This development also gave a strong hand to climate change deniers, and allowed for coal and oil industry lobbyists to manipulate the American public and the US Congress against any international commitment or national regulations to reduce emissions. However, one should not forget that China is the biggest exporter of the goods that the developed world is using and consuming. In the current legal order, the calculations of greenhouse gas emissions do not consider this dilemma. No matter who consumes the goods, the exporting country is responsible for the emission of GHGs rather than the consumers. This means that the Chinese carry the environmental burdens of producing GHG emissions while the rest of the developed world uses Chinese exported goods.

Meanwhile, pivotal developing countries such as India, Brazil, Russia and Mexico continue to produce greenhouse gasses since they are not constrained by any mandatory global-level framework. In this respect, it is civil society activists that are the main fighters in this arena, yet they have few resources or institutional authority to transform their concerns into a legally binding framework. Their main roles are those of *global* advocacy and civic action, which has an impact on public opinion that can, at times, alter debate on policy within states. It is notable that during the most recent climate change conferences in Copenhagen, Cancun and Durban, the governmental side of the summit kept civil society representatives out of official negotiations, removed them from the deliberations of governments, and their voices were silenced in the formal proceedings. Yet the transnational civil society consensus strongly supported an approach to legally binding and mandatory reduction of carbon emissions that would distribute the economic burdens fairly and in accord with global, rather than national, wellbeing.

What can be observed from global climate change diplomacy is that a global rule of law is subordinated to the primacy of global economic and national economic interests. This means that the norms will be implemented if they correspond with economic priorities rather than in response to the global threat and will be ignored if they do not. In effect, the essence of the rule of law is being violated with respect to the most important planetary and human concerns, because there exists a significant economic and climatic inequality.

However, concerns are growing more serious as the climate change agenda threatens human wellbeing in a number of different ways. For most of the modern era, states were legally unaccountable for what was done internally to individuals or to their natural resources, including the ultimate deprivations associated with slavery, dispossession, genocide and environmental destruction (or more appropriately ecocide). The state, if the conditions were appropriate, was legally responsible only to other states, but was sovereign with respect to its own population. After the Second World War, there was strong public pressure for a global human rights framework. Indeed, the United Nations provided the auspices for the Universal Declaration of Human Rights, and later facilitated the negotiation of the two Human Rights Covenants. These developments generated global norms. But it was clear that there was no intention to provide mechanisms of enforcement (Falk 2008).

Similar global ethical rules are still in the form of 'soft' law, with little or no enforceability in relation to environmental destruction. In the case of climate change, developed countries should be held accountable because of their historical responsibility for greenhouse gas emissions starting from the Industrial Revolution. However, the existing legal framework does not allow such retroactive responsibility. Moreover, according to existing traditional international rules, countries cannot be held responsible if they excessively destroy their natural resources because of economic pressure. Considering the most recent climate change negotiations, developed countries are pushing for the voluntary regulatory option and for market-based solutions. Instead, it should be mandatory that any reduction system for greenhouse gas emissions should be based on 'common but differentiated responsibility' as a means to address if not solve inequality amongst the states. Moreover a global carbon tax should be implemented, although it will be strongly resisted by the global corporate lobby and conservative governments.

As mentioned above, market-based solutions are too slow to respond, especially to the abrupt impacts of climate change. These impacts are significantly damaging not only to low-income people throughout the world, but also to low-income countries.

Responses to the environmental challenge

If the political preconditions for global law are missing, are there any alternatives available to build a reasonable system to overcome global problems?

The first option I call the hegemonic or dominant response, e.g. enforcement of norms by leading states as was tried in the 2009 Copenhagen Climate Change Summit, excluding the entire member states of the UN and only including a few states (United States, China, Brazil, India, South Africa) under the leadership of US President Obama. This initiative led to a backlash at the 2010 Cancun Climate Change Summit, which revitalized the multilateralism of the UN, but not enough to find solutions for an effective legally binding agreement on climate change. The 2011 Durban and 2012 Doha Summits promised (but have yet to deliver) a legally binding agreement for all countries.

A second option involves promoting regionalism, providing it is used with respect to equity and social justice. For example, the European Union provides a regional and comprehensive framework of procedures, norms and institutions for the establishment of regional law. The EU acts more responsibly as compared to the United States in response to climate change. Yet, the recent financial crises, and pressure from the United States, did undermine the EU's leadership on climate change diplomacy.

A third option is associated with the common interests of states in stable interactions that have produced impressive dispute settlement mechanisms in the areas of trade, banking and international business transactions, with a record of compliance by governments, whether weak or strong. This solution reflects the power of global economic institutions and well-organized capitalist interests. However, economic crises in the United States and Europe and the recent failure to establish a competitive alternative clean technology market give little promise for this option. This option can only work if a new institutional reform is put forward, such as creating a World Environmental Organization (WEO) modelled after the WTO – an idea that has been in the reform agenda for a long time. There are several options on the table, from reforming the UNEP by giving it more power, to founding a new body. Needless to say, such an institution should embody the principles of global democracy, such as equal participation, transparency, and accountability of states and peoples in international institutions.

These three options are interacting. In a decentralized, fragmented world, it is possible that these options could be used together. To use them in an effective way, however, first and foremost, it is necessary to shift away from the state-centric, national interests and growth-oriented free market principles that shape our current world order. Yet how would this happen? What has historically broken this pattern in the past is the shock effect of a *climatic catastrophic event*. Many of the major environmental agreements or engaged public consciousness came after disasters such as Chernobyl, Bhopal, Exxon Valdez, Hurricane Katrina and the Deepwater Horizon oil rig explosion: incidents that created huge publicity over environmental destruction. However, the impact of climate change, except for extreme weather, comes slowly, sporadically, and most of the time it does not have a significant resonance at the global level.

Moreover, a successful global campaign run by *climate sceptics* – financially supported by big multinational energy companies – has had enormous influence through the global mainstream media on governmental decision-makers. There is still a significant disbelief amongst the US public who continue to be influenced by the right-wing political establishment. Their message is clear: that climate change is a big lie to destroy American capitalism. This unfortunate campaign uses the false rhetoric of scientific uncertainty and delays major policy initiatives against the dangerous effects of climate change at local, national and global levels.

Unfortunately, it will be too late, if there is no immediate action to stop the adverse effects of climate change. Already we are experiencing its adverse impacts in various parts of the world, such as Russian fires, floods in Pakistan and Australia, recent global food crises and extreme weather events in the Midwest, and the mega-storm Hurricane Sandy (November 2012) that significantly damaged the East Coast of the United States.

By far the most visible wake-up call for the American public was Hurricane Sandy. It was also a tangible example of how – as Naomi Klein (2012) put it in a recent article – 'shameless disaster capitalists' acted in the aftermath. Their suggestions for recovery were in the form of 'public–private partnerships' or more precisely 'privatization' and liberalization, e.g. creating 'free trade zones in hard-hit areas in which all normal regulations, licensing and taxes are suspended'. This corporate free-for-all would 'better provide the goods and services victims need'.[8]

By contrast a more desirable path to justice would be based on human rights and a new juridico-political framework involving effective legal structures to protect the environment and to fight against climate change. The key lies in translating human rights as aspirations or moral claims into enforceable demands. The virtue of human rights to a healthy environment would be universal, irrespective of the arbitrariness of economic circumstance or geographic location. At this stage of history, environmental rights are widespread, but there is no generally accepted human right to a sustainable environment. Especially since countries such as the United States are still negotiating accepting economic and social rights as human rights. There are some developments here and there in this general direction such as the Stockholm and Rio Declarations; the African Human Rights Charter (Article 24); the Aarhus Convention (a regional agreement prepared by the UNECE on procedural rights of access to information, public participation in decision-making and access to justice in environmental matters); and the resolutions of the UN Human Rights Council.[9] There are also some promising international and domestic court decisions, such as decisions of the European Court of Human Rights (*Lopez Ostra* v. *Spain*); the decisions of the International Court of Justice on Nuclear Weapons and Transboundary River Cases (specifically Judge Weeramentary's opinions); and the *Inuit Case* against the United States in the Inter-American Commission on Human Rights. However, bringing a human rights concept to the centre of the climate change debate is not an easy task.

---

[8] Russell S. Sober, *New York Times* Online Forum, November 2012 [cited in Klein 2012].

[9] On human rights and climate change, the most recent one is Resolution 18/22 adopted by the Human Rights Council on 17 October 2011.

In June 2012 several UN experts and the High Commissioner of Human Rights called for a Rio+20 framework to ground global commitments in human rights and for double accountability mechanisms to be put in place to ensure that countries are held responsible for their actions. 'Human rights and accountability are the hallmarks of the "best practices" we have, locally and globally, for achieving genuinely inclusive, pro-poor and environmentally sensitive outcomes' (De Schutter 2012). According to the UN Human Rights Council expert on Food Security, governments should be accountable for their international commitments in relation to climate change. They also should complement this with their own domestic accountability systems.

Global environmental justice also raises questions of intergenerational justice. Therefore, to represent and protect rights of future generations, the establishment of a global ombudsman mechanism was proposed. Not surprisingly, there is significant resistance from governments and corporations who expect that opening the door to human rights litigation will have serious adverse effects on their infrastructure projects and on government decisions about energy and environmental resources.

In sum, according to Sammy Adelman, there is a need to establish a new global meta- or fundamental right to combating climate change that is trans-boundary, intergenerational and cross-sectoral. Even if one allows that some human rights are core, fundamental and more basic than others, climate change requires a different approach because of the truly universal nature of the threat it poses (Adelman 2010: 173). Given the scale of urgency of the threat, it is vital to think a new global *Grundnorm* as Hans Kelsen proposed a long time ago (see Chapter 4, this volume).[10] In the end, the future of the world depends on superseding the global limitations of a world of states with a new world political structure based on equity, morality and justice, with people at its centre, allied to regional cooperation premised on global solidarity and the celebration of cosmopolitan ethics and effective norms of global reach.

---

[10] Cited in Adelman (2010: 174).

Part VI

Globalization from below and prospects for a just new constitutionalism

Part VI seeks to highlight some potential for moving beyond new constitutionalism and to develop alternative or insurgent forms of constitutionalism in order to advance a more just, democratic and progressive world order. The main themes involve:

1. *Constitutionalism as critique* or critical perspectives on the new constitutionalism.
2. The importance of linking the critical approach to 'globalization-from-below' scholarship to challenge and transcend the epistemological dominance of neo-liberalism.
3. The political tensions and ethical contradictions between the constitution of the global political economy and the geopolitical practices and institutions that underpin and extend it.
4. The need to transform the double standards, geopolitical contradictions and normative inadequacies of the new constitutional global order by means of a 'just new constitutionalism', for example as anchored in the 'radical promise' of the UN Declaration of Human Rights.

Gavin Anderson in Chapter 17 seeks to demonstrate how critical perspectives can generate new knowledge in constitutional theory. In doing so he draws special attention to the operation of constitutional discourse at two different levels. At one level constitutional discourse develops the foundational procedures governing the exercise of political power. At a second level, 'over the rules', it plays the crucial role of setting parameters for 'how politics is contested' as well as 'what is deemed politically contestable'. That is, as Anderson notes, 'constitutional discourse is always more than the rules that it generates or legitimates, performing also a crucial "framing function"'. He argues that *constitutionalism as critique* allows for reconnecting this framing function of constitutional discourse to the power dynamics that influence our ability to imagine alternative, insurgent or, in his words, 'post-imperial' forms of constitutionalism.

In contrast with the liberal tradition of constitutional theory that justifies an unproblematic distinction between the 'economic' and the 'political' as part of the common sense of capitalist society and its dominant constitutional discourses, Anderson emphasizes that *constitutionalism as critique* places questions of political economy at the centre, not the margin, of constitutional discourse. 'Constitutionalism as critique', according to him, 'demonstrates not just that the legal forms through which neo-liberal globalization unfolds affect the scope of the domestic regulation of fundamental economic activities, but also reshape in important ways those issues conventionally encompassed within domestic constitutional law'. Thus a critical perspective – as also illustrated in Chapters 10 and 11 by Schneiderman and Sinclair – reveals how the neo-liberal juridical regimes that govern the liberalization of trade and investment beyond the scope of domestic regulation also involve 'the question of social justice in the form of the distributive consequences of constitutional choices' – in particular, questions of increasing social inequalities at both the national and global levels (see also Part V).

In this respect, Anderson stresses that crucial tasks for critical perspectives on new constitutionalism in the present era of globalization are to *both* problematize the dominant *constitutionalism as project* and to challenge the 'common sense' of neo-liberal economic orthodoxy. He underlines specifically the importance of connecting *constitutionalism as critique* with the 'globalization-from-below' studies that seek to move beyond top-down methodological approaches and disclose 'a rich empirical landscape of resistance to neo-liberalism, one that is largely focused on social movement activity in the global South'. One crucial purpose of the latter is to contest and transcend the 'epistemological imperialism of constitutional thinking that is framed by neo-liberalism and positivism' as well as its project to establish the legitimacy of neo-liberal rules and procedures as the only valid knowledge for economic and political development and regulation. This perspective can thus open up key epistemological categories 'to [help] find the agency for political change' in ways that expand 'who or what is included within constitutional discourse'. Such openings help to not only highlight a wide range of social movements (including the Zapatista rebellion, the G8 protests and the establishment of the World Social Forum) as constitutive of global governance, but also to widen our imaginary potentials in developing what Richard Falk in Chapter 18 calls a 'just new constitutionalism'.

The wide-ranging chapter by Falk focuses on the new constitutional world order 'writ large', to underline the point that the new constitutional frameworks alone are insufficient to explain the global constitution of power. Geopolitical power is used, albeit in contradictory, selective and often ethically unjustifiable ways, to reinforce the disciplinary dimensions of new constitutionalism and disciplinary neo-liberalism – a relationship that cannot be acknowledged, at least publicly, by the powerful. Falk therefore outlines the ways in which this geopolitical 'other' of new constitutionalism is (re-)produced by dominant powers and interests, often to circumvent international legal mechanisms, and how they seek to legitimate their arbitrary and hierarchically determined use of organized violence and interventionism.

In other words, the new constitutionalism, which is represented in liberal discourse as neutral and legitimate, is actually underpinned by selective applications of the laws to excuse dominant actors from various measures of accountability for wrongful and criminal acts–as well as by governing mechanisms that 'lock in' the powers and disciplines of capital in social relations, in ways linked to the primacy and related geopolitical endeavours and economic interests of the United States. Falk therefore brings the constitutional metaphors generated and favoured by economic and political elites in an era of neo-liberal globalization into the light of normative inspection and ethical-political critique. For Falk, the law can function dialectically, not only as an instrument manipulated for the benefits of dominant forces, but also as 'a counter-hegemonic soft power instrument' that can be harnessed by popular forces from below to challenge the legitimacy of the top-down, selective and unethical systematization of norms, practices and institutional procedures in world order.

Falk then explores a series of complex global policy debates. One concerns the uses of force to prevent genocide or massive crimes against humanity. Here the distinction between legality and legitimacy was initially introduced in the 'old' constitutional concepts of self-determination and sovereign territory under the UN Charter. The Independent International Commission on Kosovo relied on this distinction to insist that the non-defensive use of force by NATO without a UN authorization was unlawful or illegal, while allowing moral and political claims that the humanitarian intervention was nonetheless legitimate. The acrimonious Kosovo debates were superseded by the 'Responsibility to Protect' (R2P) norm in 2005. Falk warns that this new customary international legal norm 'opens a loophole for the pursuit of geopolitical projects associated with uses of force'. Falk then shows how the new constitutionalism has been extended to encompass the organically interrelated issues of security, criminal accountability and environment. He underlines the selective application of legitimacy criteria and the operation of double standards with regard to:

1. Situations of counter-proliferation management in the nuclear weapons regime and the post-9/11 counterterrorist challenge;

2. Accountability mechanisms of international criminal law; and
3. Carbon trading schemes (see also Chapter 3) and a lack of ecologically responsible concern about climate change and sustainability.

Based upon these discussions, Falk contends that the US-led imperial or global dominance project has not only violated the fundamental principles of human rights and democracy, particularly through exercising 'emergency' measures in a permanent war economy, but also transformed the United States into an 'authoritarian democracy'. Indeed, this project has been intended to grant 'unmediated discretion for the dominant power and its allies in crucial spheres of action' while imposing unequal and discriminatory limits on the policy and activities of geopolitical subordinates.

Nevertheless, the legality and desirability of accommodating a legal framework with the interests and preferences of geopolitically dominant actors has been contested by a variety of social forces from below. They seek to develop a 'just new constitutionalism' with a coherent sense of legitimacy that draws on the moral and political principles of 'humane global governance'. In this respect, Falk suggests that the longer-term potential for such people-oriented resistance initiatives to fulfil their normative goal is contingent on a vigorous dialectic *between* the necessary centralization of functions to tackle challenges of global scope, such as climate change and nuclear weaponry, *and* the decentralization of power from the central government of sovereign states to lower levels of authority and community through a determined politics of subsidiarity and dispersion.

17 Constitutionalism as critical project: the epistemological challenge to politics

Gavin W. Anderson

Introduction

This chapter addresses the significance of critical perspectives on new constitutionalism [hereafter *constitutionalism as critique* (Schneiderman 2010)] as a new terrain of knowledge from the perspective of constitutional theory.[1] It matters how we talk about constitutionalism as it operates at two different levels – it not only provides the basic rules and procedures that govern the exercise of political power (Lane 1996: 4), but it also, and more fundamentally, embodies foundational principles of societal organization (Teubner 2004), providing the framework for how these are made, and moreover, transformed. This chapter will therefore initially focus upon these underlying foundational dimensions of constitutional discourse, rather than new constitutionalism as it is referred to elsewhere in this book as a concrete set of neo-liberal procedures, processes and structures within capitalist societies. It then introduces the emancipatory and novel epistemological perspectives on constitutionalism associated with theories emanating from the global South, sometimes referred to as 'globalization from below'. It is argued that *constitutionalism as critique* is enriched and politically strengthened by the new forces and movements associated with these novel epistemological perspectives, which enable a new approach to the construction of foundational principles.

A key aspect of this enterprise addresses the continuities between old and new forms of constitutionalism. Thus, *constitutionalism as critique* emphasizes how the separation between the economic and the political characterizes new constitutionalism, a separation that was fundamental

---

[1] Thus, *constitutionalism as critique* is referred to in this chapter primarily in terms of the *literature* on the legal dimensions of global governance inspired by radical political economy analyses of neo-liberalism, rather than the analysis of the ideas and socio-material forces associated with the juridical and legal processes and structures of the global political economy per se (referred to throughout this book as the new constitutionalism of disciplinary neo-liberalism, or *constitutionalism as project*).

to the operation of liberal constitutionalism within the nation state, and that now is taken to a zenith by neo-liberalism. Neo-liberalism seeks to remove processes of marketization and commodification from political contestation and constitutional revision globally, thus removing the market from greater democratic control, taking further, on *transnational* and *global* levels, the processes of commodification documented extensively by Karl Polanyi in *The Great Transformation*, when capitalist market society was being established in the nineteenth century at the *national* level in England. The manner by which critical constitutional theory seeks to re-establish questions of (global) political economy at the heart of constitutional discourse is elaborated in the first section below.

Critical constitutional theory also provokes discussion regarding connections between the old and the new constitutionalism at an epistemological level. However, here the narrative perhaps involves more elements of continuity, indeed some of the generally positivistic epistemological assumptions, which have underpinned understandings of how constitutions operate at the national level, are often carried over into debates over constitutionalism beyond the state. However, to the extent those assumptions reinforce the constraining character of classical or traditional constitutionalism, they exist in tension with the political, transformative ambitions of the critical constitutional perspective. Thus the ways in which constitutionalism frames (global) society's foundational principles needs to be opened to scrutiny on epistemological grounds.

With this in mind, the final section addresses how we might move beyond these issues and imagine alternative constitutional forms. Applying the critical insight that it is 'within changes in thought' that we can '[re-]configure action' (Gill 2003: 16), we connect recent theoretical reconstructions of acts of resistance to neo-liberal globalization, particularly those emanating from the global South, to the prospects for the critical constitutional approach. This supports the contention that where the core epistemological tenets of constitutionalism that straddle the domestic and global context have been successfully confronted, the green shoots of an alternative – insurgent – paradigm of globalization and *constitutionalism as critique* can be found. In other words, the key lesson of critical scholarship on new constitutionalism is that the framing function of constitutionalism itself has to be the object of scrutiny and critique.

Political economy and constitutionalism

In general terms, constitutions discharge certain tasks that modern societies have come to regard as essential (Thornhill 2010). Through processes of 'recognizing, co-ordinating [and] assimilating' law and politics, constitutions enable different groups within society to negotiate their diverse interests, thereby stabilizing expectations and managing social plurality (Chalmers 2000). The classical constitutional discourse – or *constitutionalism as project* – that emerges from these interactions performs a 'double role' (Schneiderman 2008: 5): as 'descriptor' it charts the outcome of these processes in providing the basic ground rules for the conduct of political life, and as 'normative guide' it confers legitimacy on those rules to the extent that they enable processes of the 'abstraction, generalization [and] positivization' of political power (Thornhill 2010: 53).

Accordingly, deepening the distinction made in the opening paragraph, constitutional disputes arise at two levels: one is 'within the rules of law', focusing on, for example, how particular constitutional provisions should be interpreted or applied, while the other is 'over the rules' (Tully 2002: 207), focusing at a foundational level concerning the basic principles and procedures for creating a constitution – or put differently on the question 'how to decide how to decide' (Walker 2008: 524). Thus, constitutional discourse is always more than the rules it generates or legitimates, performing also a crucial 'framing function' (Christodoulidis in Teubner *et al.* 2011: 209), setting the parameters not just for how politics is contested, but what is deemed politically contestable.

One of the enormously significant contributions of *constitutionalism as critique* to constitutional discourse is to reconnect this fundamental framing function to questions of power and political economy in the context of globalization. The argument presented within this section therefore is that this critical political economy perspective on constitutionalism advanced by *constitutionalism as critique* is at the core, not the periphery, of constitutional theory, and moreover, that it highlights the importance of what is included or excluded from the framing function discussed above in terms of our ability to imagine alternative forms of constitutionalism. Ultimately theories of *constitutionalism as critique* are seeking (in the phraseology of Richard Falk in Chapter 18) to develop alternative forms of theory and practice that can help create a 'just new constitutionalism'.

Viewing constitutionalism as a set of underlying frameworks that shape political struggle also helps address some threshold questions, and highlights some key continuities between the nation state and global contexts. For example, Saskia Sassen in Chapter 7 shows the complexity of the relations between the two, in so far as some aspects of the capitalist state particularly in the executive branch are strengthened through their association with the transnational regulation of capital. By contrast, for some thinkers, discussing constitutionalism in the context of globalization raises a definitional *quaere*, as the former is seen as only capable of subsisting in the nation state (Walker 2008: 521).[2] However, there is no compelling reason why we should continue to conceive of the frame for politics within national bounds if political power itself is exercised across borders.

An examination of the constitutional question as something that both operates within as well as transcends nation states, brings to light connections between ostensibly different strands of scholarship under the rubric of *constitutionalism as critique*. One such strand focuses on the spread of constitutional charters of rights and the increasing prominence of courts in settling political disputes (Hirschl 2004b; Mandel 1998; Chapter 6, this volume). The second strand takes as its point of departure the new frameworks for the institutionalization of liberalization, marketization and privatization through new transnational structures for property rights, investment, trade and finance (Cutler 2012; Gill 2000; Schneiderman 2008). While emerging from different disciplines – law, political economy and international relations – and addressing different scales (the local, national and the global) each addresses how the framework within which political options can be pursued is being narrowed to make the principal criterion of legitimacy the degree to which policy and action conform to the strictures of neo-liberalism (Arthurs 1999: 27).

At the crux of such critical constitutionalist analysis, however, is an even more striking claim, namely that we are presently witnessing an attempt to make permanent changes to the constitutional mainframe. Some take up Karl Polanyi's key argument concerning the 'double movement' in *The Great Transformation* (1944/1957), seeing what is at issue as an 'attempt to set up one big self-regulating market' (Munck 2007: 14) while seeking to reduce to virtually negligible levels the prospect of a countermovement. In Loïc Wacquant's vivid turn of phrase, if successful, this would amount to the rise of a 'true *neoliberal international*', which 'presents the world made by the multinational corporations as the final stage of history and the commodification of everything existing as the highest achievement of humanity' (2004: 100, emphasis in original). What an 'end of history' perspective misses out, however, is how Polanyi theorized the second half of the double movement: as spontaneous counter-forces that encompassed workers, producers on the land and in the cities, as well as capitalists who sought to institute various forms of protection from the pure market disciplines that were atomizing society and destroying ecological structures.

---

[2] See Glossary.

The fundamental question this discussion poses for constitutional theory is whether we can rescue constitutional theory and scepticism from nihilism in an age of globalization.[3] It is possible to argue that in the context of neo-liberalism, constitutionalism has reached the stage where it has become a barrier to redirecting political power to any form of social good since it facilitates the expansion of capital and private accumulation rather than simply codifies and restrains public and private power. This is a crucial difference between the old and the new in new constitutionalism and it raises a central question concerning the basic functions of a constitution – a constitution is often traditionally associated with curbing excesses of public power. Adverting to its role in facilitating private accumulation seems to change this basic understanding. A progressive form of constitutional scepticism, by contrast, while highly dubious about the political credentials of prevailing forms of constitutionalism, believes that there can be a different constitutional future to the constitutional present.

In this context, the central argument advanced here is that *constitutionalism as critique* provides an important focus of theoretical resistance to such nihilism, and by extension neo-liberalism itself, by reopening questions about how constitutionalism carries out its fundamental framing function, which neo-liberalism wishes to remove from scrutiny and challenge. However, it needs to go further than resistance and become a key force in the reconstitution of global political power, which itself is partly contingent upon new epistemological perspectives on constitutionalism – such as those discussed in the final section of this chapter under the broad rubric of globalization from below.

How *new* is new constitutionalism?

To many observers, constitutional discourse in the twentieth century operated within relatively clear and settled contours. Put briefly, this regarded the primary task of constitutions as creating and establishing the institutions of the nation state, and regulating the relationship between those institutions and citizens. As discussed in the introduction to this volume, this traditional understanding focused almost exclusively on issues concerning the hierarchy between institutions, checks and balances between them, judicial protection of individual rights and appropriate amending formulae.

For this approach, critical perspectives on political economy have very limited relevance for constitutional lawyers: within the disciplinary division of labour, questions of economic power may be the concern of

[3] I am indebted to Upendra Baxi for this formulation.

corporate or commercial law as determined by state institutions acting within the constitution, but are not part of constitutional law. However, this ostensibly scholarly consensus conceals often frantic efforts beneath the surface to repel consideration of ideological and theoretical questions within constitutional discourse prompted by critical perspectives on political economy.

The background to this ideological dimension is provided by Ellen Meiksins Wood's analysis of capitalist society in terms of its unique separation between the economic and the political. Whereas previously, coercive powers were vested in military or political hands, and exercised directly over labourers and tenants, Wood finds in the transition to capitalist society a new form of coercive power. Accordingly, while the state remains the ultimate guarantor of the capitalist order, on a practical level, the daily business of regulating production and distribution, and, given the increasingly commodified nature of social life, much else besides, is secured by the indirect or structural power of the market. Crucially, though, this is not seen as political power, with the result that it is not subject to the mechanisms of democratic accountability that apply to the formally discrete political sphere (Wood 1995: 10–12).

For liberals, this distinction between 'the exploitative powers of the capitalist and the coercive powers of the state' (*ibid.*: 10) is unproblematic in terms of constitutional theory. It simultaneously explains and justifies the public institutional default mode of enquiry, with the political domination of the state marked out as a special category requiring constitutional limitation. Moreover, it provides liberals with the means of responding to problems of economic exploitation while remaining within the public–private divide. Thus, liberals concerned about excessive concentrations of private power might advocate the regulation of (parts of) civil society by the political institutions of the state. Here, constitutional law is seen to provide the framework for the conduct of politics: subject to respecting basic rights, the constitution is seen as neutral as to how political power, once legitimately acquired, is to be exercised (Beatty 2004: 161). Accordingly, it is open to those so concerned to advocate greater constraints on private power.

However, although this has become the dominant view within the legal academy, there has always been a dissenting tradition that has drawn on critical approaches to political economy in order to problematize the public–private divide. For example, historical analyses of liberal constitutionalism have argued that rather than providing neutral baselines, the entrenchment of individual rights impedes the capacity of the state to constrain power constitutionally allocated to the market (Beard 1921/1941; Hirschl 2004b). Legal realists undermined the key constitutional division of labour by showing how coercion and domination were equally likely to have a private as public provenance, and that in the modern administrative state, the analytical distinction between the two spheres lacked any coherence (Hale 1935). Critical legal analyses of contemporary governance have sought to demonstrate how private entities such as corporations are powerful political actors in their own right, often inverting in practice their supposedly subordinate position to the state in liberal theory (Hutchinson 1995: 125–8). *Constitutionalism as critique* can thus be located within this tradition through its depiction of global economic rules as accelerating and embedding the constitutional protection of private power from democratic supervision. Moreover, its particular mode of argumentation insists that in the global era, critical analyses of political economy are central, not marginal, to constitutional scholarship.

Constitutionalism as critique demonstrates not just that the legal forms through which neo-liberal globalization unfolds affect the scope of the domestic regulation of fundamental economic activities, but also reshape in important ways those issues conventionally encompassed within domestic constitutional law. For some, this requires a fundamental rethink of our conceptions of, for example, sovereignty (Nicol 2010: 28), citizenship (Sassen 1996: 31–58) and representation (Tully 2002: 213), to accommodate the extent to which global economic rules privilege investors and technocratic rule, thereby displacing traditional (majoritarian) political relations between individuals and the state. Others emphasize that we can only fully comprehend what power the state has, and how this can be exercised, by reference to the global economic dimension. Thus, for example, in applying rights provisions of domestic constitutions, courts are required to take into account how their potential interpretation may be constrained by international property law regimes (Nicol 2010: 128–51). Accordingly, neo-liberal globalization underlines that constitutional law does not simply limit the power of the state, but also manages relations between states and markets, allocating power between them (Schneiderman 2008: 8).

Constitutionalism as critique also makes questions of political economy hard to avoid by placing to the fore, and raising to the global level, the question of social justice in the form of the distributive consequences of constitutional choices. Such questions tend to be downplayed in the national context, subsumed within a liberal discourse of freedom and individual rights. However, an important critique of the new constitutionalism is that it involves phenomena that systematically contribute to uneven global distributive patterns, and moreover, effectively impede remediable action through constitutional change. In particular, the new constitutionalism constrains the capacity of states to resist neo-liberalism by pursuing non-market-based public policies with regard to the allocation of resources – whether by attacking social conceptions of property (Schneiderman 2008: 137–47) or placing prohibitive costs on policies of nationalization, socialization or redistribution (Nicol 2010: 117–20; Chapters 10–12, this volume). Thus, while the new constitutionalism of disciplinary neo-liberalism is seen to constrain internal redistribution in the West (Arthurs 1999: 67), viewed globally, the global South is cast as the net importer of new constitutionalist measures, and accordingly bearing a disproportionate burden of the costs of neo-liberalism (Santos 2002: 179). Accordingly, questions of global inequality are necessarily constitutional questions.

It follows that for critical perspectives on new constitutionalism, challenging the 'common sense' of neo-liberal economic orthodoxy is the key constitutional battleground of the present era. As such, it provides an important point of contrast with other theoretical approaches to constitutionalism beyond the state. Applying David Schneiderman's terminology, much of the literature on 'post-national constitutionalism' can be seen as 'constitutionalism as project' (2010) in seeking to translate notions of responsible government to the transnational level to address perceived deficits of democratic accountability at the transnational level (Walker 2002). Accordingly, it regards the solutions to problems of global governance as adapting constitutional discourse as developed in the nation state (Buchanan 2006: 6).

Constitutionalism as critique therefore highlights that the consequence of this continuity is to remove the global distributive and social justice questions outlined above from the constitutional frame; while in the national context, *constitutionalism as project* provided the default setting for liberal scholarship, in the global context, it must now be seen as a political choice.

How then can we take the critical constitutionalist perspective forward so that it is more epistemologically robust and connected to the material forces and movements seeking to transform global politics from the bottom up? In this regard, it is important to observe that while the neo-liberal constitutional project sought to reduce the scope for alternative constitutional forms, *constitutionalism as critique* necessarily implies a renewed constitutional project. Moreover, it is vital that the new, insurgent project is clearly differentiated from the (in the words of the Introduction) 'supremacist' project of the past. It is therefore crucial that the 'just constitutionalist' project is attuned to the ways in which political closure is reinforced by epistemological closure around a hierarchical conception of constitutionalism and law (Smart 1989: 4) that is 'formal, positive and singular' (Buchanan 2006: 3).

This is an important part of the response to those objections, documented in the Introduction, which find the new constitutionalist concept to be too structuralist, solid and impenetrable to transformation by countervailing forces. If *constitutionalism as critique* were to be read as transcribing a hierarchical conception of law from the national to the transnational context, this in itself could create an impasse, whether advertently or not, in closing down space for pursuing the critical constitutional project (Anderson 2012: 369–72). In the final section, we instead outline ways in which *constitutionalism as critique* can be read instead as moving alternative models of social organization into the once seemingly solid domain of neo-liberalism, thereby emphasizing the inherent contestability of the constitutional with a view to 'rous[ing] citizens into action' (Schneiderman 2008: 5).

Struggles over hegemony: imagining post-imperial new constitutional forms

In this final section, we canvass an alternative reading of critical constitutionalist scholarship, highlighting connections between it and a series of diverse studies that have been grouped under the rubric of 'globalization from below' (Santos and Rodríguez-Garavito 2005). The argument advanced here is that bringing these various strands of scholarship together is vital for taking forward the critical constitutional project, in ways that can be seen to transcend and go beyond the epistemological imperialism of constitutional thinking that is framed by neo-liberalism and positivism, which is the problem-solving perspective of 'constitutionalism as project'.

This latter scholarship rests on two highly relevant claims for present purposes. The first claim is that top-down methodological approaches, some of which may be informed by positivistic constitutional epistemology, may result in various methodological blind spots that miss key developments in globalization (Santos and Rodríguez-Garavito 2005: 6). The second claim is that correcting this problem reveals a rich empirical landscape of resistance to neo-liberalism, one that is largely focused on social movement activity in the global South, which amounts for some to an alternative, subaltern paradigm of globalization (Santos 2002: 180–2). There are important parallels here with some cognate aspects of the *constitutionalism as critique* literature: for example, A. Claire Cutler details the shortcomings of positivism in charting the extent of transnational merchant law beyond the state (Cutler 2003: 79), while Stephen Gill sees in protest and social movements, such as those that disrupted the Seattle G8 meeting, 'new potentials [for] global political agency' (2003:

218). For example, Cutler, Gill and Isabella Bakker in their respective chapters – as well as others who have contributed to this volume – seek to challenge the self-evidence of the neo-liberal 'common sense' that serves to frame many of the actual practices of the new constitutionalism within global capitalism and global governance.

For Boaventura de Sousa Santos, for example, developing the perspective of globalization from below addresses the links between knowledge and power in the global age (Santos *et al.* 2008). He sees neo-liberal globalization as having important epistemological, as well as economic and political dimensions, with the former's dominance dependent on establishing itself as the only valid type of knowledge for economic and political development. This imperialist attempt to establish epistemic singularity has been forcefully challenged over the past decade or so by grass-roots struggles, conducted by a myriad of non-governmental actors, which draw on a more pluralist 'ecology of knowledge' (Santos *et al.* 2008: xlv) based in ideas of economic solidarity, multicultural human rights and participatory democracy (Santos and Rodríguez-Garavito 2005: 19–23). Two important points emerge from these studies. First, where dominant analyses of globalization emphasize institutional restraint to the occlusion of extra-institutional opposition, this in itself narrows the constitutional frame, limiting what we speak about in constitutional terms. Second, and related, to the extent that the mobilization Santos recounts predicates 'global social justice' on the promotion of 'global cognitive justice' (Santos *et al.* 2008: xix), this suggests opening epistemological debate is a precondition for the transformation of the constitutional frame.

The importance of the epistemological dimension in promoting or confronting the interests of the powerful is underscored by a genealogical perspective on constitutionalism (see also Chapter 5, this volume). For example, James Tully has shown that colonialism was as much an epistemological as a political project, as establishing the legitimacy of European imperial rule entailed the marginalization and suppression of native understandings of authority and governance (1995). The epistemological quality of colonialism though may be the more enduring, as habituating colonial elites to ideas of Western supremacy has resulted in relations of tutelage subsisting today, long after formal political decolonization, with deep-seated consequences when the virtues of neo-liberalism are extolled to former colonies (Tully 2008: 72–5).

However, the other side of Tully's analysis is that political domination was never translated into epistemological closure, as subjugated peoples retained a sense of their right and capacity to make the world differently (1995: 99–101). This is expressed today in challenges to monist assumptions about political order, which run through Western constitutionalism, leading some to speak of a 'resurgence' of indigenous law. While political success has been partial and incremental, where it has occurred this has been through creating epistemological fissures in the ostensibly monolithic edifice of modern constitutionalism, through which the practical implications of indigenous difference have been elaborated (Macklem 2002).

Generalizing from this, globalization from below can be viewed as a fundamental epistemological challenge to the global constitutional orthodoxy and to the new constitutionalism. In terms of the classical distinction referred to in the Introduction to this volume, it represents an insurgent form of global *constituent power* – that is the power to make and, if necessary, break constitutions – in contrast with the constraints of neo-liberalism's *constituted power*, understood as the current 'formal framework of rule' (Tully 2007: 317).[4] This formulation is helpful, as it underscores that the various social movements that make up globalization from below are as constitutive of global governance as the global institutional framework they seek to challenge. Moreover, it is in the interface between constituent and constituted power that constitutional knowledge is produced. For a number of writers, extending the constitutional frame to include globalization from below provides the basis of an alternative knowledge of constitutionalism, one that opens epistemological categories to help find the agency for political change.

This occurs first by expanding who or what is included within constitutional discourse, so that the critical project can include entities such as the World Social Forum, credited with 'broadening and democratizing the public debate over transnational norms' (Buchanan 2006: 9). It also gives us a broader account of constitutional processes, involving a mix of the formal and informal, institutional and non-institutional, with none necessarily privileged as a means of instigating social change: an important corollary of this is that what some critics may see as 'hegemonic legal tools', such as litigation over rights, can be put to 'non-hegemonic use' as part of a larger struggle (Santos 2002: 466–7). For Tully, the net result of this activity is to enlarge the range of epistemological resources that the critical constitutional project can draw upon, reorienting our knowledge of constitutionalism and globalization to 'practices of creating non-imperial customary normative orders' (Tully 2007: 338).

The argument that epistemological openings are an important prelude to political change can be amplified by returning to the Polanyian *problématique* discussed above. Ronaldo Munck argues that in the rise of global

---

[4] On these two terms, see Glossary.

social movements, we can find the beginnings of a 'new great countermovement' (2007: 34–9). Munck's take on globalization 'foregrounds complexity' over the 'type of binary opposition' he suggests characterized initial debates. This complexity 'refuses all static and reductionist readings of globalization', whether blind faith in, or demonization of, the market (*ibid.* 2007: 3, 2). This more complex world though still requires governing, but the form of global governance that is emerging is a more 'decentralized and fragmented' (*ibid.*: 11) enterprise than in the territorial heyday of the nation state. For Munck, it is this new governance paradigm that 'lets the social movements back in' (*ibid.*: 13), by presenting them with a range of opportunities to intervene in order to shape the course of globalization. His account of the multifarious ways in which social movements have responded to these opportunities (from the Zapatista rebellion of 1994 through the G8 protests to the advent of the World Social Forum) leads him to the conclusion that they are as constitutive of global governance as the global institutional framework whose actions they often challenge. Thus, where critical new constitutional perspectives bring the neo-liberal enterprise of embedding society in economy within scrutiny in constitutional analysis, globalization from below adds 'the social counter-power to the unregulated free market as a means of transforming' disciplinary neo-liberalism (*ibid.*: 141).

This state of affairs is ripe for a renewal of Polanyi's thesis of the double movement for the global age. In its original formulation, Polanyi addressed the underlying logic of the societal shift to industrialization, namely that 'instead of economy being embedded in social relations, social relations are embedded in the economic system' (2001: 60). Taken to its conclusion, unlimited commodification would have hugely destructive consequences for society, but, and crucially in Polanyi's reading of economic history, a countermovement would likely develop from within society to protect itself from the worst excesses of the market. Indeed, as Gill (2008: 163) has noted, what Polanyi called a 'stark utopia' of a worldwide self-regulating market system can never be realized because of its inbuilt contradictions. Applying this framework to contemporary political economy, Munck suggests that the Polanyi problematic has now reappeared in a 'magnified and more intense form', with global economic liberalization now representing the culmination of the previously mentioned nineteenth-century attempts to establish a single self-regulating market (2007: 14). However, alongside this, can we now see in the rise of social activism new, transnational forms of social protection that can resist the neo-liberal agenda?

Giving a qualified positive answer to this question does not underestimate the scale of the neo-liberal advances nor is it unaware of the reactionary character of some social movements, nor of the risk of co-option, particularly on the part of NGOs who opt to exert influence within the establishment tent. However, we can locate in transnational social movements the enormous potential to 'build up aspects of the social counter-power to the unregulated free market' (*ibid.*: 141). The key to realizing this potential lies in social movements' capacity to break open some deeply rooted ideas and practices animating legal and political discourse. In this regard, Munck claims that the 'enduring legacy' of new social movements is that 'the rules of the political game and even what now counts as politics are open to question' (*ibid.*: 28). This change is in large part attributed to the entry of new voices, such as the indigenous peoples' movement, and new ideas, flowing in particular from the global South, into debates over democratic struggle (Anderson 2011). While new to many in the West, a Polanyian perspective enables us to locate these voices, and the ground-level political struggles they represent, as a necessary part of broader historical processes, thus reversing their previous marginalization.

A number of studies highlight ways in which the constituted power of neo-liberal globalization has been challenged and remade, whether indigenous peoples forcing oil corporations to relinquish drilling rights in Colombia (Arenas 2007), transnational networks campaigning for affordable antiretroviral drugs for South Africans in the face of restrictive global intellectual property rights regimes (Klug 2005), or the mobilization of public opposition to dam-building projects in India (Rajagopal 2003: 125–6). It is important though not simply to analyze these cases in terms of gains and losses – the victories they achieve vis-à-vis neo-liberalism are often tentative and uneven (Munck 2007: 136). Rather, by advancing and reinforcing the idea that 'another world is possible' in place of the neo-liberal mantra that 'there is no alternative', globalization from below becomes an important catalyst for political experimentation and transformation. In so doing, it refutes directly the argument that we have reached the end of constitutional history – and may well provide the embryonic stirrings of its next chapter.

Conclusion

A major achievement of critical perspectives on new constitutionalism is to open the key framing function performed by constitutional discourse to scrutiny and debate. Its highly persuasive critique of the constitutionalizing effects of neo-liberalism ensures that the public institutional focus that marked the constitutional project of the nation state cannot simply by default be translated to the global setting. *Constitutionalism as critique* makes very clear, and moreover requires justification of, the political choices involved in terms of what we bring within, or leave out of, the constitutional frame.

Unravelling the liberal constitutional frame, though, soon reaches epistemological questions about the very nature of constitutionalism, whose resolution informs the political outcomes achievable within it. If, however, critical perspectives on new constitutionalism draw on positivistic constitutional epistemology as developed in the modern state, they will set limits to how far we can not only prise apart but transform the constitutional frame. This is because we can at the same time see in other strands of thought the basis for a new and radical understanding of constitutionalism *as* knowledge, and as argued above, this type of knowledge necessarily destabilizes positivistic assumptions about the nature of constitutionalism.

In short constitutionalism can now be seen as 'a becoming not a being' (Allott 2001: 139). It is by focusing on what constitutionalism is becoming and can become through the efforts of those operating outside institutional milieu or Western conceptions of law that we move closer to resolving the tension between constitutionalism as project and as critique.

18 New constitutionalism and geopolitics: notes on legality and legitimacy and prospects for a just new constitutionalism

Richard Falk

New constitutionalism is the complex framework that systemizes the norms, prevailing practices and institutional procedures designed to produce order favoured and generated by dominant economic and political elites, whether presiding over governmental structures or administering a range of non-state actors, especially those that are market based. Stephen Gill articulates this innovative and prescriptive orientation towards constitutionalism with a primary reference to the operational logic of the world economy in this era of neo-liberal globalization (1998b, 2008: 161–76).[1] Here I propose extending the scope of new constitutionalism to encompass security, criminal accountability and environment, especially as policy and behaviour of others are impacted by the global domination project of the United States in the early twenty-first century.[2] I regard these issue areas to be organically linked, as an extension of global economic disciplinary policies, procedures and institutional arrangements designed to liberalize trade, facilitate investment, encourage resource exploitation and take advantage of commodity markets. These initiatives would have a secondary objective of diverting public attention from environmental deterioration, and containing mounting opposition to political moves that diminish prospects for profitability and capital accumulation.

Indeed, new constitutionalism depends heavily on the selective application of global norms and procedures and the adaptation of the institutional arrangements set up after the Second World War under the sway of the *old constitutionalism*, e.g. as associated with the UN Charter. New constitutionalism operates on the basis of double standards that exempt geopolitical actors from many mechanisms of accountability for wrongful and criminal acts. As such, world order structures combine states, markets and the geopolitical control mechanisms with a pervasive bias

---

[1] See particularly the Introduction to this volume.
[2] Following Ronnie Lipschutz's (2009) important book, I have a preference for the terminology of 'domination project' to differentiate the American global projection of power from prior projections discussed as hegemony, imperialism or colonialism.

toward privatization to underpin the new constitutionalism. Nonetheless, these top-heavy features of globalization are being challenged mainly from below by rising popular forces dedicated to a more equitable distribution of the benefits of economic development, a more or less regulated world order in relation to political violence, and a visionary endorsement of global democracy as necessary and attainable.[3]

Points of departure

It is my contention that the distinctiveness of new constitutionalism is as a governmentalizing instrument dedicated to promoting private sector market-driven goals and finance capital. It operates in a variety of respects additional to, although interconnected with, the subject matter of trade, investment and markets. For instance, new constitutionalism has recently exerted its influence in the security domain by way of a large-scale reliance on tendencies toward interventionary diplomacy, the outsourcing of war, and increasing the governmental role in controlling worldwide energy reserves and trade routes. Paramilitary entrepreneurs such as Blackwater, operating at the interface between the formal military and civilian society, are the sinister mercenary side of war in its privatized aspects; the same tasks can often be performed by professional military forces at a fraction of what is paid to a private security firm (Scahill 2007).

Privatization, aside from considerations of the profitable and deliberately asocial deployment of capital, involves a reduced political and moral accountability to the electorate and a diminished oversight by representative institutions, which can constrain non-defensive war making by a show of concern about mounting casualties and costs. Fully acknowledged battlefield losses and funding are far less politically saleable to a democratic public, even in American society, despite its disposition to support wars of choice. It is also the case that evasions of accountability for these undertakings have frequently been achieved by relying on covert operations and secret sources of funding kept off the books, and thus almost totally exempt from legislative and media scrutiny (Scott 2010). Some states may rely on transnational security firms to avoid the humiliation of having to accept the presence of foreign troops to uphold their security interests, thereby acknowledging their lack of governing capacity. There have emerged various forms of dependence

---

[3] The Government of Argentina expropriated YPF, a Spanish company, of its interest in the latter's oil company. This is an example of a continuing effort by countries in the South to retain control over national resources.

on neo-colonialist structures and techniques, and even reliance on the superior weaponry of the former colonial powers to police ex-colonies.

Similarly, the US push of a few years ago to regulate carbon emissions by trading mechanisms ('cap and trade') is another example of seeking private sector solutions to collective goods challenges of global scope that should be assessed as costs of production and not passed onto society. There tends to be an uncritical refusal to comprehend the nasty mind game at work: selling rights to pollute does not so much restrict emissions as marketize and commodify the process. Whether this approach has any bearing on preventing the build-up of greenhouse gasses beyond the safe thresholds of 320–360 ppm (parts per million), or even the internationally embraced more permissive ceiling of 400 ppm, is never seriously addressed, but scepticism about such a capitalist approach to global warming seems fully warranted (Orr 2009). Private interests have counter-attacked, launching a well-funded campaign of climate scepticism that seems designed to avoid putting any burden whatsoever on major emitters of greenhouse gasses. The result has been to confuse public opinion sufficiently as to discourage any meaningful response in the United States and elsewhere. It ignores the overwhelming scientific consensus, which insists that the carbon build-up is causing present harm (extreme weather events, food insecurities, polar melting and acidification of the oceans) and poses severe future threats to human wellbeing, despite the fact that American geopolitical ideologues continue to put forward national claims to provide the world with beneficial leadership even in the face of mounting indications of its inability to do so (Brzezinski 2012; Kagan 2013; Mandelbaum 2005). Leadership appropriate for human security presupposes a repudiation of the current ideological content of new constitutionalism, and its replacement by a people-oriented *just* new constitutionalism (Falk 1999).

Distinguishing legality and legitimacy

Reliance on the distinction between legality and legitimacy attempts to subject the constitutional metaphor to normative scrutiny in an era of neo-liberal globalization, and in doing so to go beyond the positivist domain of law as rules and procedures generated through the consent of governments acting on behalf of sovereign states (Falk *et al.* 2012). In some respects, this enquiry considers the symbiotic coexistence of *old* and *new* constitutionalism. By situating concerns about legitimacy within the ambit of new constitutionalism the intention is to bring to bear ordering and limit notions that derive their authority from a consideration of contextual factors that mandate action or restraint beyond the strict boundaries of law. It purports to act on the basis of moral or humanitarian claims while obscuring the causal significance of geo-economic and geostrategic factors such as securing energy reserves or protecting military bases. For instance, international uses of force outside of sovereign territory, where there is absent an authorization by the UN Security Council, may still be justified by a normative argument given the imminence of genocide or in reaction to massive crimes against humanity. Contrariwise, the unavailability of sufficient forces to carry out a protective mandate on behalf of those being victimized counsels against intervention even if the required political support exists in the Security Council. The legalization of proactive legitimacy considerations has been formalized in recent years by enactment of the Responsibility to Protect (R2P) norm. R2P represents a doctrinal attempt to justify various interventionary responses to internal strife, including military action, which had been previously rationalized as 'humanitarian intervention' (Vincent 1974; Wheeler 2000). Whether R2P reflects a more genuine collective response by the international community to alleviate the suffering of the vulnerable and marginal, or is a semantic cover-up for obtaining approval for a disguised geopolitical ploy that is, in its main effect, a disciplinary use of force helpful to new constitutionalism but not acknowledgeable as such, remains to be determined. Recent UN practice invoking R2P, particularly the 2011 NATO War committed to achieving regime change in Libya, seems to support the sceptical view that R2P is old wine in a new bottle.

To illustrate further, suppose a genocidal sweep was expected to take place internal to a large state, with a population exceeding 100 million, the moral argument for acting to protect the vulnerable population might be very persuasive, even compelling, but if there were insufficient capabilities available to make a protective mission credible, then it would be prudent and 'legitimate' to opt for inaction. Such passivity is one of the tragic consequences of geopolitical pluralism, given the hierarchal features of the persisting state system in which dominant states are exempted from interventionary challenges for *practical* reasons associated with the costs and uncertainties of intervention rather than for *legal* reasons associated with conformity to the strict limitations imposed by international law on claims to use force for non-defensive purposes or to circumvent the use of a veto by a permanent member of the Security Council.

The totality of contextual factors that affect decisions on global policy, which vary depending on the issue area, is embraced by the legality/legitimacy duality, and gives substance and structure to my interpretation of the new constitutionalism. In effect, law is an ingredient of new constitutionalism, is operative at the interface between soft and hard power, and is often manipulated for the benefit of dominant forces. It cannot be consistently relied upon to address all geopolitical calls for action in the world of the twenty-first century, given the cross-purposes of major state actors in some settings, e.g. Syria since 2011. Law can also be invoked as a counter-hegemonic soft power instrument, as in the UN and civil society efforts to challenge the legitimacy of Israeli policies in occupied Palestine.

International law and the 'old' constitutionalism

The distinction between legality and legitimacy can be constructed in several different ways and its application varies with the substantive context and the global setting in its various temporal phases. The specific articulation of the distinction emerged initially in the course of the policy debate occasioned by the Kosovo War, then later in articulating the mandate and mission associated with the NATO War in Libya. It also underlies the UN and global debate on how the international community should respond to the mayhem that has been experienced in Syria since early 2011. The Kosovo debate concerned whether a non-defensive use of force by NATO was justified by a claim of humanitarian intervention that was rather widely endorsed by public opinion in Europe and North America but never authorized by the UN Security Council. Without UN authorization, a use of force other than as self-defence against an armed attack is categorically unlawful even if done under the auspices of a regional arrangement.

Against this background of tension between what was legal and what was widely believed at the time in Europe and North America to be a humanitarian imperative that justified protective action by means of intervention, the Independent International Commission on Kosovo struggled to find a way to evaluate the action taken by NATO. The Commission formally introduced this distinction between legality and legitimacy, accepting that the use of force by NATO was unlawful or illegal, but nevertheless legitimate. The role of the distinction was to admit the clear violation of the UN Charter associated with NATO recourse to war without a mandate from the Security Council while accepting the moral and political arguments as justifying preventive action to avoid further Serbian atrocities and threatened ethnic cleansing against the Muslim majority population of Kosovo (Holbrooke 2004; Independent International Commission on Kosovo 2000).[4] The Commission discussion lamented the existence of this gap between the legal and the legitimate, recommending its prompt

---

[4] I should acknowledge my membership on this Commission.

closure by Charter amendment or interpretative resolution. It concluded that until this gap was closed by formal revision of the interpretation of the legal norms prohibiting the use of force in a manner that was more responsive to humanitarian claims, it was preferable to carve out a zone of privileged exception to the constraints of international law as it presently exists.

A seemingly different alternative to this approach, also stimulated by the acrimonious Kosovo debate, was subsequently developed by a Canadian initiative in 2000, the formation of the International Commission on Intervention and State Sovereignty. The report of this Commission influentially proposed the abandonment of the terminology of 'humanitarian intervention' and the adoption of the language of 'a Responsibility to Protect' that was to be located in the organized international community (International Commission on Intervention and State Sovereignty 2001). By stages, Responsibility to Protect has emerged as a new customary norm of international law due to its adoption by the UN Security Council, but whether this development has really altered the nature of this fundamental difficulty of identifying the limits of *legal* authority remains in doubt (Chomsky 1999). We need also to reflect upon the choice between the legality/legitimacy approach and that associated with reliance on R2P.

It is my view that the latter prods the UN to act for the sake of vulnerable peoples but opens a loophole for the pursuit of geopolitical projects associated with uses of force. It weakens the domestic jurisdiction inhibitions of Article 2(7) that were an integral component of the political contract embedded in the UN Charter back in 1945. It also evades the injunction of the Preamble to the Charter 'to save succeeding generations from the scourge of war', while purporting to take growing account of the emergence of human rights as a challenge to earlier notions of an unconditional sovereign right (Booth 1995). R2P also does not explicitly consider whether a proposed course of action is politically feasible or not with respect to the relation of means and ends.

Assuming that unconditional deference to law is not an acceptable resolution of the difficulty posed by states abusing their own people, some mode of principled reasoning to identify the scope of permissible action is needed. Of course, whenever we dilute the clarity of restraints on force we almost certainly lend encouragement to geopolitically shaped decisions, expressed through the selective application of legitimacy criteria and an acceptance of the implication of double standards. As has been noted, there is a greatly different approach taken by the UN to the various popular uprisings and regime responses in Libya, Bahrain and Syria, as well as others that have taken place during 2011–12 (Obama 2011).

The law/legitimacy tension with regard to a contested use of force has been invoked directly and indirectly in two ways with respect to the 2011 NATO role in Libya. Unlike Kosovo there was an initial authorization provided by the UN Security Council for a broadly conceived No Fly Zone framed in language that suggested that the goal was civilian protection, especially in and around the besieged city of Benghazi. This mandate by the Security Council, although weakened by five abstentions from important members, gave the intervention under NATO auspices an initial cover of legality. The military undertaking was then greatly expanded beyond the apparent scope of UN authorization with the obvious intention of helping the rebels prevail in a civil war and cause the collapse of the Qaddafi regime (UN Security Council Resolution 1973, 2011). The Libyan debate concerns whether the expansion of the No Fly Zone beyond its initial mandate subsequently made the NATO operations unlawful, as well as creating a controversial precedent that inhibited a more vigorous international response a few months later to the slaughter of civilians in Syria. Some supporters of the Libyan operations, despite the failure to abide by the original mandate, nevertheless viewed the actions as legitimate, even as a positive model, because of the desirability of regime change given the oppressive policies and recourse to crimes against humanity by the dictatorial Qaddafi leadership, or from a more sinister viewpoint, considering the relevance of controlling Libyan oil prices and reserves.[5]

The contours of the Libyan debate are more complicated, as it could be contended that the intervention was illegitimate from the outset because reliance on air-power to achieve regime change was not an acceptable means to reach such a goal, and therefore the *political* dimension of the undertaking failed the test of legitimacy. It might also have failed the test because of the absence of a credible alternative to the Qaddafi leadership that had reasonable expectations of providing effective governance for the country as a whole, a concern fully justified by the post-intervention failures to establish order and uphold rights in Libya. Beyond this, even if politically feasible, an intervention in an ongoing civil war challenged the *moral* dimension of legitimacy by its refusal to abide by the logic of self-determination that enjoys normative priority in the post-colonial imaginary. Thus, whether lawful or not, the intervention in Libya could and should be viewed as illegitimate for reasons of means, goals and overall effects, although it was definitely rationalized in the Security Council

---

[5] The legitimacy factor can be treated as relevant in a different manner by according primacy to the logic of self-determination, invalidating all interventions that are not credibly associated with the prevention of genocide or massive crimes against humanity.

debate by invoking the R2P norm, although even that was invoked to achieve the more modest objective of protecting threatened Libyan civilians, and not regime change. It has been argued by proponents of the Libyan intervention that the authorization of 'all necessary means' in the resolution delegated almost unlimited discretion to the intervening NATO forces. This seemed radically inconsistent with the language used, the reasonable expectations of the abstaining governments, and more institutionally, with the constitutional responsibility of the Security Council to do all that it can to avoid war in conflict resolution situations and interpret any mandate to use force in a self-limiting manner. It is especially relevant to decide whether the benefit of the doubt should be given to geopolitically governed uses of force that purport humanitarian and restricted aims (Slaughter 2011), especially to the extent that their effect is to reinforce the disciplinary dimensions of the new constitutionalism in the service of world capitalist interests.

Despite this, the legality/legitimacy distinction seems discursively useful, however, as pointing to situations where the legal assessment cannot be allowed to end responsible enquiry into preferred action. In this regard, the distinction offers us useful, even illuminating, modalities of discourse, although it can offer only exceedingly limited decisional guidance (Independent International Commission on Kosovo 2000). It does alert us to the possible deficiencies of adopting a legalist posture with respect to global policy debates under conditions of extreme challenge, suggesting that *responsible* global policy needs also to take flexible account of relevant moral and political considerations without being oblivious to geopolitical motivations. This is the case, especially, when exceptional conditions are present, although all the difficulties of granting 'a right of exception' in the context of the UN emerge. Such reasoning should also be extended to the application of new constitutionalism standards to national situations of stress and emergency associated with economic crises and natural disasters.

In this regard, the law should not be applied mechanically. Put differently, the stability of international interactions strongly favours adherence to legality, especially in war/peace settings, but with the proviso that an appeal to legitimacy is allowable provided it is fully explicated, and more controversially, credible as a *necessary* right of exception. This insistence on imposing a heavy burden of persuasion to uphold a claimed right of exception seems particularly important with respect to second-guessing or diluting legal restraints on the use of force in *old constitutionalism* as these were embodied in the UN Charter and affirmed as also descriptive of contemporary international law in the *Nicaragua* decision of the International Court of Justice (International Court of Justice 1986). It is almost always the powerful states, and particularly in recent decades, the United States, that seek to legalize policies that go beyond the supposed limits of legality to validate their controversial behaviour; weak states may be as inclined to violate, but recognizing their lack of political leverage, rarely make an effort to cloak their departure from law in garments of an enlarged legality, but appeal directly to moral justifications or political necessity, usually on the basis of very self-serving rendering of the factual conditions.

The legality/legitimacy distinction also has security applications in the context of counterterrorism and counter-proliferation, two other aspects of the new constitutional world order that have been unfolding in recent decades, especially since the end of the Cold War, with some bearing on the global political economy. What is consistently excluded from mainstream discourse are the multiple connections between geopolitical patterns invoking humanitarian rationalizations and protection of the property interests of a neo-liberal world economy. Such protection includes opposing movements of resistance that are motivated by social justice. It has become important for critics of new constitutionalism to connect these dots, thereby delegitimize the new rationales for Western uses of force in non-Western countries in the altered discursive setting of the post-colonial milieu.

Managing nuclear weaponry and new constitutionalism

If we are considering the constitutionalism of hard power at its supreme high end of nuclear weapons we initially take note of the interface between an unequal Non-Proliferation Treaty (1968) and its 'unlawful' geopolitical enforcement by the United States in the name of counterterrorism.[6] The peak instance of such enforcement was the 2003 attack on and occupation of Iraq on the principal grounds of preventing the regime of Saddam Hussein from acquiring nuclear and other weapons of mass destruction. In effect, the dubious legality of the NPT was linked via contrived and false intelligence briefings to unabashed aggression to validate recourse to war against Iraq by an American-led 'coalition of the willing' despite the prior rejection by the UN Security Council of the American request for authorization.[7]

---

[6] The New Haven School of International Law merged what is legal with a sociological sense of 'reasonable expectations', thereby purporting to close the gap between law and geopolitics (McDougal and Feliciano 1961).

[7] Editors' note: upon victory over Saddam's forces, the United States installed the Iraq Coalition Provisional Authority or CPA headed by L. Paul Bremer III, which then issued 88 Orders, i.e. 'binding instructions or directives to the Iraqi people that create

The tangled structure of the new constitutionalism in relation to the nuclear weapons regime suggests the contours of the prevailing structural hierarchy: nuclear weapons states possess the weaponry, disregarding their treaty commitment to engage in nuclear disarmament in good faith; some states are allowed to acquire nuclear weaponry without adverse consequences, such as India, Pakistan and Israel; other states, such as Iraq, North Korea and Iran, are faced with military threats and economic sanctions if they seek to acquire such weaponry to uphold their national security; the NPT gives every state a legal right to withdraw from the treaty or to refuse to become a party, but this status can be overridden by the means by which the geopolitical goals of counter-proliferation are pursued; in no area of international political life is US diplomacy more evident than in administering this complex and contradictory law/geopolitics regime that has been established to guard dominant political interests with respect to weaponry of mass destruction. And as the case of Iraq illustrates, this is connected to dominant economic interests in control over the substantial Iraqi and Iranian oil deposits and in geopolitical access to Gulf reserves, and more subtly in many other settings where threats and uses of force help stabilize trade and investment profitability, although these new constitutionalism goals can never be avowed.

We have considered the relationship between law and geopolitics in the setting of counter-proliferation, but what about the connection with legitimacy? Here, again, from a conceptual perspective the issue is rather distinctive. Unlike humanitarian interventions where in the background there is agreement amongst relevant political actors that genocide and crimes against humanity are *global* wrongs, the issue of proliferation gives rise to contradictory legitimacy interpretations. The mainstream Western view argues that proliferation is intrinsically dangerous, increasing the risks of catastrophic war, and hence is illegitimate and should be prevented by all possible means, even if certain allowances are made for strategic exceptions (Brzezinski 2012). US willingness and capabilities to prevent unwanted proliferation add feasibility to the counter-proliferation undertaking. The contrarian view insists that proliferation goals should be subordinated to the security needs of sovereign states, a position that is reinforced by the unacceptability of the two-tier structure of

---

penal consequences or have a direct bearing on the way Iraqis are regulated, including changes to Iraqi law'. Most of these orders were designed to privatize and liberalize the Iraq economy and open it up to foreign investors, measures modelled precisely on neo-liberal new constitutionalist principles. See for example Order 39 on Foreign Investment: CPA/ORD/19 September 2003/39: iraqcoalition.org/regulations/20031220_CPAORD_39_~Foreign_Investment_.pdf.

discrimination that has persisted for decades. Some states are allowed to possess, develop and threaten the use of these weapons, and others are unconditionally prohibited from acquisition. Nowhere are such double standards more prominently exhibited than in the contrast between Western acceptance of Israel's arsenal of nuclear weapons and its reliance on its military superiority to deny other regional actors a comparable nuclear option. The articulation of these policies never admits or discusses new constitutionalism dimensions.

In effect, then, carrying counter-proliferation initiatives beyond the limits of the NPT, and perhaps even disregarding these limits, is tainted with illegitimacy. Additionally, to the extent that counter-proliferation justifications for non-defensive and unlawful uses of force are relied upon, their function is also related to geo-economic imperial goals directly linked to control of natural resources, as was the case in Iraq and Iran. In effect, counter-proliferation camouflages economically motivated uses of force that are not only unlawful, but also illegitimate, which necessitates inventing ways to protect the global dispersion of capitalist investments and interests that do not offend post-colonial sensibilities. One such way is to invoke humanitarian justifications in contexts where the true motivation is geo-economic (Orford 2003).

International criminal accountability

This same complexity is also present in relation to the emergence of international criminal law as providing mechanisms for holding individually accountable political and military leaders of sovereign states. Such accountability is vital to the existence of a robust global rule of law, which, it should be emphasized, is quite at odds with the geopolitically oriented hierarchies of the new constitutionalism. Let me clarify the distinction: according to the rule of law equals are treated equally, or what might be called a 'just new constitutionalism', and as such no actors are practically or conceptually exempt from accountability; by contrast, in new constitutionalism hard and soft power is deployed by dominant actors to encode double standards, producing a variety of discriminatory and selective applications of the law. In this regard, a given application under the auspices of new constitutionalism may be *procedurally* consistent with rule of law and due process standards, giving defendants a fair opportunity for mounting their defense and a decision that reflects a conscientious application of legal norms, while being *substantively* selective by granting impunity to the criminality of the powerful and their 'friends' (Cheng 2012).

A stark illustration involved the refusal to enquire into the legality of the strategic air attacks on German and Japanese cities during the Second World War, as well as the atomic attacks on Japan, during the Nuremberg and Tokyo War Crimes Tribunals set after the Second World War. Famously, the American prosecutor, Justice Robert Jackson, promised that in the future the principles of accountability applied to the defendants from defeated Germany would apply to those countries whose representatives were sitting in judgment.[8] This Nuremberg Promise, implicitly designed to allow a just new constitutionalism, has never materialized: the Nuremberg Promise has been broken beyond repair. It is also relevant to observe that this discriminatory application of law crudely used to encode power relations in old constitutionalism provided a template for the more sanitized role of international law in new constitutionalism.[9]

The post-9/11 counterterrorist challenge

Turning to counterterrorism, the complexity and contradiction are somewhat differently situated, but wide-ranging in character and impact. There are two primary issues: relying within the state on detention and homeland security practices that exceed permissible legal limits, and encroaching upon widely shared commitments to democracy and human rights; violently engaging beyond the state, with or without consent of the targeted country, in a number of interventionary practices that violate sovereignty and international human rights standards. The American domestic scene since 9/11 well illustrates the first cluster of issues, which have been extensively examined (Cole and Lobel 2007; Wittes 2008). It includes the torture debate, the impact of the Patriot Act, the reliance on Guantanamo as an enclave beyond the reach of law, and recent legal justifications of targeted killing, including of Americans, anywhere in the world, as well as indefinite detention of anyone on suspicion of a connection with terrorist activity: instruments of coercive legality that result in pressures upon the legitimate use of governmental authority even in relation to citizens. The cumulative effect of these 'emergency' measures is to create a political climate, especially if combined with the politics associated with growing economic inequality, that has transformed the United States into a new political category: the first *global authoritarian democracy* (Wolin 2008). Such a reality is reinforced by the US role as enforcer of the new constitutionalism, which as a declining empire has few geopolitical

[8] The celebrated German philosopher Karl Jaspers (1967) argued that Nuremberg could only become 'just' if in the future those who sat in judgment when Nazi leaders were convicted would submit to the same kind of legal regime to assess their actions.
[9] It would be a useful exercise to compare the roles of law in the *old constitutionalism*, in the *new constitutionalism* and in what I am calling a 'just new constitutionalism'.

assets of prestige and respect to rely upon, and so is induced to rely on its military machine, which is globally situated, but increasingly unable to attain desired political outcomes and acceptable results. This same militarist mentality also explains moves on the home front to thwart any future insurgent anti-capitalist resistance of the sort prefigured in Seattle in 1999 and by the Occupy Wall Street Movement in 2011.

When considering the transnational dimensions of counterterrorism there are obvious tensions between the legal principles of a state-centric or Westphalian world order and the insistence on a borderless global battlefield for counterterrorism operations, which include covert activities by special forces units, black sites for the interrogation of witnesses, transnational drone missions and other attacks carried out in defiance of territorial sovereignty. The 1 May 2011 execution of Osama Bin Laden in his hideout at Abbottabad, not far from the Pakistan capital of Islamabad, is emblematic of these concerns. The killing of Bin Laden by a Navy Seal unit was carried out in a foreign country, possibly in a manner that violates fundamental human rights with respect to the prohibition of extra-judicial executions, and as such seems both illegal and illegitimate. Thinking otherwise, it is possible to contend that Bin Laden alive and at large was a global menace, and that exceptional methods would be justified in killing him. Bin Laden had himself declared war on the West, and arguably his execution was an act of war authorized by the American commander-in-chief acting in his combat role despite the targeted person being the beneficiary of a tacit right of sanctuary in Pakistan. Whether the transnational realities of large-scale terrorism are such as to make it legitimate to override the normal constraints of territorial sovereignty is a large hovering question that clouds the nature of global governance, and relates closely in the political imagination to the borderless world preferred by the chief strategists of transnational corporations and banks.

And suppose the security claims are persuasive, are these tactical claims being conferred on a reciprocal basis? That is, if a non-state party to such an asymmetrical war were to manage to execute political leaders of their opponents, would that be treated as an act of war rather than of terror? Are the constraints on the conduct of military or violent operations applicable to both sides in the so-called 'long war' or is only the non-state side so constrained? Note that in normal warfare the conduct rules of the law of war apply to aggressor and non-aggressor equally, although as discussed accountability mechanisms are not. Even within a Westphalian framework, it is doubtful that United States', and to a certain extent Israel's, claims to kill their opponents in third countries is seeking to establish a legal precedent available to others similarly situated. Surely,

Iran and many other foreign governments and non-state actors would have a strong basis for attacking individuals in Israel or the United States if the contours of permissible behaviour are determined by the logic of *reciprocity* rather than by the geopolitical logic of *hierarchy*.

Imperial new constitutionalism

The argument here is that these settings pose serious issues involving the non-economic dimensions of the new constitutionalism, as well as highlighting the relevance of the distinction between legality and legitimacy. Ronnie Lipschutz, in his important book, connects these enquiries into the sort of authority structure fashioned in a 'constitutional' form by the overall domination project that continues to be pursued by the United States despite the setbacks of recent years: 'The constitution for a new hybridized political structure such as Imperium is not an off-the-shelf product, and it most certainly will not be written "in Congress gathered".' Indeed, as the product of long and constant struggle amongst various centres of power and authority, the Constitution of Imperium is unlikely ever to appear as a single text. Nevertheless, a hundred years hence 'it is likely to be as "real" as any similar document under glass today' (Lipschutz 2009: 92). Lipschutz's formulation, although concerned with the rewriting of the American Constitution to serve the purposes of running a global empire, is relevant in its realization that a constitution may be composed of diverse elements that cannot be reduced to a text or series of texts, but involves geopolitical norms of action and instrumentalized norms of authority designed to facilitate the maintenance of structures of domination. Similar to the Gill conception of new constitutionalism is the complementary Lipschutz insight that one instrument of imperial geopolitics is the *comprehensive* refashioning of the overall authority structure governing uses of power by and within states in light of new discursive limits associated with the post-colonial imaginary. It is this comprehensive refashioning that is what makes it appropriate to describe the process in the language of constitutionalism.

It is important to take note of two features of this constitutional restructuring of world order:

1. Domestic authority structures are shaped by a permanent war economy exercising continuing emergency powers in ways inconsistent with human rights and political democracy, descending into an 'authoritarian democracy'.
2. International imperial authority on behalf of a post-colonial West-centric hegemonic worldview that administers a dualistic legal system,

involving unmediated discretion for the dominant power and its allies in crucial spheres of action, is coupled with legal constraints as set forth by international law to regulate the behaviour of geopolitical outliers.

Neo-liberal globalization and the new constitutionalism

In the aftermath of the Second World War, there was a definite plan to establish a world-encompassing legal and economic architecture of institutions and practices that would benefit all, but especially the industrial capitalist countries of the North. This architecture has demonstrated its resilience by continuously being adapted to serve these same interests despite changing global circumstances, especially the collapse of the colonial order. John Ikenberry (2011) has emerged as the leading champion of the virtues of this world economic order, contending that it will remain a benevolent framework for the foreseeable future.

However, the clear imbalance between rich and poor was accentuated after the end of the Cold War, commonly referred to as 'the Washington Consensus' in which neo-liberal ideology created a capital-oriented approach to development based on property rights and financial markets, which favoured the rich and punished the poor and vulnerable, especially many of the very poor (Falk 1999). That is, as Stephen Gill (2008) and others have argued, international law has played a regulatory role that validated financial institutions and markets at the expense of the peoples of the world, premised on promoting ecologically non-sustainable consumerist lifestyles, and undisturbed by impending petroleum and water scarcities, widening income disparities and persisting enclaves of extreme poverty.

Legitimacy in this setting of globalization needs to be understood primarily in terms of a contrarian people-oriented development, or what I have referred to in the past as globalization from below, and what Gill (2008) characterizes as the 'post-modern Prince'. In this respect, Gill points to 'the Battle of Seattle' as an epic expression of this encounter between the forces of law and the forces of contrarian legitimacy, between the scheduled meetings of bureaucrats and officials within the offices used by the IMF and the demonstrations by citizens in the streets (Mittelman 2010). Here legitimacy is associated with resistance and legality with the established order. It is legitimate resistance because of the failures of the new constitutionalism to achieve either the appearance or reality of fairness in developmental economics, especially with regard to the distributional benefits of growth, as well as the less emphasized failure to impose ecologically responsible constraints on production and consumption patterns or to manage force in accord with a scrupulous regard for the legal framework set forth in the UN Charter. More specifically, from the perspective of environmental concerns about climate change and sustainability, new constitutionalism is exhibiting a lack of capability and a weakness of political will to protect the global public good of present and future generations.[10]

Conceptually, then, law and legality are identified with the contradictory mixture of institutions, procedures, norms and practices associated with the established order and the prevailing ideology associated with neoliberalism. In opposition are a body of ideas that form a coherent sense of legitimacy that draws upon a morally and politically based critique that is premised upon the principles of humane global governance and ideas of global justice, a world order that provides for the needs and dignity of all the peoples and persons living on the planet and is sensitive to the claims of future generations (Falk 1995; Rawls 1999).[11] To a significant degree, prospects for humane global governance rest on the promise of authoritative instruments of international law, especially in the field of human rights, but only if applied without geopolitical selectivity. As with the use of force, however, geopolitics has managed to narrow the effective scope of human rights in such a way as to relegate its more far-reaching norms to the never-never land of utopian aspiration. Populist forces that invoke international law in counter-hegemonic moves are seeking its maximal reappropriation from below (Rajagopal 2003, 2008). These social forces are mounting on some occasions a law-centred resistance that overlaps with claims of legitimacy. Although this can be confusing, it is existentially compelling as reflective of contemporary political practice.

Let me illustrate this critical advocacy of a just new constitutionalism by reference to some provisions of the Universal Declaration of Human Rights, which amount to a utopian Trojan horse that entered by stealth from residues of *old constitutionalism*. Articles 25 and 28 of the Universal Declaration are provisions of a formal instrument that is generally treated as expressive of customary international law and, overall, a seminal achievement of human rights, but has been so far effectively

---

[10] Well illustrated by the failure of annual UN conferences on climate change to adopt policies regulating emissions that take responsible account of the scientific consensus.

[11] It is important to distinguish two types of legitimacy: the first justifying various forms of otherwise unacceptable behaviour in accord with new constitutionalism by invoking 'legitimacy' and the second, circumventing strict legal guidelines, as with intellectual property rights, to provide medicine and food to impoverished societies in accord with just new constitutionalism.

neutered with reference to global economic justice by the contrary operating principles of the new constitutionalism.

Article 25 posits 'the right of a standard of living' adequate for individual and family basic needs, including 'the right to security in the event of unemployment, sickness, disability, widowhood, old age or any lack of livelihood in circumstances' beyond control. Article 28 is even more encompassing and radical: 'Everyone is entitled to a social and international order in which the rights and freedoms set forth in this Declaration can be fully realized.' It is so obvious as to require no exposition that the new constitutionalism embodying the logic of neo-liberalism is dramatically at odds with these provisions of international human rights law. In this regard, the law as understood from above contradicts the law as affirmed from below (Rajagopal 2003). This gap can also be explained as establishing a legal order that accommodates hierarchies of power and wealth via new constitutionalism while a second legal order, a necessary utopia or just new constitutionalism seeks to align this exploitative structure with prevailing ideas of justice, including considerations associated with equality and inequality, in its quest for legitimacy (Falk 2009: 13–24). This legitimating struggle has not been adequately theorized and is mainly ignored. Its radical promise of global justice for the poor is obviously at odds with the way the world is being organized both horizontally (inequality amongst states) and vertically (hierarchical patterns of control), but it underlies, usually implicitly, the imaginary of resistance that adopts such norms of legitimacy as foundational for its hopes and struggles, and as reflective of its ethical belief in the unity of people: 'the sky has many stars, but the earth has only one human family'.

Here the legality/legitimacy interplay is used to contrast ideas of what is *lawful* in the sense of being in accord with what 'the law' prescribes, with ideas about what is *legitimate* in the sense of what accords with ideas of justice and practicality (or political feasibility). There is a fundamental tension between legality and legitimacy in all those settings where the law is aligned with the interests and preferences of the geopolitically dominant political and economic actors. As far as economic globalization has encoding neo-liberal ideology, this tension is a crucial instance. Legality constitutes institutional arrangements (most prominently, the Bretton Woods institutions) that prescribe rules and procedures that favour investment interests and capital efficiencies regardless of human consequences, which is concretely expressed in widening disparities between rich and poor within and amongst states and regions, as well as by the failure of the system to satisfy the needs of those living in extreme poverty. The 'legality' of neo-liberal globalization is contested by a variety of resistance initiatives premised upon the 'illegitimacy' of its process and substance (ranging from conditionalities to structural adjustment mechanisms).

A concluding comment

In conclusion, there are various ways to conceptualize what I am calling here the just new constitutionalism. It has often in the past been associated with discussions of 'humane global governance' or 'progressive global governance'. The guiding idea is to find a way to identify the overall outlook of what I have in the past called 'horizons of desire', or more modestly, with what would be the implications of a world order constructed on the principles of a human rights culture based on realizing the aspirations of Articles 25 and 28 of the Universal Declaration of Human Rights. In the end, fulfilling the normative potential of any just form of constitutionalism in the near future will depend on a robust dialectic between functional centralization to meet problems of global scope (e.g. climate change, nuclear weaponry, world poverty, water scarcity, food insecurities, pandemics) and a determined politics of subsidiarity and dispersion, shifting power from the governmental centre in sovereign states to lower levels of authority and community. This will also involve a struggle to wrest the discourse of legitimacy from the geopolitical manipulators acting on behalf of neo-liberal and imperial new constitutionalism. The overriding goal of global reform must become a just new constitutionalism.

Glossary

Bilateral Investment Treaties (BITs): International agreements entered into between two governments that limit a host state's ability to develop policies or legislation that impair the interests of foreign investors.

Billion: 1,000,000,000, or one thousand million.

Cap and trade: Cap and trade is a method for regulating the amount of pollution emitted into the atmosphere. Regulators establish a cap on emissions and grant facilities a certain number of permits that function like pollution credits. Facilities that are able to operate below their cap are thus able to sell their remaining permits to others. This creates a commodity out of the right to emit carbon and other harmful emissions by allowing permits to be traded on the market.

Capital accumulation: The growth of a sum of money by regular and various combinations of rent, interest, subsidies, transfers generating surplus profits; the potential for future accumulation is reflected in market capitalization of stocks.

Capital mobility: The ability to move funds and assets across borders unrestricted by policies or legislation.

Collateralized Debt Obligation (CDO): A financial asset that provides a flow of payments that are funded by underlying combinations of bonds, mortgages or other forms of debt. Senior tranche holders are paid first. If defaults occur in the underlying payment assets (e.g. mortgage defaults), junior holders of lower-ranked tranches therefore suffer the initial losses.

Commodification: The process of transforming social relations and processes, things (e.g. life-forms land, natural resources) or ideas into commodities or goods that can be bought and sold in capitalist markets. Thus work is transformed into the commodity labour power; ideas and concepts are transformed into intellectual property rights.

Commodity fetishism: The tendency to attribute to commodities a power and a life that really inheres only in the social relations and activity (work of human beings) expended to create commodities.

Commodity form: The commodity form is the most elementary and fundamental form that capital or wealth takes in capitalist society. Commodities are exchanged in the market for a value determined by their relationship to other commodities – commodities have exchange value rather than use value. In a capitalist economy, this commodification process extends to human beings as well – work is turned into the commodity labour power that is bought and sold in the labour market.

Commodity form of law: The principal form that law takes in capitalist society. This legal form mirrors the commodity form by creating private property rights that are enforceable on behalf of commodity owners. Owners/individuals are deemed to be juridical equals in contracts and in market exchanges.

Constituted power: A form of power whereby dominant forces – who may have come to rule by violence – transform their power and domination into rule and prestige that appears as rightful governing authority, for example in the state. Constituted power is consolidated in governing institutions, positions, processes and norms, codified through constitutions and laws that set boundaries on the nature of political action.

De facto:	A situation or condition that exists in reality, as fact.
De jure:	A situation, entitlement or claim that exists by right or law.
Diachronic:	Relating to social, political or broadly the historical conditions promoting change or structural transformation.
Direct power of capital:	Direct aspects of business power and influence over governments and labour in capitalist societies. These include capital's greater power relative to organized labour with respect to: its financial resources, expertise, contacts with and representation in government, and control over much of the media. Business or capital therefore has a privileged ability to influence governments, e.g. through lobbying to gain particularly beneficial tax breaks, subsidies, laws, regulations or even military interventions to protect its assets and interests.
Disciplinary neo-liberalism:	A term used to describe the socio-economic project of capital to expand the scope and increase the power of market-based structures and forces so that governments and other economic agents are disciplined by market mechanisms, increasingly on a world scale.
Dispute settlement mechanisms:	Institutions that arbitrate disputes concerning whether measures and actions taken by governments are consistent with international economic law. Only member governments can initiate disputes in the GATS and the WTO, and dispute settlement decisions are binding. However, binding dispute resolution is available to non-state actors, such as transnational corporations, under NAFTA and BITs. If a government that loses a case fails to bring their inconsistent measures into conformity with the GATS within a reasonable period,

316   Glossary

Exercise of governmental authority: the complaining party can try to negotiate satisfactory compensation. If no satisfactory compensation can be negotiated, the complainant can impose equivalent trade penalties on the offending member. The WTO allows 'cross-retaliation' so penalties may be imposed on trade in any area.
The General Agreement on Trade in Services (GATS) applies to all services except those provided 'in the exercise of governmental authority'. This has been defined narrowly to mean only those services that are provided neither on a commercial basis nor in competition with other service suppliers.

Feudal entailments: Restrictions designed to preserve large estates during the feudal period, which limited inheritance for several generations.

Fictitious commodities: Things, processes or ideas that are not produced for sale on the market, such as labour or land, but that are treated as if they are commodities when they are exchanged (bought and sold) in the market.

Global governance: A contested term often used to describe how patterns of rule and authority operate on a global scale to regulate forms of human interdependence across political jurisdictions.

Governmentality: A concept used to emphasize the union between governmental practices and mentalities of rule. It directs our attention to (1) the politico-strategic rationalities underlying the exercise of political rule and authority, (2) the tactics, techniques and mechanisms that are deployed by those who seek to govern others, and (3) the utopian ends for which these practices of government are carried out.

Grundnorm: The norm that precedes any further and developed characteristics of the law. It is prior to the law even if it concerns the law. Without the *Grundnorm* that law is the

Glossary

	(best) manner by which behaviour should be constrained/shaped, the idea of a legal system would not be possible. The *Grundnorm* can only be justified by a normative or political commitment that is not part of the legal system.
Hegemony:	Hegemony combines coercion and consent, force and persuasion in an ethical, cultural and political process whereby the principal ideas, institutions and material potentials of the leading social forces are legitimized, mobilized and extended. Hegemony, which is rarely if ever achieved or approximated, particularly at the international level, involves the fundamental relationship between leaders and led, and is manifested as both material and cultural power, and intellectual and moral leadership, within and across states. Hegemony differs from *supremacy*. In the latter coercion rather than consent comes to the fore.
Insurgent power:	A mode of *constituent* power that activates the self-actualizing potential of subordinated classes or peoples, involving their ability to act and organize politically so as to transform their political possibilities relative to *constituted power*, that is against the powers that rule or dominate them. Such a mode of power could promote either violent or peaceful strategies for change.
International anarchy:	The absence of centralized government in international affairs.
Investor–state dispute settlement:	This mechanism allows foreign investors to directly initiate arbitration claims against states under investment treaties. Investors do not need to seek consent from their home

governments and are not obliged to try to resolve a complaint through the domestic court system of the foreign government. Arbitral tribunal decisions are final, although they may be reviewed on narrow procedural grounds in the domestic courts. While tribunals cannot force a government to change inconsistent measures, they can award monetary damages, enforceable in the domestic courts, to investors.

Judicial review: A process of adjudication carried out by judges when the general rules of legislation are applied to a specific case. Adjudication or review is concerned with whether state practice(s) or its legislation is consistent with constitutional principles. If laws or government and civil service activities are found to be in breach of constitutional standards, laws can be repealed and the government made to undertake remedial action.

Jurisdiction: The official power to make legal decisions and judgments as a consequence of a state's sovereign ability to establish the laws by which it will be governed and to hold those within its territorial jurisdiction to those rules/laws. Although a state may claim extra-territorial or even universal jurisdiction for any of its laws, its legitimate ability to enforce such laws remains limited to its (internationally recognized) territorial limits.

Legal form: The expression of the principal legal structures and relations, in terms of rights, obligations, norms and procedures, for legal adjudication and redress in a particular jurisdiction.

Leverage: When investors or banks use money they have borrowed to make multiple loans in order to make greater returns on an investment. Historically, banks have been subject to capital requirements to hold a minimum percentage of deposits as base capital (e.g. 7–10 per cent of total assets or loans) as a prudential requirement, so as to ensure the overall safety of deposits. Such controls limit the degree to which banks or investors can use leverage, but such restrictions have gradually been lifted over recent decades and do not apply to all investors.

Lex mercatoria:	A Latin term, literally 'law merchant', for private trading principles governed by customary commercial law, used in Europe since the Middle Ages. It was enforced by the merchants, in their own courts, along major trade routes. Its goals were to protect freedom of contract and private property, and to enlarge trade, and, in doing so, served to increase economic activity and therefore local tax revenues for states and principalities. Such self-regulation by merchants has expanded in the modern world, creating private international courts of arbitration for commercial disputes across jurisdictions, e.g. associated with the International Chamber of Commerce.
Market access:	Market access has two meanings under services and investment treaties. In a general sense, it refers to the right of a service supplier or investor to supply a service or invest in a foreign market. More specifically, it refers to treaty obligations (modelled after GATS Article XVI) that prohibit government *measures* that limit the number of service operations, the value of service transactions or assets, the number of operations or quantity of output, the number of persons supplying a service the participation of foreign capital, and also any requirements for specific types of legal entities. Such *measures* are prohibited even if they apply equally to foreign and domestic service suppliers.
Market civilization:	An individualized, consumerist and energy-intensive social order associated with late twentieth-century and early twenty-first-century capitalism, in which the allocation of goods, services, life chances and culture are mediated and arbitrated by capitalist market mechanisms, forces and values. Its characteristic perspective on the world is ahistorical, economistic, materialistic, egotistical, short-term and ecologically myopic.

320 Glossary

Market-preserving federalism: A formalization of the neo-liberal approach to federalism developed by economist Barry Weingast. It seeks to create policy competition between different subnational jurisdictions in order to lock in neo-liberal policies.

Measures: Government laws, regulations, rules, procedures, decisions, administrative actions or any other form of government action associated with trade and investment treaties. The GATS, NAFTA and BITs cover measures by all levels of government and any non-governmental bodies exercising authority delegated by government.

Methodological nationalism: The tendency to reduce the analysis of social and historical problems and the principal object of analysis of social science to the container of the nation state.

Most-favoured-nation (MFN) treatment: A trade discipline that requires that governments 'immediately and unconditionally' extend the best treatment given to *any* foreign service or services suppliers to *all* like foreign services and service suppliers, both in law (*de jure*) and in fact (de facto).

National treatment: A trade discipline that requires that governments give foreign services and service providers the best treatment given to like domestic services and service suppliers, both in law (*de jure*) and in fact (de facto).

New constitutionalism: The politico-juridical project associated with disciplinary neo-liberalism and market civilization that seeks to lock in the power of capital through a series of pre-commitment mechanisms and disciplines such as multilateral trade agreements and structural adjustment programmes. These mechanisms – and others – serve to constitute the limits of political possibility and inspire the confidence of investors by increasing the role and scope of market values and disciplines.

Normativity: A condition relating to a standard or norm. Law's normativity concerns its ability to shape, influence and inform behaviour; that is,

	its ability to function as an 'ought' rather than a 'should'.
Organic intellectual:	An intellectual who is either (1) linked to the preservation of the existing mode of production and relation between rulers and ruled who seeks to foster and organize ruling class *hegemony*; or (2) counter-hegemonic intellectuals who seek to transform the existing order and who lead and organize subaltern forces, for example, workers' organizations and struggles for the emancipation, rights and livelihood of peasants and indigenous peoples.
Policy competition:	A situation where capital is mobile and different political jurisdictions must compete for investment by providing the types of policies that investors demand.
Possessive individualism:	A conception of the individual as one who owns his/her own person, capacities or wealth (comprising his/her property) and who owes nothing to society. This individual enters into relations with others in ways designed to further his own interest. A human society of possessive individuals would principally consist of market relations, and the function of politics would be to provide limited government to protect the individuals' property and to sustain mechanisms of exchange. Although the possessive individual cannot alienate all elements of his/her property, s/he may alienate his/her capacity to work as wage labour.
Praxis:	Theoretically informed practices that are transformative of fundamental social relations.
Private transnational governance:	Regulatory and governance institutions and processes that are being designed and enforced across international borders involving a variety of non-state entities, including transnational business corporations, private industry associations and private individuals.

Professionalization: Professionalization is the allocation of a wider range of social tasks to specialized and highly trained groups of people. Professions seek to establish clear rules of recognition for the legitimate and reliable delivery of a quality of service by accredited individuals, based on educational qualifications, training and experience.

Public reason: A mode of thought and deliberation for solving public problems. Rooted in Kant, the term was used by Rawls to describe a mode of reason applied to an entire society rather than a particular element of it. It imagines there can be a shared common reason amidst individuals with different interests and backgrounds.

Quaere: Latin word that is the imperative of *quaerere*, meaning to seek or to question; it is used to introduce a question about something that is doubtful.

Reservations: Reservations (or limitations) in investment treaties are country-specific exceptions that protect otherwise non-conforming measures from the investment and services obligations of trade treaties. *Bound* reservations exempt existing measures, but these measures can only be amended to make them more consistent with the treaty. If an exempted measure is amended or eliminated, it cannot later be restored. *Unbound* reservations protect existing non-conforming measures and also allow governments to take new measures that would otherwise be inconsistent. They therefore provide governments with more policy flexibility in an exempted sector.

Rule of law: The rule of law involves a legal system's key formal and normative content, institutional components and prevailing legal practices. Nevertheless, it remains an essentially contested concept with no consensus about its general significance or meaning in national or global politics.

Social reproduction: The ways in which any society produces, consumes and reproduces, and how it conceptualizes, understands and justifies its particular pattern of historical development. Feminists note that it involves crucial gender dimensions that concern biological reproduction, the reproduction of the labour force, household divisions of labour, and caring institutions for education, health and welfare.

Soft law: Rules that do not have the binding force of legislation, but that are nevertheless influential in shaping behaviour. In international law, soft law such as the Organisation for Economic Co-operation and Development Guidelines for Multinational Enterprises contrasts with the hard law of the international treaties.

Spot currency transactions: Foreign exchange transactions that involve the purchase of one currency against the sale of another at an agreed price for delivery on a specified date, usually the trade date plus two working days. The agreed price is called the 'spot value', which more or less corresponds with the market exchange rate between the two currencies at the moment of the transaction.

Structural power: A form of power embedded in historical structures and/or institutions that set the parameters or the limits and conditions of possibility for action in any given age.

Structural power of capital: The ability of capital to shape policy and beneficial conditions for accumulation in the long term, associated with the structural features of capitalism and the capitalist state. Under capitalism, governments usually operate from the premise that it is private investment that provides growth, prosperity and jobs, and seek to foster a hospitable investment climate by business-friendly policies. However, if policies are perceived by business as undermining such a climate, individual investors may spontaneously decide to postpone investment or to invest in other countries. The investment strike is a case of structural power, uniquely available to business to discipline governments and unions, a power strengthened by free capital mobility across jurisdictions. It works primarily through the market mechanism in capitalist economies. By contrast, if organized labour opposed government policies and collectively organized a general strike, the strike would likely be treated as if it was an attack upon society itself and be met with opposition from and possibly coercion on the part of the capitalist state.

Supremacy: Rather than a politics of justice or *hegemony*, a situation of supremacy involves increasingly coercive forms of rule by a non-hegemonic bloc of social and political forces in and across societies. This supremacist bloc exercises dominance for a period over apparently fragmented populations until a coherent form of opposition emerges.

Synchronic: Relating to social and political conditions that reinforce stability or stasis.

Transfer pricing: The practice of settling (cross-border) transactions between entities of the same multinational company at a certain price. The prices of these intra-firm transactions can be manipulated to create and distribute profits and losses and, in so doing, minimize tax owing in the involved countries.

Transformative agency: A form of collective action aimed at transforming relations of power, privilege and authority while seeking to constitute a new social order with a different set of political possibilities and relations of power.

Transnational laws: Laws that operate across international borders.

Trillion: 1,000,000,000,000, or one million million.

Variegated neo-liberalization: In contrast to convergence-based understandings of neo-liberalization, this conceptualization emphasizes the systemic production of geo-institutional differentiation across places, territories and scales during the process of regulatory restructuring.

Glossary

Weather derivatives: Financial instruments to hedge against weather-related financial risks. The firm or party that sells a weather derivative bears this risk for a premium and stands to earn a profit if the weather remains relatively stable, predictable or normal. If the weather does turn bad, then the party that purchases the derivative claims an agreed amount. Temperature is the most commonly used underlying weather factor, 18 degrees Celsius (65 degrees Fahrenheit) is a standard baseline from which deviations are measured, but any other measurable weather-related event can be used as an underlying factor for a weather derivative.

Withholding tax: An amount of money levied at the source of income. In many cases – e.g. a bank's interest payments on a customer's bank account – the paying agent directly withholds the tax and transfers it to the government.

Appendix

In preparation for this volume, the following questions were outlined and authors were requested to address some of them in their chapters:

Key questions and issues

1. How do you define new constitutionalism? How does it relate to the main conceptual and theoretical developments in your discipline or field?
2. What is old and what is new about constitutionalism/governance/world order in your area or domain of interest?
3. What are the origins and lineages of new constitutionalism?
4. What are the main transformations occurring in the global political economy and geopolitics, and what is their relationship to its principal governance arrangements?
5. How does the new constitutionalism relate to the direct and structural power of capital?
6. How does the 'rule of law' relate to global capitalism and the new constitutionalism?
7. What material and social forces either support or oppose new constitutionalism and why?
8. Identify, evaluate and critique those legal, institutional and normative aspects of new constitutionalism that can be associated with mechanisms to extend pro-market and self-regulatory reforms, e.g. through 'best practices', norms of 'good governance' or 'global standards' as well as the institutionalization and extension of private property rights.
9. How are social and political relations changing, e.g. through redefinitions of the public and private spheres, and how is this related to new constitutionalism?

Present and future prospects

These might be addressed in light of:

1. The context of an era of global crises, particularly the most severe crisis of global capitalism since the 1930s; and
2. New and emergent forms of subaltern, emancipatory and democratic politics.

Key questions

1. What legitimacy concerns does new constitutionalism raise in light of ongoing crises, and how far and in what ways may they be resolved?
2. Do you see any potential for alternate forms of constitutionalism – local, national, regional, global – to emerge?
3. If so, what forms are they taking or might they take in the foreseeable future?
4. How might this relate to prospects for continuation of contemporary world order patterns or perhaps to the creation of a new form of world order?

Bibliography

Abbott, Andrew. 1988. *The System of Professions: An Essay on the Division of Expert Labour*. University of Chicago Press.
Adelman, Sammy. 2010. 'Rethinking Human Rights: The Impact of Climate Change on the Dominant Discourse'. In *Human Rights and Climate Change*, edited by Stephen Humphreys. Cambridge and New York: Cambridge University Press, 159–79.
AEI. 2000. 'The AEI Federalism Project'. Washington, DC: American Enterprise Institute for Public Policy Research. AEI Online.
Akram-Lodhi, A. H. 2007. 'Land, Markets and Neoliberal Enclosure: An Agrarian Political Economy Perspective'. *Third World Quarterly*, 28 (8): 1437–56.
al Attar, Mohsen and Miller, Rosalie. 2010. 'Towards an Emancipatory International Law: The Bolivarian Reconstruction'. *Third World Quarterly*, 31 (3): 357–63.
Albritton, Robert. 2009. *Let Them Eat Junk: How Capitalism Creates Hunger and Obesity*. Winnipeg: Arbeiter Ring.
Allott, Philip. 2001. *Eunomia: New Order for a New World*. Oxford University Press.
Althusser, Louis. 1971. 'Ideology and Ideological State Apparatuses: Notes Towards an Investigation'. In *Lenin and Philosophy*. London: New Left Books, 127–86.
Altvater, Elmar. 1993. *The Future of the Market: An Essay on the Regulation of Money and Nature After the Collapse of 'Actually Existing Socialism'*. London: Verso.
Alvaro, Mercedes. 2009. 'Ecuador President Seeks to End Investment Protection Agreements'. *Dow Jones Newswire*. Available online at: www.nasdaq.com/aspx/stock-market-news-story.aspx?storyid=200910281854dowjonesdjonline000871&title=ecuador-president-seeks-to-end-investment-protection-agreements.
Amin, Ash. 2009. 'Extraordinarily Ordinary: Working in the Social Economy'. *Social Enterprise Journal*, 5 (1): 30–49.
Amin, Samir. 2008. *The World We Wish to See: Revolutionary Objectives in the Twenty-first Century*. New York: Monthly Review Press.
Anderson, Gavin W. 2011. 'Human Rights and the Global South'. In *The Legal Protection of Human Rights: Sceptical Essays*, edited by Tom Campbell, K.D. Ewing and Adam Tomkins. Oxford University Press, 357–64.
    2012. 'Beyond "Constitutionalism Beyond the State"'. *Journal of Law and Society*, 39: 359–83.

Anonymous. 2012. 'Swiss Bank Secrecy: Don't Ask, Won't Tell'. *The Economist*, 11 February.
Appadurai, A. 1986. *The Social Life of Things: Commodities in Cultural Perspective*. Cambridge University Press.
Aranson, Peter. 1990. 'Federalism: The Reason of Rules'. *Cato Journal*, 10 (1): 17–38.
Arenas, Luis Carlos. 2007. 'The U'wa Community's Battle Against the Oil Companies: A Local Struggle Turned Global'. In *Another Knowledge is Possible: Beyond Northern Epistemologies*, edited by Boaventura de Sousa Santos. London: Verso, 120–47.
Arthurs, Harry W. 1999. 'Constitutionalizing Neo-Conservatism and Regional Economic Integration: TINA x 2'. In *Room to Manoeuvre? Globalization and Policy Convergence*, edited by Thomas J. Courchene. Montreal and Kingston: McGill-Queen's University Press, 17–74.
   2007. 'Labour and the "Real" Constitution'. *Les Cahiers de Droit*, 48 (1–2): 43–64.
Assadourian, Erik. 2005. 'The State of Corporate Responsibility and the Environment'. *Georgetown International Environmental Law Review*, 18: 571–94.
Australia, Department of Foreign Affairs and Trade. 2011. 'Gillard Government Trade Policy Statement: Trading Our Way to More Jobs and Prosperity'.
Australia, Productivity Commission. 2010. 'Bilateral and Regional Trade Agreements'. Available online at: www.pc.gov.au/__data/assets/pdf_file/0010/104203/trade-agreements-report.pdf.
Bachrach, Peter and Baratz, Morton S. 1962. 'Two Faces of Power'. *American Political Science Review*, 56 (5): 947–52.
Baily, Martin, Lund, Susan and Atkins, Charles. 2009. *Will US Consumer Debt Reduction Cripple the Recovery?* Brussels, London, San Francisco, Shanghai and Washington, DC: McKinsey Global Institute.
Bakker, Isabella. 2002. 'Fiscal Policy, Accountability and Voice: The Example of Gender-Responsive Budgeting'. Background Paper. *United Nations Human Development Report 2002*. New York and Oxford: UNDP.
   2003. 'Neoliberal Governance and the Reprivatization of Social Reproduction'. In *Power, Production, and Social Reproduction*, edited by Isabella Bakker and Stephen Gill. Houndmills and New York: Palgrave Macmillan, 66–82.
   2005. *Gender Budget Initiatives: Why They Matter in Canada*. Ottawa: Canadian Center for Policy Alternatives. Available online at: www.policyalternatives.ca.
   2007. 'Social Reproduction and the Constitution of a Gendered Political Economy'. *New Political Economy*, 12 (4): 541–56.
Bakker, Isabella and Gill, Stephen. 2003. *Power, Production, and Social Reproduction: Human In/Security in the Global Political Economy*. Houndmills and New York: Palgrave Macmillan.
   2008. 'New Constitutionalism and Social Reproduction'. In *Beyond States and Markets: The Challenges of Social Reproduction*, edited by Isabella Bakker and Rachel Silvey. London and New York: Routledge, 19–33.

Bakker, Isabella and Silvey, Rachel, eds. 2008. *Beyond States and Markets: The Challenges of Social Reproduction*. London and New York: Routledge.
Balakrishnan, Rhadika, Elson, Diane, Heintz, James and Lusiani, Nicholas. 2011. 'Maximum Available Resources and Human Rights'. *Working Paper*. Rutgers: Center for Women's Global Leadership.
Balbus, Isaac. 1977. 'Commodity Form and the Legal Form: An Essay on the "Relative Autonomy" of the Law'. *Law & Society*, 11 (17): 571–88.
Barberis, Eduardo, Sabatinelli, Stefania and Bieri, Anngret. 2010a. 'Rescaling Processes in Europe: Convergence and Divergence Patterns: Towards Multilevel Governance'. In *Rescaling Social Policies: Toward Multilevel Governance in Europe*, edited by Yuri Kazepov. Farnham: Ashgate, 367–88.
  2010b. 'Social Assistance Policy Models in Europe: A Comparative Perspective'. In *Rescaling Social Policies*, edited by Yuri Kazepov. Farnham: Ashgate, 177–202.
Barker, Alex. 2011. 'EU Taxman has London in Sight'. *Financial Times*, 27 November.
Barlow, Maude and Clarke, Tony. 2001. *Global Showdown: How the New Activists are Fighting Global Corporate Rule*. Toronto: Stoddart.
Bartell, Laura. 2008. 'From Debtors' Prisons to Prisoner Debtors'. *Emory Bankruptcy Developments Journal*, 24 (1): 15–40.
Bauman, Zygmunt. 2001. *The Individualized Society*. Cambridge, UK, and Malden, MA: Polity Press.
  2002. *Society under Siege*. Cambridge: Wiley.
Baxi, Upendra. 2005. 'Market Fundamentalisms: Business Ethics at the Altar of Human Rights'. *Human Rights Law Review*, 5 (1): 1–26.
  2006. *The Future of Human Rights*, 2nd Edition. New Delhi: Oxford University Press.
Beard, Charles. 1921/1941. *An Economic Interpretation of the Constitution of the United States*. New York: The Macmillan Company.
Beatty, David. 2004. *The Ultimate Rule of Law*. Oxford University Press.
Beck, Ulrich. 2000. *What is Globalization?* Cambridge, UK, and Malden, MA: Polity Press.
Beck, Ulrich and Beck-Gernsheim, Elisabeth. 2002. *Individualization: Institutionalized Individualism and its Social and Political Consequences*. London and Thousand Oaks: SAGE.
Been, Vick and Beauvais, Joel C. 2003. 'The Global Fifth Amendment: NAFTA's Investment Protections and the Misguided Quest for an International "Regulatory Takings" Doctrine'. *New York University Law Review*, 78: 30–143.
Benatar, Solomon R., Gill, Stephen and Bakker, Isabella. 2009. 'Making Progress in Global Health: The Need for New Paradigms'. *International Affairs*, 85 (2): 347–72.
Bickley, James. 2011. 'Value-added Taxes as a Revenue Option: A Primer'. Washington, DC: Congressional Research Service.
Binder, C. and Schreuer, C., eds. 2009. *International Investment Law for the 21st Century: Essays in Honour of Christoph Schreuer*. Oxford University Press.
Bindreiter, Uta. 2001. 'Presupposing the Basic Norm'. *Ratio Juris*, 14 (2): 143–75.

Birch, Kean and Mykhnenko, Vlad. 2010. 'Introduction: A World Turned the Right Way'. In *The Rise and Fall of Neo-liberalism: The Collapse of an Economic Order*, edited by Kean Birch and Vlad Mykhnenko. London: Zed Books, 1–20.

Blyth, Mark. 2010. 'Ideas, Uncertainty and Evolution'. In *Ideas and Politics in Social Science Research*, edited by Robert Cox and Daniel Beland. Oxford University Press, 83–101.

2013. 'This Time it Really is Different: Europe, the Financial Crisis, and "Staying on Top" in the 21st Century'. In *The Third Globalization: Can Wealthy Nations Stay Rich in the Twenty-First Century?* edited by Danny Breznitz and John Zysman. Oxford University Press, 207–31.

Bockman, Johanna and Eyal, Gil. 2002. 'Eastern Europe as a Laboratory for Economic Knowledge: The Transnational Roots of Neoliberalism'. *American Journal of Sociology*, 108 (2): 310–52.

Böhm, Franz, Eucken, Walter and Grossman-Doerth, H. 1936. 'The Ordo Manifesto of 1936'. In *Germany's Social Market Economy: Origins and Evolution*, edited by Alan Peacock and Hans Willgerodt. London: Macmillan, 15–26.

Bond, Patrick. 2009. 'Realistic Postneoliberalism'. *Development Dialogue*, 51 (1): 193–211.

Booth, Ken. 1995. 'Human wrongs in international relations', *International Affairs*, 71(1), 103–26.

Borras Jr., S. M., Carranza, S. and Franco, J. C. 2007. 'Anti-poverty or Anti-poor? The World Bank's Market-led Agrarian Reform Experiment in the Philippines'. *Third World Quarterly*, 28 (8): 1557–76.

The Boston Globe. 2006. 'Debtors' Hell'. 30 July (online edition).

Bourdieu, Pierre. 1987. 'The Force of Law: Toward a Sociology of the Juridical Field'. *Hastings Law Journal*, 38 (5): 805–53.

Bourdieu, Pierre and Wacquant, Loïc. 2005. 'The Cunning of Imperialist Reason'. In *Pierre Bourdieu and Democratic Politics*, edited by Loïc Wacquant. Cambridge: Polity Press, 178–98.

Bouton, Terry. 2001. 'Review: Whose Original Intent? Expanding the Concept of the Founders'. *Law and History Review*, 19 (3): 661–71.

Brady, David, Beckfield, Jason and Seeleib-Kaiser, Martin. 2005. 'Economic Globalization and the Welfare State in Affluent Democracies, 1975–2001'. *American Sociological Review*, 70 (6): 921–48.

Braedley, Susan and Luxton, Meg. 2010. *Neoliberalism and Everyday Life*. Montreal and Kingston: Queens University Press.

Brand, Ulrich, Gorg, Christoph, Hirsch, Joachim and Wissen, Markus. 2008. *Conflicts in Environmental Regulation and the Internationalisation of the State: Contested Terrains*. London: Routledge.

Braudel, Fernand. 1980. *On History*. University of Chicago Press.

1994. *A History of Civilizations*. New York: Allen Lane.

Brennan, Geoffrey and Buchanan, James M. 1985. *The Reason of Rules: Constitutional Political Economy*. Cambridge University Press.

Brenner, Neil. 2004. *New State Spaces: Urban Governance and the Rescaling of Statehood*. Oxford and New York: Oxford University Press.

Brenner, Neil, Peck, Jamie and Theodore, Nik. 2010. 'Variegated Neoliberalization: Geographies, Modalities, Pathways'. *Global Networks*, 10 (2): 182–222.
Brodie, Janine. 2003. 'Globalization, In/Security and the Paradoxes of the Social'. In *Power, Production, and Social Reproduction*, edited by Isabella Bakker and Stephen Gill. Houndmills and New York: Palgrave Macmillan, 47–65.
   2004. 'Globalization and the Social Question'. In *Governing Under Stress: Middle Powers and the Challenge of Globalization*, edited by Marjorie Cohen and Stephen Clarkson. London: Zed Books, 12–32.
   2007a. 'Reforming Social Justice in Neoliberal Times'. *Studies in Social Justice*, 1 (2): 93–107.
   2007b. 'The New Social "isms": Individualization and Social Policy Reform in Canada'. In *Contested Individualization: Debates about Contemporary Personhood*, edited by Cosmo Howard. London: Routledge, 12–32.
   2008. 'The Social in Social Citizenship'. In *Recasting the Social in Citizenship*, edited by Engin Isin. University of Toronto Press, 20–43.
   2010. 'Globalization, Canadian Family Policy and the Omissions of Neoliberalism'. *North Carolina Law Review*, 88 (5): 1559–92.
   2012. 'Social Literacy and Social Justice in Uncertain Times'. *The Trudeau Foundation Papers*, Volume IV. Montreal: The Pierre Elliott Trudeau Foundation.
   2014. Forthcoming. 'Elusive Equalities and the Austerity Hypothesis'. *International Journal of Law in Context*.
Brodie, Janine, and Bakker, Isabella 2008. *Where are the Women? Gender Equity, Budgets and Canadian Public Policy*. Ottawa: Canadian Centre for Policy Alternatives.
Broomhill, Ray and Sharpe, Rhonda. 2009. 'The Problem of Social Reproduction under Neoliberalism's Reconfiguring the Male-Breadwinner Model in Australia'. In *Remapping Gender in the New Global Order*, edited by Marjorie Cohen Griffin and Janine Brodie. London and New York: Routledge, 85–108.
Brown, Meta, Haughwout, Andrew, Lee, Donghoon and van der Klaauw, Wilbert. 2010. *The Financial Crisis at the Kitchen Table*. New York: Federal Reserve Bank of New York.
Brown, Richard D. 1983. 'Shays' Rebellion and Its Aftermath: A View from Springfield, Massachusetts, 1787'. *The William and Mary Quarterly*, 40 (4): 598–615.
Brown, Wendy. 2003. 'Neo-liberalism and the End of Liberal Democracy'. *Theory and Event*, 7 (1): 1–19.
   2005. *Edgework: Critical Essays on Knowledge and Politics*. Princeton University Press.
Brzezinski, Zbigniew. 2012. *Strategic Vision: America and the Crises of Global Power*. New York: Basic Books.
Buchanan, James. 1991. *The Economics and Ethics of Constitutional Order*. Ann Arbor: Michigan University Press.
   1995. 'Federalism as an Ideal Political Order and an Objective for Constitutional Reform'. *Publius: The Journal of Federalism*, 25 (2): 19–27.
   1995/1996. 'Federalism and Individual Sovereignty'. *Cato Journal* 15 (2–3): 259–68.

Buchanan, Ruth. 2006. 'Legitimating Global Trade Governance: Constitutional and Legal Pluralist Approaches'. *Northern Ireland Legal Quarterly* 57: 1–19.
Bugra, Ayse. 2007. 'Polanyi's Concept of the Double Movement and Politics in the Contemporary Market Society'. In *Reading Karl Polanyi for the Twenty-First Century: Market Economy as Political Project*, edited by Ayse Bugra and Kaan Agartan. University of Chicago Press, 173–90.
Bull, Carolyn. 2008. *No Entry Without Strategy: Building the Rule of Law under UN Transitional Administration*. Tokyo: UN University Press.
Bumpus, A. and Liverman, D. 2008. 'Accumulation by Decarbonization and the Governance of Carbon Offsets'. *Economic Geography*, 84 (2): 127–55.
Burchell, Graham. 1996. 'Liberal Government and Techniques of the Self'. In *Foucault and the Political Reason: Liberalism, Neo-Liberalism and Rationalities of Government*, edited by Andrew Barry, Thomes Obsborne and Nikolas Rose. University of Chicago Press, 19–36.
Carim, Xavier. 2012. 'A South African Perspective on International Investment Agreements'. Speech by the Deputy Director General, Department of Trade and Industry, South Africa, at the WTO Public Forum, Geneva, 25 September. South Centre, *SouthViews*, No. 46, 5 December.
Carothers, Thomas. 2006. 'The Rule-of-Law Revival'. In *Promoting the Rule of Law Abroad: In Search of Knowledge*, edited by Thomas Carothers. Washington, DC: Carnegie Endowment for International Peace, 3–14.
  2009. 'Rule-of-Law Temptations'. *Fletcher Forum on World Affairs*, 33 (1): 49–61.
Castles, Francis. 1998. 'The Really Big Trade-off: Home Ownership and the Welfare State in the New World and the Old'. *Acta Politica*, 33 (1): 5–19.
Castree, Noel. 1995. 'The Nature of Produced Nature: Materiality and Knowledge Construction in Marxism'. *Antipode*, 27 (1): 12–48.
Cerny, Philip G. 1997. 'The Paradoxes of the Competition State: The Dynamics of Political Globalization'. *Government and Opposition*, 32 (2): 251–74.
Cerny, Philip G., Menz, G. and Soederberg, Susanne. 2005. 'Different Roads to Globalization: Neoliberalism, the Competition State, and Politics in a More Open World'. In *Internalizing Globalization*, edited by Philip G. Cerny, G. Menz and Susanne Soederberg. Basingstoke: Palgrave, 1–30.
Chalmers, Damian. 2000. 'Post-nationalism and the Quest for Constitutional Substitutes'. *Journal of Law and Society*, 27: 178–217.
Chang, Ha-Joon. 2002. 'Breaking the Mould: An Institutionalist Political Economy Alternative to the Neo-Liberal Theory of the Market and the State'. *Cambridge Journal of Economics*, 26: 539–59.
  2004. 'Regulation of Foreign Investment in Historical Perspectives'. *The European Journal of Development Research*, 16: 687–715.
Chavez, Rebecca B. 2003. 'The Construction of Rule of Law in Argentina: A Tale of Two Provinces'. *Comparative Politics*, 35: 417–37.
Cheng, Christine. 2012. 'Charles Taylor Trial Highlights ICC Concerns'. *Al Jazeeera English*, 27 April.
Chimni, B. S. 2003. 'Third World Approaches to International Law: A Manifesto.' In *Third World and International Order: Law, Politics, and Globalization*, edited by Anthony Anghie, Bhupinder Chimni, Karin Mikleson and Obiora Okafor. Boston: Martinus Nijhoff, 47–73.

Chomsky, Noam. 1999. *New Military Humanism: Lessons from Kosovo*. Monroe: Common Courage Press.
Choudhry, Sujit. 2006. *The Migration of Constitutional Ideas*. New York: Cambridge University Press.
Christodoulidis, Emilios. 2009. 'Strategies of Rupture'. *Law and Critique*, 20 (1): 3–26.
Clarke, John. 2004. *Changing Welfare Changing States: New Directions in Social Policy*. London: Sage Publications.
— 2007. 'Subordinating the Social? Neo-liberalism and the Remaking of Welfare Capitalism'. *Cultural Studies*, 21 (6): 974–87.
— 2008. 'Living with/in and without Neo-liberalism'. *Focaal: European Journal of Anthropology*, 51 (1): 35–147.
Clarkson, Stephen. 2002. *Canada's Secret Constitution: NAFTA, WTO and the End of Sovereignty?* Ottawa: Canadian Centre for Policy Alternatives.
Clarkson, Stephen and Mildenberger, Matto. 2011. *Dependent America? How Canada and Mexico Construct U.S. Power*. University of Toronto Press.
CMS Gas Transmission Company c. República Argentina. 2005. (Award) ICSID Case No. ARB/01/08, International Legal Materials 44, 1205–63 (12 May).
Coase, Ronald. 1960. 'The Problem of Social Cost'. *Journal of Law and Economics*, 2: 1–40.
Cohen, Marjorie Griffin and Brodie, Janine. 2009. *Remapping Gender in the New Global Order*. London and New York: Routledge.
Cole, David and Lobel, Jules. 2007. *Less Safe, Less Free: Why America is Losing the War on Terror*. New York: New Press.
Conference Board of Canada. 2011. 'Working-age Poverty'. Available online at: www.conferenceboard.ca/hcp/details/society/working-age-poverty.aspx.
Corbera, Esteve and Brown, Katrina. 2010. 'Offsetting Benefits? Analyzing Access to Forest Carbon'. *Environment and Planning A*, 42 (7): 1739–61.
Cornia, Giovanni A. 2005. *Policy Reform and Income Distribution*. Vol. *DESA Working Paper No.3*, ST/ESA/2005/DWP/3, October. New York: United Nations.
Corporate Europe Observatory. 2009. 'EU Trade Talks: A Covert Push for Water Privatisation?', March. Available online at: http://archive.corporateeurope.org/docs/covertpush.pdf (accessed 11 July 2013).
Corrigan, Philip and Sayer, Derek. 1985. *The Great Arch: English State Formation as Cultural Revolution*. Oxford: Blackwell.
Courchene, Thomas. 1995. 'Glocalization: The Regional/International Interface'. *Canadian Journal of Regional Science*, 18 (1): 1–21.
Cox, Robert W. 1987. *Production, Power, and World Order: Social Forces in the Making of History*. New York: Columbia University Press.
— 1992. 'Global Perestroika'. *The Socialist Register: New World Order?*, 28 (1): 26–43.
— 1996 [1981]. 'Social Forces, States, and World Orders: Beyond International Relations Theory'. In *Approaches to World Order*, Robert Cox with Timothy Sinclair. Cambridge and New York: Cambridge University Press, 85–123.

Crouch, Colin. 2009. 'Privatised Keynesianism: An Unacknowledged Policy Regime'. *British Journal of Politics and International Relations*, 11 (2): 382–99.
Cumming, Gordon D. 2008. 'French NGOs in the Global Era: Professionalization "Without Borders"?' *Voluntas*, 19 (4): 372–94.
Cutler, A. Claire. 2003. *Private Power and Global Authority: Transnational Merchant Law in the Global Political Economy*. Cambridge University Press.
  2005. 'Gramsci, Law, and the Culture of Global Capitalism'. *Critical Review of International Social and Political Philosophy*, 8 (4): 527–42.
  2008. 'Toward a Radical Political Economy Critique of Transnational Economic Law'. In *International Law on the Left: Re-examining Marxist Legacies*, edited by Susan Marks. Cambridge University Press, 199–210.
  2009a. 'Constituting Capitalism: Corporations, Law, and Private Transnational Governance'. *Saint Anthony's International Review*, 5 (1): 99–115.
  2009b. 'Unthinking the GATS: Toward a Radical Political Economy Critique of Private Transnational Governance'. In *Business and Global Governance*, edited by Morten Ougaard and Anna Leander. New York and London: Routledge, 78–96.
  2010. 'The Legitimacy of Private Transnational Governance: Experts and the Transnational Market for Force'. *Socio-Economic Review*, 8: 113–30.
  2012. 'Private Transnational Governance and the Crisis of Global Leadership'. In *Global Crises and the Crisis of Global Leadership*, edited by Stephen Gill. Cambridge University Press, 56–70.
Dardot, P. and Laval, C. 2009. *La nouvelle raison du monde – essai sur la societé néolibérale*, Paris La Decouverte: Ed. le monde.
Davies, Rob (Minister of Trade and Industry, South Africa). 2012. 'Investment Policy Framework Speech', 27 July. Available online at: www.trademarksa.org/news/davies-investment-policy-framework-speech (accessed 14 August 2012).
Dean, Jodi. 2009. *Democracy and Other Neoliberal Fantasies*. Durham, NC: Duke University Press.
Dean, Mitchell. 1999. *Governmentality: Power and Rule in Modern Society*. London: Sage Publications.
De Angelis, Massimo. 2004. 'Separating the Doing and the Deed: Capital and the Continuous Character of Enclosures'. *Historical Materialism*, 12 (2): 57–87.
  2007. *The Beginning of History: Value Struggles and Global Capital*. London: Pluto Press.
Demirović, Alex. 2011. 'Materialist State Theory and the Transnationalization of the Capitalist State'. *Antipode*, 43 (1): 38–59.
Denord, Francois. 2009. 'French Neoliberalism and its Divisions: From the Colloque Walter Lippmann to the Fifth Republic'. In *The Road from Mont Pelerin: The Making of the Neoliberal Thought Collective*, edited by Philip Mirowski and Dieter Plehwe. Cambridge, MA: Harvard University Press, 45–67.
Derrida, Jacques. 1992. 'Force of Law: The "Mystical Foundation of Authority"'. In *Deconstruction and the Possibility of Justice*, edited by D. Cornell, M. Rosenfeld and D.G. Carlson. New York: Routledge, 3–67.

Dezalay, Yves and Garth, Bryant. 2002. *The Internationalization of Palace Wars: Lawyers, Economists and the Contest to Transform Latin American States*. University of Chicago Press.
    2011. *Lawyers and the Rule of Law in an Era of Globalization*. Abingdon: Routledge/Glasshouse.
    eds. 2002. *Global Prescriptions: The Production, Exportation and Importation of a New Legal Orthodoxy*. Ann Arbor: University of Michigan Press.
DFAIT. 2011. 'Canada Welcomes Agreement with Dow AgroSciences'. Ottawa: Department of Foreign Affairs and International Trade.
Dibadj, Reza. 2008. 'Panglossian Transnationalism'. *Stanford Journal of International Law*, 44 (2): 253–99.
Dickenson, Donna. 2004. 'Consent, Commodification and Benefit-sharing in Genetic Research'. *Developing World Bioethics*, 4 (2): 109–24.
Dierckx, Sacha. 2012. 'Emerging Markets and International Capital Mobility: Beyond New Constitutionalism?' Presented at the conference on 'Rising Powers and the Future of Global Governance?', University of Sussex, Brighton, 16–17 May.
    2013. 'After the Crisis and Beyond the New Constitutionalism? The Case of the Free Movement of Capital.' *Globalizations*. Published online: 12 August. DOI: 10.1080/14747731.2013.814450 http://dx.xoi.org/10.1080/14747731.2013.814450.
Di Muzio, Tim. 2008. *Towards a Genealogy of Militant Liberalism*. Unpublished PhD thesis. Toronto: York University.
    2011. 'Capitalizing a Future Unsustainable: Finance, Energy and the Fate of Market Civilization'. *Review of International Political Economy*, 19 (3): 363–88.
    2012. 'The Crisis of Petro-market Civilization – the Past as Prologue?' In *Global Crises and the Crisis of Global Leadership*, edited by Stephen Gill. Cambridge and New York: Cambridge University Press, 73–88.
Domingo, Pilar and Sieder, Rachel. 2001. *Rule of Law in Latin America: The International Promotion of Judicial Reform*. London: Institute of Latin American Studies.
Donzelot, Jacques. 2008. 'Michel Foucault and Liberal Intelligence'. *Economy and Society*, 37: 115–34
Dressel, Björn. 2012. 'Thailand: Judicialization of Politics or Politicization of the Judiciary?' In *The Judicialization of Politics in Asia*, edited by Björn Dressel. New York: Routledge, 79–97.
Dworkin, Ronald. 1990. *A Bill of Rights for Britain*. Ann Arbor: University of Michigan Press.
Dymski, Gary. 2009. 'Racial Exclusion and the Political Economy of the Subprime Crisis'. *Historical Materialism*, 17: 149–69.
Ebbesson, Jonas and Okowa, Phoebe. 2009. *Environmental Law and Justice in Context*. Cambridge University Press.
The Economist. 2012. 'New Cradles to Graves'. 8 September. Available online at: www.economist.com/node/21562210.
Edelman, Bernard. 1979. *Ownership of the Image: Elements for a Marxist Theory of Law*. London: Routledge.
Editorial. 2009. 'No Time for Tobin'. *The Times*, 11 December.

Elias, Stephen. 2006. *The New Bankruptcy: Will it Work for You?* Berkeley: Nolo Press.

Elkin, Stephen and Soltan, Karol. 1993. *A New Constitutionalism: Designing Political Institutions for a Good Society.* University of Chicago Press.

Elson, Diane. 1997. 'The Economic, the Political and the Domestic: Businesses, States and Households in the Organisation of Production'. *New Political Economy,* 3 (2): 189–208.

Elson, Diane and Cagatay, Nilufer. 2000. 'The Social Content of Macroeconomic Policies'. *World Development,* 28 (7): 1347–64.

Elver, Hilal. 2012. 'The Emerging Global Freshwater Crisis and the Privatization of Global Leadership'. In *Global Crises and the Crisis of Global Leadership,* edited by Stephen Gill. Cambridge University Press, 107–25.

Esping-Andersen, Gøsta. 1990. *The Three Worlds of Welfare Capitalism.* Cambridge: Polity Press.

Esty, Daniel C. 2006. 'Good Governance at the Supranational Scale: Globalizing Administrative Law'. *The Yale Law Journal,* 115: 1490–562.

EU. 2010. 'Conclusions on a Comprehensive European International Investment Policy'. 3041st Foreign Affairs Council Meeting of the Council of the European Union. Luxembourg: European Union.

EU/Canada. 2011. 'EU–Canada Trade Sustainability Impact Assessment. 2011. A Trade Sustainability Impact Assessment Relating to the Negotiation of the Comprehensive Economic and Trade Agreement (CETA) between the EU and Canada, Draft Final Report: Summary Report'. Brussels: EU. Trade 10/B3/B06 (March). Available online at: http://trade.ec.europa.eu/doclib/docs/2011/march/tradoc_147754.pdf.

EU General Affairs Council. 2011. 'Text of the Mandates'. Available online at: www.s2bnetwork.org/themes/eu-investment-policy/eu-documents/text-of-the-mandates.html.

European Commission. 2010. 'Communication From the Commission to the Council, The European Parliament, the European Economic and Social Committee and the Committee of the Regions: Towards a Comprehensive European International Investment Policy'. Brussels: EC.

   2011. 'Proposal for a Council Directive on a Common System of Financial Transaction Tax (FTT) and Amending Directive 2008/7/EC'. Brussels: EC, 28 September.

   2011. 'Reflections Paper on Services of General Interest in Bilateral FTAs (Applicable to both Positive and Negative Lists).' Revised 28 February 2011. Brussels: Eruopean Commission. www.epsu.org/IMG/pdf/Reflections_Paper_on_SGIs_in_Bilateral_FTAs.pdf.

   2012. 'Enhanced Cooperation on Financial Transaction Tax – Questions and Answers'. Brussels: EC, 23 October.

Fairclough, Norman. 2006. *Language and Globalization.* London and New York: Routledge.

Falk, Richard. 1995. *On Humane Global Governance: Toward a New Global Politics.* Cambridge: Polity Press.

   1999. *Predatory Globalization: A Critique.* Malden: Polity Press.

   2008. 'The Power of Rights and the Rights of Power: What Future for Human Rights?' *Ethics and Global Politics,* 1(1–2): 81–96.

2009. *Achieving Human Rights*. New York: Routledge.

2011. 'Horizons of Global Governance'. Lecture delivered at the conference 'The Future of Global Governance?', York University, Toronto, 25 May. Available online at: http://stephengill.com/news/2011/07/re-imaging-the-future-videos-of-yorks-the-future-of-global-governance.html (accessed 13 July 2011).

Falk, Richard, Juergensmeyer, Mark and Popovski, Vesslin, eds. 2012. *Legality and Legitimacy in Global Affairs*. New York: Oxford University Press.

Federici, Sylvia. 2004. *Caliban and the Witch: Women, the Body and Primitive Accumulation*. New York: Autonomedia.

2010. 'Feminism and the Politics of the Commons'. Available online at: www.thecommoner.org.

Ferguson, E. James. 1979. *The American Revolution: A General History, 1763–1790*. Homewood: The Dorsey Press.

Ferguson, James and Gupta, Akhil. 2002. 'Spatializing States: Toward an Ethnography of Neoliberal Governmentality'. *American Ethnologist*, 29 (4): 981–1002.

Ferguson, Niall. 2011. *Civilisation: The West and the Rest*. London: Allen Lane.

Finkel, Jodi. 2008. *Judicial Reform as Political Insurance: Argentina, Peru, and Mexico in the 1990s*. University of Notre Dame Press.

Fiorina, Morris P. 1982. 'Legislative Choice of Regulatory Forms: Legal Process or Administrative Process'. *Public Choice*, 39: 33–66.

Fishbein, Allen J. and Woodall, Patrick. 2006. *Subprime Locations: Patterns of Geographic Disparity in Subprime Lending*. Washington, DC: The Consumer Federation of America.

Fitzpatrick, Peter. 2006. '"The New Constitutionalism": The Global, the Postcolonial and the Constitution of Nations'. *Law, Democracy and Development*, 8: 1–20.

Florio, Massimo. 2004. *The Great Divestiture: Evaluating the Welfare Impact of the British Privatizations 1979–1997*. Cambridge, MA: MIT Press.

Folbre, Nancy. 1994. *Who Pays for the Kids?* New York: Routledge.

Folbre, Nancy and Nelson, Julie. 2000. 'For Love or Money or Both?' *Journal of Economic Perspectives*, 14: 123–40.

Foucault, Michel. 1976. 'Two Lectures'. In *Power/Knowledge: Selected Interviews and Other Writings 1972–1977*, edited by Colin Gordon. New York: Pantheon, 78–108.

1977. *Discipline and Punish*. Toronto: Random House of Canada.

1978/2003. 'What is Critique?' In *The Essential Foucault: Selections from Essential Works of Foucault, 1954–1984*, edited by Paul Rabinow and Nikolas Rose. New York: The New Press, 264–78.

1984/2003. 'The Ethics of the Concern of the Self as a Practice of Freedom'. In *The Essential Foucault: Selections from Essential Works of Foucault, 1954–1984*, edited by Paul Rabinow and Nikolas Rose. New York: The New Press, 25–42.

1990 *The History of Sexuality, An Introduction*. Translated by Robert Hurley. Volume 1. New York: Vintage Books.

2003a. 'Society Must be Defended'. In *Lectures at the Collège de France, 1975–1976*, edited by Mauro Bertani and Alessandro Fontana. New York: Picador, 1–272.

2003b. *The Essential Foucault: Selections from Essential Works of Foucault, 1954–1984*. Edited by Paul Rabinow and Nikolas Rose. New York: The New Press.

2007. *Security, Territory, Population: Lectures at the Collège de France, 1977–1978*. Translated by Graham Burchell. Houndmills: Palgrave Macmillan.

2008. *The Birth of Biopolitics: Lectures at the Collège de France, 1978–1979*. Translated by Graham Burchell. Houndmills: Palgrave Macmillan.

Foucault, Michel, Burchell, Graham and Gordon, Colin. 1991. *The Foucault Effect: Studies in Governmentality, with Two Lectures by and an Interview with Michel Foucault*. University of Chicago Press.

Fox, Judith. 2012. 'Do We Have a Debt Collection Crisis?' *Loyola Consumer Law Review*, 24 (3): 354–88.

Friedenberg, Daniel. 1992. *Life, Liberty and the Pursuit of Land: The Plunder of Early America*. Buffalo: Prometheus Books.

Friedman, Milton. 1962. *Capitalism and Freedom*. University of Chicago Press.

Friedrich, Carl J. 1955. 'The Political Thought of Neo-Liberalism'. *American Political Science Review*, 49 (2): 509–25.

Froud, Julie, Sukhdev, Johal, Montgomerie, Johnna and Williams, Karel. 2010. 'Escaping the Tyranny of Earned Income? The Failure of Finance as Social Innovation'. *New Political Economy*, 15 (1): 147–64.

Fukuyama, Francis. 1992. *The End of History and the Last Man*. New York: Free Press.

G20. 2012. 'G20 Leaders Declaration'. June 19. www.whitehouse.gov/the-press-office/2012/06/19/g20-leaders-declaration. (accessed 26 October 2013).

Gardner, James A. 1980. *Legal Imperialism: American Lawyers and Foreign Aid in Latin America*. Madison: University of Wisconsin Press.

Garrett, Geoffrey. 1998. 'The Politics of Legal Integration in the European Union'. *International Organization*, 49: 171–81.

Genschel, Phillip and Schwarz, Peter. 2011. 'Tax Competition: A Literature Review'. *Socio-Economic Review*, 9 (2): 339–70.

Ghai, Yash. 1999. 'Rights, Social Justice and Globalization in East Asia'. In *The East Asian Challenge for Human Rights*, edited by J.R. Bauer and D. A. Bell. Cambridge University Press, 241–63.

Gilbert, Neil. 2004. *Transformation of the Welfare State: The Silent Surrender of Public Responsibility*. Oxford University Press.

Giles, Chris. 2009. 'Brown Floats Global Bank Tax'. *Financial Times*, 8 November.

Gill, Stephen. 1992a. 'The Emerging World Order and European Change: The Political Economy of European Union'. In *New World Order? Socialist Register 1992*, edited by Ralph Miliband and Leo Panitch. London: Merlin, 157–95.

1992b. 'Economic Globalization and the Internationalization of Authority: Limits and Contradictions'. *Geoforum*, 23 (3): 269–84.

1995a. 'Globalisation, Market Civilisation, and Disciplinary Neoliberalism'. *Millennium: Journal of International Studies*, 23 (3): 399–423.

1995b. 'The Global Panopticon – the Neoliberal State, Economic Life, and Democratic Surveillance'. *Alternatives: Social Transformation and Humane Governance*, 20 (1): 1–49.

1998a. 'European Governance and New Constitutionalism: Emu and Alternatives to Disciplinary Neo-Liberalism in Europe'. *New Political Economy*, 3 (1): 5–26.

1998b. 'New Constitutionalism, Democratisation and Global Political Economy'. *Pacifica Review: Peace, Security and Global Change*, 10 (1): 23–38.

2000. 'The Constitution of Global Capitalism'. Paper presented to the International Studies Association Annual Convention, Los Angeles. Available online at: http://lapdoc.ru/docs/22/index-977868.html.

2002. 'Constitutionalizing Inequality and the Clash of Globalizations'. *International Studies Review*, 4 (3): 47–65.

2003. *Power and Resistance in the New World Order*. Basingstoke and New York: Palgrave Macmillan.

2004. 'Towards a Stark Utopia?'. In *Global Tensions: Opportunities and Challenges in the World Economy*, edited by Lourdes Berneria and Savitri Bisnath. New York: Routledge, 13–27.

2005. 'Contradictions of US Supremacy'. In *The Empire Reloaded*, edited by Leo Panitch and Colin Leys. London: Merlin Press, 23–45.

2008. *Power and Resistance in the New World Order*, 2nd Edition. Basingstoke and New York: Palgrave Macmillan.

ed. 2012. *Global Crises and the Crisis of Global Leadership*. Cambridge and New York: Cambridge University Press.

Gill, Stephen and Bakker, Isabella. 2006. 'New Constitutionalism and the Social Reproduction of Caring Institutions'. *Theoretical Medicine and Bioethics*, 27 (1): 35–57.

2011. 'The Global Political Economy and Global Health'. In *Global Health Ethics*, edited by Solomon R. Benatar and Gillian Brock. Cambridge University Press, 221–38.

Gill, Stephen and Law, David. 1988. *The Global Political Economy: Perspectives, Problems, and Policies*. Baltimore: Johns Hopkins University Press.

1989. 'Global Hegemony and the Structural Power of Capital'. *International Studies Quarterly*, 33 (4): 475–99.

1993. 'Global Hegemony and the Structural Power of Capital'. In *Gramsci, Historical Materialism and International Relations*, edited by Stephen Gill. Cambridge University Press, 93–126.

Gillman, Howard. 2002. 'How Political Parties can use the Courts to Advance their Agendas: Federal Courts in the United States, 1875–1891'. *American Political Science Review*, 96: 511–34.

Ginsburg, Tom. 2002. 'Economic Analysis and the Design of Constitutional Courts'. *Theoretical Inquiries in Law*, 3: 49–87.

2003. *Judicial Review in New Democracies: Constitutional Courts in Asian Cases*. New York: Cambridge University Press.

2006. 'Locking in Democracy: Constitutions, Commitment, and International Law'. *Journal of International Law and Politics*, 38: 707–59.

Ginty, Molly. 2010. 'In Subprime Fallout, Women Take a Heavy Hit'. *Women's ENews*, 14 January.

Goodman, John. 1992. *The Politics of Central Bank Independence*. London: Cornell University Press.

Gordon, Colin. 1991. 'Governmental Rationality: An Introduction'. In M. Foucault et al. *The Foucault Effect: Studies in Governmentality, with Two Lectures by and an Interview with Michel Foucault*. University of Chicago Press, 1–51.

Gorz, André. 1989. *Critique of Economic Reason*. London and New York: Verso.

Government of India. 2012. Letter to the UN Financing for Development Office. Available online at: www.un.org/esa/ffd/tax/2012ICTM/LetterIndia.pdf (accessed 14 May 2012).

Grabel, Irene. 2000. 'The Political Economy of "Policy Credibility": The New-Classical Macroeconomics and the Remaking of Emerging Economies'. *Cambridge Journal of Economics*, 24 (1): 1–19.

Gramsci, Antonio. 1971. *Selections from the Prison Notebooks of Antonio Gramsci*. Translated and edited by Q. Hoare and G. N. Smith. New York: International Publishers.

Gray, John. 1999. *False Dawn: The Delusions of Global Capitalism*. London: Granta Books.

Green, Duncan and Griffith, Matthew. 2002. 'Globalization and its Discontents'. *International Affairs*, 78 (1): 49–68.

Greve, Michael. 2000. 'The AEI Federalism Project'. *Federalist Outlook, AEI Online*, no. 1.

Griffin Cohen, Marjorie. 2004. 'Globalization's Challenge to Feminist Political Economy and the Law: A Socialist Perspective'. In *New Socialisms: Futures beyond Globalization*, edited by Robert Albritton. London: Routledge, 33–49.

Griffiths, Martin, Roach, Steven and Solomon, Scott M. 2009. *Fifty Key Thinkers in International Relations*. London: Routledge.

Grown, Caren. 2010. 'Taxation and Gender Equality: A Conceptual Framework'. In *Taxation and Gender Equity*, edited by Caren Grown and Imraan Valodia. Abingdon: Routledge, 1–22.

Grunberg, Isabelle. 1998. 'Double Jeopardy: Globalization, Liberalization and the Fiscal Squeeze'. *World Development*, 26 (4): 591–606.

Hale, Robert. 1935. 'Force and the State: A Comparison of "Political" and "Economic"'. *Columbia Law Review*, 35: 149–201.

Hall, David. 2010. 'Challenges to Slovakia and Poland Health Policy Decisions: Use of Investment Treaties to Claim Compensation for Reversal of Privatisation/Liberalisation Policies'. *Journal of Constitutional Law in Eastern and Central Europe*, 17 (1): 85–110.

Hanlon, Gerard. 1999. *Lawyers, the State and the Market: Professionalism Revisited*. Basingstoke: Macmillan Business.

Harcourt, Bernard E. 2011. *The Illusion of Free Markets*. Cambridge, MA: Harvard University Press.

Harmes, Adam. 1998. 'Institutional Investors and the Reproduction of Neoliberalism'. *Review of International Political Economy*, 5 (1): 92–121.

  2006. 'Neoliberalism and Multilevel Governance'. *Review of International Political Economy*, 13 (5): 725–49.

  2007. 'The Political Economy of Open Federalism'. *Canadian Journal of Political Science*, 40 (2): 417–37.

  2012. 'The Rise of Neoliberal Nationalism'. *Review of International Political Economy*, 19 (1): 59–86.

Hartmann, Eva. 2011. 'International Law and Politics: A Difficult Relation. The Legal Turn from a Critical IPE Perspective'. *New Political Economy*, 16 (5): 561–84.
Harvey, David. 1989. *The Condition of Postmodernity*. Blackwell.
    2003. *The New Imperialism*. Oxford University Press.
    2004. 'The "New" Imperialism: Accumulation by Dispossession'. In *The New Imperial Challenge: Socialist Register*, edited by Leo Panitch and Colin Leys. London: Merlin Press, 63–87.
    2005. *A Brief History of Neoliberalism*. Oxford University Press.
Hauter, Wenonah. 2007. 'The Limits of International Human Rights Law and the Role of Food Sovereignty in Protecting People from Further Trade Liberalization under the Doha Round Negotiations'. *Vanderbilt Journal of Transnational Law*, 40: 1069–168.
Hay, Colin, Watson, Matthew and Wincott, Daniel. 1999. 'Globalisation, European Integration and the Persistence of European Social Models'. *Working Paper 3/99*. University of Birmingham: POLSIS.
Hayek, F. A. von. 1939. 'The Economic Conditions of Interstate Federalism'. In *Individualism and the Economic Order (1948)*, edited by F. A. Hayek. University of Chicago Press, 255–72.
    1944. *The Road to Serfdom*. University of Chicago Press.
    1960. *The Constitution of Liberty*. London: Routledge and Kegan Paul.
Helleiner, Eric. 2009. 'Crisis and Response: Five Regulatory Agendas in Search of an Outcome'. *Internationale Politik und Gesellschaft* I/2009: 11–26.
Herrera, Gioconda. 2008. 'States, Work and Social Reproduction Through the Lens of Migrant Experience: Ecuadorian Domestic Workers in Madrid'. In *Beyond States and Markets: The Challenges of Social Reproduction*, edited by Isabella Bakker and Rachel Silvey. London and New York: Routledge, 93–107.
Higgott, Richard and Weber, Heloise. 2005. 'GATS in Context: Development, an Evolving *Lex Mercatoria* and the Doha Agenda'. *Review of International Political Economy*, 12 (3): 434–55.
Hilbink, Lisa. 2008. 'Review Article: Assessing the New Constitutionalism'. *Comparative Politics*, 40 (2): 227–45.
Hille, Kathrin. 2011. 'Love You and Leave You'. *Financial Times*, 4 February.
Hirschl, Ran. 2004a. 'The Political Origins of the New Constitutionalism'. *Indiana Journal of Global Legal Studies*, 11: 71–108.
    2004b. *Towards Juristocracy: The Origins and Consequences of the New Constitutionalism*. Cambridge, MA: Harvard University Press.
    2005. 'Preserving Hegemony? Assessing the Political Origins of the EU Constitution'. *International Journal of Constitutional Law*, 3: 269–92.
    2008. *Towards Juristocracy: The Origins and Consequences of the New Constitutionalism*. 2nd Edition. Cambridge, MA: Harvard University Press.
    2009. 'The Socio-Political Origins of Israel's Juristocracy'. *Constellations*, 16: 476–92.
Hirst, Paul Q., Thompson, Grahame and Bromley, Simon. 1999. *Globalization in Question: The International Economy and the Possibilities of Governance*. 2nd Edition. Cambridge, UK, and Malden, MA: Polity.
Holbrooke, Richard C. 2004. *To End a War*. New York: Random House.

Holland, Anne-Christin. 2005. *Water Business: Corporations versus the People*. London: Zed Books.
Holland, Peter A. 2011. 'The One Hundred Billion Dollar Problem in Small Claims Court'. *Journal of Business & Technology Law*, 259: 259–87.
Holloway, John. 2002. *Change the World Without Taking Power: The Meaning of Revolution Today*. London: Pluto Press.
Holton, Woody. 1999. *Forced Founders: Indians, Debtors, Slaves and the Making of the American Revolution in Virginia*. Chapel Hill: University of North Carolina Press.
   2005. 'Divide et Impera: Federalist 10 in a Wider Sphere'. *The William and Mary Quarterly*, 62 (2): 175–212.
   2009. 'Primitive Accumulation'. *Labour: Studies in Working-Class History of the Americas*, 6 (13): 21–36.
Homans, Charles. 2011. 'Just What Is a Just War?' *Foreign Policy*, 189: 34–5.
Honoré, Tony. 1998. 'The Basic Norm of Society'. In *Normativity and Norms: Critical Perspectives on Kelsenian Themes*, edited by Stanley Paulson and Bonnie Paulson. Oxford: Clarendon Press, 89–112.
Houde, Marie-France, Akshay, Kolse-Patil and Miroudot, Sébastien. 2008. 'The Interaction Between Investment and Services Chapters in Selected Regional Trade Agreements'. *OECD Trade Policy Working Paper No. 55 now OECD Trade Policy Papers*. ISSN: 1816-6873 (online at www.oecd-ilibrary.org/trade/the-interaction-between-investment-and-services-chapters-in-selected-regional-trade agreements_054761108710;jsessionid=18tcnlkiklbmh.x-oecd-live-01 (accessed November 14, 2013)
Houlder, Vanessa. 2012. 'Osborne to Act on Corporate Tax Avoidance'. *Financial Times*, 5 November.
Hunt, Alan. 1993. *Explorations in Law and Society: Towards a Constitutive Theory of Law*. New York: Routledge.
Huntington, Samuel P. 1991. *The Third Wave: Democratization in the Late Twentieth Century*. Norman: University of Oklahoma Press.
Huston, James L. 1993. 'The American Revolutionaries, the Political Economy of Aristocracy, and the American Concept of Distribution of Wealth, 1765–1900'. *The American Historical Review*, 98 (4): 1079–107.
Hutchinson, Allan C. 1995. *Waiting for Coraf*. Toronto and Buffalo: University of Toronto Press.
ICSID. 2009. 'Ecuador Submits a Notice under Article 71 of the International Centre for the Settlement of Investment Disputes Convention'. Available online at: http://icsid.worldbank.org/ICSID/FrontServlet?requestType=CasesRH&actionVal=OpenPage&PageType=AnnouncementsFrame&FromPage=Announcements&pageName=Announcement20.
Ikenberry, G. John. 2011. *Liberal Leviathan: The Origins, Crisis, and Transformation of the American World Order*. Princeton University Press.
ILO. 2011. 'World Social Security Report 2010/11: Providing Coverage in Times of Crisis and Beyond'. Geneva: ILO.
Independent International Commission on Kosovo. 2000. *Kosovo Report*. Oxford University Press.
Inside U.S. Trade. 2011. 'Member States Mandate Strong Investor Rights for EU-Wide Deals'. 23 September.

Inter-American Court of Human Rights. 2006. 'Sawhoyamaxa Indigenous Community v. Paraguay'. 29 March.
International Commission on Intervention and State Sovereignty. 2001. *The Responsibility to Protect*. Ottawa: International Development Research Centre.
International Court of Justice. 1986. 'ICJ Reports, *Nicaragua v. United States*', 27 June.
Ivison, Duncan. 2008. *Rights*. Montreal: McGill-Queen's University Press.
Jackson, Vicki C. 2010. *Constitutional Engagement in a Transnational Era*. New York: Oxford University Press.
Jaspers, Karl. 1967. *The Future of Germany*. University of Chicago Press.
Jensen, Erik G. and Heller, Thomas C. 2003. *Beyond Common Knowledge: Empirical Approaches to the Rule of Law*. Stanford Law and Politics/Stanford University Press.
Jenson, Jane. 2008. 'Citizenship in the Era of "New Social Risks": What Happened to Gender Inequalities?'. In *Gendering the Nation-State: Canadian and Comparative Perspectives*, edited by Yasmeen Abu Laben. Vancouver: UBC Press, 185–202.
Jessop, Bob. 2000. 'Globalisation, Entrepreneurial Cities, and the Social Economy'. In *Urban Movements in a Globalising World*, edited by Pierre Hamel, Henri Lustiger-Thaler and Margit Mayer. London: Routledge, 81–100.
  2002. 'Liberalism, Neoliberalism and the Urban Governance: A State-Theoretical Perspective'. *Antipode*, 2: 452–72.
  2010. 'From Hegemony to Crisis? The Continuing Ecological Dominance of Neoliberalism'. In *The Rise and Fall of Neoliberalism: The Collapse of an Economic Order*, edited by Kean Birch and Vlad Mykhnenko. London: Zed Books, 171–87.
Joerges, Christian. 2003. 'Europe as Grossraum? Shifting Legal Conceptualisations of the Integration Project'. In *Darker Legacies of Law in Europe: The Shadow of National Socialism and Fascism over Europe and its Legal Traditions*, edited by Christian Joerges, Ghaleigh Joerges and Navraj Singh. Oxford: Hart Publishing, 167–91.
  2005. 'What is Left of the European Economic Constitution? A Melancholic Eulogy'. *European Law Review*, 30: 461–89.
  2008. 'A New Alliance of De-Legalisation and Legal Formalism? Reflections on Reponses to the Social Deficit of the European Integration Project'. *Law and Critique*, 19: 235–53.
Johannesen, Niels and Zucman, Gabriel. 2012. 'The End of Bank Secrecy? An Evaluation of the G20 Tax Haven Crackdown'. *Working Paper 2012-04*. Paris: Paris School of Economics.
Johnson, Jon R. 2002. 'How Will International Trade Agreements Affect Canadian Health Care? Discussion Paper No. 22', edited by the Commission on the Future of Health Care in Canada: The Romanow Commission. Available at http://qspace.library.queensu.ca/bitstream/1974/6884/19/discussion_paper_22_e.pdf.
Kagan, Robert. 2013. *The World America Made*. Random House Digital, Inc.
Kahn, Paul. 1999. *The Cultural Study of the Law: Reconstructing Legal Scholarship*. University of Chicago Press.

Katzenstein, Peter J. 1985. *Small States in World Markets: Industrial Policy in Europe*. Ithaca: Cornell University Press.

Kay, Barbara. 2010. 'Debtor's Prison for Dads'. *National Post*, 16 November.

Kazepov, Yuri. 2010. 'Rescaling Social Policies toward Multilevel Governance in Europe: Some Reflections on Processes at Stake and Actors Involved'. In *Rescaling Social Policies: Toward Multilevel Governance in Europe*, edited by Yuri Kazepov. Farnham: Ashgate, 32–72.

Keating, Michael. 1998. *The New Regionalism in Western Europe: Territorial Restructuring and Political Change*. Cheltenham: Edward Elgar.

Kelsen, Hans. 1923 [1998]. '"Forward" to the Second Print of *Main Problems in the Theory of Public Law*'. In *Normativity and Norms: Critical Perspectives on Kelsenian Themes*, edited by Stanley Paulson and Bonnie Paulson. Oxford: Clarendon Press, 3–22.

 1945 [1999]. *General Theory of Law and State*. Translated by Anders Wedberg. Union, NJ: The Lawbook Exchange.

 1982. 'The Concept of the Legal Order'. *American Journal of Jurisprudence*, 27: 64–84.

Kennedy, David. 2009. 'The Mystery of Good Governance'. In *Ruling the World? Constitutionalism, International Law and Global Governance*, edited by Jeffrey L. Trachtman and Joel P. Dunhoff. Cambridge University Press, 37–68.

Kennedy, Duncan. 1985. 'The Role of Law in Economic Thought: Essays on the Fetishism of Commodities'. *The American University Law Review*, 34: 939–1001.

 1993. *Sexy Dressing Etc.: Essays on the Power and Politics of Cultural Identity*. Cambridge, MA: Harvard University Press.

Kingsbury, Benedict and Casini, Lorenzo. 2009. 'Global Administrative Law Dimensions of International Organizations Law'. *International Organizations Law Review*, 63 (2): 319–58.

Kingsbury, Benedict, Kirsch, Nico and Stewart, Richard. 2005. 'The Emergence of Global Administrative Law'. *Law and Contemporary Problems*, 68: 15–61.

Kirby, John. 1970. 'Early American Politics – The Search for Ideology: An Historiographical Analysis and Critique of the Concept of "Deference"'. *The Journal of Politics*, 32 (4): 808–38.

Klabbers, Jan. 2004. 'Constitutionalism Lite'. *International Organizations Law Review*, 1 (1): 31–58.

Klein, Naomi. 2012. 'Hurricane Sandy: Beware of America's Disaster Capitalists'. *Guardian*, 6 November.

Klug, Heinz. 2005. 'Campaigning for Life: Building a New Transnational Solidarity in the Face of HIV/AIDS and TRIPs'. In *Law and Globalization from Below: Towards a Cosmopolitan Legality*, edited by Boaventura de Sousa Santos and César A. Rodríguez-Garavito. Cambridge University Press, 118–39.

Knight, Angela, Cummings, Chris, Metcalfe, Richard, Saunders, Richard and Thoresen, Otto. 2012. 'Financial Transaction Tax is Unworkable: The Letter in Full'. *Telegraph*, 12 February.

Kobrin, Stephen Jay. 2004. 'Multinational Corporations, the Protest Movement and the Future of Global Governance'. In *Leviathans: Multinational*

Corporations and the New Global History, edited by Alfred Chandler and Bruce Mazlish. Cambridge University Press, 219–36.
Kommers, Donald P. 1997. *The Constitutional Jurisprudence of the Federal Republic of Germany*. 2nd Edition. Durham, NC: Duke University Press.
Koskenniemi, Martti. 2007. 'The Fate of Public and International Law: Between Technique and Politics'. *Modern Law Review*, 70 (1): 1–30.
  2009. 'The Politics of International Law – 20 Years Later'. *European Journal of International Law*, 20 (1): 7–19.
  2011. *Politics of International Law*. Oxford: Hart Publishing.
Krahmann, Elke. 2008. 'Security: Collective Good or Commodity?' *European Journal of International Relations*, 14 (3): 379–404.
Krugman, Paul. 2009. *The Return of Depression Economics and the Crisis of 2008*. New York: W. W. Norton and Company.
  2010. 'Making Financial Reform Fool-Resistant'. *The New York Times*, 4 April.
  2012. *End This Depression Now*. New York: Norton.
Kurtz, Jürgen. 2011. 'The Australian Trade Policy Statement on Investor–State Dispute Settlement'. *ASIL Insights*, no. 22, available online at: http://ilreports.blogspot.ca/2011/08/kurtz-australian-trade-policy-statement.html.
Kysar, Douglas A. 2012. 'Transnational Environmental Law'. *Public Law Working Paper No. 244*. Yale Law School.
Laczko, Frank and Aghazarm, Christine, eds. 2009. *Migration, Environment and Climate Change: Assessing the Evidence*. Geneva: International Organization for Migration.
Lamont, James. 2010. 'India Resisted Bank Tax to Favour Inclusion'. *Financial Times*, 19 July.
Lane, Jan-Erik. 1996. *Constitutions and Political Theory*. Manchester University Press.
Lang, Andrew. 2005. 'Beyond Formal Obligation: The Trade Regime and the Making of Political Priorities'. *Leiden Journal of International Law*, 18: 403–24.
Larner, Wendy. 2000. 'Neo-Liberalism, Policy, Ideology, Governmentality'. *Studies in Political Economy*, 63: 3–25.
Laslett, Peter and Brenner, Johanna. 1989. 'Gender and Social Reproduction: Historical Perspectives'. *Annual Review of Sociology*, 15: 381–404.
Law, David. 2005. 'Generic Constitutional Law'. *Minnesota Law Review*, 89: 652–742.
Law, David and Versteeg, Mila. 2011. 'The Evolution and Ideology of Global Constitutionalism'. *California Law Review*, 99: 1163–258.
Leathley, Christian. 2011. 'What will the recent entry into force of the UNASUR Treaty mean for investment arbitration in South America?'. *Kluwer Arbitration Blog*. Reprinted in *Just Investment Newsletter*, April 2011. Online publication: justinvestment.org/2011/04/ (accessed 6 July 2011).
LeBaron, Genevieve. 2011. 'The Political Economy of the Household: Neoliberal Restructuring, Enclosures and Daily Life'. *Review of International Political Economy*, 17 (5): 889–912.
LeBaron, Genevieve and Roberts, Adrienne. 2012. 'Confining Social Insecurity: Debt, Prison and the Rise of the Neoliberal Debtors' Prison'. *Politics and Gender*, 8 (1): 25–49.

Lee, Marc. 2010. 'Canada's Regulatory Obstacle Course – The Cabinet Directive on Streamlining Regulation and the Public Interest'. Ottawa: Canadian Centre for Policy Alternatives.

Lee, Marc and Campbell, Bruce. 2006. 'Putting Canadians at Risk: How the Federal Government's Deregulation Agenda Threatens Health and Environmental Standards'. Ottawa: Canadian Centre for Policy Alternatives.

Legislative Assembly of New Brunswick. 2004. Select Committee on Public Auto Insurance, *Final Report on Public Auto Insurance in New Brunswick*, First Session, Fifty-fifth Legislature, April 2004 available online at: www.gnb.ca/legis/business/committees/reports/2004auto/PDF/Main_Report-e.pdf (accessed 14 November 2013).

Lehavi, Amnon. 2010. 'The Global Law of the Land'. *University of Colorado Law Review*, 81: 425–71.

Lemke, Thomas. 2001. 'The Birth of Biopolitics: Michel Foucault's Lectures at the Collège de France on Neo-Liberal Governmentality'. *Economy and Society*, 30: 190–207.

Lesage, Dries and Vermeiren, Mattias. 2011. 'Neo-liberalism at a Time of Crisis: The Case of Taxation'. *European Review*, 19 (1): 43–56.

Lesage, Dries, McNair, David and Vermeiren, Mattias. 2010. 'From Monterrey to Doha: Taxation and Financing for Development'. *Development Policy Review*, 28 (2): 155–72.

Leubuscher, Susan. 2004. 'The Displacement of International Obligations: BITs and the Commodification of the Environment'. *American Society of International Law Proceedings*, 98: 280–3.

Levy, David and Prakash, Aseem. 2003. 'Bargains Old and New: Multinational Corporations and Global Governance'. *Business and Politics*, 5 (2): 131–50.

Linebaugh, Peter. 2008. *The Magna Carta Manifesto: Liberties and Commons for All*. Berkeley: University of California Press.

Lipschutz, Ronnie D. 2009. *The Constitution of Imperium*. Boulder: Paradigm Publishers.

Liverman, Diana M. and Vilas, Silvina. 2006. 'Neoliberalism and the Environment in Latin America'. *Annual Review of Environment and Resources*, 31: 327–63.

Loughlin, John. 2007. 'Reconfiguring the State: Trends in Territorial Governance in European States'. *Regional and Federal Studies*, 17 (4): 385–403.

McCarthy, James. 2005. 'Commons as Counterhegemonic Projects'. *Capitalism Nature Socialism*, 16 (1): 9–24.

McCarthy, James and Prudham, Scott. 2004. 'Neoliberal Nature and the Nature of Neoliberalism'. *Geoforum*, 35 (3): 275–83.

Macartney, Huw. 2009. 'Disagreeing to Agree: Financial Crisis Management within the Logic of No Alternative'. *Politics*, 29 (2): 111–20.

Macartney, Huw and Shields, Stuart. 2011. 'Space, the Latest Frontier? A Scalar-Relational Approach to Critical IPE'. In *Critical International Political Economy: Dialogue, Debate, Dissent*, edited by Stuart Shields, Ian Bruff and Huw Macartney. Houndmills: Palgrave Macmillan, 27–42.

McCubbins, Mathew, Noll, Roger and Weingast, Barry. 1987. 'Administrative Procedures as Instruments of Political Control'. *Journal of Law, Economics and Organization*, 3: 243–77.

1989. 'Structure and Process, Politics and Policy: Administrative Arrangements and the Political Control of Agencies'. *Virginia Law Review*, 75: 431–82.
Macdonald, Keith. 1995. *The Sociology of the Professions*. London: Sage Publications.
McDougal, Myres S. and Feliciano, Florentino P. 1961. *Law and Minimum World Public Order*. New Haven: Yale University Press.
Macklem, Patrick. 2002. *Indigenous Difference and the Constitution of Canada*. Toronto and Buffalo: University of Toronto Press.
McMichael, Philip. 2012. 'The Land Grab and Corporate Food Regime Restructuring'. *The Journal of Peasant Studies*, 39 (3/4): 681–701.
McNally, David. 2011. *Global Slump*. Winnipeg: Fernwood Publishing.
Madison, James. n.d. 'Records of the Federal Convention'.
    1996 [1787]. 'The Federalist No. 10: The Utility of the Union as a Safeguard Against Domestic Faction and Insurrection (continued)'. Available online at: www.constitution.org/fed/federa10.htm (accessed 7 September 2013).
Magalhaes, Pedro. 1999. 'The Politics of Judicial Reform in Eastern Europe'. *Comparative Politics*, 32: 43–59.
    2003. 'The Limits to Judicialization: Legislative Politics and Constitutional Review in the Iberian Democracies'. Unpublished PhD dissertation. Ohio State University.
Magen, Amichai and Morlino, Leonardo. 2009. *International Actors, Democratization and the Rule of Law: Anchoring Democracy?* London: Routledge.
Mahon, Rianne. 2008. 'Varieties of Liberalism: Canadian Social Policy from the "Golden Age" to the Present'. *Social Policy & Administration*, 42 (4): 342–61.
Main, Jackson Turner. 1966. 'Government by the People: The American Revolution and the Democratization of the Legislatures'. *The William and Mary Quarterly*, 23 (3): 391–407.
Makarenko, Jay. 2007. 'Child Care in Canada: An Introduction'. Available online at: www.mapleleafweb.com/features/child-care-canada-introduction.
Mandel, Michael. 1998. 'A Brief History of the New Constitutionalism, or "How We Changed Everything so that Everything Would Remain the Same"'. *Israel Law Review*, 32 (2): 250–300.
Mandelbaum, Michael. 2005. *The Case for Goliath: How America Acts as the World's Government in the Twenty-first Century*. New York: Public Affairs.
Mander, Jerry. 2003. 'Intrinsic Negative Effect of Economic Globalization on the Environment'. In *Worlds Apart: Globalization and the Environment*, edited by James Gustave Speth. Washington, DC, and London: Island Press, 109–30.
Mann, Howard. 2005. 'The Final Decision in *Methanex* v. *United States*: Some New Wine in Some New Bottles'. *International Institute for Sustainable Development*. Available online at: www.iisd.org/pdf/2005/commentary_methanex.pdf.
Marks, Susan. 2007. 'International Judicial Activism and the Commodity-Form Theory of International Law'. *European Journal of International Law*, 18 (1): 199–211.
Marx, Karl. 1974 [1858]. *Grundrisse: Foundations of the Critique of Political Economy*. Translated by Martin Nicolaus. Harmondsworth: Penguin.

1976 [1867]. 'The Fetishism of the Commodity and its Secret'. In *Capital: A Critique of Political Economy*, Volume 1. London: Penguin, 138, 163–76.
Mattei, Ugo and Nader, Laura. 2008. *Plunder: When the Rule of Law is Illegal*. Oxford: Blackwell Publishing.
May, Christopher. 2011. 'The Rule of Law: What is it and Why is it "Constantly on People's Lips"?' *Political Studies Review*, 9 (3): 357–65.
Meiksins Wood, Ellen. 2005. *Empire of Capital*. London: Verso.
Meinzer, Markus. 2012. 'The Creeping Futility of the Global Forum's Peer Reviews'. Tax Justice Briefing. Brussels: Tax Justice Network.
Merry, Sally Engle. 1995. 'Resistance and the Cultural Power of Law'. *Law and Society Review*, 11 (1): 11–27.
Michaelowa, Axel. 2012. 'Can New Market Mechanisms Mobilize Emissions Reductions from the Private Sector?' Harvard Project on Climate Agreements. Cambridge, MA: *Harvard University Discussion Paper ES* 12-1: 1–19.
Miéville, China. 2005. *Between Equal Rights: A Marxist Theory of International Law*. Leiden and Boston: Brill.
  2008. 'The Commodity-Form Theory of International Law'. In *International Law on the Left: Re-examining Marxist Legacies*, edited by Susan Marks. Cambridge and New York: Cambridge University Press, 92–132.
Mirowski, Philip and Plehwe, Dieter, eds. 2009. *The Road from Mont Pelerin: The Making of the Neoliberal Thought Collective*. Cambridge, MA: Harvard University Press.
Mishra, Asit Ranjan. 2011. 'India Rejects Clause on Litigation'. *Mint*, 4 July.
Mittelman, James H. 2010. *Hyperconflict: Globalization and Insecurity*. Palo Alto: Stanford University Press.
Mold, Andrew. 2007. 'Between a Rock and a Hard Place – Whither EU Development Policy?' In *EU Development Policy in a Changing World*, edited by Andrew Mold. Amsterdam University Press, 237–69.
Montgomerie, Johnna. 2013. 'America's Debt Safety-Net'. *Public Administration*. Online publication. Doi: 10.1111/J.1467-9299.2012.02094.X
Montgomerie, Johnna and Young, Brigitte. 2010. 'Home is Where the Hardship is: Gender and Wealth (Dis)Accumulation in the Subprime Boom'. *CRESC Working Paper Series: No. 79*. Available online at www.cresc.ac.uk/publications/home-is-where-the-hardship-is-gender-and-wealth-disaccumulation-in-the-subprime-boom (Accessed 17 November 2013).
Moore, Mike. 2001. 'Liberalization? Don't Reject It Yet'. *Guardian*, 26 February.
Moravcsik, Andrew. 2000. 'The Origins of Human Rights Regimes'. *International Organization*, 54: 217–52.
Morgenson, Gretchen and Story, Louise. 2011. 'In Financial Crisis, No Prosecutions of Top Figures'. *New York Times*, 14 April (online edition).
Müller-Armack, A. 1956. 'Soziale Marktwirtschaft'. *Handwörterbuch der Sozialwissenschaften*, 9: 390–2.
  1965. 'The Principles of the Social Market Economy'. *The German Economic Review*, 3 (2): 87–114.
Munck, Ronaldo. 2007. *Globalization and Contestation: The New Great Counter-Movement*. London: Routledge.
Murray, Charles. 2012. *Coming Apart*. New York: Crown Publishing.

NAFTA. 1998a. '*Ethyl Corporation* v. *Canada*, UNCITRAL'.
  1998b. '*S.D. Myers Inc.* v. *Canada*, UNCITRAL'.
  1999. '*Methanex* v. *United States*, UNCITRAL'.
  2000. '*Metalclad Corporation* v. *Mexico*, ICSID'.
  2008. '*Dow Agrosciences PLC* v. *the Government of Canada*'.
  2010. '*AbitibiBowater Inc.* v. *Canada*'.
Narula, Smita. 2012. 'The Global Land Rush: Markets, Rights, and the Politics of Food'. Paper presented at the International Conference on Global Land Grabbing II. 17–19 October, Cornell University, Ithaca, NY.
Nedelsky, Jennifer. 1990. *Private Property and the Limits of American Constitutionalism: The Madisonian Framework and its Legacies*. University of Chicago Press.
Negri, Antonio. 1999. *Insurgencies: Constituent Power and the Modern State*. Minneapolis: University of Minnesota Press.
Nesvetailova, Anastasia and Palan, Ronen. 2010. 'The End of Liberal Finance? The Changing Paradigm of Global Financial Governance'. *Millennium: Journal of International Studies*, 38 (3): 797–825.
Ngugi, Joel M. 2005. 'Policing Neo-Liberal Reforms: The Rule of Law as an Enabling and Restrictive Discourse'. *University of Pennsylvania Journal of International Economic Law*, 26 (3): 513–99.
Nicol, Danny. 2010. *The Constitutional Protection of Capitalism*. Oxford and Portland: Hart.
Nikiforuk, Andrew. 2012. *The Energy of Slaves: Oil and the New Servitude*. Vancouver: Greystone Books.
Nolan, Michael. 2012. 'Venezuela Withdraws from World Bank's International Centre for the Settlement of Investment Disputes'. *Milbank's Litigation Group*, 30 January.
North, Douglass and Weingast, Barry. 1989. 'Constitutions and Commitments: The Evolution of Institutions Governing Public Choice in Seventeenth-Century England'. *Journal of Economic History*, 29: 803–33.
North-South Institute. n.d. 'The Currency Transactions Tax'. Available online at: www.nsi-ins.ca/wp-content/uploads/2012/10/2008-The-Currency-Transaction-Tax-A-Bold-Idea-for-Financing-Development.pdf.
Oakes, James L. 1981. '"Property Rights" in Constitutional Analysis Today'. *Washington Law Review*, 56 (3): 583–626.
Oates, Wallace E. 1972. *Fiscal Federalism*. New York: Harcourt Brace Jovanovich.
Obama, Barack. 2011. 'Speech on Middle East Policy to AIPAC', 4 March Available online at: www.cfr.org/united-states/obamas-speech-aipac-march-2012/p27549 (accessed 6 September 2013).
OECD. 2001. Trade Committee. *Open Services Markets Matter*. TD/TC/WP(2001)24/PART1/REV. 3 September.
  2008. *Growing Unequal? Income Distribution and Poverty in OECD Countries*. Paris: Organisation for Economic Co-operation and Development.
  2009. *Social Expenditure Database*. Paris: OECD.
  2011a. *Growing Income Inequality in OECD Countries: What Drives It and How Can Policy Tackle It?* Paris: OECD.
  2011b. *Society at a Glance 2011: OECD Social Indicators*. Paris: OECD.

2011c. 'Divided We Stand: Why Inequality Keeps Rising'. Remarks by Angel Gurria, OECD Secretary General, Paris, 5 December. Available online at: www.oecd.org/social/dividedwestandwhyinequalitykeepsrisingspeech.htm.

2012. 'Social Spending After the Crisis'. Available online at: www.oecd.org/social/soc/49170768.pdf.

OECD/DAC. 1997. 'Expert Group on Aid Evaluation. Evaluation of Programs Promoting Participatory Development and Good Governance – Synthesis Report'. Paris: Organisation for Economic Co-operation and Development/Development Assistance Committee.

Oguamanam, Chidi. 2006. *International Law and Indigenous Knowledge: Intellectual Property, Plant Biodiversity, and Traditional Medicine*. University of Toronto Press.

Onuki, Hironori. 2009. 'Care, Social (Re)production and Global Labour Migration: Japan's "Special Gift" toward "Innately Gifted" Filipino Workers'. *New Political Economy*, 14 (4): 489–516.

2012. *The Everyday Spaces of Global Labour Migration: Migrant Workers as Political Agents in Japan*. Unpublished PhD thesis. York University.

Orford, Anne. 2003. *Reading Humanitarian Intervention*. Cambridge and New York: Cambridge University Press.

2012. 'Constituting Order'. In *The Cambridge Companion to International Law*, edited by James Crawford and Martti Koskenniemi. Cambridge University Press, 271–89.

Orr, David. 2009. *Down to the Wire: Confronting Climate Collapse*. New York: Oxford University Press.

Osberg, Lars. 2011. 'Why Did Unemployment Disappear from Official Macro-Economic Policy in Canada?' *New Directions for Intelligent Government in Canada: Papers in Honour of Ian Stewart*. Edited by Fred Gorbet and Andrew Sharpe, Ottawa: the Centre for the Study of Living Standards (www.csls.ca/stewartfestschrift.asp), 127–163.

Palan, Ronen, Murphy, Richard and Chavagneux, Christian. 2010. *Tax Havens: How Globalization Really Works*. Ithaca and London: Cornell University Press.

Panel Report. 2004. 'Mexico – Measures Affecting Telecommunications Services, WT/DS204/R'.

Panitch, Leo. 1996. 'Rethinking the Role of the State'. In *Globalization: Critical Reflections. International Political Economy Yearbook*, Volume 9, edited by James Mittelman. Boulder: Lynne Rienner Publishers, 83–113.

2004. 'Globalization and the State'. In *The Globalization Decade: A Critical Reader*, edited by Leo Panitch, Colin Leys, Alan Zuege and Martijn Konings. London: Merlin, 60–93.

Parker, Owen. 2008. 'Challenging "New Constitutionalism" in the EU: French Resistance, "Social Europe" and "Soft" Governance'. *New Political Economy*, 13 (4): 397–417.

Pashukanis, Evgeny. 1978. *Law and Marxism: A General Theory*. London: InkLinks.

Patomäki, Heikki. 2012. 'The EU Proposal for a Financial Transaction Tax: Problems and Prospects'. Geneva: United Nations Research Institute for Social Development.

Paulson, Stanley L. and Paulson, Bonnie Litschewski, eds. 1998. *Normativity and Norms: Critical Perspectives on Kelsenian Themes*. Oxford: Clarendon Press.

Peacock, Alan and Willgerodt, Hans. 1989. 'Overall View of the German Liberal Movement'. In *German Neo-Liberals and the Social Market Economy*, edited by Alan Peacock and Hans Willgerodt. London: Macmillan, 1–15.

Peck, Jamie. 2002. 'Political Economies of Scale: Fast Policy, Interscalar Relations, and Neoliberal Workfare'. *Economic Geography*, 78 (3): 331–60.

— 2008. 'Remaking Laissez-Faire'. *Progress in Human Geography*. Available online www.bing.com/search?q=Jamie%20Peck%20%22remaking%20laissez-faire%22%20progress%20in%20human%20geography&pc=conduit&ptag=A495F4CCE0D9F45F7BBF&form=CONBDF&conlogo=CT3210127&ShowAppsUI=1 32(1): 3–43.

— 2010. *Constructions of Neoliberal Reason*. Oxford University Press.

Peck, Jamie and Tickell, Adam. 2002. 'Neoliberalizing Space'. *Antipode*, 34: 380–404.

Peck, Jamie, Theodore, Nik and Brenner, Neil. 2010. 'Postneoliberalism and its Malcontents'. *Antipode*, 41: 94–116.

— 2012. 'Neoliberalism Resurgent? Market Rule after the Great Recession'. *South Atlantic Quarterly*, 111 (2): 265–88.

— 2013. 'Neoliberal Urbanism Redux?' *International Journal of Urban and Regional Research*, 37 (3): 1091–9.

Peerenboom, Randall. 2004. *Asian Discourses of Rule of Law*. London: Routledge.

Perelman, Michael. 2000. *The Invention of Capitalism: Classical Political Economy and the Secret History of Primitive Accumulation*. Durham, NC: Duke University Press.

Perkin, Harold. 1990. *The Rise of Professional Society: England since 1880*. London: Routledge.

Petersman, Ernst-Ulrich. 2002. 'Constitutionalism and WTO Law: From a State-centred Approach towards a Human Rights Approach in International Economic Law'. In *The Political Economy of International Trade Law: Essays in Honour of Robert E. Hudec*, edited by Daniel M. Kennedy and James D. Southwick. Cambridge University Press, 32–67.

Peterson, Luke Eric. 2004. 'Bilateral Investment Treaties and Development Policy Making'. *International Institute for Sustainable Development*. Available online at: www.iisd.org/pdf/2004/trade_bits.pdf.

— 2010. 'Philip Morris Files First-Known Investment Treaty Claim Against Tobacco Regulations'. *Investment Arbitration Reporter*, 3 March.

— 2011. 'In Policy Switch, Australia Disavows Need for Investor–State Arbitration Provisions in Trade and Investment Agreements'. *IA Reporter*. Available online at: www.iareporter.com/articles/20110414.

— 2012. 'Investor Announces Victory in Intra-EU BIT Arbitration with Slovakia Arising out of Health Insurance Policy Changes'. *IA Reporter*, 10 December. Available online at: www.iareporter.com/articles/201212104 (accessed December 2012).

Philip Morris International. 2010. 'Submission of Philip Morris International in Response to the Request for Comments Concerning the Proposed

Trans-Pacific Partnership Trade Agreement'. Available online at: www.tobacco.org/news/311851.html (accessed 11 May 2010).
Picchio, Antonella. 1991. *Social Reproduction: The Political Economy of the Labour Market*. Cambridge University Press.
Pickard, Jim. 2009. 'Turner Stands Firm after Tobin Tax Backlash'. *Financial Times*, 30 August.
Pignal, Stanley. 2011. 'Trichet Urges EU to Drop Tobin Tax Plan'. *Financial Times*, 30 June.
Pijl, Kees van der. 1998. *Transnational Classes and International Relations*. London and New York: Routledge.
Plehwe, Dieter. 2009. 'Introduction'. In *The Road from Mont Pelerin: The Making of the Neoliberal Thought Collective*, edited by Philip Mirowski and Dieter Plehwe. Cambridge, MA: Harvard University Press, 1–44.
Polanyi, Karl. 1944/1957. *The Great Transformation: The Political and Economic Origins of Our Time*. Boston: Beacon Press.
Pollock, A. M. and Price, D. 2000. 'Rewriting the Regulations: How the World Trade Organisation Could Accelerate Privatisation in Health-care Systems'. *The Lancet*, 356: 1995–2000.
Porter, David and Craig, David. 2004. 'The Third Way and Third World Poverty Reduction'. *Review of International Political Economy*, 11 (2): 387–423.
Post, Charles. 2011. *The American Road to Capitalism: Studies in Class Structure, Economic Development and Political Conflict, 1620–1877*. Leiden: Brill.
Powledge, Fred. 2001. 'Patenting, Piracy, and the Global Commons'. *BioScience*, 51 (4): 273–7.
2006. 'The Millennium Assessment'. *BioScience*, 56 (11): 880–6.
PRA. 2010. 'Setting the Bar. Setting the Record. 2010 Annual Report'. Portfolio Recovery Associates.
Prausmueller, Oliver and Wagner, Alice. 2011. '"Services of General Interest in Bilateral Free Trade Agreements" – Reflection Paper of the European Commission'. *Arbeiterkammer Europa*, 24 March. Available online at: www.akeuropa.eu/_includes/mods/akeu/docs/main_report_en_170.pdf (accessed 6 July 2011).
Prudham, Scott. 2007. 'The Fictions of Autonomous Invention: Accumulation by Dispossession, Commodification and Life Patents in Canada'. *Antipode*, 39 (3): 406–29.
2008. 'Commodification'. In *A Companion to Environmental Geography*, edited by Noel Castree, David Demeritt, Dianna Liberman and Bruce Rhoades. Sussex: Wiley, 123–42.
Przeworski, Adam. 1999. 'Minimalist Conception of Democracy: A Defense'. In *Democracy's Value*, edited by Ian Shapiro and Casiano Hecker-Cordon. New York: Cambridge University Press, 23–55.
Ptak, R. 2009. 'Neoliberalism in Germany'. In *The Road from Mont Pelerin: The Making of the Neoliberal Thought Collective*, edited by Philip Mirowski and Dieter Plehwe. Cambridge, MA: Harvard University Press, 98–138.
Rabkin, Jeremy A. 1998. *Why Sovereignty Matters*. Washington, DC: AEI Press.
Rajagopal, Balakrashnan. 2003. *International Law from Below: Development, Social Movements and Third World Resistance*. Cambridge University Press.

2005. 'The Role of Law in Counter-hegemonic Globalization and Global Legal Pluralism: Lessons from the Narmada Valley Struggle in India,' *Leiden Journal of International Law* 18 (3): 345–387.

2008. 'Counter-hegemonic International Law: Rethinking Human Rights and Development as a Third World Strategy'. In *International Law and the Third World*, edited by Richard Falk, Balakrishnan Rajagopal and Jacqueline Stevens. Oxford: Routledge Cavendish.

Ramos, Francisco. 2006. 'The Establishment of Constitutional Courts: A Study of 128 Democratic Constitutions'. *Review of Law and Economics*, 2 (1): 103–135.

Ramseyer, J. Mark. 1994. 'The Puzzling (In)dependence of Courts: A Comparative Approach'. *Journal of Legal Studies*, 23: 721–47.

Rawls, John. 1971. *A Theory of Justice*. Oxford University Press.

1999. *The Law of Peoples*. Cambridge, MA: Harvard University Press.

Razzaque, Jona. 2004. 'Trading Water: The Human Factor'. *Review of European Community & International Environmental Law*, 13 (1): 15–26.

Reid, John Philip. 1988. *The Concept of Liberty in the Age of the American Revolution*. University of Chicago Press.

Richardson, David. 1996. 'Unnatural Selection: Care is Needed to Ensure the Survival of Crop and Livestock Varieties'. *Financial Times*, 3 January.

Rixen, Thomas. 2011a. 'From Double Tax Avoidance to Tax Competition: Explaining the Institutional Trajectory of International Tax Governance'. *Review of International Political Economy*, 18 (2): 197–227.

2011b. 'Tax Competition and Inequality: The Case for Global Tax Governance'. *Global Governance*, 17 (4): 447–67.

Robé, J.-P. 1996. 'Multinational Enterprises: The Constitution of a Pluralistic Legal Order'. In *Global Law Without a State*, edited by Gunther Teubner. Aldershot: Dartmouth, 45–76.

Roberts, Adrienne. 2013. 'Financing Social Reproduction: The Gendered Relations of Debt and Mortgage Finance in 21st-Century America'. *New Political Economy*, 18 (1): 21–42.

Robinson, Allens Arthur. 2011. 'Written Notification of Claim by Philip Morris Asia Limited to the Commonwealth of Australia pursuant to Agreement Between The Government of Hong Kong and the Government of Australia for the Promotion and Protection of Investments' (June 22). [Unpublished.]

Rose, N. 1999. 'Inventiveness in Politics'. *Economy and Society*, 28 (3): 467–93.

Rubin, Robert E. 1999. 'Don't Give Up On Russia'. *New York Times*, 21 September.

Ruckert, Arne. 2009. 'A Decade of Poverty Reduction Strategies in Latin America: Empowering or Disciplining the Poor?' *TRAVAIL, capital et société*, 42 (1/2): 56–81.

Ruggie, John Gerard. 1983. 'Continuity and Transformation in the World Polity: Toward a Neorealist Synthesis'. *World Politics*, 35 (2): 261–85.

Saad-Filho, Alfredo. 2010. 'Neoliberalism in Crisis: A Marxist Analysis'. *Marxism 21*, 7 (1): 247–70.

Sabatinelli, Stefania. 2010. 'Activation and Rescaling: Interrelated Questions in Social Policy'. In *Rescaling Social Policies: Toward Multilevel Governance in Europe*, edited by Yuri Kazepov. Farnham: Ashgate, 75–102.

Sadeleer, Nicolas de. 2009. 'The Precautionary Principle as a Device for Greater Environmental Protection: Lessons from EC Courts'. *Review of European Community & International Environmental Law*, 18 (1): 3–10.

Sahlins, Marshall D. 1972. 'The Original Affluent Society'. In *Stone Age Economics*, edited by Marshall D. Sahlins. London: Routledge, 1–39.

Sally, Razeen. 1996. 'Ordoliberalism and the Social Market: Classical Political Economy from Germany'. *New Political Economy*, 1: 233–57.

Salzman, James and Ruhl, J. B. 2000. 'Currencies and the Commodification of Environmental Law'. *Stanford Law Review*, 53 (3): 607–94.

Santos, Boaventura de Sousa. 2002. *Toward a New Legal Common Sense*. London: Butterworths.

Santos, Boaventura de Sousa and Rodríguez-Garavito, César A., eds. 2005. *Law and Globalization from Below: Towards a Cosmopolitan Legality*. Cambridge University Press.

Santos, Boaventura de Sousa, Nunes, João Arriscado and Meneses, Maria Paula. 2008. 'Opening up the Canon of Knowledge and the Recognition of Difference'. In *Another Knowledge is Possible: Beyond Northern Epistemologies*, edited by Boaventura de Sousa Santos. London: Verso, xix–lxii.

Sassen, Saskia. 1996. *Losing Control? Sovereignty in an Age of Globalization*. New York: Columbia University Press.

  2002. 'Women's Burden: Counter-geographies of Globalization and the Feminization of Survival'. *Journal of International Affairs*, 53 (2): 503–35.

  2004. 'Global Cities and Survival Circuits'. In *Global Woman: Nannies, Maids and Sex Workers in the New Economy*, edited by Barbara Ehrenreich and Arlie Russell Hochschild. New York: Henry Holt, 254–74.

  2007. *A Sociology of Globalization*. New York: W.W. Norton.

  2008. *Territory, Authority, Rights: From Medieval to Global Assemblages*. Princeton University Press.

  2010. 'A Savage Sorting of Winners and Losers: Contemporary Versions of Primitive Accumulation'. *Globalizations*, 7 (1–2): 23–50.

  2013a. 'The Global City'. In *Democracy, Citizenship and the Global City*, edited by Engin F. Isin. London: Routledge, 48–61.

  2013b 'When Territory Deborders Territoriality.' *Territory, Politics, Governance*, Vol 1, Issue 1, 2013: pp. 21–45.

Sauer, S. 2009. 'Market-Led "Agrarian Reform" in Brazil: A Dream Has Become a Debt Burden'. *Progress and Development Studies*, 9 (2): 127–40.

Scahill, Jeremy. 2007. *Blackwater: The Rise of the World's Most Powerful Mercenary Army*. New York: Nation Books.

Scherrer, Christoph. 2005. 'GATS: Long-Term Strategy for the Commodification of Education'. *Review of International Political Economy*, 12 (3): 484–510.

Scheuerman, William. 1999. 'Economic Globalization and the Rule of Law'. *Constellations*, 6: 3–25.

Schill, Stephan W. 2007. 'Tearing Down the Great Wall: The New Generation Investment Treaties of the People's Republic of China'. *Cardozo Journal of International and Comparative Law*, 15: 73–118.

Schmitt, Carl. 1985. *The Crisis of Parliamentary Democracy*. Translated by Ellen Kennedy. Cambridge, MA: The MIT Press.

Schneiderman, David. 2000. 'Investment Rules and the New Constitutionalism'. *Law and Social Inquiry*, 25 (3): 757–87.
  2005. 'Banging Constitutional Bibles: Observing Constitutional Culture in Transition'. *University of Toronto Law Journal*, 55 (3): 833–55.
  2006. 'Property Rights, Investor Rights, and Regulatory Innovation: Comparing Constitutional Cultures in Transition'. *International Journal of Constitutional Law*, 4: 371–91.
  2008. *Constitutionalizing Economic Globalization: Investment Rules and Democracy's Promise*. Cambridge University Press.
  2010. 'A New Global Constitutional Order?' In *Research Handbook on Comparative Constitutional Law*, edited by Rosalind Dixon and Tom Ginsburg. Gloucester: Edward Elgar, 1–19.
  2013. *Resisting Economic Globalization: Critical Theory and International Investment Law*. Basingstoke: Palgrave Macmillan.
Schutter, Olivier de. 2012. 'Human Rights and Accountability Will Ensure the Road to Rio isn't a Dead End'. *Guardian*, 18 April. Available online at: www.guardian.co.uk/global-development/poverty-matters/2012/mar/27/human-rights-accountability-rio-summit?intcmp=239 (accessed 19 April 2012).
Schwartz, Herman. 2009. *Subprime Nation*. Ithaca: Cornell University Press.
Schwartz, Herman and Seabrooke, Leonard. 2009. *The Politics of Housing Booms and Busts*. New York: Palgrave Macmillan.
Scott, Peter Dale. 2010. *American War Machine: Deep Politics, the CIA Drug Connection, and the Road to Afghanistan*. Lanham: Rowman & Littlefield.
Serres, Chris and Howatt, Glenn. 2011. 'In Jail for Being in Debt'. *Minnesota Star Tribune*, 17 March.
Sharman, Jason C. 2006. *Havens in a Storm: The Struggle for Global Tax Regulation*. Ithaca and London: Cornell University Press.
  2008. 'Regional Deals and the Global Imperative: The External Dimension of the European Union Savings Tax Directive'. *Journal of Common Market Studies*, 46 (5): 1049–69.
Sharp, Lesley A. 2000. 'The Commodification of the Body and its Parts'. *Annual Review of Anthropology*, 29 (1): 287–328.
Shelton, Dinah. 2009. 'Soft Law'. In *Routledge Handbook of International Law*, edited by D. Armstrong. London: Routledge, 68–80.
Shihata, Ibrahim. 1991. 'The World Bank and "Governance" Issues in its Borrowing Members'. In *The World Bank in a Changing World: Selected Essays*, Volume I, compiled and edited by Franziska Tschofen and Antonio R. Parra. Dordrecht: Martinus Nijhoff Publishers, 53–96.
Sikkink, Kathryn. 2002. 'Transnational Advocacy Networks and the Social Construction of Legal Rules'. In *Global Prescriptions: The Production, Exportation and Importation of a New Legal Orthodoxy*, edited by Yves Dezalay and Bryant G. Garth. Ann Arbor: University of Michigan Press, 37–64.
Silver-Greenberg, Jessica. 2011. 'Welcome to the Debtors' Prison, 2011 Edition'. *Wall Street Journal*, 17 March.
Sinclair, Scott. 2000. 'How the WTO's New "Services" Negotiations Threaten Democracy'. Available online at: www.policyalternatives.ca/sites/defaul/files/uploads/publications/National_Office_Pubs/gats.pdf.

2010a. 'NAFTA Chapter 11 Investor–State Disputes'. Canadian Centre for Policy Alternatives. Available online at: www.policyalternatives.ca/publications/reports/gats.

2010b. 'Negotiating from Weakness – Canada–EU Trade Treaty Threatens Canadian Purchasing Policies and Public Services'. Canadian Centre for Policy Alternatives. Available online at: www.policyalternatives.ca/sites/default/files/uploads/publications/reports/docs/Negotiating%20From%20Weakness%20EU%20Canada.pdf (accessed 6 July 2011).

2011. 'The WTO and its GATS'. In *The Handbook of Globalisation*, 2nd Edition, edited by Jonathan Michie. Cheltenham: Edward Elgar, 423–32.

Sinclair, Scott and Grieshaber-Otto, Jim. 2002. 'Facing the FATS: A Guide to the GATS Debate'. Canadian Centre for Policy Alternatives. Available online at: www.policyalternatives.ca/publications/reports/facing-facts (accessed July 2011).

Slaughter, Annie-Marie. 2004. *A New World Order*. Princeton and Oxford: Princeton University Press.

2011. 'Fiddling While Libya Burns'. *New York Times*, 13 March.

Smart, Carol. 1989. *Feminism and the Power of Law*. London: Routledge.

Soederberg, Susanne. 2007. 'Freedom, Ownership, and Social (in)Security in the United States'. *Cultural Critique*, 65: 94–114.

2013. 'The US Debtfare State and the Credit Card Industry'. *Antipode*, 45 (2): 493–512.

Somers, Margaret R. 2008. *Genealogies of Citizenship: Markets, Statelessness, and the Right to Have Rights*. Cambridge University Press.

Sornarajah, M. 2008. 'A Coming Crisis: Expansionary Trends in Investment Treaty Arbitration'. In *Appeals Mechanism in International Investment Disputes*, edited by Karl P. Sauvant and Michael Chiswick-Patterson. Oxford University Press, 39–77.

South Africa, Department of Trade and Industry. 2009. 'Bilateral Investment Treaty Policy Framework Review: Government Position Paper' (June). Available online at: www.thedti.gov.za/ads/bi-lateral_policy.pdf.

Sriram, Chandra Lekha, Martin-Ortega, Olga and Herman, Johanna. 2011. *Peacebuilding and the Rise of Law in Africa: Just Peace?* Abingdon: Routledge.

Stavins, Robert N. 2003. 'Market-Based Environmental Policies: What Can We Learn from U.S. Experience?' Available online at: www.elssociety.org/searlecenter/jep/advanced/Stavins_Market_Based.pdf (accessed 3 April 2012).

Steinbrück, Peer. 2009. 'Tax Trade to Share the Cost of the Crisis'. *Financial Times*, 24 September.

Stephan, Paul B. 2002. 'Institutions and Elites: Property, Contract, the State and Rights in Information in the Global Economy'. *Cardozo Journal of International and Comparative Law*, 10: 305–17.

Stephenson, Matthew. 2003. '"When the Devil Turns…": The Political Foundations of Independent Judicial Review'. *Journal of Legal Studies*, 32: 59–89.

Stiglitz, Joseph E. 2003. *The Roaring Nineties: A New History of the World's Most Prosperous Decade*. New York: W. W. Norton.

2010. *Freefall: America, Free Markets, and the Sinking of the World Economy*. New York: W.W. Norton & Company.
Stone Sweet, Alec. 2006. 'The New *Lex Mercatoria* and Transnational Governance'. *Journal of European Public Policy*, 13 (5): 627–46.
Strange, Gerard. 2002. 'Globalisation, Regionalism and Labour Interests in the New International Political Economy'. *New Political Economy*, 7 (3): 343–65.
—— 2006. 'The Left against Europe? A Critical Engagement with New Constitutionalism and Structural Dependence Theory'. *Government and Opposition*, 41 (2): 197–229.
—— 2011. 'China's Post-Listian Rise: Beyond Radical Globalisation Theory and the Political Economy of Neoliberal Hegemony'. *New Political Economy*, 16 (5): 539–59.
Strauss, Debra. 2009. 'The Application of TRIPS to GMOs: International Intellectual Property Rights and Biotechnology'. *Stanford Journal of International Law*, 45: 287–320.
Streit, Manfred E. 1994. 'The Economic Constitution of the European Community'. *Constitutional Political Economy*, 5: 319–53.
Streit, Manfred E. and Werner Mussler. 1995. 'The Economic Constitution of the European Community: From "Rome" to "Maastricht"'. *European Law Journal* 1 (1) 5–30.
Streit, Manfred E. and Wohlgemuth, Michael. 2000. 'The Market Economy and the State: Hayekian and Ordoliberal Conceptions'. In *The Theory of Capitalism in the German Economic Tradition: History, Ordo-Liberalism, Critical Theory, Solidarism*, edited by Peter Koslowski. Berlin: Springer, 225–69.
Swank, Duane. 2002. *Global Capital, Political Institutions, and Policy Change in Developed Welfare States*. Cambridge University Press.
Swyngedouw, Erik. 2004. 'Globalisation or "Glocalisation"? Networks, Territories and Rescaling'. *Cambridge Review of International Affairs*, 17 (1): 25–48.
—— 2005. 'Dispossessing H_2O: The Contested Terrain of Water Privatization'. *Capitalism Nature Socialism*, 16 (1): 1–16.
Sydney Morning Herald. 2011. 'Plain Cigarette Packaging to Start in 2012'. Available online at: www.smh.com.au/national/plain-cigarette-packaging-to-start-in-2012-20111121-1nqbo.html.
Taibbi, Matt. 2011. 'Why Isn't Wall Street in Jail?' *Rolling Stone*, 3 March.
Tarrow, Sidney. 2011. 'Why Occupy Wall Street is Not the Tea Party of the Left'. *Foreign Affairs*. Available online at: www.smh.com.au/national/plain-cigarette-packaging-to-start-in-2012-20111121-1nqbo.html.
Taylor, Paul, Kochhar, Rakesh, Fry, Richard, Velasco, Gabriel and Motel, Seth. 2011. *Twenty-to-One: Wealth Gap Rises to Record Highs between Whites, Blacks and Hispanics*. Washington, DC: Pew Research Center.
Teubner, Gunther. 2004. 'Societal Constitutionalism: Alternatives to State-Centred Constitutional Theory?' In *Transnational Governance and Constitutionalism*, edited by Christian Joerges, Inger-Johanne Sand and Gunther Teubner. Oxford and Portland: Hart, 3–28.
Teubner, Gunther, Lindahl, Hans, Christodoulidis, Emilios and Thornhill, Chris. 2011. 'Debate and Dialogue: Constitutionalizing Polycontexturality'. *Social & Legal Studies*, 20 (2): 209–52.

Thirkell-White, Ben. 2009. 'Dealing with the Banks: Populism and the Public Interest in the Global Financial Crisis'. *International Affairs*, 85 (4): 689–711.

Thompson, E. P. 1975. *Whigs and Hunters: The Origin of the Black Act*. New York: Pantheon.

Thornes, J. E. and Randalls, S. 2007. 'Commodifying the Atmosphere: "Pennies from Heaven"?' *Geografiska Annaler: Series A, Physical Geography*, 89 (4): 273–85.

Thornhill, Christopher. 2010. 'Legality, Legitimacy and the Constitution: A Historical-Functional Approach'. In *Normative and Sociological Approaches to Legality and Legitimacy*, edited by Christopher Thornhill and Samantha Ashenden. Baden-Baden: Nomos, 29–56.

Tickell, Adam and Peck, Jamie. 2003. 'Making Global Rules: Globalization or Neoliberalization?' In *Remaking the Global Economy: Economic-Geographic Perspectives*, edited by Jamie Peck and Henry Wai-chung Yeung. London: Sage, 163–81.

Tigar, Michael E. 2000. *Law and the Rise of Capitalism* (New Edition). New York: Monthly Review Press.

Tilly, Charles and Tarrow, Sidney. 2007. *Contentious Politics*. Boulder: Paradigm Publishers.

Tribe, K. 2009. 'The Political Economy of Modernity: Foucault's Collège de France Lectures of 1978 and 1979'. *Economy and Society*, 38 (4): 679–98.

Trubek, David M. 1972. 'Max Weber on Law and the Rise of Capitalism'. *Wisconsin Law Review*, 3: 720–53.

  2006. 'The "Rule of Law" in Developmental Assistance: Past, Present, and Future'. In *The New Law and Economic Development: A Critical Appraisal*, edited by David M. Trubeck and Alvaro Santos. Cambridge University Press, 74–94.

Trubek, David M. and Santos, Alvaro. 2006. 'Introduction: The Third Moment in Law and Development Theory and the Emergence of a New Critical Practice'. In *The New Law and Economic Development: A Critical Appraisal*, edited by David M. Trubek and Alvaro Santos. Cambridge University Press, 1–18.

Tully, James. 1995. *Strange Multiplicity: Constitutionalism in an Age of Diversity*. Cambridge University Press.

  2002. 'The Unfreedom of the Moderns in Comparison to their Ideals of Constitutional Democracy'. *Modern Law Review*, 65: 204–28.

  2007. 'The Imperialism of Modern Constitutional Democracy'. In *The Paradox of Constitutionalism: Constituent Power and Constitutional Form*, edited by Martin Loughlin and Neil Walker. Oxford University Press, 315–38.

  2008. 'On Law, Democracy and Imperialism'. In *Public Law and Politics: The Scope and Limits of Constitutionalism*, edited by Emilios Christodoulidis and Stephen Tierney. Dartmouth: Ashgate, 69–101.

Tushnet, Mark. 2009. 'The Inevitable Globalization of Constitutional Law'. *Virginia Journal of International Law*, 49: 985–1006.

Tversky, Amos and Kahneman, Daniel. 1981. 'The Framing of Decisions and the Psychology of Choice'. *Science*, 211: 453–8.

UN. 1966. *International Covenant on Economic, Social and Cultural Rights* (ICESCR). Available online at: www.un-documents.net/icescr.htm.

2009. 'Report of the Commission of Experts of the President of the United Nations General Assembly on Reforms of the International Monetary and Financial System'. New York: United Nations.

UNCTAD. 2009. *Trade and Development Report*. New York and Geneva: United Nations Conference on Trade and Development.

2010. 'Denunciation of the ICSID Convention and BITs: Impact of Investor–State Claims'. *IIA Issues Note*. Available online at: www.unctad.org/diae.

2011. *World Investment Report 2011: Non-Equity Modes of International Production and Development*. New York and Geneva: United Nations Conference on Trade and Development.

UN LDC (Office of the High Representative for the Least Developed Countries). 2003. *Climate Change Report 2003: Mainstreaming Adaptation to Climate Change in Least Developed Countries*. Edited by Saleemul Huq, Atiq Rahman, Mama Konate, Youba Sokona and Hannah Reid. London: International Institute for Environment and Development.

Van Apeldoorn, Bastiaan and Overbeek, Henk. 2012. 'Introduction: The Life Course of the Neoliberal Project and the Global Crisis'. In *Neoliberalism in Crisis*, edited by Henk Overbeek and Bastiaan van Apeldoorn. Houndmills: Palgrave Macmillan, 1–22.

Van Harten, Gus. 2007. *Investment Treaty Arbitration and Public Law*. Oxford University Press.

2010. 'Investment rules and the denial of change.' Comparative Research in Law and Political Economy Research Papers. Volume 6 Number 14. Toronto: Osgoode Law School. Available at: http://ssrn.com/abstract=1612345.

Vanberg, V. J. 1998. 'Freiburg School of Law and Economics'. In *New Palgrave Dictionary of Economics and the Law*, edited by Peter Newman. London: Macmillan, 172–9.

Vandevelde, Kenneth J. 1992. 'The BIT Program: A Fifteen-Year Appraisal'. *American Society of International Law Proceedings*, 86: 532–40.

2007. '*Aguas del Tunari, S.A. v. Republic of Bolivia*. ICSID Case no. ARB/02/3. Jurisdiction. 20 ICSID Review'. *The American Journal of International Law*, 101 (1): 179–84.

Vidal, John. 2011. 'Oxfam Warns of Spiraling Land Grab in Developing Countries'. *Guardian*, 22 September.

Vincent, R. J. 1974. *Nonintervention and International Order*. Princeton University Press.

Voigt, Stefan and Salzberger, Eli M. 2002. 'Choosing Not to Choose: When Politicians Choose to Delegate Powers'. *Kyklos*, 55: 289–310.

Vucetic, Srdjan. 2011. 'Genealogy as a Research Tool in International Relations'. *Review of International Studies*, 37: 1295–312.

Wacquant, Loïc. 2004. 'Critical Thought as Solvent of *Doxa*'. *Constellations*, 11 (1): 97–101.

Wälde, Thomas. 2009. 'Interpreting Investment Treaties: Experiences and Examples'. In *International Investment Law for the 21st Century: Essays in*

Honour of Christoph Schreuer, edited by Christina Binder, Ursula Kriebaum, August Reinisch and Stephen Wittich. Oxford University Press, 724–81.

Walker, Neil. 2002. 'The Idea of Constitutional Pluralism'. *Modern Law Review*, 65: 317–61.

2008. 'Taking Constitutionalism Beyond the State'. *Political Studies*, 56: 519–43.

Wallerstein, Immanuel. 2008. 'The Demise of Neoliberal Globalization'. Available online at: http://mrzine.monthlyreview.org/2008/wallerstein010208.html (accessed 28 October 2012).

Warren, Elizabeth. 2009. 'Feminomics: Women and Bankruptcy'. *New Deal 2.0*, 17 December.

Warren, Mark. 1989. 'Liberal Constitutionalism as Ideology: Marx and Habermas'. *Political Theory*, 17 (4): 511–34.

Watson, Matthew. 2009. '"Habitation vs. Improvement" and a Polanyian Perspective on Bank Bail-Outs'. *Politics*, 29: 183–92.

Weingast, Barry. 1993. 'Constitutions as Government Structures: The Political Foundations of Secure Markets'. *Journal of Institutional and Theoretical Economics*, 149: 286–311.

1995. 'The Economic Role of Political Institutions: Market-Preserving Federalism and Economic Development'. *Journal of Law, Economics & Organization*, 11 (1): 1–31.

Wheeler, Nicholas. 2000. *Saving Strangers: Humanitarian Intervention in International Society*. Oxford University Press.

White, Ben, Borras Jr., Saturnino, Hall, Ruth, Scoones, Ian and Wolford, Wendy. 2012. 'The New Enclosures: Critical Perspectives on Corporate Land Deals'. *The Journal of Peasant Studies*, 39 (3/4): 619–47.

White, Michelle J. 2007. 'Bankruptcy Reform and Credit Cards'. *The Journal of Economic Perspectives*, 21 (4): 175–200.

Whittington, Keith. 2005. '"Interpose Your Friendly Hand": Political Supports for the Exercise of Judicial Review by the United States Supreme Court'. *American Political Science Review*, 99: 583–96.

Wigan, Duncan. 2010. 'Credit Risk Transfer and Crunches: Global Finance Victorious or Vanquished?' *New Political Economy*, 15 (1): 109–25.

Williams, Sir John Fischer. 1928. 'International Law and the Property of Aliens'. *British Yearbook of International Law*, 9: 1–30.

Williams, Randal. 2011. 'Rethinking Investment Treaty Law: A Policy Perspective'. *London School of Economics Transnational Law Project*. Available online at: www2.lse.ac.uk/newsAndMedia/videoAndAudio/channels/publicLecturesAndEvents/player.aspx?id=1014.

Williams, Raymond. 1977. *Marxism and Literature*. Oxford University Press.

Wittes, Benjamin. 2008. *Law and the Long War: The Future of Justice*. New York: Penguin.

Wolf, Martin. 2011. 'How the Crisis Catapulted us into the Future'. *Financial Times*, 2 February.

Wolford, W. 2007. 'Land Reform in the Time of Neoliberalism: A Many-Splendored Thing'. *Antipode*, 39 (3): 550–70.

Wolin, Sheldon S. 2008. *Democracy Incorporated: Managed Democracy and the Specter of Inverted Totalitarianism*. Princeton University Press.

Wood, Ellen Meiksins. 1995. *Democracy Against Capitalism*, edited by Ellen Wood. Cambridge University Press.
   2005. *Empire of Capital*. London: Verso.
Wood, Gordon S. 1969. *The Creation of the American Republic: 1776–1787*. Chapel Hill: The University of North Carolina Press.
World Bank. 1996. *From Plan to Market: World Development Report 1996*. New York: Oxford University Press.
   1997. *The State in a Changing World: World Development Report, 1997*. New York and Oxford: Oxford University Press.
World Economic Forum. 2011. *Global Risks Report 2011*, 6th Edition. Davos: World Economic Forum.
Yackee, Jason. 2008. 'Bilateral Investment Treaties, Credible Commitment, and the Rule of (International) Law: Do BITs Promote Foreign Direct Investment?' *Law and Society Review*, 42: 805–25.
Young, Iris Marion. 1990. *Throwing Like a Girl and Other Essays in Feminist Philosophy and Social Theory*. Bloomington: Indiana University Press.
Zeldin, Cindy and Rukavina, Mark. 2005. *Borrowing to Stay Healthy*. New York: Demos.
Žižek, Slavoj. 2009. *First as Tragedy, then as Farce*. London and New York: Verso.
   2010. *Living in the End Times*. London and New York: Verso.

Index

9/11, 263, 279, 306

Aarhus Convention, 275
AbitibiBowater, 39, 186
Achmea, 188
Adelman, Sammy, 276
Africa, 83, 226, 270
  Sub-Saharan, 52, 136, 270
African Human Rights Charter, 275
agency, 1, 4, 11, 14, 17–18, 20, 26, 48, 61, 65, 156, 185, 278, 289, 290–1
agribusiness, 30, 40, 52
alienation, 39, 59, 64
Alliance for Water Stewardship, 268
Althusser, Louis, 36, 48
Amazon, 39
American Enterprise Institute, 151, 241
American Revolution, 86, 92
anarchy, 87, 89
  international, 3
Andean Community, 60
Andorra, 206
Appalachians, the, 88
appropriation, 16, 25, 45–6, 49, 53, 58, 60–1, 310
Aquino, Benigno III, 103
Arab Spring, 42, 104
Argentina, 56, 188
  financial crisis, 173
Arroyo, Gloria Macapagal, 103
Arthurs, Harry, 212, 231, 284, 288
ASEAN, 105
Asia, 60, 74, 136, 178
Asia-Pacific Economic Cooperation, 191
austerity, 9–10, 41–2, 200, 221, 236, 249, 259–60
  expansionary, 215, 259
Australia, 54, 160, 173, 177–8, 190, 275
Austria, 206, 208

Bahrain, 300
Balbus, Isaac, 46, 48

Bank for International Settlements, 137
Bank of America, 244
bankruptcy, 168, 186, 214, 240–1, 244
Beard, Charles, 86
Bechtel, 189
Beck, Ulrich, 251
Becker, Gary, 167, 169
Bentham, Jeremy, 57
Bhopal
  chemical leak, 263
Bilateral Investment Treaties, 39–40, 50, 56, 175–6, 192, 198, 313, 315, 320
Bin Laden, Osama, 307
Black Act, 58
Bolivarian Alliance for the Americas, 61
Bolivarian Revolution, 61
Bolivia, 43, 56, 58, 60, 98, 189, 192
Bourdieu, Pierre, 70–1, 165
Brazil, 10, 43
  land reform, 51
Bretton Woods, 127–8, 137, 311
BRICs, 190
Britain, 5, 67, 88–9, 104, 127–8
  empire, 77, 86, 90
Brown, Gordon, 203
Buchanan, James, 38, 112, 143, 146–7, 150–3, 227–8
Burma, 267
Bush, George W., 174, 191

Canada, 13, 39, 54, 59, 160, 173, 175–7, 182, 185–6, 191–2, 194–5, 235, 252, 257, 264
Canadian Charter of Rights and Freedoms, 102
cap and trade, 267, 313
capital accumulation, 15–16, 30, 38–9, 48, 110, 129, 212, 222, 227–8, 295, 313
carbon economy, 26
carbon offsets, 26, 55
carbon trading, 55, *see also* cap and trade

363

Catholic
monasteries, 31
central banks, 7, 13, 41, 104, 110, 117, 119–20, 124, 146, 222, 224, 232
CEO Water Mandate, 268
Chartist Movement, 144
Chernobyl
nuclear meltdown, 263, 274
Chiang Kai-shek, 101
Chicago Mercantile Exchange, 226
Chicago School, 33
Chile
under Pinochet, 33
Chimni, Bhupinder, 58
China, 32, 49, 59, 104, 163, 177, 190–1, 203, 207, 252, 271, 273
Citibank, 244
citizenship, 34, 68, 106, 117, 125, 146, 160, 172, 182, 198, 215, 227, 250–1, 256, 287
civil society, 1, 4, 6, 14, 23, 29–31, 34, 36, 38, 72, 111, 178, 192, 195, 202, 227, 267, 271–2, 286, 299
Clarke, John, 256
class
working, 122, 246
class conflict, 91–2
class war, 90, 92
Clean Development Mechanisms, 266, 271
climate change, 55, 123, 162, 196, 211, 216–17, 261–2, 265, 268–76, 280, 310, 312
Clinton, Bill, 33
Cold War, 5, 14, 24, 27, 42, 263, 303, 309
colonialism, 39, 216, 265, 290, 295
Colombia, 60
commodification, 11, 20, 25, 33–5, 45–7, 49–51, 53, 55–6, 59, 62, 128, 131, 141, 145, 161, 212–13, 222, 225, 227–8, 248, 282, 284, 292, 314
common sense, 9, 18, 23, 26, 30, 44, 45–6, 59–60, 69, 165, 175, 200, 219, 278, 288, 290
commons, 43, 58, 225–7, 261
communism, 6, 70, 168
constitutionalism, 310
consumerism, 30, 262
Corona, Renato, 103
corporate social responsibility, 267
corporations, 4–5, 13, 16, 20, 24, 32, 35–6, 40–1, 51–3, 55, 58, 60–1, 64, 68, 71, 84, 96, 105, 145, 154, 161–2, 180, 183–5, 191, 194–5, 197–202, 204, 213, 216, 220, 222, 228, 250, 258, 261, 263–4, 266–8, 271, 276, 284, 287, 293, 307, 315, 321

Cox, Robert, 2, 7, 161, 185
crimes against humanity, 279, 298, 301, 304
Crown
British, 31
Czechoslovakia, 188

De Angelis, Massimo, 49, 226
debt
collection, 93, 214, 235, 242–4
consumer, 236, 243–4
criminalization, 243
public, 10, 182, 196, 200, 259
democracy, 10, 13, 27, 33–4, 37, 39, 41–4, 58, 63, 67–9, 75, 78–9, 84, 89, 96–7, 100–2, 106–7, 125, 144–5, 170, 274, 280, 290, 296, 306, 308
Denmark, 252
deregulation, 121, 124, 163, 171, 182, 201, 238, 248, 253, 263–4
developing countries, 27, 40, 52–3, 73, 183, 187, 190–1, 195, 208–9, 216, 224, 226, 262–4, 266, 271–2
Diggers, the, 31
disarmament, 106, 304
disaster capitalism, 275
disciplinary neo-liberalism, 27, 211, 214, 233, 261, 320
dispossession, 18, 24–5, 31–2, 39, 42–3, 55–6, 94, 105, 225, 228, 272
Dow Chemical
Bhopal, 265

ecology, 1, 3, 21, 211, 217, 231, 290
Ecuador, 56, 60, 160, 176, 192
Egypt
demonstrations, 42
enclosure, 25, 31, 39, 45–6, 49, 52, 54, 57, 61, 212, 225–6, 228
Encore Capital Group, 243
English Bill of Rights, 104
European Central Bank, 10, 200, 203–4
European Commission, 10, 174, 191–3, 203–4, 230
European Convention on Human Rights, 104
European Court of Justice, 79, 105
European Union, 10, 42, 73, 79, 100, 115, 163, 174, 191–2, 230, 264, 273
exploitation, 32, 36, 42–4, 150–1, 153, 180, 195, 231, 266, 286, 295
Exxon Mobil, 267
Exxon Valdez, 274

fascism, 33
feminists, 20, 228, 234

Index

Ferguson, Niall, 63
financial crises, 13, 56, 263, 274
financial derivatives, 201, 204, 238
financial markets, 117, 145, 199–201, 226, 259, 309
financial transaction tax, 163, 202–3, *see also* Tobin Tax
First World War, 33, 123
fiscal austerity, *see* austerity
fiscal squeeze, 211–13, 220, 222, 224
food crisis, 226
fossil fuels, 31, 87
Foucault, Michel, 67, 82, 159, 166–72
France, 72, 88, 163, 166–7, 176, 202–3, 260
free trade, 12, 146, 160, 173, 180, 190–1, 222
Friedman, Milton, 41, 112, 143, 146–7, 149–50, 167, 169

G7, 37
G8
  protests, 278, 289, 292
G20, 41–2, 163, 202–3, 207, 210, 215, 230, 259
Geithner, Timothy, 203
gender, 106, 213–14, 228, 230–2, 234, 239, 241, 323
General Agreement on Tariffs and Trade (GATT), 137, 161, 180, 182
General Agreement on Trade in Services (GATS), 12, 50, 56, 161, 180–1, 183–5, 187–90, 192–3, 315–16, 319–20
genocide, 272, 279, 298, 301, 304
Germany, 163, 171, 176, 202–3, 207–8, 210, 306
Ginsburg, Tom, 100–1
global financial crisis, 58, 140, 162, 197, 207, 209–10, 211, 215, 221, 224, 235, 243–5, 249
Glorious Revolution, 31, 104
gold standard, 33
Gramsci, Antonio, 30, 41, 48, 58, 197
Great Depression, 33, 149, 156, 173, 250, 259
Great Recession, 215, 258, 260
Greece, 10, 42, 102, 236
Grundnorm, 26–7, 63, 65–6, 70, 74–5, 276, 316
Guantanamo, 306

Hanlon, Gerald, 71
Harvey, David, 49, 55, 133
Hayek, Friedrich von, 38, 41, 112, 143, 146–7, 149–50, 171, 227
health, 323

Henry VIII, 31
Henry, Patrick, 89
HIV/AIDS, 40
Hobbes, Thomas, 64
Hong Kong, 104, 178, 206
housing, 214, 223, 225, 236, 239
humanitarian intervention, 279, 298–300, 304
Hussein, Saddam, 303

Ikenberry, John, 309
India, 10, 51, 59–60, 100, 163, 175, 190–1, 203, 209, 252, 272–3, 293, 304
indigenous peoples, 31, 43, 264, 293, 321
Indignados, the, 260
Indonesia, 252, 267
International Centre for the Settlement of Investment Disputes, 173, 176
International Court of Justice, 275, 302
international financial institutions (IFIs), 17, 38, 55, 160, 173, 183, 235, 247, 260
International Labour Organization, 224
International Monetary Fund (IMF), 55, 145, 235
Iran, 304–5, 308
Iraq, 6, 177, 303–5
Ireland, 236
Israel, 102, 304–5, 307

Jackson, Robert, 306
Japan, 103, 191, 264, 305–6
Jefferson, Thomas, 88
JPMorgan Chase, 244

Kahn, Paul, 70
Karamanlis, Constantine, 102
Keating, Michael, 255
Kelsen, Hans, 65–6, 70, 276
Kennedy, Duncan, 48
Keynesianism, 116–17, 119, 136–7, 141, 156, 170, 198, 219, 222, 237, 249
Klein, Naomi, 275
Kosovo, 279, 299–302
Kyoto Protocol, 26, 54–5, 153, 268, 271

laissez-faire, 57, 250
land reform, 51
Landless Workers' Movement, 43
Latin America, 6, 34, 73, 136, 262
least developed country, 265, 271
legitimacy, 1, 3, 10–11, 14, 16–17, 20, 27, 58, 60, 66, 69, 94, 110, 117, 133, 162, 179, 196, 200, 245, 250, 260, 278–80, 283–4, 290, 295, 297–304, 308–12, 327

Levellers, the, 31
lex mercatoria, 2, 319
liberalization, 3, 12, 20, 24, 39, 41, 63–4, 66, 68, 70–1, 74–5, 96, 109, 126, 129–42, 145, 171, 189–90, 193–4, 196, 220, 222, 224, 229, 233, 248–9, 253–4, 256–8, 261, 263, 275, 278, 324
Libya, 298–301
Liechtenstein, 206–7
Lipschutz, Ronnie, 308
Locke, John, 25, 53
London, 203–5, 260
Lovelace, Sandra, 59
Lula, Luiz Inacio da Silva, 43
Luxembourg, 206–7

Maastricht Treaty, 83,
 see also European Union
Madison, James, 89–92, 148
Magen, Amichai, 74
Maldives, 98
Mandel, Michael, 13, 33–4, 68, 84, 107, 121, 284
Mao Zedong, 32
market civilization, 6, 23–5, 29–36, 42, 44, 45–6, 57, 67, 84, 96, 211, 247, 251, 262, 319
Marks, Susan, 59
Marlboro, 178
Marx, Karl
 commodification, 47, 49
 exploitation, 36
 primitive accumulation, 31, 49, 225
 rights, 59
 species being, 221
Marxism, 96
Mason, George, 89
MERCOSUR, 105
Mexico, 6, 51, 61, 102, 182, 187, 272
Miéville, China, 59
Monaco, 206
monetary policy, 222, 224, 232
Mongolia, 101
Monroe, James, 89
Morlino, Leonardo, 74
Morocco, 103
Müller-Armack, Alfred, 170
Multilateral Agreement on Investment, 39, 83, 181
Munck, Ronaldo, 291
Murray, Charles, 241
Musharraf, Pervez, 104

Naramada Dam project, 59
Nazism, 168, 170
Netherlands, 98, 188–9
New Zealand, 54, 191
Nigeria, 266
non-governmental organizations (NGOs), 60, 191, 257
Non-Proliferation Treaty, 303
North American Free Trade Agreement (NAFTA), 12, 146, 160, 173, 180, 222
North Atlantic Treaty Organization (NATO), 279, 298–9, 301
North Korea, 304
Northern Ireland, 229
Norway, 252
Nuremberg Promise, 306
Nuremberg War Crimes Tribunal, 306

Obama, Barack, 191, 273, 300
Occupy Wall Street, 175, 213, 229, 246, 260, 307
organic crisis, 9, 19, 25, 34, 43–4, 211–12, 222
Organisation for Economic Co-operation and Development (OECD), 39, 55, 67, 74, 136–7, 153, 190, 193, 206–7, 209–10, 213, 219, 221, 223, 229, 236, 252, 260, 265, 267

Pakistan, 104, 275, 304, 307
Pakistan People's Party (PPP), 104
Palestine, 299
panopticism, 38, 233
Paraguay, 174
Pashukanis, Evgeny, 48–9
Perkin, Harold, 70
Peru, 60
Peter Jackson, 178
Philip Morris International, 160, 173, 178
Philippines, 51–2, 173, 178, 252
Pinochet, Augusto, 33
plutocracy, 9, 14
Poland, 188
Polanyi, Karl, 30–1, 57, 112, 128, 144–5, 156, 169, 172, 250–1, 282, 284, 292
Portugal, 10
post-modern Prince, 25, 309
private property rights, 6, 14–17, 20, 23–4, 26, 30, 35–7, 39, 45, 48–9, 61, 68, 113, 128, 162, 197, 212, 225, 227, 314, 326
privatization, 6, 24, 33, 38–9, 42, 50, 52, 55–6, 59–61, 109, 121, 124, 136, 140, 182–3, 188, 194–5, 219–20, 225, 227, 229, 233–5, 237, 241, 248, 253, 262–3, 268, 275, 296
proletarianization, 24, 32, 43
public–private partnerships, 275

Qaddafi, Muammar, 301

Rawls, John, 98
Reagan, Ronald, 167, 171
resistance, 4–5, 10, 24, 26, 29, 32, 39–40, 42–4, 45–6, 49, 56–9, 66, 68–9, 75, 87, 90, 131, 160–1, 175, 189–90, 196, 211–14, 216, 219, 222, 228, 244, 266, 276, 278, 280, 282, 285, 289, 303, 307, 309–12
Responsibility to Protect (R2P), 279, 298
Rio Declaration, 275
Rio Summit, 263, 267
R. J. Reynolds, 160, 173
Rubin, Robert, 33
ruling classes, 9, 78–9
Russia, 33, 207, 272

Sahlins, Marshall, 98
San Marino, 206
Santos, Boaventura de Sousa, 290
Sarkozy, Nicolas, 202
Seattle
 protests, 191, 267, 289, 307, 309
Second World War, 32–3, 83, 97, 119, 127–8, 156, 180, 272, 295, 306, 309
securitization, 238
Serbia, 299
sex trafficking, 43
Shakespeare, William, 35
Shays, Daniel, 92
Shinawatra, Thaksin, 103
Sierra Leone, 266
Singapore, 103, 175, 206
slavery, 93, 272
Slovakia, 188
social dislocation, 9, 32, 57
social provisioning, 219, 221–2, 228, 234–6, 240–1, 246
social reproduction, 8–9, 11, 20, 23–4, 32, 34, 44, 82, 85–6, 161, 211–14, 216, 219–22, 224–5, 227–9, 231, 233–7, 239, 246, 250–1, 322
South Africa, 56, 102, 160, 176, 191–2, 273, 293
South America, 56, 60, 192
South Korea, 101, 252
Soviet Union, 33, 83
Spain, 10, 42, 102, 236, 275
Stavins, Robert, 267
Steinbrück, Peer, 202
Stockholm Declaration, 275
Sudan, 270
Sundaravej, Samak, 103

surrogacy
 commercial, 43, 213, 228
sustainability, 19–20, 34, 40, 175, 211, 214, 229, 280, 310
sustainable development, 56, 261, 263
Sweden, 103, 252
Switzerland, 206–7, 210
Syria, 299–301

Taiwan, 101
tax havens, 200, 205–10, 212
Thailand, 103, 252
Thatcher, Margaret, 5, 41, 167, 171
Thompson, E.P., 26
Three Mile Island, 263
Tigar, Michael, 64
Tobin Tax, 202, 230
Tokyo War Crimes Tribunals, 306
trade barriers, 150, 152
Trade-Related Aspects of Intellectual Property Rights (TRIPS), 12, 40, 61, 146, 228
trade unions, 41, 197
Trichet, Jean-Claude, 203
Tully, James, 290
Turkey, 103

Union Carbide, 263, 265
United Kingdom (UK), 176
United Nations, 15, 59–61, 64, 165, 209, 217, 224, 230–1, 268, 270, 272
United States of America, 83, 93, 193
 debt, 211
 Patriot Act, 122
Universal Declaration of Human Rights, 60, 272, 310, 312
Uruguay Round, 56

Venezuela, 56, 60
Via Campesina, 40, 43

Washington Consensus, 137, 171
Washington, George, 89
Weber, Max, 64
Weingast, Barry, 150
welfare state, 170, 190, 198, 234, 248–9, 251–2
Whig dynasties, 31
Wood, Ellen Meiksins, 286
World Bank, 3–4, 7, 13, 17, 25, 27, 39, 41, 51–2, 55–6, 60, 64, 68, 83, 128, 136–7, 146–7, 154, 160, 173, 192, 226–7, 263–4, 268
world order, 1–3, 5, 14, 18, 20–1, 23, 27, 29–30, 34, 42, 44, 77, 79, 83–4, 130, 274, 277–9, 295, 303, 307–8, 310, 312, 326–7

World Social Forum, 141, 267, 278, 291–2
World Trade Organization (WTO), 12, 14, 40, 53, 105, 110, 119, 122, 128, 137, 146, 152, 161, 180–3, 185, 189–90, 193, 196, 228, 263–4, 266, 274, 315–16

World Water Council, 56, 268

Yeltsin, Boris, 33

Zapatista
  rebellion, 278, 292